ENDORSEMENTS

A Course in Miracles guided by my mentor and spirit sister, Danét.

I met Danét in 2015. From that first meeting, I experienced a profound knowledge that we were destined to travel together and that she would be my spiritual guide.

I had been a student of conversations with God for three years and was hungry for a deeper personal experience of the Divine.

After many hours of deep conversations with Danét and listening to her personal experiences through her twenty-eight years of study and teaching *A Course in Miracles*, I was hooked.

On Dec 7, 2015, I received the first of many emails that would come daily from Danét. In this email, I felt a profound shift in my spirit and a feeling that I would be changed forever. In this email I read these words, "Since it is so close to the first of the year, I love the idea of joining energetically with the millions all over the world whom will be starting Lesson 1, January 1st."

Every morning, Danét would send the daily lesson followed by an in-depth summary of her personal experience as a result of her meditation on the lesson. She would always include a way for me to think about and apply that lesson. I could imagine the scenario she painted for me and then understand the simplicity of the lesson.

Reading each day's lesson on my own was confusion to say the least.

Now I felt I was being given the gift of a high-speed train to the world of the Divine. Love is the world in which I choose to dwell today. All the false thoughts and beliefs have fallen from my mind and I live today in the joy of knowing that I am the perfect Love of God expanding and creating Love.

Spirit-sister-friend,
Shar Pittman

Danét is so clear with her understanding of *A Course in Miracles*. When Danét shares her wisdom, it melts into your soul that it is true and understandable. . . . It feels yummy! Yes, she has helped me know when I'm in ego or spirit by the way I feel! That has helped me in so many ways! Danét walks her talk! Danét has a way with her hugs, kindness, and humor when you are in her presence. She is living in love! It is a pleasure to know her and call her a friend!

Cynthia Holman-Schmidt

I am a witness to Danét, as a living example of *A Course in Miracles*. She genuinely loves everyone. She radiates goodness, light, peace, joy, and LOVE. To be with her is so uplifting and awe inspiring. A teacher extraordinaire. She helps the student see clearly the point being made, with knowledge, inspiration, and humor. She lives her life totally in tune with spirit. Danét is truly an example of a GOD-like person. She is beautiful. One only needs to be in her presence to see the truth of who she is.

Merann Hegemann (most fortunate friend)

After forty-three years of study of *A Course in Miracles*, Danét is a teacher who stands out as one who helps the course principles sink deeply into our souls! Danét is an example of the course becoming the way we live our lives, not just a series of intellectual concepts, and compassion becomes our first priority. Thank you Danét, for your gentle, funny, incredible understanding of our greatest study. Thanks for believing in me.

Diane Cook

Transforming from day one!!

Renelle Smith, Amazon reader

I enjoy the simplicity of a hard write becoming an easy read. It's a place to go when I think I am lost. Just reconnect to the divine within me, and it's truly amazing!

Kathy Griego, Amazon reader

Guides a mindset to create your own pathway to the divine. Beautifully shared. Relatable.

Cass, Amazon reader

I love how Danét keeps it simple and understandable. I have found a new way of looking at my thoughts. Love this book.

Stacey, Amazon reader

COFFEE
WITH THE
DIVINE

A YUMMY GUIDE TO DAILY MIRACLES

Lauren —
You are a miracle — Keep shining
your Light!

Love + Joy
Danét

DANÉT PALMER

THE YUMMY WAY

To the Divine, in whom I rest, and dance the yummy life of Love, in peace—Who shows me my true face in every face, and my purpose in each moment—Present Happiness is all there is.

Paperback ISBN: 978-1-7355472-0-6
Ebook ISBN: 978-1-7355472-1-3

OCC011020 BODY, MIND & SPIRIT / Healing / Prayer & Spiritual
SEL032000   SELF-HELP / Spiritual
OCC019000   BODY, MIND & SPIRIT / Inspiration & Personal Growth

Cover illustration by Annika Burton
Cover design by Lisa Barbee
Typeset by Kaitlin Barwick
Published by Authors Who Lead

www.TheYummyWay.com

CONTENTS

CONTENTS

FOREWORD

I first met Danét at an intersection of my life, on the corner of "What the—?" and "Oh My God! What have I been thinking?" Our meeting was a true display of opposites, a comic duality.

We had both grown up in the same spiritual tradition. But she had rebelled, and I had cherished it, hook, line, and sinker. She had opted for life experience; I, for following the rules. It may have *appeared* that she had made mistakes in life. It may have *appeared* that I had actually pulled something off. She did arrive wearing a helmet and riding a scooter, after all, while I came in fashion in a fancy car. She showed up, having played the part of "the bad girl," with some real savoir faire under her belt. I entered stage right as the "good girl," having played it safe, never veering off the chosen path.

So, let's be honest.

She had done everything wrong. And I had done everything right. (I'm just saying.)

But still. Here we were, literally at the same crossroads; I, a cyclone of know-it-all passion, she, a peace (sic) of stillness. I was a real yapper! She, a listener. So, who knew that from such disparate paths we could have come together in one place to recognize the other half of our silly Selves?

Since then, our journeys have taken us in waves of experience, uphill and down, and around the bend. Yet we have never lost the awareness of being two sides of a coin, two perfect expressions of the same Lifestream. We have learned in our separate ways, (with true communion) the great lesson of life:

That each life lived is *equal in value* to experience.

I have personally benefited from Danét's stunning and formidable path, the organic nature of it, her empirical depth of wisdom as a counselor and life coach. And I was there when Danét married Larry Palmer. She—once again—had taken the high road, using all her successive "present moments" as an experiment in unconditional love.

I, of course, observed from the sidelines. But don't get me wrong. I've learned a lot from simply observing the "yumminess" of Danét Palmer's existential pragmatism.

Danét and I share a love affair with *A Course in Miracles* and have consecutively been both student and teacher throughout the years. And now I am proud to introduce this beautiful manifesto on living the principles of *A Course in Miracles*—the Yummy way—how to let Life choose for us—our next experience, our next Holy Instant. All it takes is "a little willingness," as it says in *A Course in Miracles*.

And the only thing *we* are privileged to do? Is to fall upon our scabby little knees and kiss the holy ground on which we stand.

Turns out, Yummy is the path (dare I say, the Only True Path?) to Love, to Life, to God.

Patricia York, a true fan

Author of a new novel, *Sabrina So Far*, former actress with 20th Century Fox Studios, stage name *Heather Young* costarring in the TV series *Land of the Giants*, playwright of three full-scale musicals including the musical version of the timeless classic *Jane Eyre*

PROLOGUE

*"There is one thought in particular that should be
remembered throughout the day. It is a thought of pure joy;
a thought of peace, a thought of limitless release,
limitless because all things are freed within it."*

(ACIM—16.6.1)

One uncompromising, wholehearted decision irreversibly altered the course of my life—from train wreck to present happiness. I made an appointment with God and showed up. That decision formulated into a daily commitment to begin each day and commune with the Divine—no matter what. At the time I made this decision, I had no idea what I was getting myself into. I didn't know what God or the Divine was or what to expect.

What I felt was an opening and a willingness to check it out. To believe there is another way to live than the one I'd been living.

So, when Betty (my Yoda) suggested I make an appointment with the Divine first thing every morning and keep it, I intuitively sensed this was the doorway to the other way. Her suggestion sparked a light in my darkened mind. I did not understand what it meant, but I felt something real awaken.

It never occurred to me to question this guidance from Betty. Or that I would fail in keeping it. (And this from someone whose life to this point was characterized by failure.) It's like I had been waiting for that suggestion—to see the fork in the road of my life, where I saw before me a beam of light revealing the path within.

The instant I said, "Yes!", some deep and loving aspect within me answered for me. A spark of curiosity ignited a desire to see what was beneath the fray of my known self. Keeping this appointment began to recalibrate my being, my orientation to what I was capable of, who I am to myself and the world.

A mysterious reckoning of Self began, an inner quest to meet myself anew. I began an inquiry for truth, to question everything I thought I knew or believed, and I ask that deeper sense of myself of its validity.

Ultimately, it was a decision to have faith in the ever-present Source of energy, power, and love that created and creates Life and to make a conscious effort to be present to this Presence. To trust that as part of this creation, I am integral, and I am in a relationship with this Divine energy.

Simply by showing up, making this coffee date with the Divine unequivocal, by no fault of my own, I was gifted an experience of immense, unconditional love, of immediate freedom, of being released from the contraction of my self-identity. I wanted desperately to know It intimately and to be worthy of the grace I'd been granted.

I gained faith in this vast love which had gifted me reprieve from the known world of my loser self and opened me to the possibility that I had been wrong about everything. I had a fraction of a mustard seed of faith that there was another way. It was enough.

So, each and every morning thereafter, I showed up, looking toward that light to see what it would reveal. Again, and again, each day invites me back.

Even now, each morning, early before the world begins, at the first sign of waking, I recognize the spark of life bringing me out of slumber, and instead of resisting and seeking the familiarity of sleep, I turn toward it. I thank Love for giving me life. I make coffee. It is a sacred act of self-love, a prayer of preparation consecrating this holy time with the Divine.

PROLOGUE

I go to my yummy room/meditation space, and as I cross the threshold, I imagine I am stepping into an infinite ocean of unconditional love and immerse myself completely. I feel the warmth rising up my legs, torso, neck, and head with each step I take. I let go and surrender myself with each breath.

Immersed in Divine love, I allow whatever will be, to be, and enter this still, spacious freedom and wait expectantly for the truth. This is the kingdom of love. Everything is perfect here. I am perfect here. Here, there are no rules or boundaries or time frame. Here, everything and everyone—past, present, and future—is welcome. Here, is oneness at peace with itself. It is love, the seat of my being.

I didn't know I had made a life-long commitment when I set the daily appointment. The purity of the decision, made from a holy place within, where my own divine Self resides, created its own morality. I have merely answered the call each day for the joy of it—happy to experience pure life. I've never missed a single coffee date with the Divine in over thirty-five years.

Crazy, because when I started this, I was someone from whom you couldn't count on to return a phone call. Someone who seemed to betray every promise I had every made to myself, punishing myself relentlessly, feeling ashamed and guilty. A boring merry-go-round of futility, always wishing something were different from what it is.

It is from this decision *A Course in Miracles* miraculously appeared in my life.

One day, not so long after I began my daily date with the Divine, a friend came to my door. He had a book in his hand. He said, "I don't know why I have this book. I don't remember where I got it. I think it belongs to you." The book was *A Course in Miracles*.

From the first moment I read the text, I experienced something magical happening. It wasn't the words. In fact, I didn't like the Christian terminology, but my heart beckoned me into the space beyond and between the words—where the truth that was already in my heart found its home in its message of awakening and love. I couldn't put it down. Something holy was happening. And I wanted to be part of it.

I've never been good at this world of fear and competition. I always felt ill equipped for the struggles and stresses of the dog-eat-dog, become-somebody world. I felt like nobody, pretending to belong—hoping to pass for normal, get a few things right, while I improved myself.

God, how that idea of self-improvement drove me. I was constantly reading self-help books, doing seminars and improvement programs to better myself. None touched the deep unworthiness I felt inside with hope. Becoming "somebody better"—always trying to make a better version didn't work for me. Trying to qualify for life by some outside, elusive authorial criteria felt pointless and meaningless and futile.

I simply could not believe, in my heart of hearts, that a life spent asking the world to tell me I am worthy of happiness could be the meaning of life. I had to either accept the pointlessness of my life or do something about it. I could see I was missing crucial elements that made life work happily. Something I lacked within my programmed framework. I had to look beneath it, to where it all began.

In the deepest part of my soul, I knew that happiness is all that life is about. I think we all do. In stepping away from the old familiar, a new way shone before me. I decided I would change my life completely. I did not understand what that would look like, but I knew one thing—shit had to go! Everything had to change. Where did this realization come from?

It was a mystery I had to pursue—a call I had answered—to know myself. That mystery led me to meet Betty, who taught me to question everything for proof of its authenticity.

Authenticity for me is a feeling of Self, of true reality—a feeling of love meeting love, sparking a feeling of joy, of wonder, and of peace of mind—which meant conflict had to go. Each idea and action must feel like I am a full participant, void of resistance. If it does not meet this criterion, I'm pretending rather than living.

Pretending is the old road. The one I'd been on all my life. The road of roles and labels and rules, promises and broken promises. It was the road away from my divine self. The one I'd already investigated. The one that failed me. So that road had to go. What didn't come from a place of a deep peace and joy had to go.

PROLOGUE

A Course in Miracles spoke to a self in me untarnished by my unworthy self-concept. It spoke *of* my self-concept but spoke *to* my Self beyond it. It spoke to the Love self within me—And I loved myself while I read. The feeling of total acceptance and love I felt reading the course, called me to return and give myself to the experience it offered as often as I could.

It's like intuitively I knew that I could never understand the course like I did college courses or even self-help books, with the intellectual part of my mind. So, I didn't try.

I let it teach the part of me it was speaking to, the one that felt connected to the message as I read. The part that felt I was in a personal conversation with the Author. I let love speak, and love listened. I love *A Course in Miracles*. Its application freed me from a life of falsehood and fear. Ha! That's the understatement of the year.

Guided by the lessons of *A Course in Miracles (ACIM)*, I learned to let my mind become still beneath the constant commentary of seemingly unbidden thoughts that ran my life, by questioning the thoughts that tried to stick and see the beliefs I kept bothering myself with. It spoke the language of my heart, undoing my programmed mind, and awakening my authentic, whole mind within. It has been my constant companion for over thirty years.

ACIM came into my life in answer to what I now understand was my honest heart-prayer to know my divine Self as I am. Instantly, I recognized a familiar inquiry to question. It helped me see that whatever I hold in my mind teaches me about who I believe I am, and it is from this identity I determine what you and the world is for me. That's some powerful shit!

Seeing this clearly lead me to make the decision the course suggests, "Teach only love for that is what you are" (6.3.2).

I learned that we never respond to stimuli, only to our interpretation of that stimuli. Every thought is a teaching and learning opportunity. One true fact stated so clearly from the course pierced my heart and became the credo for my life. It is this: "Everything is love. Every loving thought is true. Everything else is an appeal for healing and help." Love is always the right response.

No words can express the gratitude and joy I have for *A Course in Miracles* and the application practice of the lessons from the *Workbook for Students*. It has given me a way to be in the world as who I am—Love. It has been a holy relationship, teaching me that all relationship is holy.

It's crazy the simplicity of it. Love, joy, and miracles have become my lifestyle. To say I am grateful is insufficient. This book comes out of a heart so full of appreciation and joy I needed somewhere to collect the overflow.

I never thought of myself as a writer. So, I was as surprised as anyone when the idea of writing a book came into being. One morning, about two years ago, my gratitude formulated itself into the ideas that became this book.

As I read and meditated on each lesson prior to writing, memories of transformation appeared as examples from my life, which took place over years of simply doing my best to apply the ideas from the *Workbook for Students* of *A Course in Miracles*, each day. The examples are not in any kind of chronological order. I wrote them as I received them, so they bounce around from the beginning to present, in my life story with the course.

This book, in the form of a daily lesson guide, is my gift to anyone seeking simple examples of how to transform your life through application of *ACIM*. If you are new to all this—feel free to ride on the light trails of my experiences as we walk this path together, this year given to the Divine, until your own wings open. They will. And you will fly!

I recommend you pick up a copy of *A Course in Miracles* and read each lesson coinciding with each lesson example here and apply it according to the instructions. Reading the text will deepen your understanding immensely. It is my deepest desire that you experience the Divine as I have and do, letting your heart read and understand. Together, we let that understanding reveal itself in our lesson practice, as I know it will.

Coffee with the Divine is my expression of gratitude for the grace in which I live today. It is my truest desire that all awaken to the imperturbable peace and present joy which belongs to us all.

PROLOGUE

I have faith that if this book is meant for you, it will find you. That you, too, will see how simple, natural, and profound it can be to live in present happiness. To leave the world of fear behind, recognizing the Love that is already always present as our Self. I pray that you, too, will let truth envelop your life such that you live each day in joyful love.

PART I
INTRODUCTION

Before we begin our year together, giving our lives to the Divine through the lessons of *A Course in Miracles*, I encourage you, if you haven't already, to get your own copy of *ACIM* and read each lesson prior to the lesson commentary and examples I have given. No one teaches this awakening material better than its author. This book is the expression of how it has transformed my life. Together we will transform the world through divine love.

I have chosen to quote the entire introduction instructions directly from the *Workbook* to read before beginning the lessons, to clearly understand what is being asked and why everything in our lives is there for our transformation, which these lessons can provide.

Enter each review day with an open and joyful heart and bring your mind along for the ride. It will all be included as we let go of fear and rise in love.

Part 1, Introduction

1. A theoretical foundation such as the text provides is necessary as a framework to make the exercises in this workbook meaningful. Yet it is doing the exercises that will make the goal of the course possible. An untrained mind can accomplish nothing. It is the purpose of this workbook to train your mind to think along the lines the text sets forth.

2. The exercises are very simple. They do not require a great deal of time, and it does not matter where you do them. They need no preparation. The training period is one year. The exercises are numbered from 1 to 365. Do not undertake to do more than one set of exercises a day.

3. The workbook is divided into two main sections, the first dealing with the undoing of the way you see now, and the second with the acquisition of true perception. With the exception of the review periods, each day's exercises are planned around one central idea, which is stated first. This is followed by a description of the specific procedures by which the idea for the day is to be applied.

4. The purpose of the workbook is to train your mind in a systematic way to a different perception of everyone and everything in the world. The exercises are planned to help you generalize the lessons, so that you will understand that each of them is equally applicable to everyone and everything you see.

5. Transfer of training in true perception does not proceed as does transfer of the training of the world. If true perception has been achieved in connection with any person, situation or event, total transfer to everyone and everything is certain. On the other hand, one exception held apart from true perception makes its accomplishments anywhere impossible.

6. The only general rules to be observed throughout, then, are: First, that the exercises be practiced with great specificity, as will be indicated. This will help you to generalize the ideas involved to every situation in which you find yourself, and to everyone and everything in it. Second, be sure that you do not decide for yourself that there are some people, situations or things to which the ideas are inapplicable. This will interfere with transfer of training. The very nature of true perception is that it has no limits. It is the opposite of the way you see now.

7. The overall aim of the exercises is to increase your ability to extend the ideas you will be practicing to include everything. This will require no effort on your part. The exercises themselves meet the conditions necessary for this kind of transfer.

8. Some of the ideas the workbook presents you will find hard to believe, and others may seem to be quite startling. This does not matter. You are merely asked to apply the ideas as you are directed to do. You are not asked to judge them at all. You are asked only to use them. It is their use that will give them meaning to you, and will show you that they are true.

Remember only this: you need not believe the ideas, you need not accept them, and you need not even welcome them. Some of them you may actively resist. None of this will matter, or decrease their efficacy. But do not allow yourself to make exceptions in applying the ideas the workbook contains, and whatever your reactions to the ideas may be, use them. Nothing more than that is required. (W-pI.in.1–9)

CHAPTER ONE
DAY 1
(Lesson 1)

"Nothing I see in this room (on this street, from this window, in this place) means anything."

(W-pl.1.1)

T his moment now, we begin anew. It is the adventure we all came into this dream life to take. The one we have been searching for all our lives. We come hardwired for it. It's like a homing beacon ticks within our psyche, until we answer its call.

We all begin with just a little willingness to venture into the unknown. *The Workbook of A Course in Miracles* lessons begin with undoing the concepts we now believe, by bringing everything we think we know into question and ultimately opening our minds to a whole new perception of everyone and everything. I believe I am a separate person, in a world of independent individuals and things. Is it true?

The adventure takes us through our perceived known ideas and beliefs and feelings, into their premise, seeing what is false and what is true, and ultimately undoing the false for the true, where we come to know our Self as we truly are. We rarely realize that fear underlies much of how we interpret everything we see. We are born pure and innocent, but our coping mechanisms kick in so fast we don't realize that it is our interpretations we are reacting to, and not the person place or event.

These first few lessons are helping us look at how we perceive the world. They use the environment we are in now. We practice them twice a day, morning and evening, and only for a minute, casually applying the lesson to whatever our eyes light upon, making sure not to leave anything out deliberately. And that's it.

"This hand does not mean anything. This wall does not mean anything." And so on.

I look around the room as I do the lesson, and my eyes light on a painting my husband, Lar, painted of New Orleans. Lar and I fell in love in New Orleans. I'm not just seeing a painting. Thoughts, feelings, and associations, come to mind immediately, which cast a shadow over my sight.

With today's lesson, my only goal is to notice, and by doing so, I open a small space in my mind, in which to apply the lesson. *"Nothing I see means anything. This painting does not mean anything."* Can that be true?

We each have signatured our world with the values we have assigned to everything. Nothing I see in my world means anything. Except to me.

The lesson, applied in the morning, is now active in my mind. I get a note from my boss saying he wants to see me in his office. My heart races. My mind spins a story, thinking I'm in trouble for something. It starts planning what to say to cover my ass.

But somehow, I notice this. I take a deep breath, and the lesson comes into that little space. "This note does not mean anything." The note itself is harmless. I just spun a story of fear around it. With the next breath, I let it go. I take a step. I walk into my boss's office with an open mind.

CHAPTER TWO
DAY 2
(Lesson 2)

"I have given everything I see in this room (on this street,
from this window, in this place) all the meaning it has for me."
(W-pl.2.1)

We have given everything all the meaning it has for us—that's every single thing! Everything! All the meaning anything has to us, has come from us—from our belief system. An ego based, survival program of self-concepts, telling us who we are compared to everyone and everything else. The Divine is whole consciousness.

Ego is separation incarnate. We experience this dynamic as dual consciousness. It plays out by sequencing time and space and separating parts out from the whole of creation. Here, the idea of a false, individual self, in opposition to Divine creation, was given birth. Where a self-concept or the false self was made to cover over our true identity as love, or our true Self.

In the ego-world, judgment seems to be a necessary tool for our survival. Then we give those judgments labels based on our past experiences, and we come to accept those judgments as reality, blocking out the awareness of the love that is present now.

The course is teaching us to recognize that *we* have given everything all the meaning it has for us. Applying the lesson as instructed opens a space in our minds to relinquish our judgment, if even for an instant. An instant is enough for love's spirit to enter, reinterpret, and direct the mind toward truth.

I look around me and wherever my eyes light, I apply the lesson. "I have given that window all the meaning it has for me." A voice in my head pipes in, "Damn, that window is filthy. I should have cleaned it yesterday like I said I was going to." I notice, and I continue applying the lesson as instructed. I take a breath, letting a little space open in my mind for the lesson to be what it is.

The door opens. It's my daughter Lin. She steps inside my meditation room. I apply the lesson. "I have given this girl all the meaning she has for me." I notice I resist. I don't want to have an open mind about the meaning Lin has for me. She is my daughter, whom I love—special. But the lesson works its magic anyway. In noticing the resistance, a space opens in my mind. The love is still there, but there is a spaciousness around it.

My initial response to everything is a defense against the unknown. When I apply the lesson in the space of acceptance, I feel neutral—open. Like a space in my psyche opens to see what emerges naturally when judgment is gone.

A little willingness to suspend what I think something is or means is all it takes to let it be what it is.

A minute in the morning and again in the evening. We simply apply the lesson and allow Spirit to begin to undo our fearful interpretations so the awareness of love's presence can emerge.

CHAPTER THREE

DAY 3

(Lesson 3)

"I do not understand anything I see in this room
(on this street, from this window, in this place)."

(W-pI.3.1)

Today we begin to clear our minds of the past associations, so we can actually see things for the first time, just as they appear right here, right now.

All these assumptions, the names and labels I have adopted as the meaning of what something is, can I really know they are true? Once I open to questioning, I see that nothing I see through a name or label is actually open to understanding. Labels are prisons, keeping me from a present, open mind.

Today's exercise opens us to the realization of how little we actually understand in our present experience. It requires willingness to suspend judgment and look directly into now. If I suspend my interpretations for just a moment and open my mind to receive the lesson today, I have a new experience of understanding.

Entertaining the idea that we might not understand what we think we understand frees us to enter the unknown, the world of curiosity and mystery—the moment now present as it is.

Yeah, it's scary. The ego fights against honest inquiry, where it is not at home. It's scary because it threatens the ego identity's very existence. But the ego is not who we are. But rather, a set of false ideas about ourselves.

I read over the lesson, looking around me and whatever my eyes light upon is the subject for my practice. I notice a tendency to be selective rather than random. But the lesson reminds me that each thing is all things. So, I don't deliberately leave anything out of my practice. It's wild to see just how much I tell myself I understand, which shuts the door on learning.

I say the lesson, *"I do not understand anything I see in this room."* Immediately, the ego jumps in, trying to derail me from having an actual experience of now. It feels like a little inner gripping to argue the point, "I *do* know; I *do* understand. I have proof."

I say the lesson again, noticing the voice argue the point. I question it. "Do I? Haven't I often found that what I thought I understood, when given more information, was wrong?" An opening emerges as I allow the idea in. I question. "Do I actually know? Isn't it truer that I assume I understand? And if I assume, I understand, am I seeing what is before me now?"

Today's idea defies everything I learned as a child. The rules that ran my life hinged on understanding what I was looking at. I look around me and apply the lesson anyway. "I do not understand this table. I do not understand the light on the pole outside this window, nor the pole."

Suddenly, I notice my reflection in the window. I apply the lesson. "I do not understand this reflection." Tears sting my eyes. I feel merged with something bigger I can't explain. Before, I always looked at my reflection and judgment run interference to seeing.

I think I understand what I see by what my judgments tell me. "You look tired, need makeup, look old . . ." I thought I understood what my reflection was for. I didn't. This time, looking deeply, my heart softens. "I do not understand anything I see." It's this instant I glimpse what the lesson is teaching me. I must empty my mind of everything I associate with the object before me, so I can see the relationship I have with it that connects me with everyone and everything.

CHAPTER FOUR

DAY 4

(Lesson 4)

"These thoughts do not mean anything.
They are like the things I see in this room
(on this street, from this window, in this place)."

(W-pI.4.1)

Today's lesson practice begins with watching the thoughts that occupy our mind. It is the first crucial step necessary for the thought reversal for which the mind-training aims. For about a minute or so, we simply note the thoughts that cross our mind. We are looking inward at the thoughts that run our lives.

The thought arises, "I've got to help Lucas with homework." This thought does not mean anything. "What time is it?" This thought does not mean anything. "I should have made that appointment yesterday. Luke lied to Laura on General Hospital." These thoughts do not mean anything."

It's crazy, how it seems like thoughts just come unbidden, and they are so random. It's like "I" am not thinking. It's like this thinking mechanism I have called my mind is more like a depot. Trains of thought come in and pass through.

I can hop on and become a passenger on a train of thought, causing a temporary unconsciousness to what is happening right now. Or I can watch them pass. I notice as I apply the lesson that some thoughts I label "good" while others I label "bad." I assign value according to the belief system of my personal identity, or what I call my "story of me." If I hop on for the ride, meaning I am thinking of it as "my" thought, "my" life, etc., and it deludes me into thinking I'm going somewhere. It obscures present possibilities from my awareness.

However, if I just notice the thoughts, it is easy to see that one is just like the other. And that they mean nothing unless I make them mean something. The course is teaching us in this lesson that all the thought trains are the same. They are leading nowhere. They are equally meaningless. Behind them is stillness—a blank screen—an open mind.

I am helping the kids with homework, and Lucas doesn't want to do his math. I notice I am feeling upset. I feel a little pop in my mind, and there's the lesson, waiting to be applied. I take a minute to look at the thoughts occurring in my mind and apply the lesson.

"If he doesn't do his homework, he'll fail." These thoughts do not mean anything. "I'll be a bad mom." These thoughts do not mean anything. Is it true? I let the thoughts arise, and I let them pass. The upset contraction in my mind unknots, simply by observing and letting it pass. A subtle acceptance that nothing is wrong but my thoughts, comes quietly into my mind from a place deep within. The feeling is freeing.

The lesson loosens the belief system of false identity and the automatic trains of thought that repeatedly recycle making our fearful thought system appear real. It is the beginning of opening the possibility of choosing a different voice or thought.

Once we see that the thoughts we think we think are only as meaningful as we have assigned, we see that the meaning we have given them has not made us happy. We come to the inevitable fork in the road of choice.

CHAPTER FIVE
DAY 5
(Lesson 5)

"I am never upset for the reason I think."
(W-pI.5.1)

I love how today's lesson points out just how specific our preferences are; how detailed and individual they are to every aspect of our lives. Just how alone and separate and victimized we believe ourselves to be. We see how we have given each upset a hierarchy of values and its need of resolution.

The course is teaching us we think we have thousands of problems. But in reality, we have only one problem. Our *one* problem is that we believe *we are separate from God*—we believe we are alone. That one problem is projected out as fear, anxiety, anger, worry, lack of support or lack of any kind, jealousy, heartache, loss, hopelessness. Need I go on?

In applying the lesson, first, we search our minds for sources of upsets and the forms which result. We use the terms like angry, anxious, afraid, frustrated, or worried in the form they appear and apply it to the situation we believe caused the upset.

I don't have to look far. I'm upset (worried) because of financial struggles. I'm upset (frustrated) because Lin spent her lunch money on earrings. I'm upset (angry) because I thought I would get a raise after the last review and didn't. I'm upset (guilty) because I wanted to have enough money for Lin to have both earrings and lunch.

I say, "I am not frustrated with Lin for the reason I think. I am not worried about money for the reason I think. I am not angry and disappointed that I didn't get a raise at work for the reason I think. I am not guilty that I am not a better provider for the reason I think." In applying the idea indiscriminately, then adding the tagline, *"There are no small upsets. They are all equally disturbing to my peace of mind,"* (W-pI.6.3) like this, I notice that the upsets were all internal reactions to events based on a set of beliefs.

I see that my beliefs around money are a huge wedge of guilt blocking the awareness of present okay-ness. At first, I find it difficult to consider not being upset by what I think is a lack in my life. It seems irresponsible not to feel guilty—like that would somehow justify something.

Noting that, I use the tagline from the lesson, considering its meaning. *"I cannot keep this form of upset and let the others go. For the purposes of these exercises, then, I will regard them all as the same"* (W-pI.6.3). And much to my surprise, I feel immediate relief. I see that my guilt is a prison. I see that it's really nothing. My guilt does not mean anything. The grip loosens and guilt dissipates.

With that realization, I let it go so that the spirit of love can reinterpret for me. These "upsets" can serve as portals of transformation. Through a little willingness to allow the possibility, I open a space within in my mind for love to show me how all upset is the same. Upset is not love. Only love is real.

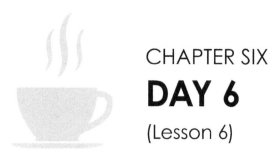

CHAPTER SIX
DAY 6
(Lesson 6)

"I am upset because I see something that is not there."
(W-pl.6.1)

Upset is always a sign I am resisting what is happening. It might look like I am upset because of something someone said or some event happening. But, would I be upset if I wasn't attached to things going the way I want?

No. My upset is a decision in my mind to resist accepting what arises just as it is. I am upset because I am interpreting now based on my past experiences and projecting them into the present moment. So, yeah, I'm upset, the second my fear-based thought system get activated.

The course is introducing us to the reality behind the illusions projected from a fear-based thought system, through the body's senses. It's teaching us what we see with our eyes is not our true reality, because everything we see and experience is an effect or projection of our past thoughts and beliefs, regardless of how real our everyday experiences seem to be to us.

Love includes all things and accepts all things. Our real life has been covered over by illusions. Today's exercise is helping us to open that space of willingness to be shown the truth that is already here within us. Everything we see is just like a motion picture of a belief system we have. It is merely showing how we perceive ourselves and the world now.

These initial lessons are what I call "leap of faith" lessons. What my eyes are showing me seems real. Because I want peace, I am willing to suspend what I think I see that I believe is the cause of my upset and apply the lesson.

I practice in faith. "I am frustrated about the kids fighting because I see something that is not there. I am worried about not having enough money this month because I see something that is not there." I'm aware of the ego voice in my mind trying to argue the point, "I do see the kids fighting. That is your last ten dollars for the month. These things are upsetting." I breathe into my faith and let those thoughts pass by.

I continue, *"There are no small upsets. They are all equally disturbing to my peace of mind. I cannot keep this form of upset and let the others go. For the purposes of these exercises, then, I will regard them all as the same."*

A new clarity emerges. The wild thing I realize is the upsets that arise aren't real feelings. They are fear from a story of what might happen. It tells me to blame someone. But no one is here, right now, to blame. It is all in my mind. I am upset because what I believe is not real. I breathe and apply the lesson, *"I am upset because I see something that is not there."* Now I see the choice. I can take the responsibility for the decision in my mind to believe in separation instead of love.

On my way to work, the main thoroughfare is congested and moving at a snail pace. I feel anxious, and a story starts spinning in my mind telling me I'll be late and in trouble. I feel angry at the circumstance where I feel powerless to do anything about it. A little space opens in my mind, "No time like the present to put my lesson into action. I am anxious because I see something that is not there. I am angry, and I feel powerless because I see something that is not there."

When looked at with a mind opened through the lesson practice, the upsets are just thoughts. The story lets go of my mind, leaving me with a spacious feeling of peace.

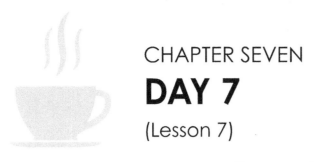

CHAPTER SEVEN

DAY 7

(Lesson 7)

"I see only the past."

(W-pl.7.1)

Practicing today's lesson brings all the lessons up to now in perfect order. If I see only the past, then what I am seeing has no meaning now, only the meaning I assigned to it. And because it is past, I do not understand what I am seeing.

The same with my thoughts, they are tethered to past associations, so they mean nothing in the reality of the present moment. No wonder I am upset. I have overlaid past fears on the present moment and judged it, apparently to keep myself safe (based on past experiences of hurt). I am upset because I am seeing something that is not there.

I come to today's lesson, and I think I am ready. Still, at first, I resist. It seems like what I'm looking now is real. Is it? Or do I just see what I believe is there?

My commitment steps forward. I look around my meditation room and apply the lesson, *"I see only the past in that candle. I see only the past in that incense smoke. I see only the past in this cushion. I see only the past in these pillows."* Wow, maybe, I don't really see now. I have decided theses are pillows but what am I really seeing without that label?

I let the question sit and look back at the other items, "What would I see if I didn't think I knew this was a candle, a flame, wax?" I do the same with the incense, the smoke, letting the question rest in my mind, "Am I really seeing this as it really is, or do I see what I have labeled it to be from past experience? I feel present in a new way.

It is a blissful glimpse of unity. I feel awake. Buzzing. I continue with the lesson. *"I see only the past in this arm. I see only the past in that curtain. I see only the past in this body."* My resistance to the idea that I see only the past has eased. I am in the glimpse of now, in the spaciousness I feel in my mind. "Maybe what I see *is* only the past."

I see how my upsets are always referenced from something I learned in my past. I don't know about you, but "upsets," in one form or another, were basically what I managed my life around. Armed with "good" judgment, I ordered my days in such a way as to keep myself safe and viewed in a favorable light, according to everything I had proudly learned from my past experiences.

Practicing the daily lesson, regardless of my resistance, opens a space in my mind where the truth can enter—like it wakes up present seeing in my mind.

I'm at work, and I have one of those aha moments with the lesson. I'm about to go to lunch and I think, "I'll ask if I can pick something up for anyone else in the office." I look over at my colleague and past thoughts start bombarding me. "She'll want me to pay for hers, like always. I don't have the money." Just like that my open-heart idea is squelched under the lies of the past.

But it's like a little pop in my mind and my lesson appears. *"I see only the past."* I start laughing. The moment is surreal. I have no idea what this moment and my idea will bring. I say, "Anyone interested in lunch? I'm going out." The look on my colleague's face is one of beautiful inclusion. I am released from any outcome because I am operating in a new zone. Love.

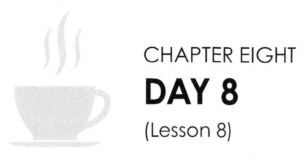

CHAPTER EIGHT

DAY 8

(Lesson 8)

"My mind is preoccupied with past thoughts."

(W-pl.8.1)

Today's lesson is at the heart of why we have such a hard time "being present." It is the reason we see only the past. We're preoccupied with it. These ideas may seem radical right now, but that is because we are undoing a carefully constructed illusion based on a timeline, from past to future. Love is beyond timelines and that's where miracles wait for us to choose. What we are seeing is always a projection of the thoughts in our mind.

I read the lesson and my first thought is, "I agree completely. My mind is always ruminating on past mistakes, guilt, and shame." But, as I actually apply the lesson, I begin to see that what's been occupying my mind isn't actually thinking. It's more like watching a replay of yesteryear.

That is the purpose for today's lesson, to begin to train our mind to recognize when it is not really thinking. It feels mind-boggling at first. I close my eyes as instructed, with as little investment as possible, I search my mind for a minute or so, merely noting the thoughts I find there. I am to name each one by the central figure of theme it contains and pass on to the next.

It's crazy to watch what my mind gets up to. I no sooner close my eyes than my mind starts up with doing the lesson right. As instructed, I say, *"I seem to be thinking about if I am doing the lesson right. But my mind is preoccupied with past thoughts."*

I see the pictures forming and they are as vivid as if my eyes are open. I watch them form and watch them pass. I've seen them all before. I notice they emerge from a spacious openness which is always present. I realize what the lesson is showing me that when I think I am thinking or seeing, I am not. I am merely replaying past associations in the "story of me."

It is increasingly apparent that the constant preoccupation with past thoughts distracts the mind from being available to recognize the presence of God. Being present and observing lets them go without attaching themselves.

The transfer of training into daily life is much more difficult. I start out feeling totally yummy from my morning practice. I'm going along with my day and I notice I feel anxious. That feeling is my invitation to stop and observe the thoughts I am preoccupied with. I notice the craziness in my mind about an upcoming event where I am to give a presentation.

What happened? The presentation's not happening now. Past thoughts of fear and unworthiness are feeding an illusion! I apply today's lesson. "I seem to be thinking I am anxious about my presentation, but my mind is preoccupied with past thoughts." An idea from the lesson comes to mind, *"The one wholly true thought one can hold about the past is that it is not here."* I feel my feet on the ground, place my hand on my heart, take a conscious breath, make myself present here, now. A smile spreads across my face as the story of anxiety leaves.

By watching my mind carefully, I recognize that beneath the "busy thinking" and "figuring out thinking" constantly running through my brain, there is an opening into stillness. A stillness which is and has been with me all along. The stillness is love.

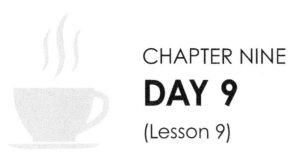

CHAPTER NINE

DAY 9
(Lesson 9)

"I see nothing as it is now."

(W-pl.9.1)

Whatever I see with the body's eyes are images reflecting what I believe I am. From there, I people my world with what supports this self-concept. What I love about these initial lessons is how they loosen the grip of the existing construct I believe to be reality. So, yeah, that part of my mind throws up active resistance in applying today's idea.

In the first paragraph of the lesson, it says that we might intellectually accept the idea, but that it's unlikely that it will mean anything to us yet. It says, *"In fact, the recognition that you do not understand is a prerequisite for undoing your false ideas."* Whew! I'm right where I need to be.

It's cool. Simply applying the lessons as instructed somehow undoes this resistance and opens our minds. It proves itself out through practice. We just show up the best we can. And it's like miracle alchemy. But we have to show up and apply the lesson. That's the deal.

Our part is to actually practice each idea each day as outlined in the lesson. The best we can. The willingness to practice allows the ideas to undo our thought system of fear or ego, leaving a clear and recognizable reflection of the truth or love in us. We are invited to go boldly into the unknown. *The truth is only known to us through our desire for it, just as it was lost to us by our desire for something else.*

As I read today's lesson, I feel immediate resistance, a clenching in my gut. "What is this terror?" I let the question sit and applied the lesson. *"I see nothing as it is now."* I thought I was doing so damn good. And it's like this lesson is pulling my covers. Oh, the terror is a sneaky little program behind the obvious.

I've served notice. I am committed to know my Self as God created me. The lessons of *A Course in Miracles* are the way for me. The terror is a sneaky voice that says, "You'll never get it."

Recognizing my true desire, I feel a release in my mind. I look around me and apply the lesson indiscriminately, *"I do not see this book as it is now. I do not see this hand as it is now."* Then further away from me, *"I do not see that window as it is now."*

There is a knock on the door. It is Lucas. "We made breakfast." I apply the lesson one more time: *"I do not see this boy as he is now."* I sparkle with joy. It's like confirmation I am seeing the truth. It is nothing, and everything. It is the spaciousness I feel around whatever appears. I feel a new acceptance that, yes, I don't see things, yet, as they really are, but I am a part of reality as it really is—love.

I am present. I can see only now. In the now, an inner Presence defines what I see. But I must make a choice. It's not exactly whether I want to quit seeing the past, but, rather, do I want to see? I want to see with love, trusting that whatever appears on the screen of my day, will be translated into miracles.

CHAPTER TEN
DAY 10
(Lesson 10)

"My thoughts do not mean anything."
(W-pl.10.1)

The first thing my mind does with today's lesson is to tell me it's a lesson I've already done. I love my mind. It totally cracks me up. The lesson answers me, *"This time the idea is introduced with 'My thoughts' instead of 'These thoughts,' and no link is make overtly with the things around you. The emphasis is on the lack of reality of what you think you think,"* I love this. It's restating that our minds are really blank. Seems crazy, right? But try to quiet your mind to meditate, right? Thoughts keep happening.

With today's lesson, I just watch and recognize the constant influx and apply the lesson. *"My thought about my thoughts does not mean anything. This idea will help release me from all that I now believe."* The lesson says, *"To recognize this is to recognize nothingness when you think you see it. As such, it is the prerequisite for vision."* Cool, right? We're being opened to the difference between ego-based perception (the way we see now) and vision, or whole-love-based perception.

I close my eyes and just watch. I feel a bubble of curiosity in my belly. Then the same ole, same ole daily thoughts start. I let each center and apply the lesson, *"My thoughts do not mean anything. This idea will help release me from all that I now believe. My thought about finances does not mean anything. My thought about the million things I must do does not mean anything."*

As each thought comes, I noticed a tendency to contract around it. Engage "figure out and fix it" thoughts. But, in noticing, I let curiosity watch and see it can pass by.

I notice how noisy the atmosphere around these kinds of thoughts is. But as I observe dispassionately, I am aware of quiet stillness behind them.

My daughter thought is harder to release. I have a more personal investment in it. It seems like my investment in that thought is bonding me with Lin, giving me a feeling of responsibility to be doing something. I apply the lesson, *"My thought about Lin's feelings does not mean anything,"* and quickly tagged it with the follow-up statement, *"This idea will help release me from all that I now believe."* It's like magic, releasing the contraction completely. Whoa, all the thoughts are equally unreal. My mind feels spacious, peaceful.

As I continue, I see how I "special-ize" myself with what the course calls "private" thoughts. Specialness or private thoughts are the part of our mind which we think we can keep to ourselves. This privacy, incidentally, also keeps them away from the light of spirit, where they can be undone, reinterpreted, and healed. They keep us from recognizing the blankness of our mind.

A little willingness to hold nothing back from applying the lesson is all that is asked. I feel the loosening, the emptying out, and blessed stillness is there. It is this experience which keeps me suiting up and showing up and giving myself over to the lesson practice—for the miracle alchemy it brings.

Without the experience, the course is just another book of beautiful prose and inspirational ideas. It is their application that brings me back to the truth—to the memory of the love I am, and you are.

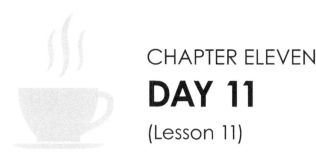

CHAPTER ELEVEN
DAY 11
(Lesson 11)

*"My meaningless thoughts are
showing me a meaningless world."*
(W-pl.11.1)

We start transformation from where the world we see begins, in our thoughts. With eyes closed, we introduce today's idea, *"My meaningless thoughts are showing me a meaningless world."* Then with eyes open we survey our environment.

The lesson idea is our constant thought, repeated over and over as we casually look around us, letting our eyes land briefly on the images we see. I love it, because this is really what we are doing in our lives; we look within first and then project what we expect to see out onto the world. This world we see is the outward picture of our inner environment.

The course teaches us that the premise of our belief system determines the appearances that show up in our lives. It says that the fidelity to premise is the law of mind. Until the course, I believed I was the messed-up person the ego identity told me I was, and the world I saw reflected the same. That was my premise.

I no longer believe the ego is real. I'm not saying the ego doesn't actively influence my daily life. It does. But that's what is so awesome about the lesson practice. Each day, each application of the lesson idea to those addictive self-concept ideas, shakes them loose. They literally can't hold solid when held to the light of truth each lesson introduces. That's forgiveness. I experience a touch of love each time.

That love experience is my new premise. It is part of the original premise. God, being Love, created me like Himself. We can do nothing to change the appearances that show up in our lives unless we change the premise in our mind.

As I begin my lesson practice, I sense an alchemy taking place behind the scenes of my perceived life. I close my eyes, and I feel a stillness in my mind as I slowly recite the lesson, *"My meaningless thoughts are showing me a meaningless world."* I open my eyes. I see the sunrise through my window, the desk with my journal open on it, the meditation cushions and pillows, the candles and incense, the wall, this body.

I slowly repeated the idea, *"My meaningless thoughts are showing me a meaningless world."* And as I do, I see how personal I have made my life and yet, how ordinary, and the sense of specialness I've attached to what I see eases. Just behind my eyes is a spacious feeling connects me with the space around the items.

I'm hanging out with the kids. I feel connected and think how special they are to me. This "special" thought is like a little tick in my mind that reminds me to practice my lesson. I close my eyes and repeat the idea slowly to myself. *"My meaningless thoughts are showing me a meaningless world."*

It almost hurts. I note I am resisting including Lin and Lucas in my encounter with meaninglessness.

Resistance hurts. I let the thought come. "I don't want my children to be meaningless. My meaningless thoughts are showing me a meaningless world. All thoughts are equal. They are just thoughts; meaningless in and of themselves." That's the release! It is my attachment to the meaning I have given them that is causing an upset.

A smile spreads across my face. Happily, I look again. I see the card game on the table, the light fixture above us, Lin, the empty chair across from me, Lucas, his skateboard next to him on the floor. *"My meaningless thoughts are showing me a meaningless world."* Instead of the resistance I had anticipated earlier, I feel a warm glow, a gracious openness beyond what my eyes are seeing. A glimpse of vision. Yummy.

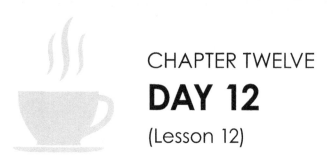

CHAPTER TWELVE

DAY 12

(Lesson 12)

"I am upset because I see a meaningless world."

(W-pI.12.1)

With today's lesson, we get to correct a major perceptual distortion. We think the world we see is how the world really is. We think we see a negative or frightening world, a satisfying or happy world, a competitive or painful world, right? Well, your adjectives might be different—which is actually the point of the lesson. As we have seen throughout the curriculum thus far, nothing we see has any inherent meaning. We give everything all the meaning it has for us. Right?

This lesson shows us we're really looking at a blank canvas, upon which we have written our fears and hopes, because of a confused identity based on the ego mindset. The ego is like a parasite that entered our minds and temporarily took control, seducing us into believing we're it.

Applying the lessons dislodges the ego's hold on the mind and that threatens its so-called life. Without our agreement, the ego can no longer siphon our life force for its purposes. The ego has no power of its own. So, the idea of a meaningless world is a threat to the ego. That's why we feel upset by the idea. But it is no threat to who we are in truth. It's empowering.

We can see, as we apply the lesson, what our history of choice and meaning is, yes? We are always looking at the effect of past thoughts, beliefs, and alignments. With today's idea, we are being guided back to the real place where correction can be made—in our mind. Our beliefs are perceptual distortions, overlaid upon the emptiness of possibility. So, the first step is to realize that what we see now does not matter. We are learning to give everything we see equal value.

As I begin my lesson practice, my mind is preoccupied with a major change in my life: changing jobs from working at a small residential recovery home for women to a large neuropsychiatric hospital.

As I read the lesson, it seems impossible not to focus on what a big change I perceive this will be in my life; the expectations that might be placed on me and the ones I place on myself. Looking at my world as meaningless and feels at once irresponsible, but also hopeful.

I think I am upset because of external and internal expectations. Noting this, I apply the lesson as instructed, looking about me and expressing whatever descriptive words come to mind, *"I think I see a world of expectations, a fearful world, a successful world, a competitive world, a world of failures and defeats, an uncaring world, a world of struggle and pain, a happy and satisfying world. But I am upset because I see a meaningless world."*

At first it feels kind of crazy, all these conflicting ideas. Then something shifts inside me as I continue to apply the lesson with neutral energy using whatever descriptive terms come to mind. The need to qualify, judge, or be right about my assessment diminishes.

I feel an inclusiveness and the terms themselves seem to lose meaning each time I repeat today's idea. It is like the big life-screen *is* blank. It is ever-present, just waiting for meaning to be given it. I feel present with something grand. I feel open. Perhaps, I can let meaning come from the awareness of spirit. I realize that meaninglessness is not threatening; it is neither good nor bad. It's an opening. This awareness is grace.

CHAPTER THIRTEEN
DAY 13
(Lesson 13)

"A meaningless world engenders fear."
(W-pl.13.1)

It is a major leap of faith for us to trust that what our body's eyes are telling us is just an illusion drawn from our own belief system. It was for me. What's so groovy about the experiential nature of just systematically applying each day's lesson is that it doesn't matter *how* it happens—that's the miracle! The ego simply cannot understand or even enter the world of spirit—the world of love. The best it can do is try to mimic and distract.

The course says that the highest thought the ego is capable of is entertaining the possibility of seeing something in a different way. And that's what we are doing with the lessons—entertaining the possibility of seeing something differently, systematically undoing the thought system that makes us unhappy and opening to where happiness rules.

I read over the lesson. Reading the words "I think I am in competition with God" feels disturbing, sacrilegious. Still, I am determined to follow the instructions to the best of my ability. I have a spacious willingness to suspend my initial reaction, because now, I have faith in the alchemy of applying the lessons.

With eyes closed, I say, *"A meaningless world engenders fear."* Looking around me, I say, *"I am looking at a meaningless world. A meaningless world engenders fear, because I think I am in competition with God."* Internally, I jump back from it. I realize a deep-seated fear to look at what is there. It feels so wrong. I want to deny, "No, say it isn't so. I don't think that. Do I?"

I let the idea settle, turning within. Something deep inside me stirs. Like I've awoken the dragon, and it's saying, "Game on." Ha! Ego's secret hideout has been exposed. I think a meaningless world is impossible. Then I see it!

I see my compulsion to be right. To have my world, my happiness, my way! I would have sworn I wasn't in competition with God. But now I see it laid bare before me. As the dust settles, the fear dissolves with the "my" belief. I want God. More than anything.

I see that the deep-seated belief that I am something I am not, guilty of betraying God, must be uprooted. That's scary shit. Pretending it's not there, didn't work. Copping to it disperses the guilty energy, and I see the belief for what it is—nothing. What is left is a blank canvas commissioned for God.

I begin my practice again, looking slowly around me, saying, *"A meaningless world engenders fear, because I think I am in competition with God."* I feel that a glimmer of truth has been revealed and there is no putting it back in its box. I am being undone. A meaningless world is only as frightening as my desire to play God.

I begin to see it everywhere. I'm in an argument with a coworker. I feel the urge to make my point—to be right. It's like a switch flips in my mind and my lesson appears. *"I am looking at a meaningless world. A meaningless world engenders fear because I think I am in competition with God."* I see that my coworker is my savior right now, showing me my mind. Gratitude fills my heart.

CHAPTER FOURTEEN
DAY 14
(Lesson 14)

"God did not create a meaningless world."
(W-pI.14.1)

I read today's lesson, and it's like a breath of fresh air—a relief and a recognition. Like, "Whew, oh, right. God's got this! He did not create a meaningless world, so, the world He has for me is still here. I've just covered over it with the illusion of fear." It's a tiny Zen bell of truth ringing in my mind.

"God is all that is. All that exists, exists within His love—and this is what I am." God is all meaning. Everything else is an illusion. My part is to see illusions as an appeal for help and healing. How could all meaning create the meaningless? What is not of God must be a dream.

With today's lesson, we are deliberately inviting into our awareness our own personal repertory of horrors, the things we live with every day. Some are shared illusions, but others are our own personal hell. It does not matter. What God did not create can only be in our own mind, seemingly apart from God's. Therefore, it's an illusion and has no meaning. Whatever is not love, is not real. Once realized, the choice for love is inevitable.

The first thing I notice as I read the lesson, though I feel the ring of truth in it, is how I am still addicted to problems and solving them. It's wild though, how just applying the lesson as instructed penetrates the cracks in my psyche and goes deep within.

I close my eyes and survey my mind, stating each horror that surfaces, as guided by the lesson. *"God did not create the traffic accident I barely missed yesterday where five people died, and so it is not real. God did not create leukemia, and so it is not real. God did not create the bullies that have been picking on Lucas, and so it is not real. God did not create the guns and gang wars, and so it is not real. God did not create a meaningless world."*

As I practice, I notice the special relationship I have in my mind with these horrors. I see how I justify hanging on to fear—it's personal! I justify judgment. I determine they make me unhappy. My mentor, Betty, has leukemia, and I don't want to lose her. Lucas, my baby—well, I want to hunt down the bullies and put an end to his suffering.

I see now how I have held these beliefs in place to make myself feel safe. In looking at each in the context of today's lesson, *"God did not create a meaningless world,"* I see I need not maintain any position, right or wrong, on illusory ideas that God did not create—regardless of how seemingly personal, or if it is a mass hallucination shared by everyone.

Love rushes in as I realize that only what God created is the "real" in the world. Not our stories. Those are subjective. It is a fundamental shift for me and all those horrors lose their weight. I feel a spark of joy expanding within me.

The lesson practice is like the energizer bunny. It keeps going, working its alchemy regardless of what my ego throws at it. It disengages my old determination to do everything on my own, my need to prove myself worthy in a stingy, competitive world—leaving a space to see the word of God written here.

CHAPTER FIFTEEN
DAY 15
(Lesson 15)

"My thoughts are images that I have made."
(W-pI.15.1)

Today's lesson starts by describing why we think what we see is real. It's because that's the function we've given the body's eyes. Their purpose is to see images we think we think. It is not seeing. It is image making. Image making is the ego's substitute for seeing or vision.

Haven't you noticed that whenever you are super focused on something, it starts to show up in all sorts of ways in your life? This is especially apparent when we are worried or afraid. It seems like the reality of those fears gets magnified, right? Thoughts are like the film in the movie projector in our mind and what we see on the screen of our lives is the projected images of those thoughts.

We have two options for viewing to choose from in deciding what film to play: truth and illusion, love or fear. The course tells us that the world of perception was made to replace the oneness of love or God. It is an outward expression of the thought of separation. Period. We believe what we see—because we see what we believe.

We are learning with today's idea to question what we see, and let it show us our thoughts. As long as we believe what we see—that we are limited persons, in bodies, in a world of physicality—the only choice we have is which lens we want to see through. Will it be fear or love?

I read over the lesson and it sparks something true in my psyche. I've had occasional episodes recently where I sensed there was light coming from behind what I was looking at, but when I try to focus on it, or figure out what was happening, it's gone. Until I read today's lesson, I'd assumed it was something biological. Like a migraine aura. Now, I'm curious about this glow surrounding everything. Had I just not noticed it before?

In applying today's lesson, the memory of these few episodes comes to mind. I state the lesson, *"My thoughts are images I have made."* I look around me, letting my eyes rest on each thing while I say, *"This carpet is an image I have made. This hand is an image I have made. This candle is an image I have made."*

It seems as if light from the candle increases, casting a glow over everything I look at. Am I making it up? I realize it doesn't matter. What I am seeing is showing me the power of my mind. *"My thoughts are images I have made."* It's like I'm watching a movie instead of being inside it. It seems my mind is shining a light on what I believe to be fact. What I see reflects what I expect to see. I see something else—a glow in and around everyone and everything. I am the light behind it all.

I'm walking through the parking lot at work. A man is walking slowly ahead of me. My first impulse is to avoid him—to feel suspicious. I notice resistance in my flow. It's almost like my vision starts to gray. Noticing, I smile and take a breath, recalling my lesson to mind. *"This unsafe man is an image I have made."* Everything seems suddenly malleable. The apprehension I felt a moment ago has left. I feel free and happy. I pick up the pace and happily greet a new friend.

CHAPTER SIXTEEN

DAY 16

(Lesson 16)

"I have no neutral thoughts."

(W-pl.16.1)

Today's lesson is reinforcing how crucial it is to watch our minds closely. It reminds us there's no such thing as "idle" thoughts. We are always either fostering the belief in the false or the truth. The lesson says, *"What gives rise to the perception of a whole world can hardly be called idle. Every thought you have contributes to truth or illusion; either it extends the truth, or it multiplies illusions. You can indeed multiply nothing, but you cannot extend it by doing so."*

I thought I was going along great—really getting this mind-training thing. Then BAM! This lesson shows up. No neutral thoughts? Turns out every single thought has the power of creation behind it, creating the life I see before me.

I've subscribed to the philosophy that our thoughts create our reality for years. Affirmations are some of my best friends—plastered on sticky notes on my desk and walls and written on the mirrors in my house. "I love and appreciate myself completely."

It's whacked how I do it, too. On the one hand, I'm throwing affirmations at the problem, because deep inside me I really *do* recognize the power of my mind. But then I want to ignore the itty, bitty, shitty thoughts, the game-changer thoughts. The ones that continuously run in the background of my mind, stabilizing my unworthy self-identity.

The thing is, and this is what today's lesson showed me, it is the thoughts I ignore that run interference, negating true change. Thoughts like, "I have to, I can't, I don't, always, this won't matter, just this once, never again." Huge awareness! I have a sneaky ego operating system!

So, I pay close attention while applying the idea. Earnestly, I follow the trails of resistance in my mind. I want to find the thoughts I am hiding from myself. I realize a habit pattern in my mind to pass over core belief thoughts— the ones that say, "I already know—so don't look any further." Fear is the arbiter.

The exercises for today are done with eyes closed. We search our mind and any thought that occurs, we attach *"is not a neutral thought,"* and finish with *"because I have no neutral thoughts." "This thought about calling back Renelle, my sister, is not a neutral thought. This thought about Doctor Joe not doing a consult today is not a neutral thought."*

The lesson says while we search our minds to *"actively seek not to overlook any 'little' thought that might tend to elude the search."* I notice subtle secondary thoughts, "I know what Renelle wants. I already know how Doc Joe is, so forget it."

In my life, it shows up looking like absent-mindedness or not caring.

I slow down and apply the lesson and finetune, watching, allowing, making friends with my little sneaky thoughts. Thoughts like, "I'll get to that later. That doesn't apply to me. It's only smart to avoid this thing that's obviously bad." I see that the fear to look is a boogieman. It's these seemingly secondary thoughts that string my thought system of fear together. Wow, *"I have no neutral thoughts!"* A roomy awareness frees something in my mind, and warm feeling—a sense of forgiveness and gratitude—floods in.

CHAPTER SEVENTEEN

DAY 17

(Lesson 17)

"I see no neutral things."
(W-pI.17.1)

We see no neutral things—because we have no neutral thoughts. Today's lesson is another step toward identifying cause and effect as it actually operates. Naturally, this lesson follows yesterday's because this is the sequence in which the world is made. What I see witnesses to what I think. The thought comes first and is projected as an image. It's never the other way around, regardless of how much I want to believe it is. It is the reversal from the way the world thinks. It's essential that we learn that it *is* the way we think.

I'm in my meditation room, applying the idea. I say to myself, *"I see no things, because I have not neutral thoughts."* I glance about me, letting my eyes rest on the pillow next to me, repeating as instructed, *"I do not see a neutral pillow, because my thoughts about pillows are not neutral. I do not see a neutral leg, because my thoughts about legs are not neutral."*

The door flies open. Lin and Lucas bust through, wrestling each other to the ground.

I notice the temptation to be upset by the interruption, but I am aware because of my lesson practice. I breathe and apply the lesson, *"I do not see a neutral child, because my thoughts about children are not neutral. I do not see a neutral interruption, because my thoughts about interruptions are not neutral."* And bingo! Everything is different.

The charge that seemed to instantly get sparked as the kids burst through the door fizzled out as I applied the lesson. A big smile spreads across my face as I watch their fun. I see how my programmed thoughts make me think I have to react in a certain way. *"I see no neutral things, because thoughts about things are not neutral."* I feel free. I feel present, joyful, aware. I jump into the mix with the kids, rolling around and tickle wrestling amongst the meditation pillows.

I am noticing something incredible happening in my psyche each day as I witness the shift taking place in my mind and—by extension—in my life. I have this increasing awareness of my mind. Like the mind-training has seeded and is training it back to love. Even as I notice myself questioning things like the need for all the repetition, I immediately remember my life, as it has been up until now, is based on the repetitious programing I denied before. The course is uncompromising. I must be also.

It is astonishing how this thing works. Even if I don't agree with the ideas, I do the exercises, do my best to apply the idea as instructed, because I made the commitment to do it. Even if I don't see how it will ever change anything. The miracle works anyway, despite my resistance. By applying the ideas to whatever shows up, a little space opens in my mind for the idea to work—it's miracle alchemy!

CHAPTER EIGHTEEN
DAY 18
(Lesson 18)

*"I am not alone in experiencing
the effects of my seeing."*
(W-pl.18.1)

Today we add an additional element to the fundamental idea that everything we see, without exception, comes from the thoughts in our mind. With today's exercises, we are shifting the focus from what we see, to how we see it. It's introducing the fact that minds are joined. So, every interpretation we make affects the whole. Isn't that astounding? We are being affected by the thoughts of everyone as a whole—every mind is one. It's incredible, yes? What we are seeing and assigning meaning to is affecting everyone. Wow.

So, believe it or not, everything we think is affecting every mind. It's hard to fathom from the separated, individual person's mind. Right? The ego mind is all about separation and cannot even comprehend oneness.

As I approach the lesson, it feels mechanical. I apply the lesson indiscriminately, letting my eyes rest briefly on each thing I see, while stating the idea. *"I am not alone in experiencing the effects of how I see this body. I am not alone in experiencing the effects of how I see that candle. I am not alone in experiencing the effect of how I see the course book."*

I don't get it. I like the idea of oneness, and I recognize a sense of synchronicity when people join in a common purpose. I experience it in AA. But the idea that my perspective, how I look at things, *always* affects the whole of humankind—Shit man!

As I keep the idea out front in my mind, I recognize that much of how I see a thing, or my interpretation of what it is and what it is for, comes from all the commonly accepted and unquestioned thinking of the world. I feel a click of understanding. "Hey, if the perceptions of the worldview affected my worldview, I have to agree that I am at least an equal player in the view of the world as we collectively see it now."

I am in a meeting at work. I feel a familiar sense to mentally checkout. But something sparks in my mind, and my lesson enters. I look around the room, briefly resting my eyes on each person and thing I see. Silently, I say, *"I am not alone in experiencing the effects of my seeing."*

I feel a curious opening like I am seeing everyone for the first time. As I look at each subject where I apply the lesson, I notice I want to feel good about what I am seeing. I am present with what is. It's like just being present brings a feeling of connectedness. I'm happy.

As I leave the meeting, I think, "What if I consciously try to only see the good, the lovely, and the beautiful? Like it says in scriptures? To let any initial judgment that might come up pass and love anyway. I don't have to believe the lies my ego mind tells me anymore just because it jumps in there with an opinion. It's like, Eureka!" That's exactly what the course is training my mind to do, to see only the truth—the love, innocence, and joy in every situation.

CHAPTER NINETEEN
DAY 19
(Lesson 19)

*"I am not alone in experiencing
the effects of my thoughts."*
(W-pl.19.1)

We are continuing today with the theme that minds are joined. It is another step in understanding the true cause and effect relationship. Today's idea is the reason we are not alone in experiencing the effects of our seeing—because we are not alone in experiencing the effects of our thoughts. With today's practice, we begin to see the impossibility of "private thoughts." Sheesh . . .

We are opening our minds to the idea that every thought affects the whole perception of the world. Every thought we have contributes either to truth or illusion, unity or separation, love or fear. We are alone in nothing. The course tells us we are teaching all the world with every thought we have.

Prior to reading the course, I hadn't thought about private thoughts. Much less that *my* private thoughts just might not be so "private." This idea seemed unfair at first. Actually, it scared the shit out of me. My so-called private, self-accusing, guilty thoughts were where I hid from the world what I judged as unsafe for their consumption.

They were my own private hell—judgmental and unforgiving. In a sick sort of way, I cherished what I thought was fact—these were *my* private thoughts. They were a sort of strategy for living. Like here, in the privacy of my own mind, I can figure out how to fix what's wrong with me, what to say and how to behave so I look normal, before taking myself to the streets. They made me feel safe.

My initial response to the lesson is fear. The ego jumps in and says, "Holy shit! I thought I was pulling off this image of normalcy, but if people know me like I do, I'm screwed." I know—a wee bit self-centered and perhaps a little on the drama-queen side.

But then a light comes on. It's not me. That false image is the ego. We've all heard that we are as sick as the secrets we keep, but this idea really busts that wide open! Every thought I have affects everyone and vice versa. I feel infused with determination to let no thought go unquestioned. Every thought I have either supports truth or fosters illusion.

Now I'm feeling like today's lesson is the way out of that spin of falseness and fear. Like, we're all in this together. I close my eyes and search my mind for the thoughts contained there—even the ones that try to scamper to the dark corners, attempting to escape my view. I apply the lesson. *"I am not alone in experiencing the effects of my thought about guilt. I am not alone in experiencing the effects of my thought about coffee. I am not alone in experiencing the effects about time. I am not alone in experiencing the effects of my thoughts about doing better."*

I notice that just paying attention to the thoughts that cross my mind, takes some of the charge out of them. It's like watching slows thoughts down enough for me to make a present choice whether I want to attach to that thought or see the situation differently and let it go. Awesome, right?

The receptionist at work doesn't look at me when I greet her. The thought comes, "She's a bitch." I see it and apply my lesson, *"I am not alone in experiencing the effects of my thoughts."* It's not true that she's a bitch. I let it go. She looks up. I smile. She smiles back.

I see the connection between the way I think about things and what shows up in my world. I am no longer being led around by unconscious ego programing. Something extraordinary is taking place.

CHAPTER TWENTY

DAY 20

(Lesson 20)

"I am determined to see."

(W-pI.20.1)

Today's idea is teaching us to invite vision to replace image making. The determination to see is all that vision requires. It is a decision we must make. We are now ready for a more structured practice. We are asked to call the lesson idea to mind every half an hour and to slowly and positively repeat the idea to ourselves. I begin the practice as instructed, saying, *"I am determined to see,"* and set the intention to remember every half hour.

This seems impossible at first. I set off for the day after my morning time with God and the lesson, determined to make my half-hour remembrances the most important thing I do. Then I forget about it most of the day. I chastise myself and promise to do better.

I write the lesson on my wrist, tie a string around my finger. Set alarms. I think, "Damn, this is hard!" Bingo! Something pops. The thought at the front of my mind is, "Remembering my practice periods is really hard! Ha! I believe it is up to me to discipline myself—to get rid of all the things I'm putting ahead of the mind-training as a priority." A light dawns. I choose to forgive that belief and give my training to the Divine—to remember for me!

The rest the day I give my practice to spirit and feel the lesson alive in me. *"I am determined to see!"* About mid-day, I'm with a client, and I feel something is off. I'm not present. I call my lesson to mind. *"I am determined to see."* It's like my exchange with this client is now lit with a present glow. I see her as she is right now. I love her.

I realize my efforts were coming from a belief in unworthiness. The more I tried to force myself into discipline, the less I let love, or the Holy Spirit, do it for me. I realize now that my willingness to have my fearful belief system undone is my part. Undoing them is the Holy Spirit's.

The lesson says the structure is not to be misconstrued as being coerced or forced. We want to be happy—and this is how to get there. We are being guided on a direct path which uncovers the happiness God wills for us. We want freedom from judgment and suffering. Our determination to see aligns our will with God's, which gives us all power in Heaven and on earth. In our determination to see, vision is given us. This is no trivial thing. It is the return to the self we are as love.

We can check our determination to see truly, by the way we feel in any situation. If I do not like how I am feeling about something, I can apply today's lesson, *"I am determined to see."* This is my prayer of willingness to let the Holy Spirit show me a different perspective. With love as guide, we need not be afraid to look directly into the source of our unhappiness, because just by looking, love reveals its falsity.

CHAPTER TWENTY-ONE
DAY 21
(Lesson 21)

"I am determined to see things differently."

(W-pl.21.1)

Today's lesson is embedded in my psyche like a light switch that flips on the instant I feel upset. *"I am determined to see things differently."* My life is the playground that shows me what is happening in my mind. What I am seeing and how I am feeling is always reflecting my state of mind. Is it love or fear? The mind is where the miracle happens.

Our physical experience is the backdrop for the mind-training. So, as we examine our minds for the many ways in which we resist life and become determined to see things differently, forgiveness becomes available to us, and through forgiveness, the awareness of present love.

With today's practice, we are searching our minds carefully for situations past, present or anticipated which arouse anger in us. The lesson says, *"The degree of the emotion you experience does not matter. You will become increasingly aware that a slight twinge of annoyance is nothing but a veil drawn over intense fury."*

This is such a powerful part of the mind-training. I fear anger. I make it something it is not, based on experiences from my past. Even in my own mind, I avoid and deny anything that resembles anger. These are the thoughts in my mind that scurry to the dark corners, trying to hide from the light of awareness.

My story on myself paints me as easygoing, non-judgmental, and pretty accepting of people and situations. Sure, I get frustrated, but not angry! I do not want to be like I believed my father was when I was a child—angry, controlling, withholding. I am afraid of anger. But I take what the lesson tells me on faith—that even mild frustration is really deep, intense rage. Accepting this idea breaks something open inside me.

My experience as I practice the lesson reveals something new. I don't know what is true. I begin as instructed, repeating the idea, *"I am determined to see things differently."* I let it work deep within me, accepting it in my heart as I close my eyes and begin searching my mind. I feel curious to see what I am denying. I am willing to cop to each irritation as covering over deep-seated rage.

Because I am committed to doing the lessons no matter what, I keep an open mind and practice in faith. The course is uncompromising, and I must be also. I want to unplug from the attack thoughts in my mind.

I search for thoughts that bring anger—even the slightest irritation. I don't have to look far. I'm pissed at a shrink at work. I'm irritated that Lin didn't put the dishes in the dishwasher. I'm angry that my dad made me afraid of anger. Whoa.

I apply the lesson, *"I am determined to see Doctor Alan differently. I am determined to see Lin differently. I am determined to see dish responsibilities differently. I am determined to see my Dad differently. Wow, I thought I did. I am determined to see anger differently."*

I feel the knotted bundle in my mind begin to unravel, exposing a whole list of unacceptable thoughts, feelings, and memories I had denied and buried. Pictures from my childhood where my father was angry arise. I offer my lesson, *"I am determined to see my dad's rage at Dirk differently. I am determined to see my guilt at not doing anything to stop it differently."*

Images of my story of my past arrive, loosen, and ease as I apply the lesson to each and leave none as I saw before. They are just images of a story of the past. I let them pass. I am at peace. I am love. I am beginning to see it differently.

CHAPTER TWENTY-TWO

DAY 22

(Lesson 22)

"What I see is a form of vengeance."
(W-pI.22.1)

As long as we hold attack thoughts in our mind, we continue to project them onto the world. As a result, we see a world where vengeance could strike at any moment. If we feel unsafe, mistrusting, and afraid, it is because attack rests at the heart of how we see the world. Because we hold attack thoughts in our mind, we see an unsafe world. We then justify attacking as self-defense.

These early lessons are the part of the mind-training course that teaches us that *projection makes perception.* Applying the ideas to our own seeing and thinking undoes the cycle of attack and defense.

Today's exercises help us get honest about the dark thoughts we have denied but that are still running our lives. We start with our perception and work backward to our thoughts. We are asked for five practice sessions of at least a minute each.

As I read today's lesson, *"What I see is a form of vengeance,"* I feel my gut clench. I'm resistant to being honest and responsible for what I don't think I like. I don't want to see that vengeance is in my mind. But I realize my very resistance to it is showing me that something miraculous is possible by accepting and applying the lesson. My gut eases through my willingness to see and accept. In fact, I'm kind of excited to uncover the scary thoughts I've previously run from.

I say the idea slowly, looking around me. "What I see is a form of vengeance." I let my eyes move slowly from one item to the next, my body, my cat, the window, the street where a car passes by. I repeat the lesson, trusting its alchemy. *"I see only the perishable. I see nothing that will last. What I see is not real. What I see is a form of vengeance."*

I take a deep breath and ask myself honestly, *"Is this the world I really want to see?"* I say aloud. "No. It is not." I know it is true—I can feel the freedom as I say it. My eyes light on the last line of the lesson. *"The answer is surely obvious."* I smile, and a warm glow spreads throughout my being and across the field of my vision.

As I go about my day, my lesson at the forefront of my mind, I am aware of little self-protective defenses in my mind. Thoughts like, "Avoid this because you might get hurt. Don't look at that, I could be uncomfortable." I see that every facet of my life has the mark of vengeance on it. And fear is the result. My beliefs that foster a reality of a fragile world and body are attack thoughts. Wow. Is it possible that the fear of vengeance I defend against is due to attack thoughts in my mind? Yep.

I'm on break at work—a great time to practice my lesson. I go out on the balcony overlooking the city. Everywhere I look is marked by my past. Each memory image that comes to mind as I look over the city is tainted with fear of vengeance. I pay attention while I apply the lesson, *"I see only the perishable. I see nothing that will last. What I see is not real. What I see is a form of vengeance. Is this the world I want to see?"* No.

I feel the loosening and release as the thoughts come and go. I buzz with joyous excitement as I continue looking over the valley. It's like the scene changes before my eyes. What I see feels fresh, bright with colors and textures. My mind is clear. I am in love. Looking directly at what is reveals a light beyond, yet within my heart.

CHAPTER TWENTY-THREE

DAY 23

(Lesson 23)

*"I can escape the world I see
by giving up attack thoughts."*

(W-pl.23.1)

I feel energized as I read the first few lines of today's lesson, *"The idea for today contains the only way out of fear that will ever succeed. [. . .] But there is indeed a point in changing our thoughts about the world. Here we are changing the cause. The effect will change automatically."*

As I begin applying today's lesson, I note that I'm not so apprehensive about what I might find lurking in my mind. I feel confident that healing is taking place within my mind. I must just keep showing up. Because the cause of fear and attack is in my mind, I'm not trapped in the mass hallucination. I can change my mind about how I see and instead see a healed and forgiven world.

The lesson describes healing as a three-step process. First, we recognize that the cause of the world as we see it now is our own thinking. Second, we must let go of how we see the now. Third, we're willing to see it differently, allowing the Holy Spirit to reinterpret and heal our mind. So, my part is really the first two and then release my mind to the Holy Spirit which brings truth to my awareness.

I look around me slowly repeating the idea, *"I can escape the world I see by giving up attack thoughts."* I close my eyes and invite attack thoughts into my awareness. As each cross my mind, I apply the idea as instructed, holding the attack thought static, while I say. *"I can escape the world I see by giving up attack thoughts about sickness, sniffles, and viruses. I can escape the world I see by giving up attack thoughts about traffic accidents. I can escape the world I see by giving up attack thoughts about the children getting harmed."*

As I do, I feel a now familiar spaciousness opening behind the thoughts in my mind. I conclude with a prayer of release, "Holy Spirit, I give my mind and all my attack thoughts to you to reinterpret and heal my mind and the world. Thank you that *I can escape the world I see by giving up attack thoughts."*

Throughout the day, I keep noticing areas where I perpetuate the unreality of a dangerous world. I catch a train of thought, "I better get some water and keep it at my desk, because I don't want to get dehydrated and get sick." Ha! I say aloud, smiling to myself. I silently say my lesson, *"I can escape the world I see by giving up attack thoughts about the vulnerability of my body."*

I notice a conflict between two coworkers and recognize that what I see is coming from attack thoughts in my mind. Joyously, I say, *"I can escape the world I see by giving up my attack thoughts about coworkers. I can escape the world I see by giving up my attack thoughts about conflict."* I realize no one is guilty. No one is to blame. I feel a spacious feeling of unified perception taking place in me, where everything is love.

CHAPTER TWENTY-FOUR

DAY 24

(Lesson 24)

"I do not perceive my own best interests."
(W-pI.24.1)

We make plans. Get our ducks in a row. Do the right thing. Know the right people, etc. Still, persistent joy eludes us. This was the formula for my life for a very long time. I truly believed it was all up to me. That if I just got it right this time or next time, I would be happy. Yet, happiness was fleeting at best, and mostly a disappointment.

As I read today's idea, *"I do not perceive my own best interests,"* I feel two things happening. On the surface, I think, "Hey, if I don't know my own best interest, who does?" But something deep within stirs. It tells me, "Well, based on the evidence of my self-initiated life, can I really argue the point? My best shot is motivated by fear, guilt and shame, worry and self-loathing, and trying to make a better me." I want to let go, giving the reins to the Divine.

Today's lesson asks for a deeper level of honesty than we are accustomed to having. I'm not sure where I'm not being honest, but I trust that practicing the lesson as honestly as I can will reveal it to me. I trust the Holy Spirit to show me what I'm missing. As instructed, I begin by repeating today's idea, *"I do not perceive my own best interests."* Then close my eyes and search for unresolved situations I'm currently concerned about.

With each concern, I apply the lesson as instructed. *"In the situation involving the kids, I want to spend quality time, to meditate together, and have fun. I want them to want to spend time with me, to want to meditate, and to want to have fun with me."* I do not perceive my own best interests in this situation. *"In the situation with my car, I want a car that is problem free, and I want it to not add extra financial strain, so no car payment. I want it to relieve my stress about getting to work and getting the kids where they need to go."* I do not perceive my own best interests in this situation.

By the time I finish this first practice period, I'm laughing. I see how all my wants conflict. I see the impossibility in the demands I am making on each situation to make me happy. It's insane.

As the day goes on, it seems everywhere I look I see the insanity of the way I have "happy outcomes" wired up and the impossibility of their accomplishment.

A client is hysterical. I want him to calm down. And I want him to have his feelings. I want to accept him with love, just the way he is, and I want him to change. I silently apply my lesson. *"I do not perceive my own best interest in this situation."* Instantly, I feel free. I am present with him just as he is. Nothing needs to change.

I see what is happening is neutral. Perfect for me. It is for my best interest. The beautiful thing is I realize I am not alone. There is a presence and power with and within me that already knows the best interest for me and everyone.

CHAPTER TWENTY-FIVE

DAY 25

(Lesson 25)

"I do not know what anything is for."

(W-pI.25.1)

Today's lesson is about purpose. It says, *"Purpose is meaning. Today's idea explains why nothing we see means anything. You do not know what it is for. Therefore, it is meaningless to you. Everything is for your own best interests. That is what it is for; that is its purpose; that is what it means. It is in recognizing this that your goals become unified. It is in recognizing this that what you see is given meaning."*

It's amazing to experience how this mind-training thing works. I always get to see the lesson idea play out in my life.

It seems like I know what things are for, right? But I'm willing to accept that maybe I don't know, because what I want above all else, is to know what God wants me to know. As instructed, I say, *"I do not know what anything is for,"* while slowly looking around at whatever my eyes light upon. *"I do not know what this cushion is for. I do not know what this arm is for. I do not know what this telephone is for."*

I feel open to the possibility that what I thought each was for, is not its real purpose. Like with the telephone, I know it is for talking with someone, but maybe what I want to communicate needs to come from a purpose greater than I yet see. I was feeling open to learning from the lesson practice.

At least that is how I was feeling during and following my first couple of practice sessions. Then, life happens. I get the mail. In it is my phone bill. As I open and look at the bill, my breath catches. It's almost $1,000 more than I expected. I'm hyperventilating. Fear, anger, and victimization wash over me like a wave. What was my lesson? I take a few deep breaths, repeating my lesson, *"I don't know what this phone bill is for."* I repeat it again, gaining some composure, then call the phone company.

I explain to the attendant I had lost my phone a couple of weeks before, and the charges aren't mine. She asks if I reported the loss. I didn't. She tells me I should have reported it immediately and suspended the service. I didn't. I tell her I don't know how I'll be able I'd pay for it. She puts me on hold. I feel victimized and unjustly treated. It's like ants crawling just under my skin.

I shake my head. "This is insanity. It cannot be what this situation is for!" My lesson comes into my mind, *"I don't know what this phone call is for. I don't know what this bill is for. I don't know what the conversation is for."* And peace begins to settle my racing heart. *"I don't know what anything is for."* It diffuses the restless energy and I breathe into the open spaciousness of that release. My focus lifts from having a problem, to wanting peace.

Ah, it totally works! I'm okay—even peaceful. I thought I needed a resolution from the phone company, but what I really want is peace of mind. It's like magic. Nothing's changed but my mind. I know everything is as it should be.

I'd nearly forgotten I was on hold when a supervisor comes on the line. She tells me they tracked the phone calls and see the incongruences in the past couple of weeks and are dismissing the charges. The groovy thing for me is that I had already found peace. Miracle.

CHAPTER TWENTY-SIX

DAY 26

(Lesson 26)

"My attack thoughts are attacking my invulnerability."

(W-pI.26.1)

Today's lesson is introducing the idea that we always attack ourselves first, because ideas of attack begin in our mind. So, if attack starts in my mind and I attack myself first, then I can escape feeling vulnerable, by giving up attack thoughts.

But first, I must take full responsibility for every experience in my life as coming from my own mind. Love creates only like itself, and there is no place that attack and love meet up. I can accept my reality as spirit—pure and innocent love, as God created me. Or I can believe that attack is real.

The first paragraph says, *"It is surely obvious that if you can be attacked, you are not invulnerable. You see attack as a real threat."* This feeling of being vulnerable to attack by forces outside ourselves is one of the first things we are taught as children.

Our parents were always teaching us that our bodies are vulnerable. "Be careful, you're going to get hurt. Don't do that or I'll be mad." So, we have our vulnerability twisted up with protecting ourselves from harm. Without the body identity, would I still feel vulnerable?

As I practice the lesson, the first thing that comes to mind is money lack, so I start with that. I say, *"My attack thoughts are attacking my invulnerability. I am concerned about not having enough money. I am afraid I won't be able to give my children what they need. I am afraid I am not being a good mom. I am afraid creditors will come after me. I am worried something will happen that I won't have the money to pay for. I am ashamed that I am not doing better financially. These thoughts are an attack upon myself."*

I notice while I am thinking of fearful possible outcomes that could attack my life, I feel the attack in my mind. My heart tightens and my mind contracts, pinpointing the fear. I say, *"This thought is an attack upon myself."* The awareness is real. *"My attack thoughts are attacking my invulnerability."*

Wow, I am having an immediate experience of what the lesson is teaching. My attack thoughts always attack me first. I see how fear and worry attack my peace of mind. I get it. I alone am doing this to myself. Suddenly, I feel a powerful presence—I am not alone. A grateful prayer fills my heart. A calm assurance and peace abide with me. I'm eager to see how it plays out in my day.

Right away I get my chance.

Lin tells me she wants to join the French Club. It costs money. I feel the initial grip reaction in my mind and gut. I breathe and I realize this is my lesson in action. A quiet voice says, "Hey, no one is attacking me here. It is my mind. I am the invulnerable child of love. *My attack thoughts are attacking my invulnerability.*" I know Lin's asking is perfect. I trust the answer comes from love. I feel at peace as I say, "Yes," trusting our invulnerability as God's children.

CHAPTER TWENTY-SEVEN
DAY 27
(Lesson 27)

"Above all else I want to see."

(W-pI.27.1)

Today's lesson asks for stronger commitment to seeing than just mere determination. We are to repeat the idea, *"Above all else I want to see,"* at least every half hour and preferably every fifteen minutes. Am I willing? Do I want vision? How much do I want it?

It is our small gift of willingness and the mighty power of God through the Holy Spirit in the mind that opens us to vision. In truth, above all else, we do want to see. We are one in Christ and we are not alone. *"Above all else I want to see."* Ask and it is given.

I love how this lesson adds to my experience in realizing that my attack thoughts show me a world where I feel vulnerable and that by recognizing them I free myself from their preoccupation in my mind. I feel open to seeing things differently. Today's lesson is the perfect next step.

It's scary to step off the ledge of the familiar and trust that something more real and substantial will emerge, but what's the alternative? For me, I want to feel joyous about everything in my life, even those areas I loop back around to fear and defense.

Today's lesson provides an opening to vision. Above all else I want to see God's love everywhere. I want to see what God sees. I am willing to let go of the familiar and trust I will be shown. The steps provided in the lesson are like steppingstones that let me open my mind and sight. I state the lesson. *"Above all else I want to see."* If I feel any resistance I say, *"Vision has no cost to anyone. It can only bless."*

The frequency to remember is like a litmus test to my resolve. And it's amazing to see how addicted to absent-mindedness I am. The first couple of hours are relatively easy. The lesson is fresh in my mind. I feel wonderful from my practice in my morning time with God, and I truly believe that above all else I want to see. But as the day wears on, I get distracted.

Before I know it, it's noon. I realize I haven't thought of the lesson for over an hour. I find a quiet place where I can be alone. I consider my lesson, *"Above all else I want to see."* I remind myself that vision is my priority and let it sink deep in my mind, *"Above all else I want to see."*

I put a rubber band around my wrist so I'll see it every time I take a patient's pulse or when I sit down to chart or make a phone call. I instruct my mind, *"Vision has no cost to anyone. It can only bless."* I sit down with a patient and as I look at them my lesson plays in my mind. *"Above all else I want to see."*

As I go home for the evening, getting in my car, I notice my lesson playing again and again, *"Above all else I want to see."* I let it play over in my mind as I head home to the kids, setting reminder markers in my mind for my time with the kids to help me remember. As I kiss the kids good night, repeating silently, *"Above all else I want to see."* It feels real, and it seems a warm glow of love surrounds our abode.

CHAPTER TWENTY-EIGHT

DAY 28

(Lesson 28)

"Above all else I want to see things differently."

(W-pl.28.1)

Today's lesson is a set of specific directives to change our mind about our mind. It is a commitment to what we want in truth. It is a loosening-up of beliefs and of "being right" about what we think we see and what it is for. With today's lesson we are making definite commitments as we apply the lesson with each practice period and throughout the day.

When we say we want to see something differently, what we are doing is we are asking the Divine *what* we are seeing. The way we have done it in the past is to project an image of separation through labels and names we don't question. It is a subtle, but monumental difference that changes everything. It is the shift from isolation to communion. It is open-mindedness.

Today we are setting aside our own ideas each time we practice, *"Above all else, I want to see things differently."* The lesson says that we could gain vision from a table if we could see the purpose behind it. Above all else is a total commitment to seeing differently.

As I practice the lesson in the morning, stating the lesson, *"Above all else I want to see things differently,"* I feel open and committed. I casually looked around, randomly picking subjects and just applying the lesson.

Holding my commitment to see everything differently at the center of my mind, I let nothing hold any particular meaning as best I can. *"Above all else I want to see this hand differently. Above all else I want to see that wall differently. Above all else I want to see this book differently."* I can feel the idea undoing what I believe things are. I don't know what anything is. I feel part of the luminous mystery all around me.

That mysterious undoing is active as I go about my day. By declaring my commitment that above all else I want to see this differently, I am withdrawing my preconceived ideas of what something or someone is, and it's like a light gets turned on in my mind and in what I am looking at.

They are all the same light. This opens my mind to accept another purpose than what I automatically prejudge that it was for. And instantly I feel at peace and trusting that I'll be shown.

I'm hanging out at a coffee shop with friends. I look around the table at each face and it feels mechanical, the way we interact, our conversations. I realize I'm not really seeing them or hearing the conversation. I have prejudged the situation, so I am not present.

A question enters my mind: "Why am I here?" My lesson opens brightly before me: *"Above all else I want to see this differently."* I look at my friends and it's like everything is in slow motion. I see the tilt of a head, a smile, a nod, a colorful opinion. I get it.

We're all the tapestry of divinity expressing itself. I don't want to miss a thing. Joy spreads across my heart and a warm glow encompasses my circle of friends, expanding and extending. I see differently because the desire for union has replaced differences. A reversal of my thought system is in effect. It is absolute joy! It's amazing how it works!

CHAPTER TWENTY-NINE

DAY 29

(Lesson 29)

"God is in everything I see."

(W-pI.29.1)

We can recognize God in everything we see, because we, and what we look at, share the purpose of the universe, and what shares the purpose of the universe, shares the purpose of its Creator.

Today's idea is inviting us to see that within all things in the universe, beyond what the eyes can see, is the purpose God has for it and us. LOVE.

Through a unified perception, love emerges. We accept that beyond the forms of what we see, is a unified purpose of love and joy. The distinctions that once seemed so separate, merge and blend within our minds and we find that we are always looking at our wholeness and oneness with everyone and everything.

As I consider today's idea, I notice a tendency to think that God is in the objects or persons I'm looking at. At first, I feel like I'm trying to sort of paste the idea that God is in this chair, or in this body, or person, onto what my body's eyes were showing me. But as I look around, saying the lesson, *"God is in this hand. God is in this window,"* I feel a slight alteration in my mind and sight.

I remember the course says everything the body's eyes see is a lie. My eyes soften and I invite spirit to see for me. I seem to look past appearances directly into the light within. I realize that regardless of what my physical eyes see, I am looking to recognize God's presence in everyone and everything. It is a wonderful exercise in trust that I take with me as I move into my day.

I'm driving to work. *"God is in this car."* The sky is clear. "God is in the sky." The sun is shining. *"God is in sunshine."* With everything I look at, I feel God's presence in everything I see.

I'm coming through the door at work and someone else is hurrying out, bumping into me. We both apologize, "Sorry." I pause and let a thought arise, *"God is in this exchange."*

I'm at the grocery store, and in front of me in line a toddler is crying. The mother is telling her to stop crying. Immediate judgment flares in my mind, "Stop being mean. She's just a little girl. She needs love, not judgment." My lesson taps me mentally, pushing pause.

I take a deep breath and apply the lesson, looking directly into the heart of what I am seeing, *"God is in this mom. God is in this little girl. God is in everything I see."* Immediately, I see the situation differently. I choke up with gratitude. I see the obvious gift to me. "That's me! Both mother and child. God is in this moment, in me, in mother and child. I am in love."

I ask if I can help take her groceries to the car. It feels amazing. *"God is in everything I see."*

CHAPTER THIRTY

DAY 30

(Lesson 30)

*"God is in everything I see
because God is in my mind."*

(W-pI.30.1)

Today's lesson is the reason vision is possible, and from it a whole new world opens for us. With today's idea, we are extending yesterday's idea that God is in everything we see, to the *reason* for it. The cause for vision comes from the fact that everything that God created is still within the one mind of God, and it shares His purpose which is love, light, joy, peace, and happiness.

Today we practice with real vision. We are to apply the lesson as often as possible throughout the day. We want to frequently pause and repeat the lesson slowly to ourselves, *"God is in everything I see because God is in my mind,"* trying to realize that the idea applies to everything we see now, or could see now if it were within the range of our sight—what is in our minds as well as physical sight.

They are all the same because God is in the mind that sees. Real vision is not limited to time and space, nor does it depend on the body's eyes at all. Divine mind is its only source.

As I apply the lesson, *"God is in that candle because God is in my mind. God is in this book because God is in my mind, God is in this body because God is in my mind,"* it feels sacred. There's no space where judgment or preconceived ideas can enter a mind opened in God.

I close my eyes, curious about what I might see and attaching the idea to each picture as it arises on the screen of my mind. *"God is in Lucas sleeping in his bed because God is in my mind. God is in Lin and our conversation last night. God is in the traffic because God is in my mind."* I notice a feeling of open-minded union with everything I look at or think about. God within is the unifying factor.

I feel as if I am walking in a beam of light, as I move throughout the day. I feel as if I am looking at everything and God's love is seeing through my mind and eyes. I'm in the break room at work. I let my eyes wander to the familiar sights and people I know, pausing for a moment with each and repeating today's idea. I feel connected with each one—in love.

I think of a coworker I haven't seen for some time and let him come into my mind's eye, and then another not in the room. I think of the charting to be done in the other room. With each thought, I repeat the idea silently, *"God is in you because God is in my mind. God is in everything I see because God is in my mind."*

Love and appreciation light my mind and the room with love's glow. I feel a new closeness with my coworkers, the hospital, and the purpose of love and healing which unites us.

Because I am not looking at my past definitions that my ego mind gave everything, the light within, the purpose, which would unify, extends a feeling of love and unity. I'm experiencing an intuitive understanding of what it means to have God in every aspect of my perception. In actively applying the idea with whatever or whomever I see or think of, I have a deep sense of union and peace. And something I never expected happens. I realize finally, I am not alone.

CHAPTER THIRTY-ONE
DAY 31
(Lesson 31)

"I am not the victim of the world I see."
(W-pI.31.1)

Imagine never feeling victimized again. It's like breathing for the first time after being under water. Right? From the first moment I began reading and contemplating the ideas in the course, I could feel the immense possibility for total release. I am humbled to realize I am naturally taking responsibility for my own mind through each day's lesson practice.

I see I can be free from feeling like a victim, powerless to forces outside myself, and eventually from my false identity. So, accepting and practicing today's idea is potent for me.

The lessons have been systematically preparing us to accept today's idea and put it into practice in our lives. *"I am not the victim of the world I see"* is a decision to see ourselves, everyone, and our life as a unified whole. It is a declaration of release from fear in the name of freedom.

Freedom is our natural inheritance. This one idea, accepted fully, is the key that unlocks the prison we have placed ourselves in, and shows us we are the jailer, and the jailed. The application, however, requires tremendous vigilance.

It is incredible to see how insidious victimhood weaves its way around in my psyche and life. Acceptance of today's idea recalibrates all the ideas that make up "the story of me," to a whole new perception. One where I see innocence where there was judgment. Where no one is guilty, and everyone is the equal. I see we are all always only doing one of two things—extending love or asking for love.

This single idea, when applied with sincere open-mindedness, has the power to immediately flip us right side up. It opens us to the oneness we share with all the world.

As I practice the lesson in the morning, I look around me, slowly repeating the idea, *"I am not the victim of the world I see,"* several times. I'm like, "I've got this. I can see that it is the way I look at a situation that makes me feel victimized or not. I can do this." As I close my eyes and survey my inner world, I remind myself my inner world causes the world I see outside. *"I am not a victim of the world I see."* I set off for the day feeling empowered and happy.

Then boom! I'm in a staff meeting. I'm trying to get a point across about a patient, and one doctor waves his hand, cutting me off, and prescribes a different form of treatment. My heart speeds up. My face gets hot and I feel sick with unfairness. The desire to justify myself and my perspective feels compulsive. I take a deep breath to prepare my defense, when my lesson whispers *"I am not the victim of this situation."*

It's like cha-chinch! I see it. The victim story is not me. It is not true. It is not real. I need do nothing but let it go. My victim story is not what is happening. Everything suddenly looks different. What is happening is a joining in the name of healing. I let it all be exactly as it is. I trust that when my input is needed, I will be able to communicate it in a way that truly helps, when the time is right. I am happy—at peace. I am free. I am open to communion.

CHAPTER THIRTY-TWO
DAY 32
(Lesson 32)

"I have invented the world I see."

(W-pI.32.1)

We are seeing that our world reflects our predominate thoughts and beliefs. Quantum physics tells us that it is the observer that shifts the tide of energy to the expectations of the one observing—and the material world begins to form around those belief expectations.

With today's lesson we are taking responsibility for the inventions we have projected on our world by the expectations in our mind—the thoughts and beliefs we value invent the world we see. Do I want a world of pain and suffering, complaints, and blame? Or do I want one of peace, harmony, joy, and unity?

We are looking at the true relationship of cause and effect; that giving and receiving are the same. Today's idea is a statement of ownership, making it clear why we are not the victim of the world we see—because we invented it. And because we invented it, we can just as easily change it. How we see the world is up to us. The world we see is literally a reflection of what we want to see.

Reflecting on today's idea during my morning time with the Divine, I see how I reinvent the world of fear every time I react with anything but love to a brother. Every time I get upset by something I see or hear on the world stage and I don't stop, recognizing it is fear and ask for truth to replace the error in my mind. Each time I get into fixing or trying to prevent problems, I am inventing a world of problems by my belief.

I quiet my mind, and, in the stillness, I invite another world into my mind. I feel the peace within and surrounding this sacred time and imagine a world of peace, where every relationship is holy ground. I imagine love bursting from heart to heart and joy compelling us to a new collaboration in a world attentive to the Divinity within all creation.

The phone rings. It's my friend Kathy. She's talking fast. She tells me her email account has been hacked and she was mean to the Microsoft employee who couldn't do what she requested. Now she thinks someone was at her back window last night trying to break in—they must have gotten her address from her email account.

Today's lesson flashes across my mind like a neon sign. *"I have invented the world I see."* I don't want to give any validity to her story of fear and worry. I want to reinforce the magnificent power of our minds. I want to break the spell she's under and offer a miracle—to invite her to join me to see things differently and envision a new world.

I feel inspired to share a joke about a guy who complains about having peanut butter sandwiches for lunch every day. When his coworker asks why he doesn't have his wife make something else, he replies, "I make my own lunch." We laugh. It's perfect.

Kathy is a student of the course. She shifts instantly, "This situation is just another form of my old belief that the world is unsafe, and people are out to get me." We laugh again, and the spell is broken. I tell her today's lesson is *"I have invented the world I see."*

We join in forgiving the old belief, looking beyond it to the truth—We are distinct consciousness, capable of direct communication with the Creator of that consciousness. We are powerful giving and receiving channels. By our decision we can see the world of love and unity, which is our inheritance.

CHAPTER THIRTY-THREE
DAY 33
(Lesson 33)

"There is another way of looking at the world."
(W-pI.33.1)

It's remarkable the way the lessons systematically undo our false, fearful belief system while infusing our mind with another way of looking at the world through applying the ideas—even when we're actively resisting. The lessons are the mind-training manual that undoes our insanity and restores us to the sanity of the love we are in truth.

As I apply today's lesson, *"There is another way of looking at the world,"* I'm looking at the things around me, the couch, my hands, a book, the carpet. I notice my inner dialogue of malcontent thoughts come immediately, "I need a new couch. These hands are looking old. I need to put that book away. The carpet needs cleaning." They are all thoughts that something needs to be different than it is now for me to be happy. I apply the idea, *"There is another way of looking at this couch. There is another way of looking at these hands, there is another way of looking at this book, there is another way of looking at this carpet."*

I smile. "Aha! These are unreal thoughts about something that is not actually happening." Applying the idea while looking at both my outer and inner world, I see how the lesson progression is effectually driving the application to the next logical awareness. I notice if I see something and I feel I lack something or think I need more or I wish something to be different from what it is, my inner world is plagued by guilt, regret, sorrow, wishful thinking, or futurizing.

But as I apply the idea, I recognize I am the cause. What I am looking at is the effects of past thinking. I realize instantly I can choose another way of looking instead of this. I can be present with love and appreciation, and immediately the scene before me changes. I feel the presence of God, of love. I feel open. *"There is another way of looking at the world."* I am present now. Everything is as it should be. I need do nothing. I feel released and at peace. There *is* another way of looking at the world. Changing nothing but the way I see, I am happy.

While dropping Lin at school, traffic is thick in the drive up to the front of the school. I feel impatient, and imagine each car is filled with impatient parents wishing like I am for things to move faster. As my mind wanders, anticipating being late for work, I note the yucky feeling I have about it, and I know immediately it is the way I see the situation causing my discomfort.

My lesson flashes in my mind, cutting through my reverie. I chuckle, *"There is another way of looking at this."* It brings me immediately present and gratitude washes over me. I catch Lin's eye. We smile. I reach over and slip my hand in hers, grateful for a few extra minutes to pause and bask in our love for each other.

I look around at the other cars and see loving parents dropping their children off as I am. I love them. We're in this together. As Lin walks up the steps into the school, my eyes fill with tears of joy. "Another way, indeed."

CHAPTER THIRTY-FOUR
DAY 34
(Lesson 34)

"I could see peace instead of this."
(W-pl.34.1)

Today's idea is so yummy. Just saying, *"I could see peace instead of this,"* feels good, yes? We go into each practice period with hope, just by repeating the idea, yeah? Peace is a state of mind. So, that covers literally everything we think or experience. The old way of looking at the world was to think that I would be peaceful if circumstances would only change to suit me. Now, we see that the way we experience everything in our life comes from our state of mind.

At first, while considering today's idea, sneaky little negative what-if thoughts creep in. I am disappointed that so many unimportant things are still occupying so much of my mind. I think I should be past this by now.

This is what the ego does. It's always grading my enlightenment for me. Aargh! I apply my lesson, *"I could see peace instead of disappointment."* Bing! My mind clears—a moment of pure release. Whoa, I can feel peace instead! Just like that. My choice! The disappointment and grading system dissolve into present peace. Even before I finish saying the words, the idea has penetrated my mind, *"I could see peace instead of this."* The feeling is immediate. Seems too easy. Right? By noticing that I am disturbing my own peace of mind, I am free to choose peace always.

The instant I notice that I don't like how I feel, I can choose peace instead. That's why it is so important to develop the habit of watching our minds incessantly. The ego hides out where we won't look. This is the mind-training, alive and well.

Even in the most horrific of circumstances, I can choose peace instead—as I found out on the morning of September 11, 2001. The TV is on in the background when I hear the news broadcast. The Twin Towers in New York have been hit. Footage of an airplane crashing into the tower. It's surreal. Unbelievable.

A voice whispers in the back of my mind. *"I could see peace instead of this."* I breathe into the peace and let fearful thoughts surface and be released. This is my part. The idea of all the lives taken and all the lives being changed by what was being called an act of terrorism, is impossible to wrap my head around.

I think of the fear and confusion that can consume a mind in such a way that a deliberate act against life could feel justified. I understand the senselessness of a mind in fear. I hear its desperate appeal for love and healing. I weep unabashedly and let the steady thrum of today's idea still my heart, *"I could see peace instead of this."*

I think of my sister and a dear friend who live in New York and all the brothers and sisters—all part of the one mind we share. As I sit with my children on the couch watching the broadcast, today's idea plays steady in the background of my mind. *"I could see peace instead of this."* I pray. "Let us see peace. Let us extend love. Let us find union and peace with each other." Peace washes over me in waves. I pray my love, offering peace through the ethers to all minds.

CHAPTER THIRTY-FIVE
DAY 35
(Lesson 35)

"My mind is part of God's. I am very holy."
(W-pI.35.1)

Today's lesson is inviting us to see through the overlays of ego self-identity that we have ascribed to for ourselves and reclaim our true identity as God created us. It is appealing to the part of our mind that knows the truth. God is the Source. We are the effect of that Source. We are as God created us. Such is our true identity. We are holy because, God, being Holy, extended His Holiness, creating what was like Him.

Holiness is accurately a description of our raw materials. It's like our spiritual DNA. We will always be what God intends us to be. No matter what we believe.

The thing is, we can decide against ourselves. We decide what we accept and what we deny. So, if we ascribe for ourselves the story that we are a particular person, in a particular life, with particular circumstances and struggles and successes, by the very nature of choosing this identity, we block from our awareness our true identity as God's holy child.

Our focus with today's idea is on the perceiver, rather than what we perceive. We state the idea, *"My mind is part of God's, I am very holy,"* then close our eyes and search our minds for the ways we describe ourselves, with equal regard to negative or positive attributes. They are all equal within the thought system of the ego and therefore equally unreal.

I begin: I see myself as confident. *"But my mind is part of God's, I am very holy."* I see myself as underappreciated. *"But my mind is part of God's, I am very holy."* I see myself as helpful. *"But my mind is part of God's, I am very holy."* I see myself as guilty. *"But my mind is part of God's, I am very holy."* I see myself as kind. *"But my mind is part of God's, I am very holy."* I see myself as worried. *"But my mind is part of God's, I am very holy."*

I take today's idea to heart in faith. I feel its truth deep within, I see where I still get caught up in confused identity. Much of my environment still seems to reinforce the core story of me as a person in a world of other persons. I recognize that much of my mind is still highly influenced by the problems and "fixing" framework. Now, I find it increasingly easier to catch the thoughts that hurt me and choose peace instead.

I get a blast in that false structure later in the day while I'm paying bills. I notice the old familiar angst that there won't be enough money arise, but with it I feel a little tickle in the back of my mind. I pause and let it speak. "Wait a minute, my mind is part of God's, I am very holy—this angst isn't real. The story of lack and guilt is false. I could feel peace instead of this.

I apply my lesson, *"I see myself as lacking, but my mind is part of God's, I am very holy."* I trust my holy mind, to heal my misperception and see that lack is impossible, since God is my Source. In this moment, I have everything I need." The effect is immediate. The sticky belief in lack blocking the awareness of my abundance releases, replaced by gratitude.

It's funny. I love paying bills now. I call them expressions of appreciation.

CHAPTER THIRTY-SIX

DAY 36

(Lesson 36)

"My holiness envelops everything I see."
(W-pI.36.1)

The idea for today begins from the premise established with yesterday's idea. We are extending holiness from the perceiver to the perceived. We are holy by birthright because our whole mind is part of God's Holy Mind. Today we are applying the idea of holiness to our sight. We must have holy sight because our sight comes from a holy mind. Holy sight is not what we see with the body's eyes but from vision, which sees everything whole and complete in the light of love.

As I work with today's idea, I realize I have only an intellectual understanding of its meaning. If I accept that my mind is part of God's, then my mind is holy. So, what I look at is seen from holiness, at least somewhere in my mind. It feels real during my practice period in my morning time with the Divine.

I continue the pattern, practicing as I go throughout my day. I'm stuck in traffic, and as fast as I feel resistance, I feel my lesson come alive in me. *"My holiness envelops this traffic."* I feel at peace in traffic with my brothers. It's the way of it. I love it.

My little boys are fighting. At first the old way of seeing springs to mind. I see them hurting themselves and each other. I want to help them deal with each other in a better way. Loving. Right? Wait. I can feel something is not right about my perception, because it feels icky to think this way. I pause and let my lesson fill my awareness, *"My holiness envelops these boys. My holiness envelops everything I see."*

I realize that my initial view from a problem mind blocked my holy vision. My premise that something is wrong could only offer a solution to affix a loving perception to what I see as a problem. There is no problem—only a belief. I release it to holiness. *"My holiness envelops everything I see."* I do nothing about the situation. I do nothing to stop or to "help." I just quit seeing anything wrong. Everything is holy.

An instant more and the boys are laughing and playing. I'm laughing too. We are bathed in love's light. We are the light that envelops everything we see with holiness. Accepting my holiness is a tuning fork to see with the eyes of love, to the truth of who we are. We are the light of God shining from the holy mind we share and enveloping everything we see in holiness.

CHAPTER THIRTY-SEVEN
DAY 37
(Lesson 37)

"My holiness blesses the world."
(W-pl.37.1)

The lesson starts out with this statement: *"This idea contains the first glimmerings of your true function in the world, or why you are here. Your purpose is to see the world through your own holiness."* Today's idea is the end of all suffering. Isn't this fantastic news? It's why we are here. This is truly our function—to bless the world through the holiness we are as God created us.

"My holiness blesses the world." There is no compromise possible between everything and nothing. Consider the implications of today's idea. It is astounding! Our holiness blesses the world! We learn to recognize our holiness by blessing the world with it! To bless is to trust. We trust the Holy Spirit to reveal our holiness in everything we look upon, within or without, as we practice the lesson today. That's everything. Nothing is excluded. It's either all holiness, or it is nothing at all.

Through our little willingness to open our mind to the idea, *"My holiness blesses the world,"* each time we practice, we bring blessings to the person or thing, and ourselves, and all the world. We see that through the holiness we share, we are all blessed, uniting our minds in truth. Holiness is the great equalizer.

Once again, I approach the practice with today's idea with faith. I am looking for an experience that confirms my belief that my holiness blesses the world. The more I practice, the more real it feels. I make a fun game out of it. I set the goal of blessing everyone I see, in every situation that occurs today, by saying silently, "My holiness blesses you" to whomever I see or think of.

My daughter, Lin, calls. It is a day amidst so many, sitting on the phone with her while she grieves. Her young husband, Eric, recently died of a heart attack. As I pick up the phone, I breathe into my lesson. *"My holiness blesses Lin."* In my ear is a whimper as she whispers, "Mommy. I can't. I can't." She is overwhelmed with grief. Her anguish seems unbearable. I am powerless to ease her pain.

My lesson, like a silent prayer, answers for me. *"My holiness blesses you. My holiness blesses Eric. My holiness blesses life. My holiness blesses everyone as one."* God is with me. I feel His grace beneath my wings and in my heart. She talks and weeps, while I silently bless everything she says. I feel the anguish ease and total calm of presence. She too has calmed. "Thank you, Mama," she whispers. "I love you."

We hang up and I feel a greater strength within. "Oh my God, I can hold the whole world." Everything is as it should be. Holiness is blessing everything, and all is well. How blessed am I to have this exquisite opportunity to hold the truth in the face of what seems an insurmountable obstacle of pain?" Not adding to the story of suffering, but letting holiness bless and transform. Holy gratitude! *"My holiness blesses the world."*

CHAPTER THIRTY-EIGHT
DAY 38
(Lesson 38)

"There is nothing my holiness cannot do."
(W-pI.38.1)

From yesterday's lesson, I see it translate naturally into today's. *"There is nothing my holiness cannot do."* I feel a presence and power within imbuing my life with holiness. Today's idea is teaching us the true power of our mind. The lesson says that through our holiness, the power of God is made manifest and made available. There is nothing the power of God cannot do. We're learning that by identifying with the holiness in our mind we are tuning into all the Power in the universe. And with that Power behind us and within us, there is nothing we can't heal and make whole.

Accepting our holiness takes us out of the time-space continuum and directly into the Source of all power. Accepting there is nothing our holiness cannot do effectively makes us a conduit of salvation in this world. It reverses all the laws of the world. It is beyond restriction of any kind, because we are identifying with the Source. Accepting today's idea can save us. The only thing there is to be saved from is our belief in an identity apart from God and apart from the holiness we are.

Our holiness undoes the false by proclaiming the truth. It's incredible to consider the implications of what our holiness can do. In fact, the ego mind cannot comprehend it. But that's not our part. Our part is to apply the lesson as instructed and let the awareness of our holiness be awakened in us.

I approach my practice with reverence, *"There is nothing my holiness cannot do."* I close my eyes and look for any sense of loss or unhappiness, then name the situation and persons involved and apply the idea, *"In the situation of time limitations in which I see myself, there is nothing my holiness cannot do. In the situation of Eric's death, there is nothing my holiness cannot do. In Lin's grief as she sees herself, there is nothing my holiness cannot do, because the power of God lies in it."* I feel the potency of this idea as I practice, accompanied by calm assurance.

This lesson is amazingly powerful for me. Not that I'm raising the dead or healing the sick, but my mind is turning in on itself and recognizing a power within me that sustains me and moves through me, changing my mind about the world and my place in it.

I am excited to practice as I visit the Hospice. I want to be with my recent friend and bless him, a young man in the advanced stages HIV. I feel different as I walk in his room. Feeling sorry for him has left my mind. I want only to see his holiness and bless this situation. I don't think about his diagnosis. My mind is filled with my lesson, *"There is nothing my holiness cannot do."* I sit at his bedside and take his hand. I see his innocence and courage. I see his love. I see his holiness.

I tell him about the lessons I'm doing in the course right now about holiness and what a blessing it is for me. I say I am practicing with him today. *"There is nothing my holiness cannot do."* He asks me to read to him. I read the lesson. The holiness of our union is palpable. We sit in silence and let it bless us. As I take my leave, he's smiling and asks if I'll read another passage the next time I come. I kiss his hand. "Yes," recognizing we are both transformed.

CHAPTER THIRTY-NINE

DAY 39

(Lesson 39)

"My holiness is my salvation."

(W-pI.39.1)

Today's lesson is teaching us that it is our investment in guilt that is keeping us from recognizing our holiness. We are posed the question, *"If guilt is hell, what is its opposite?"* Do I believe that guilt is hell? Hell, yes! We're being invited to explore a deeper level of honesty with ourselves. I feel ready. Where am I still addicted to guilt? What am I hiding from myself?

During my four 5-minute practice sessions, I open my mind, attempting to get to the real answer. I begin, *"My Holiness is my salvation."* Instantly I think of work—the charting I skimped on yesterday. I feel fearful, blaming, and guilty. I say, *"My unloving thoughts about work are keeping me in hell. My holiness is my salvation."*

My twin brother comes to mind. I haven't called him back. Guilty again. Unease spreads like heat through my veins. I say, *"My unloving thoughts about Dirk and returning phone calls are keeping me in hell. My holiness is my salvation."*

Anticipating an upcoming conversation with a friend, I feel defensive, insecure and a need to be right (attack). I apply my lesson. *"My unloving thoughts about my friend, about communicating and defending my point of view are keeping me in hell. My holiness is my salvation."* Ah, it is from these unloving and guilty thoughts that I need to be saved. I ask myself, "If guilt is hell what is the opposite?" I feel the answer—holiness.

Guilt is hell! I can attest to that. Guilt is the ego's right-arm man, and hell is the result. As I examine my mind more closely, I see I'm haunted with specialness thoughts. I have a hierarchy of worthiness and I rank myself and everyone on the scale. I feel guilty for wanting to have more status than someone else. I feel guilty for not being further up the scale. Pure hell!

This unloving scale of justice in my mind, feeling guilty about mistakes, afraid of being "in trouble" or perceived as foolish, irresponsible, insignificant, irrelevant, or fraudulent, are ways I keep myself in hell. It's like: "OMG! Specialness is my religion. I am addicted to thinking I am somehow better or worse than someone else."

I'm attacking my mind with the belief in separation! *"These unloving thoughts are keeping me in hell. My holiness is my salvation."* My specialness story dissolves. I pose the question from the lesson. *"If guilt is hell, what is it's opposite?"* Amazing love spreads through me. I realize this is my holiness. This is my salvation! My holiness is my salvation.

For moments of unplanned time throughout the day, I try to relax my mind, be still and not think at all, as the lesson asks. It's like mini coffee breaks with God. It's still not easy to quiet my mind with life coming at me. But I love the times it clicks, and I sit in the wonder of it. Life seems to follow, slowing down around me, like it knows these moments are sacred.

I'm on the patio off the cafeteria, sitting quietly by myself. I hear the sliding door open. "Shit," I think without looking. "Don't come out here and mess with my mojo." Instantly, I laugh inside. *"My unloving thoughts put me in hell. My holiness is my salvation."* I pat the space next to me and say, "Join me?" I don't look up to see who it is but feel a presence next to me. I think how my holiness is this brother's holiness and joined our holiness is the salvation of the world.

CHAPTER FORTY
DAY 40
(Lesson 40)

"I am blessed as a Son of God."
(W-pl.40.1)

Today we claim the truth. We are blessed as a Son of God. Beneath the surface of our dream of exile is the never-ending blessing of God's Love. We are a part of this blessing, now, always, already. The only thing keeping it from our awareness is that we have denied the truth of our reality as a child of love—the Son of God. God is present within us always, so we're blessed constantly by love's presence.

There isn't anything in creation that is not the presence of God. By acknowledging this today, we remember what we forgot. We learn the truth by letting the truth flow through us. This is the mind-training of *A Course in Miracles*.

There is a different world for us to experience, and it is already present in our mind, now. It's just that it goes unrecognized because of our attachment to our self-identity in the dream. But we are the dreamer of the dream, and we can wake up to the Self, which is God's Son, complete with all His blessings, through applying each consecutive lesson. The natural outcome is we are blessing the world with our Holiness.

The practice for today feels awesome even as I read the lesson and declare, *"I am blessed as a Son of God."* I let all the yummy attributes I associate with the Son of God, a child of love, come to mind and claim them as my own. *"I am blessed as a Son of God. I am love. I am happy, joyous, and free. I am peaceful and serene. I am loving and lovable. I am contented and satisfied. I am enthusiastic and energetic. I am calm, quiet, assured, and confident."* I close my eyes then open them, letting the feelings of wonderment and joy expand.

We are to apply them to ourselves frequently throughout the day—like every ten minutes or so. It's like the best kind of game to play today. Can we do it? Can we think loving, happy thoughts about ourselves every ten minutes? I'm damn sure going to try.

I set guides for myself as little triggers to tell myself of how blessed I am as a child of God. Every time I change from standing to sitting, get in the car, stop at a light, or walk into a room, I remind myself that I am blessed as a Son of God. I am love and light and joy. I am happy and free.

Then I have this totally unexpected, amazing experience. I'm walking into Starbucks for a coffee. A scroungy-looking elderly woman grabs my arm and asks me for spare change. She is someone I would have usually passed right by. But it is so sudden, and my mind is so primed for love, that my ego doesn't have a chance to get in there with its commentary.

Immediately, I turn and look right into her eyes, saying silently, "We are children of love, you and I, and we are blessed. You are light and joy and so am I." This incredible feeling of love and unity waves through me. I'm sure she feels it, too.

What I do next is completely out of my wheelhouse. I invite her to join me for coffee and sweets. She gladly does. We have a wonderful conversation about motherhood. We enjoy an hour or so together, blessing each other as holy Children of Love. It's funny, we have so much in common. Who'd have known? Our holy Self, that's who.

CHAPTER FORTY-ONE
DAY 41
(Lesson 41)

"God goes with me wherever I go."
(W-pI.41.1)

Today's idea feels good, just saying it or thinking about it, yes? But here's the thing, God *does* go with us wherever we go. Whether we are aware of it or not, whether we believe it or not, whether we believe in God or not. God being love, it's the one true thing in all the world. Imagine what our lives would be like if we trusted that God goes with us wherever we go? Whenever we feel afraid, anxious, worried, or alone, we remember, "God goes with us wherever we go."

The method we use for today's exercise introduces a new level of experience. The results are virtually unlimited. We are literally leaving the world today and joining with God where He resides always and forever in our mind.

It is the springboard for recognizing God is with us. It is 100% possible to reach God. The fact is, it's the most natural thing in the world. The way opens if we believe that it is possible. Ultimately, we will succeed in in experiencing God, because that is God's will. It is our true will.

So, we can relax and sincerely let our mind sink down, leaving the world of thoughts and enter God's presence. This is the beginning of recognizing the voice of God within our mind, and ultimately, that God goes with us and speaks to us wherever we go and in all circumstances. But we can't hear His voice and listen to the ego simultaneously. That's impossible.

My morning time with God is a sacred time and today it is enlightening. I say, *"God goes with me wherever I go,"* and let my mind drop behind all the thinking to a single point of light deep within. It is perfectly still, even the constant hum in the background quiets. I am in total peace and love. I am in God. After resting here a while, a question arises, "Do I go with God, wherever I go? Or am I off spinning stories of separation, insecurity, doubt, and fear, then asking God to fix it for me?"

Bingo! That's it. I see what it means to live in God's world of love. It means trusting whatever happens is for my best interest and because God is within me, I am being guided. I repeat the lesson, *"God goes with me wherever I go,"* and make the goal be centered in His world of love, trusting wherever I go I will know what to do.

I'm driving on the freeway heading to work. I'm feeling God within me and I'm filled with love and peace. I'm thanking God for my holiness and for being ever-present within me and going with me wherever I go. Often, I feel vulnerable on the freeway. Like at any minute, someone could pull in front of me and well, a thousand, painful scenarios emerge.

But none of this is in my heart and mind this morning as I drive. So, when a car pulls in front of me, barely missing my front bumper, instead of being gripped with fear or getting pissed at the other driver, I take it in stride. I know I am safe. Wow!

One idea permeates my mind, filling me with peace. *I AM WITH YOU.* There isn't even a moment where I think I'll get hurt or I need to be saved from an accident. I'm in the flow. Gratefully I declare, *"God goes with me wherever I go."* Thank you. Thank you. Thank you.

CHAPTER FORTY-TWO
DAY 42
(Lesson 42)

"God is my Strength. Vision is His Gift."
(W-pI.42.1)

Isn't this series of lessons yummy? They remind us that whatever we need to live our lives comes from the Source within us. They zero us in on the fact that God is our Source of strength, vision, clarity, joy, happiness, and all the things we want or need.

It is not up to us to have the solution to any perceived problem. It is not up to us to have the wisdom, peace, and compassion we need. God is within us. All power and wisdom are at the ready when perceived issues arise. His Strength is ours.

My little willingness is my gift to God. That's how I see that everything is God's gift to me. This is so powerful. We allow the Holy Spirit within our mind to teach us that God is within us. He is our Strength. So, there's nothing to fear. It is our willingness to not interfere, by replacing our self-evaluation in place of God's.

This awareness changed my life and continues to amaze me daily. The message that my willingness is enough first came as a shock to me. I was addicted to "effort-ing." Prior to my lesson practice, my first response to any difficulty was to try to figure it out or blame myself for doing something wrong.

But as I sit with God in the morning, with today's lesson, I realize how much of my thinking now includes the ideas from the lessons. I am infused with feeling that God is my Source and the true answer.

I'm working with a patient. He's a big, elderly guy. I feel a little apprehensive as I sit down with him. I remind myself, *"God is my Strength. Vision is His gift."* He is in for early stage dementia or Alzheimer's. His voice is raised as he tells me he is upset at his children for putting him in the hospital and how unfair it is that he should have his freedom taken after all he has done for his children.

I keep eye contact. I listen, silently calling on God's strength, asking for guidance. I'm not sure how to respond. I am relying on God's gift of vision and strength. As he spills, I touch his hand gently. He begins to calm, and tears fill his eyes. He tells me how scary it is to be forgetting things that he knows he knows. He squeezes my hand and says, "I'm afraid I'm losing my mind."

Compassion washes over me, filling the room with love. As tears fill my eyes, I see this brother is myself. We gaze into each other's eyes and I know his call for love is my own. I see that I, too, fear losing my mind. I feel an inner chuckle. Actually, losing my mind is exactly what is happening in a gentle, systematic way through *A Course in Miracles*, and the mind-training. I tell him I believe that the only real thing in this world is the love we share and have shared, and I don't believe we can ever lose what is real.

He takes a deep breath and smiles, "I agree. That's comforting. After it's all said and done, that's the only thing that going matter, isn't it? I know love is what's behind the kids putting me here. I know they're scared too. I guess I can cut them a break from here on out. Hope I remember!" It is a holy encounter. A witness to God's strength and the vision He gives.

CHAPTER FORTY-THREE

DAY 43

(Lesson 43)

"God is my Source. I cannot see apart from Him."

(W-pI.43.1)

God is our Source. In reality, we cannot see apart from Him and exist. We can only *dream* we see apart from Him. That's perception. It's relative. Perception is not an attribute of God, where pure knowledge and oneness is experienced. God doesn't need to see, being all in all. Perception was made by the ego as a way of keeping our attention away from God, by keeping us focused on impossible problems.

The Holy Spirit's uses what the ego made to bring us back to the light of truth within our mind. All this is possible because of today's idea. *"God is our Source. We cannot see apart from Him."*

Today's lesson heals the split in our mind. We are learning to look only with love on everything we see. God is our Source for sight, we cannot be without Him. We look first to our Source, choosing to see only the truth. Simultaneously, we withdraw our belief in the reality of the ego thought system as we rely on God for vision.

When looking from the ego perspective, as persons or bodies in this world of time and space, we are not actually seeing. It's like we have our eyes glued to the peephole of this world of separation, loneliness, and scarcity, while there is the huge ocean of joy, abundance, unity, and peace all about us. We're so busy looking for scraps of it through the peephole, that we don't realize we can simply withdraw our eyes from the peephole and open up to the beauty around us.

I have one of those aha moments with today's lesson where it all becomes clear. There is a new display of paintings in the reception area at the hospital. They are those magic-eye paintings, where they appear on the surface to be one thing, but there is a whole different picture hidden within the same painting, for eyes that can see.

I'm looking at one of these magic-eye pictures. It is a picture of the sea, with a mountain visible in the background. I keep staring at it, thinking, "What's the deal? It's a sea and mountain. What else could it be?" The more I try to focus on it, the more solid the image is to me. Suddenly, I think, "Hey, what if I'm not really seeing what I think I am seeing?" and I naturally soften my eyes. The image of the mountain and sea seem to dissolve as a sailboat emerges, almost in 3D, right before me. I am delighted. My little enlightenment into what vision is.

This magic-eye experience is my metaphor for vision. As I soften my mind, detaching from what my body's eyes are telling me, I see what eluded me before. *"God is my Source. I cannot see apart from Him."* From a mind filled with love, the real purpose of what I am looking at emerges in 3D—more real than what I assumed before.

That's all it takes—a willingness to soften into the Holy Spirit's reinterpretation, which is always love and always feels peaceful. It's a miracle-mind-meld.

CHAPTER FORTY-FOUR

DAY 44

(Lesson 44)

"God is the light in which I see."

(W-pl.44.1)

Today's lesson begins with the premise that the light of creation is found within our mind. It is inherent in our creation. So, light is literally the way we see life at all. Darkness doesn't actually exist. Only in the illusion of separation did darkness come into play. The ego depends on darkness and shadows to remain in our mind so we can be controlled by fear.

But, once we see the light in our own mind, the ego's days of smoke and mirrors is nearly gone. Truth has dawned in our minds, and its appeal is undeniable. We are drawn back to it ever-increasingly until all the dark, false thoughts that occupied our minds have been uncovered, forgiven, and dispelled.

Applying today's idea leads us to the truth—let there be light—and it is so. The truth is the light within. We are attempting to reach the light within and training our minds to recognize our natural state of light. We are training our mind to turn to truth.

Today's exercise is one of my favorite meditation practices. It gives a focal point that never fails. The light of God is within our mind. The lesson instructs, *"Try to sink into your mind, letting go every kind of interference and intrusion by quietly sinking past them. Your mind cannot be stopped in this unless you choose to stop it. It is merely taking its natural course. Try to observe your passing thoughts without involvement and slip quietly by them. [. . .] Salvation is your happiest accomplishment."*

Seeing the light in our mind is actually the most natural thing in the world for us to do.

I approach my practice in reverence. I am attempting something very holy. I am ready. I have been training my mind for this. After reading the lesson, I repeat the idea, *"God is the light in which I see,"* saying it several times as I close my eyes and let my mind sink down within.

A tiny pinpoint of light emerges out of the darkness as I repeat the idea, letting my mind sink down deep down, past everything I seem to believe, beneath the insane thoughts, feelings, and judgments that make up the darkness of this world, seeking only what I am instructing my mind to find, and into the light I am in truth.

The point of light seems to naturally guide me past resistance, releasing my mind from darkness into light. I see the light glowing and expanding as I see only it, filling my whole my mind with light and my being with a tremendous feeling of love and warmth.

My sight is lit with love's light as I move through my day. I'm doing an intake on a resistant patient. The thought, "Give it a break, buddy. We're just trying to help," flashes on the screen. I can feel the darkness closing in as I judge. I silently invite my lesson to fill my mind. *"God is the light in which I see."*

Instantly, I see the guy is just in fear and darkness. I smile, extending the light I know is within, mentally reaching to join the light in him. He smiles back, and visibly relaxes. I look around us. Everyone and everything seem connected, infused, and surrounded by light. It is still and peaceful and whole. *God is the light in which I see.* It is a new sense of seeing which brings with its immediate peace, lighting my mind with love. I carry the light of life, blessing everything in holy sight.

CHAPTER FORTY-FIVE

DAY 45

(Lesson 45)

"God is the Mind in which I think."

(W-pl.45.1)

The lessons *God is my Source, I cannot see apart from Him; God is the light in which I see;* and today's lesson, *God is the Mind in which I think,* describe the true cause and effect relationship. We exist because we are part of God, and all our life is sourced by Him. We see because the Source of vision, the light within our mind, is within the Mind which Sources it. We think because God is the Mind which makes thinking possible.

All the thoughts *we think we think* are merely supporting characters for the ego-directed self-concept. They are kept active because of our belief in their reality. They are the barrier to recognizing the pure, creative mind we share with God. Each is kept in place by a present decision of the mind to value what *we think we think,* over what God would have us think.

The lesson says, *"Today's idea holds the key to what your real thoughts are. They are nothing that you think you think, just as nothing that you think you see is related to vision in any way."* We are reminded throughout the course that the past is gone, and if we weren't repeating the same decision to believe the false in this present moment, we would recognize the truth already in our mind. The truth is what we are trying to reach in our lesson practice today. We are trying to recall our eternal reality with God.

It is a miracle when this dawns in my mind. I have been preoccupied for days with an upcoming performance review. It's like an ongoing loop that leads nowhere.

I'm mountain biking up in the hills above the valley before work. This mind loop is driving me mad. I remember the peace I felt with my morning practice and crave it now. The sun is just reaching above the mountains east of where I am. *"God is the Mind in which I think,"* plays across my mind. I feel reverence for what it is teaching me. It is a perfect moment for my lesson practice.

I approach it, as the lesson suggests, as I would *"an altar dedicated in Heaven to God the Father and to God the Son. For such is the place I am trying to reach."* I sit down on a boulder to take in the view. Then, closing my eyes, I watch my mind, observing the circular thoughts. I'm worried about the review, afraid I've missed something I did wrong. I wonder what is so important as to drive the incessant, needless ruminating. It'll go how it goes. I instruct my mind, *"My real thoughts are in my mind. I would like to find them now."*

All my obsessive discomfort leaves as I draw my single focus on today's idea. *"God is the Mind in which I think."* I let my mind sink deep within, past all the unreal thoughts that cover the truth in my mind, reaching to the eternal. It's like the thoughts slow, breaking apart and dissolving. My mind fills with awareness of a Divine Presence, wondrous well-being. There is no future and no past. Only now—only the divine present.

I open my eyes, my mind, is open to this present moment which extends forever. I feel alive with wonder. This instant is the portal to eternity, to the truth—to the thoughts I think with God.

I get up, put on my helmet. The sun makes its way across the valley. I'm off to meet the wizard of a brand-new day.

CHAPTER FORTY-SIX

DAY 46

(Lesson 46)

"God is the Love in which I forgive."

(W-pI.46.1)

To say today's lesson idea has saved my life would be an understatement. God is the Love in which I forgave what I once believed to be unforgivable. God is the Love which makes the impossible, possible. God is the Love in which I forgive myself completely! Each word speaks to me of release and comfort. God is the Love in which I recognize my Self as Love. God is the Love I am, which allows me to release all fear and condemnation from my mind.

Forgiveness is the grand prize of the mind-training, leaving only the awareness of the Love we are as God created us. Forgiveness is the way out of the matrix of fear. It unplugs us from fear, and we recognize the reality of Love.

A Course in Miracles defines forgiveness as the recognition that what we thought our brother did to us, never occurred in truth. So, we're not even looking at the specific "wrong" that we feel occurred, we're looking past it to the error in our mind that projected it onto our brother. Forgiveness allows us to release him and ourselves from the false ideas imprisoning us both. It doesn't matter how huge the error may seem.

What is not love is not real. We have peopled our world with our own thought system. So, it is always our mind which we are dealing with. The so-called enemies that we think have wronged us are our saviors because they show us, we are identifying with an error within our mind. Thank God, because once we have projected it "out there," we think it is being done *to us, right?*

Forgiveness lets us release condemnation and fear from our mind completely. By bringing each grievance to the light of awareness, we allow the Love of God to shine through it and dispel the false from our mind.

Sometimes things happen that seem to assign a life sentence of guilt. This was the case for me—the catalyst for my total surrender to God. Forgiveness gave me life around a situation I felt there was no hope for me. Only God— the Love in which I forgive, could have released me from the guilt prison I put myself in, because of choices I made which I deemed unforgivable.

I put my children's lives in danger, resulting in my boyfriend burning my son's hands. I didn't feel I deserved forgiveness. Hell, I didn't feel I deserved to live. But God, being Love, had other plans. Plans to forgive and awaken me to my Self as Love. *God is the Love with which I forgive myself.*

I review my unforgiving thoughts about the event, trusting the alchemy of miracles as I apply the lesson. *"God is the Love in which I forgive you, Rick. God is the love in which I forgive myself my ignorance."* I see that my guilt distorted the way I see my children drawing a veil of pity over the face of Christ. *"God is the love in which I forgive myself for pitying my children because of what happened."* It dissolves instantly in the light of awareness. I see their bright shiny faces of love and purity—and I know it is mine. *"God is the Love in which I forgive the whole story of guilt."*

The guilt story burns up in a blazing light of forgiveness. *"God is the Love in which I forgive myself."* Peace washes over me. I am released. Only love is real! *"God is the Love in which I have already been forgiven. No fear is possible in a mind beloved of God. God is the Love in which I love myself."* Hallelujah!

CHAPTER FORTY-SEVEN
DAY 47
(Lesson 47)

"God is the strength in which I trust."
(W-pI.47.1)

If we are trusting in our own strength, no wonder we feel insecure, worried, and afraid. Reality is whole. On our own, we have no way to predict or control anything. We do not have access to all the information in the universe, past, present, and future. So, we are always operating at a deficit. By giving up our agenda, and trusting God, we are given the strength to handle each situation that arises as it arises.

Through our willingness to trust God's Strength, we open ourselves to the Holy Spirit within our minds which has all the information, effectively giving us the power of the universe for the strength, we need.

I was smack dab, face-to-face with the "grand-disillusionment" of my life when I began the mind-training of *A Course in Miracles.* I used to pride myself on my strength, my ability to handle any situation, to pull myself up by my bootstraps and press on, to put my shoulder to the wheel.

But I never felt successful, even when it looked that way on the outside. I never once felt I was enough. "I'm smart, and I know how to work hard. Maybe next time." That was my story, and it got me to the brink of despair. I felt a failure relying on myself for everything. The thing is, that it was my best effort at life. The sense of aloneness was excruciating. I could not trust myself. I had no strength in myself from which to draw. But now I see that alone am nothing, because I am not alone.

So, when I come to today's lesson, having had miracles of awakening through the lessons leading to it, I give myself completely to the lesson practice. Aware that doing it on my own leaves me feeling like a failure, lets me unplug from my strategic mind as I repeat the idea, *"God is the Strength in which I trust."*

I search my mind for situations I have invested with fear, worry, regret, or anxiety. Work, the kids, finances. As each situation comes into my mind, I apply the lesson, *"God is the Strength in which I trust."* I let my mind sink beneath all my concerns, including my sense of my own inadequacy. "God is the Strength in which I trust." I feel drawn deeper within—toward release and light. A compelling force is with me. A peaceful confidence settles over me, with a trust whole and complete.

I feel Love's confidence and trust as I set out for a trip to Park City with the kids. We're halfway there, in the middle of nowhere, when the car starts puttering. I pull to the side of the road. Before, I can even start panicking, my lesson dances across my mind. *"God is the Strength in which I trust."* It seems we're all alone. This is before cell phones. But I know what to do. I invite the kids to join me in a prayer thanking God for strength we can trust and the clarity to know what to do. We play "I spy" games and wait, trusting help will come.

Within minutes a friend, heading to Park City, pulls over to help. Turns out, he works on his own cars and he spots the problem—a disconnect in the wiring—and fixes it straight away. I chuckle to myself as we get back in the car, "Yep, it's just like my mind. When there is a disconnect in the wiring of love, I stall out, and need the Strength of God to see me through." A miracle adventure!

CHAPTER FORTY-EIGHT
DAY 48
(Lesson 48)

"There is nothing to fear."
(W-pl.48.1)

Fear is the domain of the ego. When we are afraid, it is a sure sign we are mistaking illusion for the truth. If we are afraid, we believe illusions are the real McCoy. Fear is a sign we have forgotten who we are and are trusting in our own strength. There's a lesson for that.

"There is nothing to fear." We want to repeat this as often as possible today. We are reminding ourselves to rely on God for everything, in all situations. Whenever we are feeling less than wholly joyous, *"There is nothing to fear."* When frustrated, worried, in a hurry, or dragging our feet, it is a reminder that in reality, *"There is nothing to fear."*

God is with us. Only what God wills for us will bring us happiness. Truth and illusion cannot coexist. God's will for us is perfect happiness. In the presence of God—or keeping God present in our mind—we realize there is nothing to fear. And we are always in His presence because we cannot be apart from Him. His love and light and joy, His strength and peace are like the spirit DNA of what we are. Where light, joy, peace, and love reside, fear has gone.

This lesson—it's rewiring my mind as I let it play on a continual loop as I go through my day, reminding myself constantly. *"There is nothing to fear."* Increasingly, I feel divine peace and well-being. I am living at peace with life itself.

In the staff meeting, I feel a familiar apprehension as the room fills with colleagues. I remind myself, *"There is nothing to fear."* Instantly, I am filled with enthusiasm and love for joining on behalf of patient care. With nothing to fear, I trust the divine union with my colleagues and patients.

Fear had always been my constant companion, before my experience with *A Course in Miracles*, the mind-training and the experience of God's love in my life. I actually thought fear was a necessary part of keeping me safe. It told me to be cautious and on the lookout.

So, as I consider today's idea, I ask myself, "How would my life look if I knew there was nothing to fear? The answer was so obvious, it busted up the fear pathways in my mind. Love is the answer! Love everything just as it is.

I am hanging with my children, reflecting on myself as a mother. With nothing to fear, I am the mother I want to be, loving, present, and playful. I no longer buy into some "good parent" script. I am myself. I recognize a deep and honest awareness within me. Love *is* enough! The power and presence of God is in me. I breathe deeply into present peace, *"There is nothing to fear,"* giving myself wholeheartedly to our time together. God is with me, beating my heart with love.

Love is the answer. What is the question?

CHAPTER FORTY-NINE
DAY 49
(Lesson 49)

"God's Voice speaks to me all through the day."
(W-pl.49.1)

Today is like a big "trust fall." We lean back in our mind, leaving our own thinking, and drop into the arms of God's love, where His Voice is the one we hear speaking to us throughout our day. It is there for us. And it takes a million forms.

The Holy Spirit will use the best possible method for each of us, according to our willingness to hear at the time. It might be an intuitive thought or action. It might be an unexpected smile, or an understanding that comes to us during an encounter with another. It might be the words to a song, a bumper-sticker, a thought picked up in a passing conversation, or remembered from another one. It could be an idea to forgive, to let go, to embrace.

Today, we try not to listen to the ego. Instead, we try to identify with the still, peaceful part of our mind. God's voice is speaking to us, reminding us we are His holy child—God's voice lovingly calling us home. It is our willingness to not think we know, but trust there is a place within us that does know. We turn toward it, which allows us to hear *"God's Voice speaks to us all through the day."* We are tuning to God's frequency, where Love speaks to Love.

During my morning time with God and the lesson, I close my eyes and listen in deep silence. My mind is open—the light within, my single focal point. I sink deep into the peace that is my eternal link with God, past all the craziness of my mind, the thoughts and images of the insane world that obscure my recognition of God's ever-present peace. Peace welcomes me with open arms and permeates my being with a feeling of God's presence. I am being guided by the loving Voice within my mind.

As I go about my day, I start questioning. "How do I know if I am receiving guidance? How can I be sure if I am really hearing the Voice for God?" I pause and repeat my lesson, *"God's Voice speaks to me all through the day."* An awareness opens in my mind. I see where the disconnect occurs. I introduce uncertainty every time I question if I'm receiving guidance, blocking the natural trust I have in the Divine.

Doubt is the way the ego gets a foothold. And it does it under the guise of wanting to hear the voice of God. Sneaky, right? Once I see it, I see that trust is uncompromising.

When I arrive at work, there is a message for me to see my boss immediately. On autopilot, I feel panic rise. My heart races. As I walk toward her office, my mind starts spinning, "What did I do wrong? Am I being reprimanded for what I said at staff meeting?" I feel insane. I try to slow my breathing. I notice the song in the background, it is Louis Armstrong singing, "It's a wonderful world." It stops me in my tracks.

My lesson instantly comes to mind. *"God's Voice speaks to me all through the day."* Tears fill my eyes as I breathe deeply into the peace and gratitude that opens my mind to quiet stillness—all the thoughts from a moment before slipping from my mind. Trust slows my heartrate.

Whatever this meeting is for is in my best interest. God's Voice will guide me. The purpose of the meeting is joining. I walk into my boss's office with an open mind. She asks me to consult on an outpatient. Of course, I'll love to. *"God's Voice speaks to me all through the day."*

CHAPTER FIFTY
DAY 50
(Lesson 50)

"I am sustained by the Love of God."
(W-pI.50)

What if we believed today's idea, *"I am sustained by the Love of God,"* without reservation? Can we imagine how it would change our life? We are always, already sustained by the Love of God. We just don't realize it. Our attention is elsewhere.

Whenever we experience anything as a problem, we have entered the domain of fear. Problems and needs are the ego's playground. The ego offers "magic cures," and would have us believe that anything *but* God is a source to sustain us. Money, stuff, medications, credentials, intellect, power, food, water, electricity, tools for defense.

As long as we believe that our problems are in the physical universe, we will seek for solutions there as well. They will ultimately fail to bring happiness.

I know for sure the miracle that comes from allowing myself to be sustained by the Love of God. It is the answer to every problem that confronts us. From worries, fears, addictions, and even childhood programming. It is the answer today, tomorrow, and throughout time.

Addiction is a mechanism that the ego uses to mimic the single-focused purpose we crave to have with God.

Here's an example of a miracle I received with today's idea. I was insane around body and food. I suffered from an addiction to body image, thinking food was the enemy. It was consuming and I was sick of it. I was tired of feeling haunted by its pull running interference in everything I did. I needed a miracle. And, just like that, I get one.

One night I wake up with a belly full of craving and a mind starving for release. In total desperation, I utter a sincere and honest prayer. "Dear God, I'd rather be 300 pounds if I could love myself just the way I am and be at peace. I just want to be happy! I know happiness is Your will for me. Please free me from this insanity. May I feel sustained by Your Love and love myself. Show me another way to see myself, my body, food, and my life."

My heart and mind calm immediately, settled by a deep peace. An image appears in my mind. The image is of me holding my infant child in my arms. My hands rise to my heart. I am transported back holding my Lucas's head right next to my heart at nursing time.

The image morphs and *I* am the infant I am holding, and it is as if God's hands hold my little head to the Divine breast of Love. It is like liquid Love pours into me, filling every cell of my being—a love beyond, yet including the incredible love I have for my children—a Love that spread its arms around my life, past, present, and future.

I realize that I never had to learn *how* to love my children, I was sustained by God's Love in that stewardship. I realized that *I* am the stewardship I am assigned to, along with my children and all my brothers who are one with me. In gratitude, I stand up from my prayer and wipe my tears. I am released—sustained by the Love of God. I know it is time to prove out God's trust in me—by trusting me to God.

That image remains forever in my mind. It stabilizes me. Anytime I feel afraid, alone or I start fixating on an outcome in worldly terms, my hands automatically go to my heart. It is a flip-switch to remember that *"I am sustained by the Love of God."*

CHAPTER FIFTY-ONE
REVIEW I: DAYS 51–60
(Lessons 1–50)

The first fifty lessons of mind-training contain the "undoing" ideas. The next ten days, we're getting a chance to review and further integrate them. I love it because we get to see how our minds are already being trained toward love.

Each day we are reviewing five of the ideas and related comments on each, contemplating each with eyes closed at the beginning and end of the day, reflecting on their central theme. Each days' five lessons have been presented slightly different from the original lesson, showing us how they each build upon the next, creating our new thought system based on love.

I write them on a 3x5 card and set the intention to contemplate at least one each hour and reflect on how it is showing up in my life at this moment.

The fun thing I notice as I stop and reflect is how many of the ideas have become a natural way of seeing my life and the world around me. When I run up against a fearful glitch in my nexus of love, I notice.

We are developing the habit of pausing and thinking with God, at regular intervals throughout our days. By reviewing five lesson ideas per day we get a chance to really integrate what we've been practicing thus far. Feel free to go back to the examples I've given previously.

I have not given specific examples for these review days, encouraging you to capture your own. It is truly healing to write down instances where we remember to pause and think of the Divine, replace fearful responses with forgiveness and love, or simply a prayer of gratitude for the increasing sense of wellbeing we're experiencing daily.

As you practice the five lesson ideas, I think you'll see something fundamental is beginning to shift in your belief system—a softening and letting go in the fear-based structure defining your life. A willingness and openness to see through the eyes of love and let love/spirit direct your thoughts. Have fun with it.

NOTES

NOTES

NOTES

NOTES

CHAPTER FIFTY-TWO

DAY 61

(Lesson 61)

"I am the light of the world."

(W-pI.61.1)

The course tells us that God created us for joy. God is the Source of Light, and in extending His Love, created us as light. Joy is God's Voice within us, our clear communication with God. We are the light of the world. It is because we are the light, that seeing is even possible in this dark world of shadows and imaginings.

Light and love are one in the same. Light is the ground of our being. It is the truth. It is the pure frequency of life. So, it literally is our only function. It is why we are here. Fear, guilt, judgments, and grievances block the light, both from our awareness, and our healing effect on the world we see.

Practicing the idea helps me to see *I* am the only thing in my way, and how simple it is to get out of the way. I used to be a self-help junkie. I was trying to get good enough to have something to offer the world. I participated in workshops on how to find your purpose in life and how to function in the world.

My purpose always ended up being somewhere in the future. But *today* I was still not enough. Something about that didn't sit right with me. Isn't there anything that I am innately meant for? Something of inherent value that could benefit the world.

Then, thank God, *A Course in Miracles* came into my life. It spoke to this part of me that nothing else had been able to access. The innocence, pure and loving Self—the Light Self. The course redefines everything I think and believe, essentially turning me back in on myself. As my guilt and fear lift from my mind and heart, I understand the light! It is my Self.

With today's lesson, I know I have finally found my purpose and function. I slowly repeat the lesson, *"I am the light of the world. That is my only function. That is why I am here,"* It feels true and natural to me. It is the best workshop ever!

The only price I pay is the release of guilt and fear through forgiveness. It asks only that I let go of anything that interferes with my being the love I am and shining that love-light with everyone I encounter. I say again, *"I am the light of the world. That is my only function. That is why I am here,"* and let it sink deep down. I realize I am uniquely qualified to be the light in my corner of the world. By doing my part, light spreads across the universe.

The sun is rising outside my window as I open my eyes. I watch mountains, sky, and backyard come to life as light wakes the sleeping world for today. Parker slips quietly in and sits on the cushion next to me. He takes my hand in his as the sun enters our yummy space.

Or is it that we are lighting the sun and world with love? I am filled joyous humility as I accept my only function as the light of the world. This is my ministry for forgiveness. My purpose. It is eternally present, now. All around everything is getting brighter and brighter, gradually waking the world from slumber and inviting me to embrace the adventure of the new day.

CHAPTER FIFTY-THREE
DAY 62
(Lesson 62)

"Forgiveness is my function as the light of the world."

(W-pI.62.1)

Today we are given the key to fulfilling our function as the light of the world. *"It is our forgiveness that will bring the world of darkness into the light."* When we forgive, the truth of what we are as Love returns to our mind. That's why forgiveness is our salvation.

Forgiveness recognizes that what we thought another did is a misperception based in misbelief of what we are. The same stands with what we think we did to another. Illusions about ourselves and others are one in the same.

That's why all forgiveness is a gift to ourselves. All attack is really an attack on the awareness of truth in our mind. It doesn't pardon sins; it sees that there is no sin. The course defines sin as a lack of love. Forgiveness returns the awareness of love to our mind.

The idea of forgiveness and happiness are brought together with today's lesson, *"Forgiveness is my function as the light of the world. I would fulfill my function that I may be happy."* We can't feel guilty and be happy in the same moment. The choice is ours.

Happiness is God's will and ours. When I am not happy, I am out of touch with God's will for me. It's like a built-in red flag, and I know a forgiveness lesson is on the table. I must be happy, or my vibration is too dense to fulfill my function as the light of the world. Forgiving lets me see myself and my brother's innate innocence, which raises my vibration.

During my basic training in the military, I'm assigned as platoon leader. The responsibility of the soldiers in my command rests on me. A couple of gals seem to take a disliking to me from the beginning and seem to go out of their way to make my position difficult. It's irritating. They show up late to formation, their uniforms incomplete, no belt, shirt untucked, or their hair not neatly tucked in their hat.

I take the hit for that, drop and give the drill sergeant twenty pushups. They blatantly disregard my authority when I attempt to talk to them. I didn't want the job in the first place! Now I'm pissed.

I'm lying in my bunk one night, thinking about the situation. It hits me. "Holy shit. I have forgotten who I am and why I am here. I need help." I pray, "Dear God, I feel like a victim. I am angry, so I know the error is in my mind. I want to see it differently, because I want to be at peace." Instantly, forgiveness takes me in its embrace—Peace spreads like the sun rising across my mind.

Today's lesson is like a marquee, *"Forgiveness is my function as the light of the world. I would fulfill my function that I may be happy."* The events of the recent experiences play in my mind, and with each I say, "I forgive." A different picture begins to emerge. I see my arrogance and self-will. As I picture the gals in question, I realize I have only seen the guilt I assigned to them, never looking for their innocence as God's kids, one with me. Joy fills my heart.

I'm dressing the next morning when I encounter the girls. I smile, I see my friends, who brought the light of forgiveness to my mind, and silently thank them. I know what to do. I ask them to be my squad leaders. Genuine smiles answer yes!

Funny thing, miracles. Not a single incident of conflict arises again. We are in this together. Our relationship changed because I changed my mind through forgiveness. I fulfill my function and happiness speaks God's will to me—I light the world with forgiveness and love.

CHAPTER FIFTY-FOUR
DAY 63
(Lesson 63)

*"The light of the world brings peace to every
mind through my forgiveness."*

(W-pI.63.1)

Today's lesson speaks to the absolute surety God has in us. Through our forgiveness, we bring peace to every mind because there is only one mind, of which we are a part. As we bring our false beliefs of fear, attack, scarcity, sacrifice, pain, and suffering to mind, and allow forgiveness to heal these false states of mind, healing is experienced in every mind.

Just look at the first paragraph in today's lesson: *"How holy are you who have the power to bring peace to every mind? How blessed are you who can learn to recognize the means for letting this be done through you! What purpose could you have that would bring you greater happiness?"* Wow.

What's so cool about forgiveness is that it takes our past story that caused us the negative states and changes the formatting. It keeps all the loving parts—the Self—and lets the rest go. Only the lessons of love remain. What I give my brother is my gift to me. This has been my ongoing experience with forgiveness. Each time, with everything, equally, all the negative charge is gone, and peace has taken its place.

As far as past events, I still have access to the story when it's useful to facilitate forgiveness in another, but in its purified form. The negative states no longer occupy my mind. The light of forgiveness immediately brings peace to the mind of both giver and receiver. This is salvation.

We have a newly appointed director of the recovery unit at the hospital. I go in the break room and everybody seems weird about it. I listen to the conversations going on around me. One counselor is afraid her group will be cut from the program. Another is fearful we won't have as much control as case managers. I feel apprehension rising within me.

Ha! Gratitude replaces unease as I realize my forgiveness opportunity. No one has actually met our new director. Yet the air is filled with fear and worry about the direction things might be going. I close my eyes and bring all my colleagues into a circle of light in my mind.

I apply my lesson, *"The light of the world brings peace to every mind through my forgiveness. I am the means God has appointed for the salvation of the world. I am love, and I trust my brother who is one with me."* I breathe deeply into the present moment, letting the false states pass through the light of awareness in my mind, and peace settles over everything.

I now engage in the conversation, sparkling with enthusiasm. I say how excited I am to have fresh blood to infuse the program with new light. I thank them for the unity and synchronicity we share due to our openness, and a true desire for the best possible help and healing for our patients. I am excited to bring our new director into our circle of light and healing. They join easily in these ideas, smiling and nodding.

The door opens. Yep, it's her. A warm welcome commences. Not surprisingly, we all fall in sync as she shares her hopes and dreams for the unit.

CHAPTER FIFTY-FIVE
DAY 64
(Lesson 64)

"Let me not forget my function."
(W-pI.64.1)

Today's idea reminds us that our function to be the light of the world is also seeing that our function is to be happy. We do this by forgiving the false ideas that block happiness from us. We are choosing to be host to God, instead of hostage to the ego.

That is the same as saying that we choose to recognize ourselves as God created us and not what we made of ourselves. We choose peace, offer peace, and accept it. We choose to be happy. Through forgiveness, we choose to recognize and reclaim the light within and our happiness.

I chose the path of unconditional happiness as my spiritual path. At the time I made that declaration, I knew it was the highest spiritual path for me, having no idea what that would entail. But here it is. Fulfilling my function of forgiveness, my light shines in joy with each step of freedom from fear. I can keep my heart open to love, and happiness is my state of being.

Here's an example from a session with a couple who are in conflict. They enter the room and sit on opposite sides of the couch, their bodies turned away from each other. "I can't trust my husband," begins the wife. "Me? I can't trust her!" replies the husband. "She doesn't listen." "He lies." They talk over each other, and the feeling present is panic. It speaks volumes.

I ask them to speak one at a time. Each tells the story of misinterpretation based in fear, hurt, blame, and mistrust. I know that story; it was once mine. My lesson plays in the background of my mind. *"Let me not forget my function. Let me not try to substitute mine for God's. Let me forgive and be happy."*

I focus only on the truth that they are love and forgive misinterpretation and misunderstanding. I silently ask what would be truly helpful. As their story drizzles out, I ask, "Have you considered that what you think the problem is, isn't the problem? That maybe you are misperceiving based on the past, where you felt hurt? Can you consider that you are reacting to your interpretations and that is causing you to see things, in a way that makes the other look suspicious to you?" Both turn toward me, forward in their seats, and toward each other.

Nodding in unison they say, "Go on." I say, "Our minds are joined. So, on some level, we always know when we are reacting with fear, rather than love, both in ourselves and the other. No matter what is being said, when the words don't match our feelings, we feel suspicious. And that starts up these old scripts that don't have anything to do with the present time."

They are visibly relaxing and move next to each other, taking hands. I place my hand on theirs, and say, "In the presence of love, where no one is to blame, we welcome forgiveness, and start fresh."

CHAPTER FIFTY-SIX

DAY 65

(Lesson 65)

"My only function is the one God gave me."

(W-pI.65.1)

Today we reaffirm our commitment to salvation. It is about our willingness to forgive and accept our function as saviors and share it, in light and joy and peace. It is our willingness to take 100 percent responsibility for our mind. Nothing outside of us can hurt us and nothing outside of us can make us happy. This realization is Heaven on earth.

Today's lesson requires a two-part application and hourly remembrances. (1) We must recognize that salvation is our only function, because through forgiveness we light all minds along with ours and bring salvation to the world. (2) We must relinquish all other goals we have cherished for the one and only function God has given us.

All meaning comes from God and comes to us through our relationship with Him—through our true identity, making everything meaningful. That's salvation's purpose.

As children of God, what is most natural to us is to live a life free from troubles or worries of any kind. As we accept the function God has given us, relinquishing all others, perpetual peace and joy become our continuous state of mind. This is the message of salvation we bring as we go about our daily lives. Each encounter becomes holy because our only function is the one God gave us.

It's one of those days I have a million things I "have" to get done. My morning time with God and my course lesson is serenely beautiful. I feel in harmony with a sense of purpose. I catch intruding thoughts during meditation, recognizing that they are goals that keep me from accepting my only function. I release them to the Holy Spirit, letting my mind still, seeing a clean slate before me to allow the day to unfold.

But by midmorning, the committee meeting is in session in my mind, "You've got to get shit handled; write that report. Call this person. Why didn't you talk to him about that when you saw him?" Yikes! I've lost my peace. I'm impatient with the guy at the post office. I'm irritated when I get a red light in traffic.

But then while sitting at that light, gratitude comes over me and I smile, thanking Divine wisdom for the pause. It's like a gift from the Holy Spirit calling me back to my only function. Two hours have passed since my last remembrance of the lesson. I'd forgotten, thinking I didn't have time to step aside from all the shit that still needed to be handled.

As I repeat my lesson, *"My only function is the one God gave me."* I see my conflicting goals. I let my get-this-shit-done list surface item by item and apply my lesson, *"This thought reflects a goal that is preventing me from accepting my only function."* I let them go easily, and my mind becomes clear: *"On this clean slate let my true function be written for me."* The light turns green, and I feel satiated as I repeat again my one goal: *"My only function is the one God gave me."*

Funny, from that clean-slate moment of remembering my commitment to God as my only function, I am in a state of absolute joy, driving without a care in the world. I have already accomplished the one thing that matters—I recognize my purpose. Everything that seemed so freaking important before is suddenly trivial.

Now I trust that what serves my purpose will get handled in the perfect order with a happy outcome for everyone concerned. And it does. Life brings what's needed right before me. I don't need to hunt anything down and "get it done."

CHAPTER FIFTY-SEVEN
DAY 66
(Lesson 66)

"My happiness and my function are one."
(W-pI.66.1)

It's 3:33 a.m. I wake in indescribable joy. Awareness says, "Good morning, love. Thank you for my life." The night before, I'd been contemplating something I read about the path of unconditional happiness as the highest spiritual path. "The Path of Unconditional Happiness!" I declare it as my own.

A Course in Miracles, through applying the lessons, provides the means for me to stay true to the way of love and joy—to clean up the beliefs I harbor that risk interfering with my true and honest state of happiness. Happiness is living as the Self as God created me. It requires that I keep my heart and mind open to love, no matter what. Forgiveness makes this possible.

Through forgiveness I see it is only my thoughts that can cause me pain. Once met with understanding, those thoughts dissolve into the awareness of Divine Mind—the love I am. God's thoughts of joy, love, and healing take their place. My happiness and my function are one.

Today, in my Divine morning time, I read today's lesson, and it feels like the most natural and real thing in the world to me. How perfectly it confirms my declaration to live the way of unconditional happiness!

Today's lesson reminds me that joy is the ground of my being as God designed. God created me for His joy. He gives only happiness. He gave my function to forgive the false and be the light of the world. I can only fulfill my function in a state of joy and peace. In this state of wholeness, I recognize the guidance continually coming from the Divine.

Gratitude and joy burst from me as I set happiness as my goal for the day. My attention is zeroed on the light within, living joyously, listening only for Voice for Love—the Holy Spirit—for guidance. I am attuned to when my flow is interrupted by fear, guilt, or judgment and I pause and honestly inquire on the thoughts occupying my mind. Seeing it is only my thoughts out of accord with what I am, I forgive and let another way of seeing come into my awareness.

I'm gathering laundry strewn around the house, humming and loving every minute as I move from room to room. Lar is out of town on business. He comes home today. I love preparing the household for his return. I make sure I have his favorite meals ready to prepare, fresh sheets on the bed, and my open heart waiting as he returns home.

An hour before, Cole and Parker start a science experiment in the kitchen. I love how they spontaneously attempt to prove to themselves what they learn from the science channel. But right now, I want everything to be clean and fresh when Lar walks in. Don't I?

That thought throws a wrench in my happy flow. I pause and look at it. Do I really believe things need to be a certain way to be happy? No! I apply my lesson, *"My happiness and my function are one because God has given me both."* I forgive the idea that I know what is in my best interest in this situation and open myself to fully appreciate life as it gifts me in my present moment.

Parker is rummaging through cupboards, gathering materials for Cole who stands at the counter with a large bowl, Playtex gloves up to the elbows, joy exuding from both. I watch, my heart bursting with joy and enthusiasm. I have no agenda—only happiness. I can't wait to see the experiment. I know Lar will too.

CHAPTER FIFTY-EIGHT

DAY 67

(Lesson 67)

"Love created me like Itself."

(W-pI.67.1)

I think of love as my true name. Love created me like itself! It's like deep within I knew that love is what I am from early in my childhood, but nothing in my environment reinforced it. That knowing just got covered over by false ideas, twisted up with human-doingness, producing a sort of amnesia, and a different identity which I came to consider myself. Through forgiveness, the memory of the love I am returns to my mind.

Today's lesson states the true and accurate statement of what we are. It is why we are the light of the world. And why God appointed us as savior to the world. In accepting or awaking to this one idea, we realize the full truth we seek. *We are love!* And here, in what we are, is our happiness fulfilled.

This is the truth that sets us free. Just saying the words slowly and meaningfully, right now—applying it to our self, and something very true and core clicks inside. Right? Can you feel it? Love created us like itself. Period. Everything in existence, without exception, is love. How could it be different? God is Love—creating Love with Love. We are that Love. How could we be anything else? Love is the raw material from which we each have our being. *"Love which created me is what I am."*

I was counseling a lot when I started practicing these lessons. What joyous fertile ground to have for applying the ideas. Many times, I'd try to help a client and feel impotent. My lesson, without fail, when I applied it, perfectly addressed whatever was happening. Through the practice of forgiveness in my own life, I learned to step back, remember I am love—*Love created me like itself*—and let the Holy Spirit counsel through me.

I'm with a client with an eating disorder. She's been through treatment, seen several counselors, nutritionists, and doctors. She tells me her story and I relate. She feels hopeless. I remember feeling that way. I love her. She is me. I sit next to her on the couch and put her hand in mine. I share with her my story. I share about my surrender in prayer and how I realized I am the love that could heal the hunger and starvation that had held me hostage for so long.

Looking in each other's eyes, I see her innocence, purity, and love. It's a miracle mind-meld and I witness the recognition of Self behind her eyes. I witness as she opens and joins me in the possibility she too, must be love. Joy brightens her face—her light and mine blend, casting a rosy glow, surrounding us in Divine Love.

A brand-new conversation begins today for us. We are joined in love, and healing is inevitable. I know it isn't my words that impact her, it is the love behind them. Healing has begun. Love which created us is what we are.

Love gave us our only real identity. What a relief and celebration it is to realize this! It has been through accepting and applying ideas like today's lesson that let me forgive my false "story of me" and open me to the obvious truth of what I, and we all, must be! It was always there, just waiting for us to let go of the false image of ourselves that caused us pain and heartache.

Forgiveness uncovers what we already are. We are love because Love created us like itself. Holiness created us holy. Kindness created us kind. Helpfulness created us helpful. Perfection created us perfect. Happiness created us happy!

CHAPTER FIFTY-NINE

DAY 68

(Lesson 68)

"Love holds no grievances."
(W-pI.68.1)

This lesson can blow our whole mind structure to bits. It starts with a compelling statement, *"You who were created by love like itself can hold no grievances and know your Self. To hold a grievance is to forget who you are."* It says that to hold a grievance is to see ourselves as a body and to let the ego rule our mind and condemn our body to death.

Grievances are what is between us and our recognition we are love. Grievances stand in the way of accepting our full inheritance of everything we want or need for perfect happiness.

So, that little resentment we're holding at our mother is no trivial thing. It is keeping us from our happiness. It is preventing us from recognizing our Self! And incidentally, that mom is me. Just saying.

Our grievances, no matter how small, keep us asleep and dreaming lives of lack and lovelessness. They prevent us from realizing that in actuality, we totally love everyone and everything in creation because that is what we are.

Grievances are the sleeping pill that keeps us dreaming we, and everyone and everything, are something that we are not. We are not fearful, angry people, in competition for the meager sustenance in the world and in need of proving our worthiness. Notice how all grievances are tied up with body identity—some imagined threat to our physical being.

Holding grievances is the ego's answer to keeping us safe from the perceived threat. This clouds our vision and our ability to see another alternative, to see that the one before us shares a common condition with us, and ultimately a common goal—to remember the love that would end all suffering for all time.

I read today's lesson, and it makes total sense. Of course, love holds no grievances, they are opposites. So, in applying the idea I'm surprised to see how I can find interference or grievances with everyone I believe I love unconditionally. With each grievance I see how I have lined up my hostages in my mind, and how it holds me hostage to feeling guilty. With each I say, *"Love holds no grievances. I would see you as my friend, that I may remember you are part of me and come to know myself."* I feel at peace.

I start on the sneaky little grievances I've thought I could live with. Things like I thinking I know what's best for someone else. This stops me in my tracks.

My daughter Lin and I are best friends. I mean, I was basically a child myself when she was born. You could say we grew up together in some ways. We've been through a lot and forgiven even more. So, I am astonished to see I hold a grievance of this sneaky sort with her. Lin's body is fat. I resent society because the judgments on obesity, like being fat is an unforgivable sin. I assumed myself separate from this culture I judged and held a grievance against.

But the instant it comes to my awareness, I see the grievance is all mine. I have felt sad for Lin. Sadness is a grievance against the truth. It blocks my awareness of perfect joy, of her absolute innocence, and my own. Instantly, I see it's the body identity belief. I gladly forgive, and my forgiveness sets me free.

It's like our bodies dissolve in my mind, and only love is there. I adore Lin just the way she is. She's perfect for me. With my whole heart I surrender, waking up to what is: present joy and happiness.

CHAPTER SIXTY
DAY 69
(Lesson 69)

"My grievances hide the light of the world in me."
(W-pl.69.1)

Check out the imagery used in today's practice. We are this incredible light—the center of life itself. But we just can't see it because we believe the false stories in our minds. Like all these heavy burdens in our lives, are merely cloud coverage that we can walk right through to our goal of peace and see the light of truth—that you and I are One. It totally works! I am the witness.

I would describe my son Parker as a free spirit—a sort of a Love Angel. From the moment he began interacting with the world, love radiated from him, infusing everyone with joy.

He is fearless and daring, joyously exploring life with complete abandon. He'd climb anything, determined to see what lies beyond the next horizon. He was always climbing up on people's laps and giving them loves, or climbing up near wherever the action was, smiling his bright, infectious smile.

It's midmorning. Lar and I are in the home office on our computers, when Parker, about four years old at the time, bustles into the room and climbs up on an antique daybed across from our desks. Lar tells him to get off, and not get on it again. I'm immediately irritated with Lar. My mind starts spinning a story about how men don't really care about children's feelings, and I feel bad for Parker.

I'm blinded by this story I concocted in childhood and reinforced with every man in my life since, so it feels real to me right now. I see Lar bullying Parker, acting as if the furniture is more important than Parker.

Parker climbs down and runs off to play elsewhere. I'm still caught up in my story and fuming silently at Lar, blaming him for my imagined tale of the plight of children at the hands of men, when here comes Parker. He climbs right back up on the bed. Lar gets pissed, yanks Parker off, telling him to not do it again.

I jump up, gather Parker in my arms and righteously leave the room, feeling violated, for both of us. It's unbearable being in my own skin. I drop to my knees gathering Parker next to me. In that instant, grace cracks open my defenses and my training kicks in.

It's almost comical, if not for the fear-ants under my skin, when today's lesson, clear as day, breaks open the dark clouds of the grievance story and offers me the answer. *"Love holds no grievances. My grievances block the light of the world in me."* I push through the clouds of falsehood in my mind. I realize I don't see the situation as it is, only my interpretation based on an ancient grievance. And in the light of willingness, I know it isn't true.

It blocks the light of the world in Lar and me from me. The story literally breaks apart like clouds in my mind as I move toward the light—the truth within—the love we are as one. Compassion and love rise within me. I look at Parker, who's scuttling off to play. He's smiling, total joyous. He absolutely glows with the light of the world. I see my innocence, and Lar's, in him. Thank you, Christ.

On autopilot, I turn around and walk back into where Lar sits. I say, "I do not want to spend one more instant not loving you completely." I tell him of the awareness of my grievance and the drama I assigned to him, now brought to the light of awareness and forgiven. I thank him for his perfect part, my heart swelling with love and appreciation. We hold each other embraced in love's light. Parker steps in next to us, and without missing a beat, slips a tiny hand in each of ours.

CHAPTER SIXTY-ONE
DAY 70
(Lesson 70)

"My salvation comes from me."
(W-pI.70.1)

Salvation is God's promise we will find our way back to Him—that we will see the light within us and realize that light is what we are as God created us.

The seeming cost of accepting today's idea is this: It means we accept that nothing outside ourselves can save us. Nothing outside ourselves can give us peace. Nothing outside ourselves can hurt us, disturb our peace, or upset us. We are responsible.

I am responsible. *My salvation comes from me.* How freeing. Whenever I think something outside myself needs to change for me to be happy, I have already decided against my salvation. I can easily tell by the way I feel.

If I feel icky, I know I have decided against the truth of what I am as love. I look again at what I think I need, and using today's lesson, I remind myself, *"My salvation comes from me. It cannot come from anywhere else. Within me is the world's salvation and my own."* It's like a prayer to call on my holiness—the light within me, the Holy Spirit within my mind. Instantly I feel better, at peace. Nothing outside me needs to change—though it appears to have changed. I have turned within, to where salvation is already waiting for me.

Today's idea, *"My salvation comes from me."* I remember I am responsible, and my salvation comes from me. I'm at an unschooling event with Cole and Parker. I'm feeling awesome after a great morning meditation and mind-training. I feel like nothing can rock me. I am happy.

The kids begin a project with rocks they gathered the day before, and I sit with the other moms, where we visit while the kids do the project. Suddenly, I hear one little girl yelling at Parker and calling him stupid. Whoa!

It only takes a minute for my whole attitude to shift from calm to total momma bear! I look sternly at the girl's mom, who doesn't even seem fazed. I jump up from my seat, hairs bristling, determined to set the girl straight.

But like a force of nature, my lesson stops me. It says, "Sit back down. Think about this. Is there really something outside of yourself that is distressing you? No. Your feelings—your responsibility!" I take a breath. "Uh . . . Honestly? Is there really anything but you that can give you peace? No. So, the upset is inside you, and you have the power to restore your mind to peace."

I take a deep breath, letting the upset pass. I sit quietly, reiterating today's idea, *"My salvation comes from me. Nothing outside of me can hold me back. Within me is the world's salvation and my own."* I settle back into love—knowing that real help comes from my forgiving and fulfilling my purpose as the light of the world.

I see the innocence we share—Parker, his friend, her mom, and myself. The upset leaves the way it came. In an instant. *"My salvation comes from me."* It is a moment of pure grace.

Filled with gratitude, I look back to the kids, who are already playing happily together.

CHAPTER SIXTY-TWO
DAY 71
(Lesson 71)

"Only God's plan for salvation will work."
(W-pI.71.1)

Since only God's plan will work and nothing else, why waste time? The prayer from this lesson is a Divine lifeline. *"What would You have me do? Where would You have me go? What would You have me say, and to whom?"* It is the perfect prayer to align our will with God's. I use it constantly! It, at once, says: I surrender my ego will, and accept God's will, in which I trust His strength, vision, and guidance.

During my coffee with the Divine, I contemplate today's lesson. *"Only God's plan for salvation will work. Holding grievances is the opposite of God's plan for salvation. And only God's plan will work."* I let my mind sink deep into the heart of the love I am as God created me, where I feel His guidance alive in me.

Transitioning from my meditative rest, I pray the divine prayer in today's lesson. Suiting up for yoga, the prayer is in the background. As I leave the studio, I hop on my little scooter, grateful for the blessed union with life all around me. I breathe in the moment, appreciating how perfect this segment of the day has gone without my interference. As I turn the key, looking at the road before me, the sun rising, casting its glow on me, I lean back in the arms of trust to carry me forward.

Once home, I anticipate the long-awaited weekend vacation with the kids I've planned. It is a much-needed weekend getaway for the kids and me. I have all my ducks in a row; the kids are packed up, the car gassed up, we have a place to stay, and we were going to Park City.

Just as we're heading out the door, the phone rings. I resist answering it because I want nothing to interfere with our plans. But I instinctively bypass that impulse and answer anyway.

It's a young mother I sponsor in AA. She's crying, sucking in words as she breaks down into my care. She's frightened, feels out of control and is afraid she will hurt her child or herself. I understand. I know the feeling of believing that insanity from the ego mind is real. I've been that young mother. I want to help, and I can easily see this is a call for love.

My mind spins in conflict. "If we don't get to my friend's condo before they leave, they'll lock up and we'll have no way to get in. There is no place we can afford to stay in Park City, my friend's invitation to stay while they are gone is what made our vacation possible. If we don't leave now, our plans will be ruined. Another broken promise to my children. Aargh. I should have just left. We're running late as it is. Why did I pick up the phone?"

It's like I hear a shushing, quieting the ego voice. *"Holding grievances is the opposite of Gods plan and only His plan will work."* Oh wow, I realize, there must be a better plan than mine. I silently pray, *"What would You have me do? Where would You have me go? What would You have me say to her?"* I know what to do.

I share the prayer with my friend, and we join in prayer together. Lin and Lucas step in on either side of me and put their arms around me. I am at peace—Park City forgotten. Lin jumps in, "Hey, let's invite Donna and her son to join us in Park City." And that's what we did.

When we arrive, there's a note on the door of the condo telling us to get the keys from the management. I see my life is by Divine plan and I trust everything that happens is for our own best interest. We have a blessed weekend with family *and* friends.

CHAPTER SIXTY-THREE

DAY 72

(Lesson 72)

"Holding grievances is an attack
on God's plan for salvation."

(W-pl.72.1)

It seems like we all hold grievances like it's a perfectly normal thing to do. And, it is—according to the ego. Of course. The ego's chief goal is to replace God in our mind. That's why all the focus on form—identifying ourselves as people in bodies, separate from other bodies. Ego = form. Spirit = content. The ego uses the body for pride, pleasure, and attack.

With God's plan, the Holy Spirit uses the body for communication, for union through love. The course tells us that everything we see with the body's eyes is an illusion. Today's lesson is asking us to recognize that to the extent that we place our attention and focus on physicality, we are putting our faith in the body as our salvation.

It's crazy to see the extent I still see my body as my home. Sure, in meditation, I have brief holy instances where I feel lifted beyond the body, but in everyday life? Not so much. The truth is, I have my body at the center of my self-concept much of the time.

I consider the message of today's lesson sincerely, willing with all my heart to let go of what I think I understand so I can be shown. Do I trust my life to God's plan? How will I make the shift to spirit-centered living full time? But here's what is so beautiful, and why I love my morning time with God and the lessons.

This is a time I have consecrated to the Divine and I willingly suspend what I think I know, so I can be shown something new. I apply the lesson as suggested and trust. I ask, *"What is salvation, Father? I do not know. Tell me, that I may understand."* Immediately I realize I don't need to know; I need only be aware of Love's presence in each present moment! It's like a click, and something fundamental shifts inside me.

Being willing to look with love at how deep the rabbit-hole of my body-identification goes, *is* my part. Not resisting looking—no longer pretending it isn't there, or that I'm past it—but forgiving and asking to be shown, that's my part. I recognize myself as Spirit, trusting and enthused to take my lesson to the streets.

As I go about my daily business, I notice a subtle shift away from form and into content. Like I'm actually looking beyond the physical dynamics and into the reason behind them. Am I looking with love and joining from a place of recognizing the truth in my brother?

For example, I'm at lunch with friends and the topic of insurance and pharmaceutical companies comes up. People are sharing the latest list of victim stories, and we're laughing, and it seemed like it's all in fun. Subtly, I notice an icky feeling creeping over me.

LESSON ALERT! I'm sharing in stories that attack God's plan for salvation—stories of victimhood, pain, suffering, the all-powerful medical complex, of right and wrong. I stop engaging and just witness my mind. I check the meaning behind the storytelling. These indirect attacks on the "collective enemy" are fertile ground for the ego to get control and blot out spirit temporarily in my mind.

The prayer from today's lesson fills my heart, *"What is salvation, Father? I do not know. Tell me that I may understand."* Another picture of this gathering unfolds before me with joyous content. I see only union with friends. I forgive our judgments and see our innocence in coming together for companionship, connection, fun, and love. I am filled with gratitude. Silently I say, "Thank you for your holiness," to each companion, and feel my own. Smiling, I rejoin the conversation from my love-Self.

CHAPTER SIXTY-FOUR
DAY 73
(Lesson 73)

"I will there be light."
(W-pI.73.1)

I have had a passionate love affair with *A Course in Miracles*. I love how peacefully sane, at home, innocent, and whole I feel when I am engaged with this beautiful text and contemplating its teachings.

Early on, I began this ongoing internal inquiry, a continuous contemplation, in the back of my mind "What if I actually have everything that would make me happy, right here, right now? What if the search really is over? What if I just apply whatever lesson I am on each day to whatever comes up and have faith that this magnificence that draws me to the course will handle the details of my life?"

A Course in Miracles is a portal of grace that let me recognize I am home. I gave myself over to its divine alchemy. I enjoy applying the lessons to whatever arises, and the feeling of trust and faith I have that by merely doing my best to implement them as instructed. And something magnificent and beautiful, of which I am an equal part, transforms all that makes no sense, into the light of understanding love.

Everything else had failed. I didn't have anything to lose. Simple, right? Not so easy. I was addicted to "figuring things out," worrying, regretting, and planning, as a way of organizing my life. It's a hard habit to break.

But, as I catch myself in those patterns, I apply the lesson as the best I can. And there has never been a single time that stopping and applying the lesson has failed to bring peace and a sense of relief. Today's lesson is a beautiful example. Declaring *"I will there be light,"* connects me with God's will for me, and lets me see the right path before me.

I am traveling to Alpharetta, Georgia for my annual sister's retreat. This is my first time using the metro train system, and I'm not sure how the whole thing works. I'm feeling apprehensive when I get on the train, hoping I'm headed in the right direction. I look around, and I can't see one friendly face to help me. My breath is shallow, and I realize I feel afraid.

I know feeling afraid is always a sign I think I am alone, that I am relying on my own strength instead than the strength of the light within. I close my eyes and tune into my lesson. *"I will there be light."* Instantly, the darkness giving me this unsafe picture on the train lifts, releasing my fear. My eyes open to a whole new experience.

A bright smile spreads across my face, as I am reminded these are my brothers, I share the train with. I instinctively know my next move. Give my brothers the chance to extend love, to be generous with me, and help me find my way. I say, "Can someone please help me with where I am going? I've never been on this kind of train and I'm not even sure I'm going the right way." The response is overwhelmingly positive. Several of my new friends turn to help. They happily point out which stop is mine and say they'll make sure I get to my destination.

People want the be the best of themselves. I love seeing this miracle of which I am a part, offered and received. We are the light emblazoned in union. Together, we enjoy a joyous ride on the Light train!

CHAPTER SIXTY-FIVE
DAY 74
(Lesson 74)

"There is no will but God's."
(W-pl.74.1)

Today's idea lands on a day where I had been secretly harboring a conflict in my heart, which I have believed needed resolution, so, as usual, it's perfect. I can't see that conflict is not real as long as I temporarily want something else.

I smile because just reading the lesson brings me back home. *"There is no will but God's,"* why wrestle with my conflict an instant longer? Only by accepting that God's will and mine are one in the same, can I see with sanity. It's so simple to see the instant that I remember what I am is love, and love and conflict cannot coexist. God is the I Am, and I am, because He is. God's will must be mine because we cannot be apart. God will's perfect peace and happiness for us. Conflict is not His will, so it is not real.

My conflict circumstance is not real. Conflict is not God's will and, hallelujah, it certainly is not mine. It's so great to see this open up in the light of day—the light of truth. It's a miracle. Up until a minute ago, I actually thought something needed to change for me to be at peace. And, I guess in a way, that is true. I needed to see things differently. Conflict is like death, it stops communication in its tracks and looks for evidence to prove that conflict is real. Only my perception makes the illusion of conflict or gives life through forgiveness and love.

So, what was the circumstance? Lar and I have a holy relationship, so we feel it when there is interference in communication. I've been sensing Lar has been wrestling with a conflict in his own heart, which he is not sharing with me. But rather than clarify with him, I judge him as withholding, placing a barrier to our communication. I have been taking his not sharing with me personally.

I let myself ruminate on this withholding idea so much that I convinced myself that his not sharing what I *imagine* he is struggling with, somehow takes something away from our love. I take it into my lesson practice, and it's just so perfect. I see that conflict is personal—that's a clue.

There is no conflict in God. It is not His will, and God's will is my real will. I'm clearly making this up. The conflict is in my mind. *I* am interrupting communion with God! I repeat my lesson, *"There is no will but God's. I cannot be in conflict. God's will and mine are one. God will's peace for His Son. I am at peace,"* letting it penetrate deep within, stilling my heart and mind. Peace settles over me like a blanket and I remember I really do trust our holy relationship.

I know the Holy Spirit is handling all seeming conflicts in our hearts. What needs to happen for our healing, can't help but happen. My part is happening right now with my lesson practice. I let my feelings and fears arise, place them on my inner altar, and forgive the unreality of conflict in the light of awareness. My heart is wide open communication, continuously extending and receiving. *"I am at peace. Nothing can disturb me. My will is God's."*

I hear a small tapping, open my eyes, and Lar walks into my meditation room. He sits next to me on the couch and says, "Do you have a minute to talk?" I love this man and this course!

71

CHAPTER SIXTY-SIX

DAY 75

(Lesson 75)

"The light has come."
(W-pI.75.1)

Today's idea resonates at a frequency that can be seen only by a forgiving mind. The perception through the ego world is too dense to see the truth. So, to resonate with present light—to see the that the light has come, right here, right now, the decision for total forgiveness of everyone and all false perception must be made. It is the way of Atonement.

The light has come! It is already here, but we can't see it as long as we hold on to the past. Today's lesson gives us the chance to make this shift to the frequency of light and entirely change the world we see.

While doing the exercise in today's lesson during my morning time with the Divine, it feels as if a new pathway to vision opens before me. I read and contemplate the lesson, *"The light has come."* Yes. I am the light. It's how I can see at all. It is in and behind everything, illuminating my projections, whether they be illusions of despair or ones cleaned of false ideas through forgiveness, therefore reflecting the truth. I offer thanks for the passing of the old and the beginning of the new, affirming, *"The light has come. I have forgiven the world."* I give my mind to this single idea, releasing the past and inviting a new vision to come.

At first, it seems shadows from my past parade across my open mind and dissolves into a light beyond. Then in a holy instant of timelessness, my entire mind is pure light, bringing with it a feeling of immense joy. I know it is Divine presence, gifted me through forgiveness. Like right during this time sequence I call my life, I am lifted out of the dream and into present light.

My world now comes back into view within my mind and all the players—my children, my work, my colleagues and clients, the stranger at the grocery store—all have a shiny brightness or aura emanating from within. I sense a dynamic buoyancy to my sight, and I feel extraordinarily happy. I have a felt sense that my world has fundamentally changed.

I'm basking in this inner glow, about to get on with my day, when Parker and Cole come in for a snuggle. It is pure love, and we are bathed in a warm rosy glow, the light of love surrounding us. I smile, *"The light has come. I have forgiven the world."*

This brightness goes with me throughout the day. I'm waiting at a crosswalk when I see a blind woman tentatively tapping the space in front of her, waiting to cross the street. Just as I think I'd like to lend a helping hand, a gentleman, seemingly out of thin air, appears next to the woman. He takes her arm and walks toward me, radiance emanating from them. It seems, all around me, others see it too, smiling and acknowledging this act of kindness as they pass by. The light has come!

CHAPTER SIXTY-SEVEN
DAY 76
(Lesson 76)

"I am under no laws but God's."
(W-pl.76.1)

Today we are challenging the very foundation of the ego's game. Protecting the body appears to be salvation. Life seems governed by laws that keep us safe; laws of nutrition and health, science, relationships, economics, and fair trade. These laws bind us to body-identity and blind us to our true identity as God created us.

Bodies are not what we are. We are as Spirit and it is only by withdrawing our allegiance from the laws of the world and trusting God's laws, we realize how they are always operating on our behalf.

His laws guarantee that our salvation is already accomplished. The only thing we need saving from is the belief we are something we are not. Under God's laws, miracles bend the quantum field to fulfill God's will for happiness for us.

When I left the traditional mental health to forge a new vision of mental health healing, it was today's lesson that bolstered my faith. Fortified by trusting God and the principles of *A Course in Miracles*, I felt inspired to dedicate myself to just working for God. It was scary, and I felt insecure a lot. But I knew these were opportunities to see where my beliefs were still stuck and to forgive and trust God.

Several colleagues and friends joined with me to create a nontraditional, spiritually based center for healing, through the recognition of the power of the Divine within each of us. We created intensive workshops; offered gatherings for *A Course in Miracles*, individual and group counseling, massage therapy, and even clairvoyant readings. It was a giant leap of faith, and there wasn't a lot of money to start—nothing I could count on from week to week.

Within the first month, my car dies. My home is ten miles from the center. I have a workshop to facilitate in two hours, and I am without transportation to get to the center. Not only that, I cannot see a way I can replace my vehicle. Everything had gone into the center.

Today's lesson rings like a bell in my mind, and before taking any self-initiated action, I settle into meditation, reminding myself, *"I am under no laws but God's."* I feel the fear lift, replaced by trust. The right thing will happen— I trust God that I am under His laws and He wants me to be happy. So, what I need, I'll have. If I don't have it, I don't need it. The phone rings and I get a ride to the workshop with one of the other facilitators. I leave the rest to Divine Providence.

At the center, I give myself entirely to God's wll for the workshop, the transportation problem gone from my mind. After the weekend workshop, one of the participants asks to speak with me. She tells me she wants to participate in the weekly follow-up group but that she doesn't have the money. She asks, "Is there was any way you would be willing to accept a motor-scooter in trade for therapy?" I smile, knowingly and answer, "Yes!" I tell her she is a miracle worker in a Divine plan!

It is a summer of slowing down and being present. Riding a scooter is like rock climbing or meditating—I can't have my mind somewhere else if I stay present and alive.

After another workshop, before the first snow fall, the husband of one participant takes me aside and says, "I noticed you drive a scooter to work. Is that your only vehicle?" I nod. He says, "I've got an old truck sitting in my driveway I'm not using, would you like it? Maybe we can work something out so my wife can keep coming here." My trust in God's laws proves itself out!

CHAPTER SIXTY-EIGHT

DAY 77

(Lesson 77)

"I am entitled to miracles."
(W-p1.77.1)

*"W*e are entitled to miracles.*"* It's sort of the reason we started this mind-training—for the miracle alchemy due us the Children of God. We are entitled to miracles because of what we are, not what we imagine ourselves to be as persons in the world. We receive miracles because of what God is. And because we are one with God, we will naturally offer miracles because they are the extension of love.

With every seeming problem that arises, here is the bottom-line ticket to our salvation. Miracles are the remedy. Period. The thing that gets in our way is the belief in a hierarchy of illusions—that some problems are more difficult for a miracle in than others. That's why the first principle of the course is *"There is no order of difficulty in miracles. One is not 'harder' or 'bigger' than another. They are all the same. All expressions of love are maximal"* (T.1.1). Miracles are the way we live in the world, identified as our True Self.

Until I accepted today's idea, I suffered, believing that some of my personal issues, though large and encompassing to me, were too small or insignificant for a miracle to answer. I felt it was up to me to fix my own shit. Which, of course, is the ego's ultimate game strategy.

I deployed all my best techniques to burn the idea that *"there is no order of difficulty in miracles"* into my mind—writing it on my mirror, the fridge, the inside of my wrist, setting timers. Because let's face it, I always need a miracle. My deserving miracles was a worthiness issue.

But as I began to see that no illusion is true, I also realized that each problem was the same error in my mind—I believe I am separate from my Source. Today's idea disputes my false unworthiness issue—I am worthy as a child of God. *"I am entitled to miracles."*

Today's lesson is the confidence we need to lean back and trust that through our willingness to trust the transformation of merely practicing the mind-training, the idea will seed itself within our mind whether we're aware of it at the time or not. We say with confidence, *"I am entitled to miracles."*

We remind ourselves we're only asking for what is rightfully ours and by asking, we bring miracles to all minds which are one with ours. Imagine our cells, and all the molecules of the world, transforming under the laws of God to bring miracles to us. Feel a powerful presence within, and I know we will no longer withhold our so-called personal problems away from the miracle that is our birthright. *"I am entitled to miracles."*

I realize a permanent shift has taken place while reorganizing my office. Under my desk calendar, I find a list from a year before. It is a list of problems in need of a miracle to solve.

- Obsessing about my body and food.
- Being afraid there won't be enough money.
- Getting angry with the kids and feeling guilty.

As I read the list, tears of joy spill from my eyes on to the page, smudging the ink. Not one thing on the list still holds my mind hostage. Each has been handled by miracles. I love myself and am at peace with my body and food. I'm doing work I love and whatever I need comes to me, so money isn't the same burden, because I trust. I don't take what the children do personally anymore, so I don't get angry, but invest myself in their unique way of seeing the world. My whole way of seeing has changed. That is the miracle: A shift in perception, from fear to love. I am humble before the miracle that has become my life.

CHAPTER SIXTY-NINE

DAY 78

(Lesson 78)

"Let miracles replace all grievances."
(W-pI.78.1)

Every thought we have that isn't love-based is actually some sort of grievance. When I meet someone, if I'm not thinking with God, I assess them as competition. I compare. I do not see.

As I give my assessment up through forgiveness, it clears my vision so I can see my brother, instead of another. I know the difference by the way I feel. When I initiate the encounter as holy, with an open mind, I feel peaceful, loving, and I want to join with them rather than try to impress or judge. They are immediately my best friend for the moment, and I see we have everything in common—we want to love and make our contribution of beauty to the world. That's why miracles replace all grievances in my mind.

Today, we have the chance to dissolve "the wall of hate" our grievances place before our sight, which blocks our vision and keeps us trapped in the dark and lonely world of our own private mind. We pick one person to represent all brothers and sisters. Someone whom we hold hostage for a grievance of hurt, anger, and judgment. I know instantly the one I'll choose. Keri. Keri is my sister whom I have given the role of lifelong antagonist. I go into the meditative exercise with not only a reservation that it will work, but also unsure I want it to.

I picture Keri in her smug, know-it-all, martyr attitude, hands on hips, chin up, looking down her nose at me. I envision times I felt she hurt me, judged me, made me feel small, thought she was better than me—all the hurts and betrayals I attach to her. I feel the sticky texture of judgment and the hollowness of my need to be right in my gut. They are the armor I have placed over my sight and heart.

I crack open the breastplate with the words from today's lesson: *"Let me behold my savior in this one You have appointed as the one for me to ask to lead me to the holy light in which she stands, that I may join with her."* Instantaneously, more than being right about being wronged by Keri, I know a miracle is all I want to see. I *want* the light of love to blaze through my dark ideas around Keri and myself.

While I hold Keri in my mind, each grievance unravels. The knot of black rope tying me to my pain and resentment unknots—until there is only a stream of light connecting us to one another—my picture story of Keri, dissolving into the light.

A vision of the little girls we were as children, before she was hit by a car and I was blamed, comes into my mind. I see our innocence and blamelessness, ease and carefree wonder, which fills and resets my heart. Miraculously, I am released from the prison I placed myself in at five years old, with she as jailor. Tears of release and forgiveness cleanse me, as love fills my heart and sight with wonderment and light.

I see Keri as she is, light emanating from within her, my sister, my friend—my savior. I feel the same light emanating from me, surrounding us both in God's brilliant love. In reverent gratitude, I thank Keri for the miracle she is and has given me.

When I think of Keri now, I see only the miracle she gave. My heart reaches out to hers, to that sweet spot where miracles have replaced grievances. I have precious fondness and appreciation for the miracle she is, and I am, as the holy child of divine love.

CHAPTER SEVENTY

DAY 79

(Lesson 79)

*"Let me recognize the problem
so it can be solved."*

(W-pI.79.1)

The course teaches that all problems that seem to arise come from one original error. We believe we are separate from our Creator. By accepting this false idea, we are now looking at a world that seems fragmented, separate from us. Today's lesson is pointing out that any problem we are having, regardless of the form it takes, is not our real problem. Our real problem is that we believe we are separate from God. This is our one and only problem. It is not true—and it never actually occurred.

Remember that the ego wants to tie our attention up with tangential, insolvable issues so we won't think to look where the problem really lies. The problem is in the mind that believed it could be separate from its Source.

Today's practice cuts through all the unnecessary chatter, zeroing us back to where a real solution to our one problem can be found. We must first recognize what the problem really is, so the answer can occur.

If I don't recognize the problem, solving it is a crapshoot at best, right? That pretty much describes my life when I'm trying to run it myself.

Practicing today's idea requires we surrender and empty our mind of what we think our problem is, that includes all the evidence we believe supports our position. It requires that we take our hands off it for good, giving it to the Holy Spirit that remembers what the error in our mind is and how to correct it. The results are profound.

I'm in a relationship with another counselor, and I use this situation as a starting point to apply the lesson. I'd been feeling inadequate and misunderstood. (No surprise there.) It seems he always has to be right and doesn't take responsibility for anything.

The way I'd been dealing with it is to write out these long, investigative inventories of my part in the problem. Then I'd present it to him hoping he'd cop to his role and meet me in that vulnerable place where we could join in a solution. Sounds reasonable, right? It never works out that way, and I leave those conversations feeling shitty because he doesn't do what I want. He's like, "Look, Danét, It's not my problem. It's your problem—your feelings, your problem."—Asshole.

As I begin my lesson practice, I place this relationship problem on the altar of my mind, for the Holy Spirit. I am aware, suddenly, of the emptiness I have felt defining my problem myself, and then trying to solve it myself.

I let go, saying, "What is the problem, Lord? I do not know. *Let me recognize the problem so it can be solved.*" Peace settles in my heart, and I feel as if the love of God beats a steady thrum of wholeness and surety. I realize *my problem* is not my problem. I have forgotten to ask God's will for happiness for me.

Now I am grateful my partner refuses to play a game where no resolution can be found. Now I see I need only to remember who I am and that I am never alone. The answer is always God! Divine union solves everything. The problem and solution are together, right in my mind, where God is. Whew!

CHAPTER SEVENTY-ONE

DAY 80

(Lesson 80)

"Let me recognize my problems have been solved."

(W-pI.80.1)

Today's lesson completes the practice we began yesterday. What good is recognizing our problem unless the answer is intrinsic in that recognition? *"Let me recognize my problems have been solved,"* is a call to awaken and be glad. Our one and only problem has been answered, and we have no other. One problem. One solution. Freedom from conflict has been accomplished.

In applying yesterday's lesson, I realized that the second I decide something is a problem, I have decided against God's plan for my happiness. What an incredible gift. It opens a space in which I see the answer.

Today's idea sits right behind yesterday's. The instant I ask to see the truth instead of a problem, I can accept everything that happens as a chance to forgive and be a light of love and healing in a situation. The idea of problems is my only problem. All my problems are one problem. They are all a result of a false self-concept. In that recognition, the solution is impossible to miss.

I am as God created me. Not a body, not even a person. These are the costumes I wear to bring the happy dream of union and joy to the world. Without my self-concept at the center of my perception, the natural union through love I share with my brothers is evident. I take my place in God's plan for salvation.

I make a decision. I don't do problems anymore.

I am excited for today's lesson. It asks that I trust that the truth is already in my mind. I am ready. It is already alive in me. During my morning practice, I repeat today's idea, *"Let me recognize my problems have been solved,"* freeing my mind of everything else. The problem game slips off me like shedding a garment. I am released into the solution always there, waiting for me to remember. My mind becomes clear and free with a feeling of deep contentment. It is the love of God.

It doesn't take long before I get my first challenge. The boys love Halloween. I've promised to take them to the Halloween Spirit store. They are already dressed and ready to go when the phone rings. It's the husband of a former client. His wife has attempted suicide and is in the hospital. He is grief stricken, crying so I can hardly understand him as he asks if I can come to the hospital.

I look over at the boys, their pleading little faces looking up at me. They seem to say, "Someone needs mommy, we'll have to wait." It's heartbreaking.

As I recognize the conflict within me, my lesson comes in on its heels. *"Let me recognize my problems have been solved."* I take a deep breath and lean into my trust that each aspect of what is happening is part of God's plan.

I know what to do. I remember this family has two children, a little older than the boys. I tell the husband to sit tight, I'll get right back with him. I squat down and take the boys hands. "How would you feel about inviting some other kids to go with us to the Halloween Store?"

Happy relief shines on the boys faces as they say, "Yes." We swing by the hospital where the family sits by her bedside and invite the children to spend the day with us. It is the perfect expression for the healing the family needs. Rather than feed the belief in problems, we went directly to a solution of unity and love.

CHAPTER SEVENTY-TWO
REVIEW II: DAYS 81–90
(Lessons 61–80)

Today we begin our second review—two lessons a day until we've reviewed all the lessons since our last review. I love these review periods. First off, because as we review of the ideas, we cover each day, we realize how the ideas have seeded themselves in our mind and become part of our love-matrix.

Also, I love the review because part of my old programming is the fear that I've missed something important that could make all the difference. Can you relate? Ha! It's like the course knows this and gives us the chance to review and feel bolstered by witnessing the influence of the ideas in a fresh way in our own lives.

It's amazing how setting the idea at the forefront of our mind as a sort of light beacon to the day before us never fails to bring witnesses to the truth of the ideas in our lives. They act as a flip-switch when the tendency to go to some dark, judgmental place about a situation or person arises.

By having that constant reminder of the truth, when the desire to react occurs, a little nudge reminds us something is off. We feel it—it's icky! The darkness of judgment, fear, and guilt no longer feel tolerable. They're becoming unnatural to us. We recall the ideas, letting them address the darkness, and the desire to harm is released from my mind.

I think of these reviews as integration periods to really establish ourselves in the ideas we've applied in the last twenty days. Each morning, we slowly read both lessons for review and the supporting ideas given for that day. Then sit for a few moments, letting them gel within us. At this stage of the mind-training we are developing the ability to be uncompromising in our intent and determination to allow the transformation for which the lessons intend.

After first spending a few moments with the whole lesson (both ideas), we again review the first idea and dedicate our morning to seeing where we can practice the idea and allow for transformation. The second half of the day will be devoted to the second lesson idea and applying it with whatever shows up.

Feel free to review the lesson examples from the original day's lesson. But also, I encourage you to use these review periods to write your own insights and examples of practice. Sometimes we don't even realize we have integrated a particular idea until we try to articulate it. It can be quite enlightening. Give it a spin. You deserve it.

NOTES

NOTES

NOTES

NOTES

NOTES

CHAPTER SEVENTY-THREE

DAY 91

(Lesson 91)

"Miracles are seen in light."
(W-pI.91.1)

We all get we are not our body, right? But, do we? The light that reveals miracles can't be seen with the body's eyes. This light is within. It is the alternative to the body-identity. Today we are asking for a real experience of our Self—the light of love.

During my morning practice, I consider today's idea and the question posed with a sincere and open heart. *"Miracles are seen in light. The body's eyes do not perceive the light. But I am not a body. What am I?"* I want to know what I don't yet realize. I know my life experience continually reinforces the body-identity.

But I'm also experiencing the grace of a greater purpose behind what happens. I am developing trust in the Divine wisdom of life which seeds my mind with the miracles forgiveness brings. As I add the statements, *"I am not limited, but unlimited. I am not weak, but strong. I do not see in darkness but in light,"* a subtle but unmistakable awareness of Divine presence rises like the sun from the center of my heart and in my soul. Filling me with Its certainty, strength, and calm assurance.

The light of miracles is within us always. It is that feeling in our heart when we feel compassion for another. It is that energetic lightness we feel when we help someone in need or spread random acts of kindness, knowing that the gift is in the giving. It is the feeling in our heart when we smile at someone who looks lonely. The impetus to offer the smile—that is the light—the guiding impulse to act with love, regardless of what the body's eyes are showing us.

Unschooling is all about trusting the light within our children is guiding their desire to learn. Cole wanted to learn about commerce and business. So, we become mystery shoppers. We pose as customers, write reviews, and get paid.

One morning we're pulling into a Sonic Drive-In. At the edge of the parking lot sits a homeless man. He's wrapped tightly in a threadbare jacket. It's windy and cold, and there are still remnants of snow on the ground. He looks freezing cold. He has a sign that says, "I'm hungry."

As we see him, in symphony, we decide to give him the food we get. We order the required menu items for the mystery shop. While we're waiting, Parker and Cole slip out of the van, walk over and make friends with this man, inviting him to warm up in the van while his food was being prepared. Past thoughts of unsafety come unbidden to my mind. But in noticing, I forgive, *"Miracles are seen in light. The body's eyes do not perceive the light. But I am not a body. What am I?"*

The boys don't see a scary guy to be suspicious of, but a call for love and the ability to answer it.

The gratitude in the man's face and the joy in boys' fill my heart as they walk back together and get in the van. Cole hands him a blanket we keep in the van for park days, to wrap around him while he eats. I order him another meal to go. He doesn't talk, just eats hungrily. But as he goes to leave, a giant smile spreads across his face, "Thank you. God bless you."

Just as we're closing the van door, Parker pipes in and asks, "Can we give him our park blanket to take with him?" He gives our new friend a big hug, handing him the blanket and sack lunch.

This is the light of miracles. We feel love's call and rise to the miracle it offers. We are the living miracle. The light within us is central to our being. We always have everything we need to be miracle workers.

CHAPTER SEVENTY-FOUR

DAY 92

(Lesson 92)

*"Miracles are seen in light,
and light and strength are one."*
(W-pI.92.1)

Following from yesterday's idea, *"Miracles are seen in light,"* today we add another dimension. *Light and strength are one.* As a result of the mind-training of *A Course in Miracles*, I see it in action all the time. It is a shift out of the darkness and into the light where I remember I am light, spirit, and love.

Miracles are the perfect remedy for everything. Every time I'm caught up in some sort of problem, where I actually think *I* need to solve whatever I seem to face, I'm identifying myself as a body, and effectively pulling shades down and blocking the light from my awareness. Our self-concept will always give us reasons we can't do something. We're not strong enough to move a car or a mountain—to enter an unknown situation and help.

But we're not a body. We are the light that brings the strength needed for each miracle. *"Miracles are seen in light, and light and strength are one."* We can tell by the way we feel. As a body we feel a heaviness, like darkness is blocking our ability to see how we can bring a miracle and prompts to turn away. Today's practice is to use these moments as the flip-switch to turn within to the light and ask for a miracle and the strength to carry it out.

I love how my life works. I just finished contemplating today's lesson when my phone rings. It's Parker. He asks what I'm doing. I tell I'm doing my course lesson, *"Miracles are seen in light, and light and strength are one,"* and we talk a little bit about what it means and how it shows up in our lives.

He says, "I had an experience like that just the other day. Anika and I had just been at the thrift shop over by my house, and when we were leaving, we see these two girls trying to push their car out of the middle of the road. But they were getting nowhere fast. We run over to them, and I say, "Hey, want some help?" And the look of relief and joy in those girls faces, Mom, it was beautiful.

We start helping them push the car, and the next thing you know, some random guy, comes out of nowhere, also starts pushing. We get the car into the parking lot easily. We all felt amazing! I love doing stuff like that."

I ask, "Why didn't you hesitate?" Parker says, "It's like your lesson says, I just knew to help, and the strength we needed would be given to us. It never occurred to me that it wouldn't." How simple.

Our light looks beyond the appearance of weakness we have of ourselves as a body, to the strength of God within us. His strength denies our weakness. When we are thinking about the strength of God within us, it dispels the idea of weakness from our mind.

Every day I devote to offering miracles. I can't do it as a body. But the strength of God within me can. Just like in the example with Parker, once we are open to seeing from the light within, we see a chance to bring a miracle, and what is needed shows up.

CHAPTER SEVENTY-FIVE
DAY 93
(Lesson 93)

"Light and joy and peace abide in me."

(W-pI.93.1)

Reading today's idea feels like it smiles back at me. Something in me, where all the true stuff is, knows. Reading or contemplating true ideas like today's is like flipping the "Light of Truth" switch, awakening us to the alternative in our mind.

The self-concept is like pulling the blinds, casting shadows across our life story, then we go chasing them. The ego loves to fascinate our attention with trivial, unsolvable problems. It's up to us to invite the truth in—to shine the light and dispel the shadows of falsehood.

The story of the little me is the ego's kingdom. Its foundation is sin and punishment. Its creed is to seek and not find. Resources are scarce, so competition of the fittest decides the winners and losers, but only to fight another day. It is a story of inevitable loss and death. In it I am the hero and the victim, forever balancing the scales of justice and worthiness, always hoping to find a little light, joy, and peace around the next corner.

Today's lesson is inviting us to make this crucial shift in our perception today. God created us whole, complete, innocent, and pure love—the only version of us God has. Nothing we have dreamed apart from His will has altered the truth of what we are as He created us, nor ever could. Divinity doesn't battle with our perception, It merely sees only what is true. Only illusions battle, and only with illusions.

I'm at work, wishing I was anywhere else. I have that awful feeling I get when I'm twisted up in my self-concept. I screwed up with a patient earlier in the day, and it weighs heavily on my mind. This patient was what we call a retread, meaning he's been in and out of treatment several times and never "gets it."

I remember him from the last time he was here, less than a month ago. While in treatment, he appeared to be sincere in his desire to get sober and live a life of sobriety. He was gregarious and friendly. I liked him. But now here he is again.

He's angry and withdrawn. I figure it is shame. I probe him to try to understand what happened. I ask him what he thinks the trigger was that made him start thinking about using again. He put his face right next to mine and says, "None of your business, bitch!" I say, "Look, it's your funeral." And leave the room.

As I play the scene over in my mind, my lesson whispers from my heart. *"Light and joy and peace abide in me."* I breathe it in, letting peace settle my restless mind until only light and joy and peace are present within me. I see the scene again, repeating, *"Light and joy and peace abide in me. My sinlessness is guaranteed by God."* I recall my client's face pressed next to mind and tell him, *"Light and joy and peace abide in you. Your sinlessness is guaranteed by God."*

Now, I recognize the call for love from both my client and myself. Love is the answer. My mind and heart lift within joy and peace. I know what to do next. Holding my lesson at the center of my heart, I go to see this brother whom I had not really seen before.

I find him in the break room. He is sitting off by himself. I walk toward him, beaming and radiant with love. He looks up, and it's like he feels the shift too. He smiles, jumps up, and says, "Oh good, you're not pissed. Sorry for being such an ass." We hug long and forgiving. Facing him, I say, "I came to say the same thing to you. Sorry for being an ass. Want to start over?" He says, "I think we just did."

CHAPTER SEVENTY-SIX
DAY 94
(Lesson 94)

"I am as God created me."
(W-pI.94.1)

This lesson is the only lesson in *A Course in Miracles* repeated several times. That is how important it is! It is the heart that makes all the other lessons finally beat true. It states a simple, unalterable fact. *"I am as God created me."* Today we are attempting to accept this eternal fact that brings confusion to an end. *"I am as God created me"* is a flip-switch, zeroing in on the Self we truly are.

This idea, *"I am as God created me,"* held singularly in our mind is enough to heal the world and everyone in it. It is God's idea of us, before time was, and the beginning and end of time. This holy idea is the word of God imprinted eternally within everyone and everything—We are as God created, and only that is true. Nothing specific in this world has meaning.

In my morning time with God, I feel a profound resonance as I repeat the ideas for today, *"I am as God created me. I am His Son eternally,"* and let my awareness sink down and deep within. I am home. I know my Self. I have a sense of being lifted up, bringing the power of God with me.

I see how my identity shapes the world I see. The world bends to the identity I hold as real for myself. This is the holy gift today's lesson offers. It says, *"The sounds of this world are still, the sights of this world disappear, and all the thoughts that this world ever held are wiped away forever by this one idea. Here is salvation accomplished. Here is sanity restored."*

During my first hourly reminder, I feel naturally drawn within, back to that whole sense of Self. I declare, *"I am as God created me. I am His Son eternally,"* and wait in quiet expectancy. I let my mind sink down beneath the humming between my ears and focus on my breathing. Each breath seems to say the lesson in its breath; Inhale—*I am as God created me.* Exhale—*I am His Son Eternally.* I am breathing, "I am love. I am loved." It's like Divine cadence. *"I am as God created me."* It is my Self. It is the atonement—the truth and the life.

I commit to holding this one idea as my only goal, the purpose of all my interactions so I won't forget. And to forgive quickly when I do.

Later in the day my commitment is challenged. I'm visiting with family members. One sister is relaying a story about an experience in the past we'd all experienced together. It seems to me she is twisting the angle so she looks like an innocent victim—a martyr.

Several things go through my mind seemingly simultaneously. First, I want to jump in. Be helpful. Invite her to "see her part," and maybe go into a little teaching spiel about how nothing can change until we take full responsibility for everything in our lives. But as quickly as that thought train arises, I feel a clutching inside.

That response is dishonest. It's some sort of ego-grandstanding. It isn't my Self. Love. Love doesn't grandstand. I pause and recall my lesson. *"I am as God created me. I am His Son eternally."* I feel the shift instantly. I catch my sister's eye, and through the eyes of love, say silently, *"You are as God created you. You are His Son eternally."* Silly ego. Memories are not reality. Soon I'm filled in the joy and entertainment of childhood stories we share, laughing and loving.

CHAPTER SEVENTY-SEVEN

DAY 95

(Lesson 95)

"I am one Self, united with my Creator."
(W-pI.95.1)

With today's lesson, we're fine-tuning our minds to keeping the truth about our Self and our relationship with the Divine ever-present in our minds. Beginning today the first five minutes of every hour are devoted to reaching the truth—*"I am one Self, united with my Creator, at one every aspect of creation, and limitless in power and in peace"*—within our minds.

This form of practice is a call to attention, an increased accountability in our practicing. We are training our minds to a constant awareness of our Self, united with our Creator. It is an important turning point.

We are invited to see how disciplined we have been up to this point—how often we remember our daily lesson throughout the day or let hours at a time pass without recalling our mind-training—how often we actually utilize the day's lesson to address any and everything that confronts us throughout the day.

Our practice is the touchstone of our awakening. We are refamiliarizing ourselves with our natural state, stripped clean of the false self-image made to obscure our awareness.

Each time I take a moment to turn toward the truth, recalling my lesson ideas and contemplate the truth, it's like a reboot. I am declaring my one desire to know my Self—the Self, as God created me, unified and whole. Each practice period, be it five minutes at the beginning of each hour, or a moment between where I recall the idea for the day and let its message take me home, gifts a miracle that plants a seed of growing awareness of "true" recognition in my mind.

Light and joy and peace abide in me for I am One Self, united with our Creator, at one with every aspect of creation and limitless in power and in peace. I write the lesson inside my wrist in purple ink as a mark of my devotion to remember.

Still, I miss my first hourly remembrance entirely. I notice this as I'm making breakfast. Immediately I feel the grip of guilt—and that's my flip-switch. As I repeat the idea, *"I am one Self,"* I realize guilt comes from a false self and blocks my awareness of the truth of today's lesson.

I laugh in happy forgiveness. Nothing can keep me from what I already am. I start thinking about each hour like Christmas when I was a kid. Like each is a present from God, I get to open. A gift of His presence and mine.

I see the practical application of today's idea a few minutes later in an encounter with Lucas. He is cramming all this papers and heaven knows what in his backpack as we get ready to leave. On autopilot, I'm just about to correct (judge) him on his behavior, and my lesson speaks to me just behind the initial response.

I pause and listen, then silently say to Lucas, *"You are one Self with me, united with our Creator in this Self. I honor you because of What I am, and What He is, who loves us both as One."* It changes everything. Now I watch him through the eyes of love. I don't want him to change a thing. It is a joy to witness and love "his way." It's perfect, just the way it is. It is miracle-awareness.

I witness too, that devoted to remembering the Self we share as one, united with God, judgment can't gain any footing. I see that we are one Self—that my interests and his are the same. We are as God created us—love—light and joy, limitless in power and in peace.

CHAPTER SEVENTY-EIGHT

DAY 96
(Lesson 96)

"Salvation comes from my one Self."
(W-pl.96.1)

We are one Self, though we experience ourselves as two: good and evil, loving and hating, mind and body. This split in identity is why we feel conflict. It becomes unbearable and ultimately we must choose one.

Only one is true. We are as God created us. Today we make the choice for truth. It is the choice for Spirit, our one Self, united with our Creator. Salvation comes from this Self within us.

We're just addicted to looking at problems and solutions as outside ourselves. That's the ego's way. And the result is confusion. Confusion ends with the choice to recognize only one Self, one Voice, one Purpose. We cannot make this decision if we try to maintain our identity as a body. The body and spirit are irreconcilable. When we react as if what we see with the body's eyes or feel with the body's senses is the real McCoy, we leave no room to recognize the truth.

In choosing to see that *"Salvation comes from my one Self,"* the body can be used by spirit as a communication device for miracles. The five-minute practice periods each hour are powerful at this point in our curriculum, because we still believe in two selves. That's why we try to "figure out," fix, and improve.

When we stop a moment and go within, seeking another way of seeing, the Self we are as God created us steps forward and the self-concept dissolves in the awareness of love's presence. The structure of the practice for five minutes each hour has literally saved me from myself.

Like the day when Lin, Lucas, and I were moving to a new home. We'd been loading furniture and boxes into a U-Haul all day. Every hour we'd stop, drink water, and I'd remind myself of the lesson, *"Salvation comes from my one Self."* Everything was moving along easily, peacefully and happy.

Finally, late in the afternoon, we lock up and drop the key in the slot. Carrying cleaning products and the vacuum, we drag ourselves down the stairs for the last time. As we walk toward the U-Haul, we see that another moving van has blocked us in. There's no one around or in the van. Aargh! The leasing office is closed for the day. Double aargh!

Now, I'm feeling tired and frustrated and helpless. Lin and Lucas have plans with friends for later that evening, and I promised they could go. They're antsy to get done. They've been such excellent help; I want them to go have fun. But we still must unload everything into the new place. I can't do it alone.

Hoping the people with the other moving van will show up soon, we wait it out in the U-Haul cab, and I try to take a nap. But, as time ticks by, I feel panicky, searching wildly in my mind for a solution so I can keep my promise to the kids.

Like an alarm bell, my lesson rings in my mind, *"My salvation comes from my one Self. Its thoughts are mine to share."* I remember nothing outside of myself can disturb me or bring me peace. I take a deep breath and let my mind settle and reach for where salvation can be found. I am not this tired body, but spirit. With each breath, I let my mind still into the light of love within, until peace is all I feel. Inhaling, *"Salvation comes from my one Self."* Exhaling, *"Its thoughts are mine to share."* I let my mind expand, imagining it was lighting a thousand minds with mine.

Suddenly, there is a knock on the window. It's three big, husky guys from the other van. They'd gone to get food before unloading their van. They apologize for blocking us in and ask if they can help us unload ours at our new place. We happily accept the help. It's perfect. With our "moving angels" we easily handle everything, and in plenty of time for Lin and Lucas to go out with their friends.

CHAPTER SEVENTY-NINE

DAY 97

(Lesson 97)

"I am spirit."

(W-pl.97.1)

I don't know about you, but today's idea instantly brings me joy! It merely states the truth, *"I am spirit."* It only accepts what is true, making no room for a split or false identity. The lesson says, *"Practice this truth today as often as you can, for it will bring your mind from conflict to the quiet fields of peace. No chill of fear can enter, for your mind has been absolved from madness, letting go illusions of a split identity."* Isn't that yummy?

In my morning time with the Divine, I am lifted beyond body identity and feel absorbed by the reality, *"I am spirit,"* filling me with boundless joy. Like a marquee, I imprint my mind with the lesson phrase, *"Spirit am I, a holy Son of God, free of all limits, safe and healed and whole, free to forgive, and free to save the world,"* so it is at the front of my mind.

I draw a little heart on the back of my hand, to remind me not to forget to be in touch hourly with spirit.

The morning is getting away from me, busy with getting the kids to school on time, when Parker announces he is supposed to bring cupcakes to his kindergarten class. Frantically, we all jump into the car to swing by the grocery store on the way to school and pick up cupcakes.

As I'm pulling out of the parking lot, "BAM!" Another car is backing out simultaneously, and we crash into each other. We both jump out, accusation in our eyes. I don't have time for this shit! Why wasn't she watching what she was doing? Why wasn't I? My heart is racing, my chest tightening, and as I lift my hand to place it on my racing heart, I see the little red heart and remember (by the grace of God), *"I am spirit!"*

It's like "poof," the frantic energy disperses, the tightening loosens, and I see our call for love. A peaceful smile smooths my face. I am spirit—resilient and free. I silently repeat the prayer from the lesson in my mind, *"Spirit are we, the holy Son of God, free of all limits, safe and healed and whole, free to forgive and free to save the world."*

I join in love and forgiveness with the woman in front of me—she is my Self. She is frantic and says, "Sorry, I wasn't looking where I was going. I'm just trying to get the kids to school on time."

I place my hand on her shoulder. Her eyes meet mine, and she joins me in the space of peace, a smile lighting her face. All malice is gone from our minds. I say, "Same with me. I was rushing to get my kids to school on time too." We look at the damage to the cars together, as friends. There's hardly a scratch on her car and just a little dent in mine where her bumper hit. We happily agree to let it go.

We hug each other and get back in our cars. It is a holy encounter. Forgiveness blessed us for we share a common goal of peace, that just happened to look like a "fender-bender" and "getting the kids to school."

Grace, the experience of peace, of ever-present spirit proves itself out. The slightest willingness to drop the façade and be shown, shifts our perception from separation to wholeness. We feel willing to let things play out however they do, while we listen for guidance. We trust that a happy and peaceful outcome is sure.

CHAPTER EIGHTY

DAY 98

(Lesson 98)

"I will accept my part in
God's plan for salvation."
(W-pI.98.1)

Today's lesson is asking for an honest accounting from us. It necessitates that we draw a line and take our stand on the side of truth, of love, of God, letting illusions go. We accept our part in God's plan for salvation, excluding all other plans. It is a day of devotion—a dedication to doing our part in the Divine Plan.

What is our part in God's plan for salvation? The course tells us that our part is to accept atonement for ourselves. So, what does that look like? We are learning, day by day, lesson by lesson, forgiveness by forgiveness. That's why the hourly reminders are so important at this stage of the curriculum. They help us stay true to ourselves and the commitment we make today.

We're asked to give five measly minutes each hour in exchange for the world. We are learning that God's will for us is perfect happiness and that the Holy Spirit needs happy learners. There's a place in the course that says that if we think we have decided for happiness and we are not feeling supremely joyous, we haven't really decided. Because all requests are answered. Today, we stand firmly with God's plan for our happiness and accept our part.

I feel "in the flow" today, remembering, hourly, *"I accept my part in God's plan for salvation."*

As I walk in the door after work, the phone is ringing. It's a bill collector calling to collect a debt from years before, which I had forgotten about. I feel my pulse speed up and defensiveness rising within me. I feel "in trouble"—ashamed.

I pause and slow my breathing and silently recall my lesson, *"I accept my part in God's plan for salvation,"* becoming calm, and ready to accept guidance as to my part in God's plan in this circumstance. I instinctively forgive all shame and doubt, certain this situation has been given a different purpose than I first imagined. My mind is clear. I listen with my heart for a true message of love and union.

I notice the nervous tension in the man's voice, and I am filled with compassion and a desire to bless and heal. He's just doing his job. It is a call for love. I say, "I think it would take a lot of courage to do your job. It seems like it would be scary. Money is such a touchy subject, yes?"

I can feel him relax. He says, "Thanks for understanding. You wouldn't believe how hard it is sometimes. A lot of people are defensive and blame me." I tell him I know the debt is mine and ask what we can do. He wants to help. I always find this to be the case when I give up defensiveness.

People want to love, to experience the Christ in themselves rise up and take the lead. He troubleshoots various options. We happily decide on one. Both of us are blessed by our holy encounter.

When I hang up the phone, I think, "I love this. I see why I got the phone call. This is my part in God's plan for salvation." The debt was just the vehicle. I see how naturally and practically today's lesson graces my life.

CHAPTER EIGHTY-ONE

DAY 99

(Lesson 99)

"Salvation is my only function here."

(W-pl.99.1)

Wait a minute, isn't forgiveness my only function here? Isn't being the light of the world my function? Isn't being happy? Isn't love? Yes, Yes, and YES! Ultimately, they are the same. Each idea reaches the confused mind from a slightly different angle since diversity is how the ego hides out.

The course refers to Salvation as a sort of borderland in the mind where our illusion thoughts meet up with the truth. This borderland is where we spend our day with today's lesson.

Today's idea can easily get shelved as theoretical, spiritual rhetoric. But with the added thought, *"God still is Love, and this is not His Will,"* it puts its practical application right smack in front of whatever situation we contrive that takes us out of peace. If it isn't love, it isn't God's will, so it isn't real.

If it isn't love, something has gone wrong. Forgiveness is required, and salvation is the borderland in my mind where the answer to it has been saved for me.

I'd been in an ongoing struggle with my landlord. Nearly every day, his parents or construction workers show up to work on the house or property, often cutting the water or power off for extended periods of time.

I decide he is disrespectful; I feel victimized and justified in my righteous indignation. And I feel like hell about the whole thing. But I don't want to see things differently. I want to be right.

Still, it feels shitty. I know I'm not fulfilling my function. I'm not seeing this brother as a savior. I'm blaming. "He doesn't deserve it. He's mistreating me. I have rights." Yada, Yada, Yada. My light is shrouded in darkness. It's like I'm deliberately hiding from the solution.

The thing is, judgment has become intolerable for me now. I have experienced the light of love. I have felt the peace of God. I have met my Self and loved it all. So, this thinking is hell. I recognize that my landlord and I share an illusion that keeps us in hell.

It doesn't take long before I'm ready to choose heaven instead. I place the entire situation, my feelings, and my brother on the altar during my morning time with the Divine. Something inside shifts, like a crack in my armor, where light streams through.

Later, during a conversation with my landlord over the phone, I get activated again. My heart tightens. My breath gets shallow. I'm about to point out, for the umpteenth time, that what he's doing is violating my privacy, but I pause.

Like a breeze filling my lungs with peace and softening my heart, and my lesson whispers, *"Salvation is my only function here. Salvation and forgiveness are the same. God still is Love, and this is not His Will."*

I breathe deeply, turning toward peace. This pause thing is incredible! It is like turning on the light of my willingness to go home to love. While my landlord talks, I pray my lesson, *"Salvation is my only function here. God still is Love, and this is not His Will."* I forgive us both in the name of love, freeing us for true communication.

I'm now willing to see the situation with love, and compassion fills my heart. I realize our mutual call for love. When it's my turn to talk, I thank him for sharing his perspective with me and helping me to see things differently. What's important is restoring peace between us.

He says he'll send an email with the upcoming dates he'll have a crew at the house, and he'll speak with his parents, too. I realize this is the borderland where all differences are brought to oneness and made whole. I can afford to be generous. After all, salvation is my only function and here is my happiness and peace.

CHAPTER EIGHTY-TWO
DAY 100
(Lesson 100)

*"My part is essential to
God's plan for salvation."*

(W-pI.100.1)

Wow! 100 days given to Divinity! Yummy, yes? Today's lesson is like a confirmation to our chosen path. *"You are indeed essential to God's plan. Without your joy, His joy is incomplete. Without your smile, the world cannot be saved."*

Joy is the unifying element which instantly connects us to each other, and we feel a natural kinship. It is our joy which unveils our wholeness as one mind, united with our Creator. The joy within us is the home of the Christ within which we all share. We each have a unique part to play which completes God's plan for salvation. It is God's will that we accept our part and find our perfect happiness. So, we can't fail.

God's will for us is perfect happiness, and ultimately, there is no will except the will of God. We want to be happy. Everything we do is geared toward it. It's just that we've been confused about who we are, and why we are here, so we have placed our happiness outside ourselves, or off in the future where it can never be found. Because the future is an illusion, too.

Today, we move beyond illusion and join in God's Joy. We are recognizing the power of our mind and learning to use our feelings as a barometer. Joy tells us we have decided to be host to God. Fear and guilt make us hostage to the ego.

Applying these lessons helped me see how my sadness, anxiety, and guilt is merely a misperception. When I feel anything by joy, it is a sign I am asking for a miracle. I pause and remember I am as God created me, and only what He wills is my real life. God's will is only happiness for me. Forgiveness lets my false self-concept beliefs slip back to the nothingness from which they came. I forgive quickly and get on with being the light of the world—a minister of love and joy.

The lesson invites me to realize my part in God's plan is to be happy, to dive deep into the ocean of joy within me, where Christ is waiting. *"My part is essential to God's plan for salvation!"* I let my mind slip past the silly thoughts that tell me how I'll fail, and into the serene depths of joy where a smile starts deep within, filling my being with overwhelming contentment—and suddenly I am being breathed—each breath infuses my cells with joy. This quiet joy is the Christ within me—the Self I am as God created me. I feel God's will for happiness for me and all the world. A happy day is inevitable.

I'm buoyant with joy. It spills over into everything I do and with everyone I meet. I can't keep the smile off my face.

Case in point. I'm at Costco, everyone I see I encounter with joyous reverence, acknowledging the Christ we share as one. Joy beams from me and it's met with warmth and immediate kinship.

As I'm checking out, the guy boxing my groceries says, "Your smile is infectious. You're radiating happiness, entirely unapologetic, not holding anything back. I saw you come in, and it made me feel so good, I've been keeping an eye while you've been shopping. Everyone you talked to left with a smile on their face, beaming, just like you are now. Thanks, you made my day."

I say, "Yay! Spread the joy! Pay it forward."

There is simply nothing that matters more than joyously meeting the Christ within! By accepting our happy essential part of God's plan for salvation we carry the joy of God with us, in our smile, a listening ear, and our warm acceptance of everyone and everything.

CHAPTER EIGHTY-THREE
DAY 101
(Lesson 101)

"God's Will for me is perfect happiness."
(W-pI.101.1)

Today's lesson answers everything for me. It is the ground of my being. It disputes the falseness of my programmed ideas about myself that get me in a fix, where I think I need something to be different to be happy.

It reminds me of the truth of what I am as God created me. What I am, is love, which is always joyous. When I am not happy, it is only because I have aligned with the ego self-concept and believe that sin is real. The malcontent I'm feeling is the punishment for my crime. Yuck! That is hell. That's my old, homey prison cell. But now, thank God, the light has dawned, and I can at least recognize that I am deluded. Forgiveness is the way out.

I'm recalling with affectionate humor an incident from my college psychology class. We're studying borderline personality disorders. I have a sick feeling in my gut throughout the lecture. As I'm cataloguing the characteristics, my mind keeps tossing up examples from my life, which, when looked at through the lens of this personality disorder, appear to qualify me. I begin to secretly fear I might have this diagnosis. (Apparently, this is a common phenomenon for students. But I take it personally. Like, no way should I be counseling other people with their lives.)

For a long moment, I have left reality and it seems darkness is closing in on me. I try to think of my positive characteristics to combat it. To remember the light. That is the tipping point—my flip-switch. I pray, "I will there be light! I am as God created me." And as quickly as the darkness and confused identity had descended, the light of truth burns through with today's lesson, *"God's Will for me is perfect happiness. There is no sin; it has no consequence,"* filling my mind with light and heart with joy!

I can't help but chuckle to myself, to see this crazy dynamic. I am a messenger for God. He wills happiness for me and His will and mine are one. I feel resilient, airy, and happy! I look back at the diagnosis on the page before me, and the gig is up! I am above the battleground and seeing the story of fear and mental confusion for the fraud it is. I am the dreamer of the crazy dream—a twisted angle on a sinner's life. Now I choose the happy dreams sanity brings. I am filled with gratitude for the instant shift in my perception. Miracle.

What's so wonderful about the way this experience happened is that I could see how letting what might seem like a little fear to go unquestioned, opens the door to entertaining the whole world of false identity and it can seem to take on a life of its own, and I feel guilty. Guilt is a sign I believe in sin.

Today's idea leaves no room for compromise. There is no sin because God did not create it. The ego did. The ego is the lie. I love the gentleness of this line from the lesson, *"Joy is just, and pain is but the sign you have misunderstood yourself."* That shines the light on the next step—Forgiveness. Our perfect happiness is inevitable.

As class gets out and my friend Mary Jo and I meet up, I say, "Dude, for a minute there, I started to identify with all those symptoms. Insane, right?" She says, "Oh, my God, I thought it was just me. I've got lots of personality traits that fit that diagnosis, too." We have a good laugh at insanity, grateful for miracles that restore sanity and happiness. I tell her about my flip-switch using today's lesson. *"God's Will for me is perfect happiness."* She joins me in happy recognition, *"God's Will for me is perfect happiness."*

CHAPTER EIGHTY-FOUR

DAY 102

(Lesson 102)

"I share God's Will for happiness for me."
(W-pI.102.1)

Today's lesson beats deep within my heart. I can measure my real life by the profound life-changing moments (miracles) where all the cogs in my psyche, my being, and even my body, seem to line up perfectly—a cosmic cha-chink, that sets everything in right alignment. Love's presence fills my awareness, and a new vision opens, revealing a slightly different path before me.

"I share God's Will for happiness for me, and I accept it as my function now." I take my stand with God for perfect happiness! When we take our stand, sharing God's will for our happiness, the ego structure starts breaking down. Everything is up for review.

The old substitutes for happiness don't satisfy. Old pleasure and pain distractions can't replace the joy of listening and being guided by the voice for happiness.

It seemed like everything fell apart at first after taking my stand. And still, if I'm not vigilant in aligning my will with God's, if the ego gets footing, things can go south fast. It's just that now, I choose to see it for what it is—temporary insanity. And there's an app for that—a daily lesson that restores me to sanity every time.

During my morning practice when I make my declaration, *"I share God's Will for happiness for me, and I accept it as my function now,"* cha-ching! It's an unswerving homecoming. I feel the presence and power of the Divine breathing me with joy and peaceful purpose—a feeling of oneness with all life permeating my being. "This is it! Joy is the way of it for me. This is my service, in gratitude to God, and the world. To keep my heart open, no matter what. Happiness is my commitment to the Divine in all of life."

It turns out to be simpler than I thought. (Not easier—simpler.) Don't get me wrong. I'm challenged to be true to my purpose with every choice I make in response to what arises in my day. It's just that I set a zero point, like a homing beacon within, for which to return.

I am peacefully happy after my morning time with God, singing while I reorganize my yummy room.

Parker bursts into the room, exuberant, jumping up and down. He's animatedly talking a mile a minute, telling me about his skateboarding adventure. He's talking so fast I have a hard time following what he is saying. I feel his joy and am instantly drawn in. I want to hear every word, picture his adventure in my mind. But I can't make out what he is saying. I tell him to slow down.

I'm trying to understand, impatience rising within me. Now I have an agenda—a criterion for listening. I'm not joining him in his joy at this moment, I'm trying to understand. I've left the present and detoured into the past. Into what's not happening.

Parker just continues joyously sharing his excitement, oblivious to my perceived need "to understand." The contrast is palpable. I pause and my lesson, like a breath of fresh air, zeros me back to presence. I bust up laughing and join Parker in present joy. *"I share God's Will for happiness for me, for Parker and everyone."*

What's wild is it that the instant I return my mind to present joy, I easily follow Parker's adventure story. Remembering my true will is happiness, I'm home. Nothing *I think I need* is worth the price of this precious encounter, attending to Parker singing his heart out. God's presence is profound. This present moment united in joy *is* the kingdom. Parker's smile is bigger than the world. And so is mine.

CHAPTER EIGHTY-FIVE

DAY 103

(Lesson 103)

"God, being Love, is also happiness."

(W-pI.103.1)

I am one of the happiest beings I know. I realize the peace behind really not caring about what happens in this world, in the sense of it being real, but in looking beyond it to the love that unites us as one mind and heart. This is the gift of forgiveness.

It is the gift that frees me to care about loving, about falling in love with everything that arises before me. I want to fully *"grok"* (love and appreciate) all the beauty and glorious wonder already given. I feel grateful because I get presents every day from everyone, everywhere, in every circumstance! Even before I open up the moment and look within, I am grateful. I love it. It's the gift I always wanted.

Happiness is an attribute of love. We cannot experience joy when we lack love for anyone or anything. Recognizing love is at the very fiber of our being, is happiness. It is our oneness with God, which is our happiness. It is the magic ingredient of enlightenment. With today's lesson, we see again that what God is, is what we are. Period. Won't we happily give five minutes an hour to remember happiness is our birthright? What's the downside?

During my morning practice contemplating today's lesson, *"God, being Love, is also happiness. To fear Him is to be afraid of joy,"* a prayer of pure desire springs from my heart, "Dear God, I know I must be afraid of joy on some level. I feel such love and gratitude, but I also see the results of my split mind showing up in my life, which demonstrates fear is there. I want only to experience my Self, just as You created me in joy. I am willing to see my fear and forgive, so nothing interferes with my function of happiness. Please, dear God, let this be the holy instant of my Ascension. Amen."

My mind, like the sky parting, opens, revealing the words from the lesson *"God, being Love, is also happiness. And it is happiness I seek today. I cannot fail, because I seek the truth."* Content, free, and happy, I'm ready for today.

The feeling stays with me as I run errands and each encounter feels holy.

As I'm driving out of the Sam's Club parking lot, behind a long line of cars trying to exit, I see a homeless woman with a sign asking for help at the exit mouth of the parking lot. I can't read the sign from where I am, but I recognize a call for help is on the table.

I keep my eyes fixed on her as we move forward. I am instantly in love with her, she is my sister-self. On impulse, I start singing "Amazing Grace" and I beam love and joy to her, grinning from ear to ear, as I make my way to the exit where she is. As I approach her, I roll my window down so I can hand her some coin, I hear her she's singing too.

Yep, you guessed it. "Amazing Grace." As our eyes meet, tears of joy spill, and holiness fills the space that contains us. She receives my tokens, a toothless grin spreading across her face. Amazing grace, undeniably.

How blessed is it to actually be available to experience holy encounters such as this—how glorious, how divine. Sacred moments like this happen every day. It is astonishing the bounty that is just waiting to avail itself, when we want nothing else. *"God, being Love, is also happiness."*

CHAPTER EIGHTY-SIX
DAY 104
(Lesson 104)

"I seek but what belongs to me in truth."
(W-pI.104.1)

We want but what belongs to us in truth. Ours is the choice for heaven and the peace of God, which is our inheritance. The thing is, we must be willing to lay our substitutes down. We must be willing to forgive whatever we have been holding in time; be it to pay penance for past mistakes, or things we feel we must solve ourselves as well as those we've held hostage for their misdeeds or deemed unworthy.

We must we be willing to place all things we value in this world of time, in the Holy Spirit's hands, so the truth can reveal its presence in our minds. This is how we recognize and accept our eternal gifts of joy and peace.

The truth is within us right now. Today's lesson practice takes us deep into the inner recesses of our psyche, where we honestly take stock of the self-made gifts we have kept tucked away, reserving them for ourselves alone. We must look honestly at what we have placed upon the altar as substitutes for accepting what is already ours. The altar where only God and His gifts belong.

Each substitution represents where we feel our worthiness lies, what we feel we deserve, and who we believe we are. Our inheritance waits for our welcome. Joy and peace are ours to accept now. We need only release our substitutes, by looking with the Holy Spirit, holding nothing back.

I think I know where the lesson is taking me when I begin my morning practice. *"I seek but what belongs to me in truth, and joy and peace are my inheritance."* Easy-peasy. I am God's holy child. I get it.

So, it takes me by surprise when I feel unease rise within me—a sort of warding me off kind of feeling. I thought I had a true awareness that love is what I am, and joy and peace are mine because I am love.

But as I explore in honesty, with my higher mind at the helm, while repeating the idea, *"I seek but what belongs to me in truth,"* I see the split. The Self that doesn't question my worth, and the self-concept that does. I notice a "trying to get something" feeling. This makes me curious. Curiosity is good for me. It tells me my mind is open.

Trying to get something conflicts with accepting what is. I repeat the idea, *"I seek but what belongs to me in truth,"* seeking clarity. The image of the little orphan from the musical Oliver comes to mind.

My eyes sting with tears and my heart aches as I realize this image represents my self-concept. My self-concept is still trying to survive—like Oliver with his bowl asking, "Please sir can I have some more?" I see self-concept is an orphan in a world of exile—always seeking.

I bring this image into my heart of forgiveness, imagine gathering her in my arms, melting her into my heart, as my being fills with abiding peace and joy.

Now my inner altar is clear to accept my inheritance. In the light of this awareness, I repeat the idea, *"I seek but what belongs to me in truth, God's gifts of joy and peace are all I want. I am as God created me."* Pure rays of light stream from my altar with the truth of my divinity as God's holy child, where joy and peace is already mine. So, yeah, easy-peasy.

CHAPTER EIGHTY-SEVEN

DAY 105

(Lesson 105)

"God's peace and joy are mine."
(W-pI.105.1)

Today, we are undoing the upside-down construct we have about giving and receiving. The one that says if we give, we lose.

We can't give something we don't have, right? Yesterday we went within, seeking the joy and peace that is our birthright. The course is teaching us that as we give the gifts of God to everyone, without reservation, we receive them for ourselves. Or, more accurately, we recognize that we have received them. So, the gifts we give are eternal. God's peace and joy.

We want to realize peace and joy in everything we do, right? But if we are withholding them from anyone for any reason (grievance), we are keeping them just outside of our own field of awareness and, therefore, our daily experience.

So, today's practice is about accepting the gifts of peace and joy by sincerely offering them to all our brothers. We are learning that to experience the certainty of peace and joy as ours by birthright, we must give it to all. This is the Law of Love. What I give my brother is my gift to me.

The way we recognize what we have is through what we give and share. Our brothers are part of our One Self. That means everyone and everything. Whatever we offer to another, we claim as our own. It is a total reversal of the laws of the scarcity and loss.

The lesson suggests that we start with thinking about our "enemies," which is anyone or situation that brings up the icky feeling of judgment. These are the parts of our One Self we have rejected and projected outward, to reestablish a sense of innocence. Honestly, we feel the loss the instant we think judgments of any kind. Judgment places a barrier to our awareness of the truth, our innocence, peace, and joy. They're not gone. We've just blocked them from our awareness.

I'm feeling disheartened in my relationship with a friend. She is a prominent figure in our circle of friends and it seems like she's is always "one-upping" me, or discounting the significance of my insights, like, "Duh, I've known that for years, and you're just getting it?" It seems like she's deliberately antagonizing. Yet, she is super sweet, and everyone likes her—including me. It's an ongoing struggle with feelings of unworthiness for me, which I continually need to forgive.

She springs to mind instantly in my morning practice. I say, *"My brother, peace, and joy I offer you, that I may have God's peace and joy as mine,"* It's almost comical to see my judgments of her, based in my own fear of inadequacy, which I projected as her response to me. With relief, I forgive her for what she never did in truth, repeating, *"My brother, peace and joy I offer you, that I may have God's peace and joy as mine,"* As I picture her in my mind, I see us both stripped of my judgment, standing in the light of peace and joy, receiving and giving as one.

When I see her at coffee later that morning, my apprehension is gone entirely. I'm filled with the joy and innocence forgiveness brings. I'm happy to see her, recognizing our oneness. We hug long and intimately, mending and healing our relationship, letting only the good and beautiful penetrate. We're accepting God's gifts of joy and peace together. So say I.

CHAPTER EIGHTY-EIGHT

DAY 106

(Lesson 106)

"Let me be still and listen to the truth."

(W-pl.106.1)

Today's idea is the very heartbeat of our lives as miracle workers. We are developing the habit that replaces all the mindless habits we have learned through the ego, designed to block the voice of truth. We are disengaging from ego's voice, and we engage the silence, listening for the truth.

In my morning practice, I close my eyes and say: *"Let me be still and listen to the truth. What does it mean to give and to receive?"* An image of a cat watching a bird comes on the screen in my mind. The cat watches with rapt, relaxed, attention and patience, ready to act when the time is right. No matter what is going on around or outside of the focused attention, it's like the cat can't hear it, only the goal at hand has her full commitment. I get it. My Self, like the cat, is rapt to the stillness; attentive only to the truth.

I am filled with wonder as I engage my day from this tranquil place within. I want to be the quiet message of love's presence as I go into my day. Right away I get to see how sincere I am, how well I have taken the practice to heart and apply it.

When I get to work, a young man is waiting to see me. He's been referred by the court for substance abuse. At the top of his chart, in red ink, are the words, "sex offender." Fear and disgust flood unbidden into my gut. My breath catches as a whoosh of judgment heats my ears. I don't think I can work with this patient. I want to "return him to sender."

I take a deep breath and recall my lesson, *"Let me be still and listen to the truth. I am the messenger of God today. My voice is His, to give what I receive."* My mind goes quiet, slowing my heartbeat and filling my being with love and acceptance. I am a messenger of love.

I sit across from the young man. His head is bowed as he speaks in whispered tones of his story of what brought him to me. "I just got out of prison, after serving five years for deviant sexual behavior, while under the influence. I'm so ashamed." A calm peace accompanies me as I listen to his history of being abused in a foster home, turning to drink, and eventually perpetrating the same act with another.

I am filled with a compassionate, peaceful presence. I ask him to take my hands and have a moment of silence with me, which he does. With eyes closed, I say, *"Let us be still and listen to the truth."* As I speak, a message comes from deep within, and I say out loud, "This alcoholic sex offender is a false identity you have mistaken for yourself. It is not your true Self and it can be forgiven completely, right here and now. This false identity has created feelings and actions that are opposed in every way to the truth. But because they are false, they can be forgiven and let go. We are all pure love, as children of the Divine. Nothing you have done or has been done to you could alter your true identity as God created you. You can forgive, for you have already been forgiven." We join in giving his life and our sessions together to the truth, which will light our way forward.

As we sit calmly in the light of forgiveness, he tells me about when he was young and living on the reservation—how he felt the Great Spirit was his constant companion, and he knew he was loved, but after he was abused, he no longer felt worthy of it.

With tear-filled eyes and a gentle smile, he says, "I feel the Great Spirit with us now. The moment we prayed together; it all came flooding back."

CHAPTER EIGHT-NINE
DAY 107
(Lesson 107)

"Truth will correct all errors in my mind."

(W-pl.107.1)

The most important gift I ever gave myself was to set a date with God as the first thing I do every day. And no matter what, I keep that appointment and do my damnedest to give myself over to the truth. I am gifted a persistent sense of certainty and okay-ness which I rely on, trusting that the guidance I need will be there as needed. Whatever situation I'm in, it is not by accident. This is the gift of the mind-training.

We're recognizing two voices in our mind: the invasive, mean one, always telling us we are something we're not—and the consistent gentle voice for Love Itself, cheering us on, reminding us of our identity as love, joyously complete. We're learning to listen only to the Voice for Truth, which reminds us of our function as a light in the world and forgive the errors which intrude upon the holy mind of God's Son.

This voice is always gently guiding us toward miracles. Today we practice certainty, trusting we walk with truth, and count on it to enter into all our choices. Truth and error cannot occupy the same space in our mind. The instant we decide we want the truth above all else, our willingness to have all errors corrected and our mind healed has been established. We will never walk alone again.

I've just left a doctor appointment and am heading to get some "routine" labs drawn. I notice anxiety about my state of health creeping in. Noting the stress as an error in my mind, I counter it with my lesson, *"Truth will correct all errors in my mind, and I will rest in Him who is my Self."*

Promptly, I have a strong sense I should reschedule the labs. I pull off the road and take a quiet moment and ask for clarity. In trust and peace, I reschedule the appointment and start driving again.

My eyes are drawn to a sign for a nail salon up ahead and I feel inspired to go there. Funny, I have a regular nail-gal, but follow the guidance. During my manicure, I begin a friendly conversation with the gal next to me. Within minutes, my new friend is crying and sharing her concerns about the relationship between her husband and son.

Our conversation morphs into one about the importance of remembering and trusting the presence of Divine guidance in our lives. She shares how afraid she's been and how she's been trying to avoid dealing with it. That she's forgotten to pray. She's grateful to remember the things we're talking about today. It is a holy encounter with the perfect message for both of us—the presence of miracles infusing us.

Suddenly, she asks, "What brought you in here today?" I tell her how I felt guided and just went for it. She says, "You were brought here for me." I say, "And me." It's lovely. This is the life of a minister of God.

Later, at my rescheduled lab appointment, I meet a frightened "big guy" waiting at the elevators. I lightly touch him on the arm and ask if he's all right. He says, "I'm scared. There's something wrong with my heart." He proceeds to tell me his whole story about his heart condition. I listen and remember my lesson, *"Truth will correct all errors in our mind."* I say a silent prayer for peace as we ride the elevator up to the lab together.

We wait together, calmly talking about how nothing is random, and he thanks me for sitting with him. I know I am here especially for this holy encounter. Another reason I was guided to reschedule my labs.

CHAPTER NINETY
DAY 108
(Lesson 108)

"To give and to receive are one in truth."

(W-pI.108.1)

During my coffee time with the Divine, I read the lesson and contemplate its meaning. Truth and light are one. *"[Vision] is a state of mind that has become so unified that darkness cannot be perceived at all."* I think I understand that to give and receive are one in truth. That the state of mind in which I see *is* the gift I give my brothers and myself.

I quiet my mind and forget what I think I know, letting my thoughts still into the lesson idea. *"To give and to receive are one in truth. I will receive what I am giving now."* A procession of people crosses my mind as I say, *"To everyone I offer joy. To everyone I offer quietness. To everyone I offer peace of mind. To everyone I offer gentleness. To everyone I offer love."* I'm feeling a quiet joy, a gentle peace, feeling love for everyone that comes to mind.

That is, until I see a news broadcast. The broadcast shows a political rally where a candidate, whom I have judged to be bigoted, seems abusive with a citizen at the rally. And, just like that, my heart knots up. Anger, sanctimoniousness, fear, and pity spill into me like a bitter taste. "Whoa. Yuck."

I freeze frame the scene in my mind, zeroing in on this candidate, and state, *"To give and to receive are one in truth. I will receive what I am giving now."* Holding him in my mind, I say, *"To you I offer forgiveness. To you I offer tranquility, freedom from fear and intolerance. To you I offer peace of mind, love, and happiness."* My heart opens. I truly want this for my brother and myself. My mind returns to serenity and a joyous state of being.

Later in the day when a friend brings up the incident at the political rally, I feel honest compassion for everyone involved. I share my experience from my morning practice with her and we join in a moment of silence with the lesson, offering peace and safety, love and unity. The joyful tranquility we share is profound.

Today's idea is the practice of the actual cause and effect principle of creation. *"To give and to receive are one in truth."* By offering acceptance and love, I look about me, and that's what I see. I love the practice of going straight to real offerings. Going for God in every experience.

I don't really know what I am looking at in any situation, until I do. But by continually giving love, joy, acceptance, and peace; looking for that Christ Spark within my brother, my Spark gets ignited! I feel joyous, generous, free, and connected! It's like magic—that's miracles for ya.

CHAPTER NINETY-ONE

DAY 109

(Lesson 109)

"I rest in God."

(W-pI.109.1)

Today's practice is the Holy Grail. I'm so grateful. These four little words can deliver me from hell in an instant and into present time. It works! It proves itself out. I lean back and rest in the peace of God and letting whatever faces me today be resolved through Him. From the tiniest incident to the seemingly major stuff. God's rest always fortifies and resolves what the mind with the problem can never see. It's a miracle.

All we need do is pause and think of God. Breathing into the silence, we accept total rest from thinking and let peace encompass us. Practicing *"I rest in God,"* in any situation, lifts us out of time and space and into eternity—the present moment. It's exactly what we need whenever we are taking things personally.

It's what we need when we're stuck in the drama of the dream, thinking something needs fixing or should be different than it is. A deep pause, *"I rest in God,"* transports us out of the dream, reminding us we are the dreamer, where we can forgive and change our viewpoint to see with Divine love instead.

Anytime I have cause to pause, like in line at the grocery store or on hold on the phone, is a flip-switch, *"I rest in God."* I contemplate that each moment I rest in God, I am calling all minds out of their frantic time-space loop, back home to rest with me, in God. It's so simple and feels so good.

When my son Parker was going through a breakup with his first girlfriend, he was beside himself with angst over breaking her heart. He slips into my yummy room and says, "I just need to sit a minute in this peaceful space. I feel terrible for Ashley. But I know I did the right thing for me."

I want to help him feel better. I pause, today's lesson fresh in my mind. "Perfect! We need the peace of God for this." Centering on the real goal pulls me back from making my own decisions about what to say to help, or devising a plan to fix, and brings me instantly into present moment peace. I center on *"I rest in God."*

It's like everything stills in reverence to God—to His rest, comfort, and love. My breathing slows and deepens, Love infusing every breath with peace. Resting in God is like a magnetic pull calling Parker's mind to peace. He takes my hand in his. Our breathing synchronizes to peace. Beyond the situation at hand, we rest in God, reminding us of the only true thing—love. We are awash in peace and love, quieting the seeming problem of hurt and heartbreak and allowing love to heal.

When we start talking again, it is about how remarkable loving is, and how loving is its own reward—the real gift is in the giving. Parker says he realizes that loving so honestly with Ashley has shown him what kind of man he is becoming.

We bring Ashley into our flow, and I say, *"We rest in God."* Together we are lifted out of the angst by peace, joining in joyous recognition that love is enough and heals all wounds. Miracle!

CHAPTER NINETY-TWO

DAY 110

(Lesson 110)

"I am as God created me."

(W-pl.110.1)

Awesome! We're at this yummy foundation lesson again! It's inspiring how the lesson *"I am as God created me"* keeps showing up at different stages of the curriculum. But of course. It is the one thought that heals everything. If we are as God created us, untouched by anything else we've mistakenly thought, believed, or done, then if we withdraw our attention from all but this one idea, we are home. Right?

Infusing our minds with this thought, *"I am as God created me. His Son can suffer nothing. And I am His Son,"* is essential. Today, we can literally shed the skin of false-identity and step into now—this present moment, where the Christ, the Self God created as His holy Child.

As I read today's lesson, I am determined to embody today's idea, *"I am as God created me. His Son can suffer nothing. And I am His Son,"* as the only truth, where no other reality even exists to comprehend. I feel the beginning of a sickening fear churn in my gut. I know this reaction by now, it's the ego fighting for its life. It starts deploying all sorts of delay tactics, "I better use the bathroom first, have some coffee, make a to-do list."

Well, I'm not having any of it. I close my eyes and dive deep into my Self, seeking the place within where Christ resides. I sink below my thoughts and let my mind still into a single point of light. It's as if I've stepped into another room—a room filled with light. A recognition of Christ rising within me and lighting me with the truth. The feeling is magnificent, complete, and glorious—love filling my entire being. As I rise from my lesson practice, I feel something fundamental has shifted. I feel present, alive to my life, and trusting whatever shows up today.

When my son Lucas calls, I feel as though a Divine thread interlaces our minds in sync while we talk. He's having difficulties in his marriage. Usually, sensing he is in pain, I try to empathize. I get into counselor, fix-it mode. But I've got my dial tuned to God, to the truth, to the identity we share as holy children of the Divine. I am interested in empathizing with strength, not weakness.

So, rather than get into the rights and wrongs and problem-solving, I let my lesson play like background music, and let it inform my responses. I am tuned to the presence of our identity in God. Any fixing or pitying responses don't even occur.

As I speak with Lucas, I trust I am being guided to what will be helpful. We readily talk universal truths. Lucas isn't specifically into the course, but truth is a universal language. Lucas is totally into Wayne Dyer. I speak Wayne Dyer. I am guided to reference my own experiences with the Wayne Dyer, creating a dynamic catalyst that's relatable for him to access the truth within himself.

It's so lovely. I anticipate nothing, just hold the truth of our identity as God created us. The rest is given as needed. We talk about his children and how pure and innocent they are. About his wife and how she is confused about her identity and has it twisted up with her addiction and is in fear.

We join in the awareness that each is still as God created them. How they deserve love because love is what they are, and that they need not qualify for love. We talk about how the only appropriate response to a call for love, is love and forgiveness. Lucas tells me how that truth also translates to himself. We hang with each other on the phone a while, resting in forgiveness and love, his self-confidence and trust reestablished.

CHAPTER NINETY-THREE

REVIEW III: DAYS 111–120
(Lessons 91–110)

We begin our third review today. We are at the stage of our mind-training where consistency in practice is key to reversing our fearful thought system and replacing it with the truth. We realize the truth by utilizing these ideas in our daily lives. The format is changing a little. We are to review two of the last twenty lessons per day, for the next ten days.

We are up leveling our integration now. Our willingness to return our minds to love—to devoting specific times throughout the day to the practice session is what matters. The format for practicing over the next ten days is thus:

We devote the first five minutes (more if it feels right) and the last five of our waking day to reviewing and considering the two ideas for that day and the supporting comments. We let them fill our minds and relate them to our perceived needs, concerns, or problems. We set our intent with the ideas at the outset of embarking on our day.

We then review—on the hour, we contemplate the first of the day's ideas, and on the half hour, contemplating the second of the ideas for the day.

The important thing is to use the ideas, thus, blessing everyone with our holiness. We are being trained to think with the Holy Spirit consistently. We are being trained to think with God.

These reviews remind us that as miracle workers, the light we need to see is not found outside ourselves, but within. The light in us is how miracles are seen. We remember we can never find the light by analyzing darkness. We can never find the answer by picking apart all the details of the problem. We cannot see in darkness, which is what we are trying to do by sorting through the past to fix things. When something disturbs our peace, instead of rehashing what went wrong so we can fix it, we are learning to turn to where a real answer can be found.

It's fun to see, at this stage, just how distracted we can become from our intended dedication. Often, we'll realize we've missed several practice periods. This isn't a chance to feel guilty. In fact, we should forgive immediately realizing we're still undoing the ego training and it'll get in through any crack in our resolve. Silly ego. What is important is to reinforce our commitment to the transformation of our minds and apply the lesson.

It is an act of faith, trusting that the wisdom of our minds which are being recalibrated through the mind-training and the Holy Spirit within our minds will assist us in our endeavors throughout the day. Our part is to listen for the messages we receive and take the opportunity as often as we can to pause and remember the ideas which are returning our minds to love.

Feel free to review examples from the previous lessons we're reviewing if it's helpful. But I encourage you to trust you own witness and each day write your own examples of trust, transformation, and awakening.

NOTES

NOTES

NOTES

NOTES

NOTES

CHAPTER NINETY-FOUR
DAY 121
(Lesson 121)

"Forgiveness is the key to happiness."
(W-pl.121.1)

When I began with *A Course in Miracles*, the way it described forgiveness captivated me—activating a core recognition deep within I didn't yet understand.

I thought I knew what forgiveness was. You know, letting shit go and getting on with things. But forgiving myself was an entirely different deal. I had things wired up in my mind that I needed X amount of time of not making mistakes, of doing worthy shit, paying penitence for my past. Talk about keeping separation alive and well.

Today's lesson shifted things for me. The exercise is precise and pure in showing the actual experience of forgiveness—it is impossible to miss once practiced. Practicing shifts our understanding that giving and receiving are the same from intellectual to actual.

I love the image of forgiveness as a key always in my hand. One that opens the door to happiness, which I keep with me all the time. When things are sticky, forgiveness is always what is needed. True forgiveness is the realization that what has seemed to happen never occurred in truth. It is never about the happening. It is about what I believe I am. When I know I am as God created me, guilt is impossible.

Today's lesson came like grace in a moment in my life I truly needed it. We're supposed to choose an enemy—somebody we're holding hostage, we judge, or are angry with. I pick my dad.

I thought my healing was done on him. He's a student of *A Course in Miracles*, and we share a common goal. So, I was surprised when recently I received a letter from him, which I perceived as his judgment.

The letter detailed his idea of the responsibilities of a "good parent," signifying ways I fall short of this ideal. Needless to say, I had a belly full of screw-you worked up, and it felt terrible. I feared he was right. Worse yet, I was ashamed that I still get activated by my dad's disapproval and feel guilty about being upset. Yuck! Perfect ground for forgiveness.

During my morning time with God, after reading the lesson, I set aside my ten minutes for the forgiveness exercise in today's lesson, twinkling with joy and trust in the alchemy of miracles I've come to expect through these lesson exercises.

I picture my dad, the one that surfaced when I read the letter, like I've seen him a million times—judging me, making me wrong. But then I look as the lesson suggests and try to see the light in him. Before I know it, the image starts to glimmer.

The image itself softens, becoming less substantial as the light grows increasingly brighter. My heart, too, softens, releasing the love I am and the holiness we share. The judgments I'd placed on my father, which I had believed he put on me, became empty words—symbols of symbols—as they pass by and disappear into the ever-growing light.

As innocence and peace replace hurt, anger, and judgment, the friend I would bring into our joining walks into the picture. It is my mentor Betty, whom, in my mind, practically walks on water. The light is magnificent, extending from the center of their joining and surrounding them, reaching out like open arms. I open entirely, receiving their light while simultaneously releasing the light within me. Our holiness shines in oneness, in union, in God.

My entire perception of my father has changed. Without fear and judgment, I see his offerings as gifts of love, or a call for love. I've let the label of Dad go. I no longer see him as my dad, but a brother with the same interests as my own. Very cool. We have a lovely relationship now. And it's a total groove that we're both in love with the course.

CHAPTER NINETY-FIVE
DAY 122
(Lesson 122)

"Forgiveness offers everything I want."

(W-pI.122.1)

"What could you want forgiveness cannot give? Do you want peace? Forgiveness offers it. Do you want happiness, a quiet mind, a certainty of purpose, and a sense of worth and beauty that transcends the world? Do you want care and safety, and the warmth of sure protection always? Do you want a quietness that cannot be disturbed, a gentleness that never can be hurt, a deep, abiding comfort, and a rest so perfect it can never be upset?"

(W-pI.1.1–5)

Yes! Yes! For me, it is yes, with no opposite. I've been down the other road—it leads to hell. During my morning practice, I feel happy anticipation as I sink into the joy and peace forgiveness offers me. I imagine lifting the veil of my false ideas about myself and the world. In the center of my mind, I see a brilliant light, which I walk toward. I feel it reaching for me, encompassing me, breathing me, and beating my heart with incredible joy. I feel light, lifted out of my body identity and into the Divine. With arms spread wide I receive, gladly accepting the gifts of God while repeating today's idea. *"Forgiveness offers everything I want. Today I have accepted this as true. Today I have received the gifts of God."*

Later in the day, I get a miracle witness to the effects of my choosing forgiveness while lecturing Lin and Lucas on being "good" kids. Some incident occurs where I compulsively feel the urge to teach the pre-wired parent script, correcting their behavior "for their own good." I was teaching them something, alright—guilt. Representing to myself, and them, that sin is real.

So, I'm feeling like hell, like I always do when I lecture the kids. But this time, it's like time stalls and I see that my feelings are showing me the error in mind. I feel shitty because I am playing out a script that is not who I am. My mind turns around on itself. I see my character-self and understand I am the one witnessing it.

I stop talking and whisper a forgiveness prayer, "I've got it wrong—I need forgiveness here." My lesson sweetly adds, *"Forgiveness offers everything I want."* In a holy instant, my perception changes completely. My heart softens. The kids feel it immediately and put their arms around me and I can feel my dad in our joining too.

I now realize I'd said my prayer out loud and they'd promptly joined me. My rant witnessed to an error in my mind about my role as a parent. And through forgiveness, I see my call to remember I am love, they are love, and we are equal, holy children of love.

My eyes, once beady little judges, open to windows of joy. I start giggling, and the kids join. In happy laughter, I see there is no problem. I can't recall what I thought was so important before. It disappeared in the light of forgiveness. It shifts my core operating system as a mom.

The world of love and joy is just beyond the curtain of false beliefs and identity. Forgiveness answers every question. We just must be willing to question each belief we hold—every role we play.

Forgiveness is the "Holy Grail" as far as I'm concerned. It has offered me everything. To be able to release myself and my brothers in an instant and return to the awareness of love's presence is pure happiness.

Forgiveness is the gift we reach for whenever we're in need of a mind shift. It is key to our new set of life skills. Forgiveness is a straight shot to the Source—to happiness and love.

CHAPTER NINETY-SIX
DAY 123
(Lesson 123)

"I thank my Father for His gifts to me."

(W-pI.123.1)

Today the focus is gratitude. The curriculum gives us this big thank you pause. It kind of lets us catch up to ourselves and pool all the love around us, filling up, and resting. Sanity has entered our minds. We have just opened our eyes and minds, so it's natural we practice living in gratitude today.

Because as we do, we see just how far we've come. We realize we can't turn back the way we came because we've felt the alchemy of miracles and truth. We uplevel our trust today as we rest in gratitude that we are God's Holy Child. We realize that all happiness is coming from our inheritance, which is already in place and just waiting for us to open and share.

After my morning time with God, I'm feeling grateful and committed to keeping gratitude ever most in my mind. With my heart open, I'm off and running in my day. I attend an early morning AA meeting, where a girl I sponsor is taking a chip for a year sobriety. A perfect opportunity to bask in gratitude and appreciation, right?

While new members take chips for a month, three, six, I let my mind wander. Instead of being present, appreciating the incredible gift we share, I think about my sponsorship times with "my girl," and how far she's come, and how much I've helped her. (Ah, the ego's favorite hook—specialness.) I get it into my head she'll be acknowledging me as this awesome, badass sponsor that helped make it all possible, right? (Expect much, Danét?)

Well, it doesn't go down like that. "My girl" doesn't so much as look at me or say anything about sponsorship—basically taking cred for it all herself. I'm bothered. Then, I'm bothered that I'm bothered, embarrassed at my pettiness.

That icky feeling is my flip-switch. My lesson, like a silent partner, interrupts my selfish reverie, *"I thank my Father for His gifts to me,"* breaking the code of special identity, and flushing my being of falsehood, leaving only blessed gratitude. "Thank you, God, for your gift to me." Tears sting my eyes as I breathe deeply into the precious gift of this moment we share, the gift of sobriety, love, and union.

Humbled, I feel only appreciation for my girl—my sister, silently thanking her for reflecting the split in my mind, which I gratefully forgive.

A distant light from deep within my soul, unveils an image of myself, years ago, when I started this journey. Desperate, sitting alone in the dark, frightened, with no idea how my life would ever change, and considering death a viable option, when the hand of AA—my sponsor, Betty, took my hand and led the way out.

In sequence, an image of meeting my friend, my sponsee, a year ago surfaces, where I reach my hand to her and share the joy of sobriety. My heart beats with the holiness we share, blessed with the gift's forgiveness and service in love, receiving and extending.

As my friend tells her story, I join her, sharing her gratitude, extending the warm glow from heart to heart, including everyone in love's soft glow.

CHAPTER NINETY-SEVEN

DAY 124

(Lesson 124)

"Let me remember I am one with God."

(W-pI.124.1)

Today we extend the length of our contemplation time to a full half hour. Imagine contemplating the holiness of being one with God! A half hour is a long time for an untrained mind to focus on one idea. But our minds have been readied for this.

Today we see with Christ's vision past appearances that cause anxiety and doubt, where pain gives way to peace because we are aware of God's presence within our mind. *Today we see only the loving and the lovable.* We are looking at the "real" world in place of what we made up.

We recognize a presence and power with us all the time, and we are learning to keep returning our minds to that place where we remember. There is nothing to fear because God is with us. Our willingness to remember we are one with God allows us to deny the ego identity and accept the oneness we share with God.

After my morning session with God, I feel like walking light. With today's lesson at the center of my mind, I am determined to remember I am one with God all day. It's perfect because it's a day I volunteer at a homeless shelter. I know I'd been tempted in the past to feel sorry for people, but today I am determined to see only the truth—to see Christ in each brother.

When I first arrive, the woman in charge asks me to pass out blankets. I think of the Christ child in each man, woman, or child I see and that we each have a gift to give and receive. As I make my rounds, I say a silent blessing of gratitude for their holiness as I approach each one. With just two blankets left, I come to a family, a mother and three children.

They don't have coats, let alone blankets. I give them the blankets and ask if there is anything else, I can do. The little girl, about five years old, asks, "Will you tell us a story?" My heart explodes with love. I sit down on the cot with her and the rest of the family gathers around. I ask if they've heard the story of the Velveteen Rabbit. They hadn't. I'm not sure I remember it right, but it's what comes and I trust I am being guided.

I tell the Velveteen Rabbit story; how the rabbit waits patiently in the nursery for the little boy to choose him as a playmate. I share that he becomes real through the child's love. I say it is how we came to be through God's Love—that God's love is in us, and we are never alone because God is part of us. I tell them every time we love someone else, they become real for us.

The kids snuggle up next to me. "Tell us more. Tell another one." I say, "How about you find another child here and share the Velveteen Rabbit story with them and pass on the yummy feeling you have right now?" They excitedly agree it is a grand idea.

The mother, with shiny eyes, says, "Thank you. That story is just what I needed. I need to remember God is always with us."

I have no doubt of the Divine guiding and blessing the entire holy encounter. My experience witnesses to just how intimately present God really is—always! His presence actually *is* closer than my breath. God's plan is already in full swing. I have answered the call, and I am His messenger. And every situation and circumstance that arises in my life is my ministry. Every encounter is holy because *I am one with God!*

CHAPTER NINETY-EIGHT

DAY 125

(Lesson 125)

"In quiet I receive God's Word today."
(W-pl.125.1)

The course is uncompromising. It says the word of God is "I am as God created me." We can hear God's voice speak of the love we are. We can feel the joy of extending that love, healing and lighting the world with love. Or, we can snooze in fear, pain, lack, and worry. These are the two worlds the course talks about.

We cannot see two worlds. One or the other individually. It is our decision. Such is the power of the Children of God. We are 100 percent responsible. In quiet—that instant we quit thinking we know—we leave the world of suffering and doubt, remaining only what we came with—our Self as God created us.

I came to the course with a habit of projecting God outside myself, wanting Him to come into my little-limited idea of myself. To fix the "me" I believed I was—trying to bring truth to my illusion.

Today during my quiet time with God, I am filled with awe to realize I no longer project God out there, because I experience the Divine as my real inner being. Even as I read the lesson, I experience an undefined, yet fundamental recognition, like a memory without images. My Self understands the meaning behind the words on the page. I feel a Divine Presence—God is always, already communicating with me.

As I contemplate today's lesson, *"In quiet, I receive God's Word today,"* I experience an immediate shift from trying to being—from illusion to truth. I stop thinking, aware of only the beat of my heart. In quiet, I receive God's Word—a recognition of holiness, certainty, peace, and freedom. "I am as God created me."

I know something profound and unalterable. I imagine my heart as a vessel continually receiving the memory of God and Self, created in His love. I see my "thinking mind" like a flap at the door of recognition. If I get into thinking rather than receiving, the flap covers over access to the Divine wisdom within. God's voice speaks only of the truth I am. If I need to know something, it is a given.

Everything I am and everything I need lives in the present moment. Nothing else is real. My so-called life is a backdrop for these present moments of love, where I can extend, heal, and make happy.

I'm at coffee with a friend and colleague, and we begin our usual bitch session about the administration at work. My gut clenches. I close my eyes briefly to the physical scene and all the thoughts from the previous conversation leave, replaced by a profound stillness. I call my lesson to mind, *"In quiet, I receive God's Word today."*

I recognize our call for love and healing and feel only love for all concerned. A loving smile comes from deep within. My friend asks, "What's with the big smile? Did I miss something?" I share my experience. I tell her how I felt a clutching feeling in my gut, which is a signal I am not being true to myself. I share how I cherish these moments when my feelings tell me to return my mind to peace. How it only takes a pause, to zero back to love.

She smiles in recognition and joins me in a moment of silence where we wait for Divine wisdom to infuse our communication. The quiet infuses our conversation with truth and joy. The conversation purpose is transformed to one of healing, of keeping the outcome of peace and happiness in mind, knowing it influences everyone concerned. From the quiet, we hear God's voice speak the happy outcome for us.

CHAPTER NINETY-NINE
DAY 126
(Lesson 126)

"All that I give is given to myself."
(W-pI.126.1)

Today's idea is the bedrock of forgiveness, showing us that giver and receiver are the same. We are learning that every experience we get is a result of what we give. This world reflects exactly what we believe it is, because of what we believe we are. Nothing is out there manipulating us.

What we give to anyone, we are simultaneously giving to ourselves. If we judge, we feel judged, or we fear we're being judged. If we offer love, we experience instantaneous union. *"All that we give is given to ourselves."* This upgrades our understanding of forgiveness and converts it to a holistic view in our minds. The course uses the symbols we made for separation and lays them out in a different arrangement. One that unites in an inclusive whole.

When we are upset with anyone, it is always because of the role we've assigned to them which we feel they aren't fulfilling. If I think someone is a bully, I am the one assigning that character to them, reinforcing attack in my mind, and blocking the awareness of our natural invulnerability.

But when we withdraw judgment, we leave a space in our mind for the truth to enter. This is forgiveness, seeing our judgment, taking responsibility, and choosing the truth instead. We now see them as they are, one with us, as God's holy child. We realize if we withdraw the role we've assigned them, they are innocent, just as we desire to know ourselves.

Today, as I read the lesson, a recent encounter with my sister Keri comes to mind, which has been festering inside me ever since. I know I can't see Keri or myself clearly. I feel disconnected from her and from myself.

I let the scene play out before me like a movie. Keri appears judgmental, guarded, and dishonest. She's crying, saying how we don't understand the demands placed on her, as one in the top one percent in her field, with so many people counting on her. That it is impossible for her to accommodate the new dates we'd agreed on for the sister's retreat.

I whisper to another sister, "Get off the cross, Keri, we need the wood." I sit as arbitrator, judging her as sick, addicted to a false persona, and in denial. (Yeah, like I've never done that before.)

But I pay Keri lip-service (and myself) saying putting our relationship first is what matters most to me. I feel the stab of attack immediately in my gut, but I ignore it. I'm loaded on righteousness. I'm right about my assessment of her!

Remembering, my gut churns. I tune in and remember my lesson, *"All that I give is given to myself. The Help I need to learn that this is true is with me now. And I will trust in Him."* Instantly, the light dawns! My Keri story is witnessing the battle waging within myself. I let the ideas sink past my judgments and deep within, recalibrating me for forgiveness.

Communication wasn't my goal. Judgment was. And judgment is what I received. My perception of Keri is *my* call for love. I forgive her for what she never did and let love heal my mind. I repeat my lesson, *"All that I give is given to myself!"* I am released.

And go figure—I actually see that Keri is my savior. I'm filled with appreciation for her. The scene shifts in my mind. Brilliant light surrounds the image of my sister and my Self—illuminating the Holiness we share—a reflection of whole-mind. My heart is bursting with love and gratitude. Cheerfully, I pick up the phone and call her.

CHAPTER ONE HUNDRED
DAY 127
(Lesson 127)

"There is no love but God's."
(W-pI.127.1)

In this world we talk about love like it's a level system, right? Like love is on a sliding scale or something—everything from loving coffee to the extraordinary love we have for our children or special relationship. Yes? Today's lesson clears this confusion once and for all. It's either God's love or illusion.

Love is not an emotion, though it can be experienced emotionally. It is not an action, but often expresses through us as such. Love is what we are. It has no levels and any exclusivity separates us from our recognition of our Self as love. Today's lesson works like a touchstone to remember the love of God is all there is. Period. There is only love, there is only the power of love, there is only the presence of love.

I used to think that since so many of the enlightened masters didn't have children it made it easier for them to live a life devoted to God. They didn't have all the daily responsibilities of another person's life to be concerned with, only their own. They could live in an ashram or meditate for days in a cave, or I don't know, but something different than me. It made me feel better about not "getting" it.

The thing I love about the mind-training of *A Course in Miracles* is it meets me exactly where I am and uses whatever I am going through to train my mind back to love. Realizing there is no love but God's, raises us above the battleground where we see the inclusivity of everyone and everything.

Today, during my morning time with God, centered on today's idea, *"There is no love but God's,"* I feel a "special" angst in my heart as a mother. Lin and Lucas have been out all night with friends. It's unusual for them to not call as it gets late or when plans change.

Night passed into early morning and fear for their safety crept in. What if something has happened to them? Every parent's nightmare, right? My mind starts spinning stories, naming their friends as villains. But even as I am tempted to blame, I am immediately filled with the spirit of today's idea, *"There is no love but God's. I bless you, brother, with the Love of God, which I would share with you. For I would learn the joyous lesson that there is no love but God's, and yours and mine and everyone's."*

I realize I must forgive my "motherly love" to make room to experience God's love, which is my own, and I let it all go into the arms of the Divine. I feel comfort and peace, returning me to my natural state of trust and faith.

I recall the old idea of gurus who never have kids and I realize my mind has totally shifted. My children *are* my ashram. I see an image of the children playing video games, and I am joined in their bliss, blessedly immersed in inclusion—in God's exuberant love. Their innocence shows me my own.

Allowing them to follow their bliss teaches me that love allows all things. As a result, I allow myself the gentle love that heals when mistakes are made, and I forgive myself. *Motherhood* is my guru. Joyous appreciation rewards me. My heart is open. God is my heartbeat.

Minutes later, the door opens and the kids come rushing in. They'd had a flat tire between Salt Lake and Wendover and no way to call for help. They were stranded until a cop came to their rescue. We have a laugh and hugs all around. Life is a miracle, blessed by God's love.

DAY 128

(Lesson 128)

"The world I see holds nothing that I want."

(W-pl.128.1)

When I first read today's lesson, I think, "Wait a minute. My life is just getting good. There have certainly been times in my life that I could say with all honesty that my world held nothing that I wanted. But now, well, my life's pretty bitching."

The lesson says what we value we make part of us as we perceive ourselves. That's why we must release it all. Am I valuing only the truth? What am I valuing, thinking I can hold on to this little thing for a while, a trinket or judgment that I am making part of myself, that interferes with recognizing only love?

I mean, that one thing—it's powerful! Why not be vigilant for pure love, for being the light of the world and bringing peace to every mind through my forgiveness and holiness? Why not value the joy of God above all else, when happiness is all we've ever sought in the end anyway? Right? What's the downside?

There is no compromise to this. We can't hold onto anything of seeming "value" out there if we want to recognize our true Self. The Self as God created us is the only thing of value. It is the *real* in this world of illusions.

As I apply the lesson *"The world I see holds nothing that I want,"* sinking beyond words, I realize the two worlds side by side within me. First off, in this place of stillness and peace, I feel whole, satisfied, loved. But, as the things I value in my world cross the threshold of my mind, I notice a sense of lack clutch in my gut, a hungry feeling, accompanied by guilt.

As I let go of my attachment to what I value, the sense of lack and guilt disappear. Joy replaces hunger as I let each value go. I swiftly release it all to the Holy Spirit for reinterpretation. I am lifted into the happy dream—a world of wholeness, joy, and love.

I realize the world I perceive when looking as if it's something outside myself, holds nothing I want. But when I view the world from the inner perspective of divine purpose, I see my ministry. I feel my place in the world as love and joy—a messenger of peace.

I'm at a garden party with my sister, Lyn. It's high society. The atmosphere is light, superficial, proper. The conversation is trite, maintaining status quo.

Back in the day, I wanted to be high society. I believed it would prove my worthiness—my value. I smile. I choose to see the divine purpose of this garden party. Though recognizing my body's eyes interpretation of the party scene, I look beyond the images and bodies and see a world of Christ light. Each person I meet is holy, each a brief and brilliant sacred encounter.

In one exchange I drop the conversation deeper and the woman unburdens herself of the conflict she's experiencing in her marriage into the healing balm of light. I am the face of love. Another joins us and shares the joy of her recovery from cancer and how it has opened her to the mystery of life and higher purpose. We unite, recognizing the divine mysticism all around us.

I can't help but think of my lesson's promise, *"Your whole perspective on the world will shift by just a little, every time you let your mind escape its chains. The world is not where it belongs. And you belong where it would be, and where it goes to rest when you release it from the world. Your Guide is sure. Open your mind to Him. Be still and rest."* I attest to this beautiful transformation of sight. I see it in the faces and love all around me at the garden party of my life.

CHAPTER ONE HUNDRED TWO

DAY 129

(Lesson 129)

"Beyond this world there is a world I want."

(W-pl.129.1)

Today, we are given a day of grace. There is a world beyond the one we see now. In this world, it seems there are simultaneously two worlds, one of fear and the world of love. By our desire, we experience one or the other. We decide upon the world we want and it happens for us. Today we choose the eternal joy of the love's world in place of the world of fear.

My experience with migraine headaches is a metaphor for what happens when I choose the world of fear. I used to get them frequently. I felt powerless. If you've experienced one, you know. They are not like regular headaches. They mess with you neurologically. They mess with you psychologically. They mess with your sight, distorting your vision. Make you question the value of life altogether.

I seemed at the mercy of the migraine until it was done having its way with me. Kind of like addiction. A lot like addiction. My experience with migraines (and addiction) is like a microcosm of the world of pain and powerlessness and fear. I feared the migraine. It was like Lord Voldemort from *Harry Potter*, He-Who-Must-Not-Be-Named. We called it M, for dread that saying migraine would summon its presence. No shit.

This morning, as I felt the aura presence of an almighty migraine descending, today's lesson flashes one pure instant of clarity—of sanity in my mind, *"Beyond this world is a world I want. I choose to see that world instead of this, for here is nothing that I really want."*

It's like a lighthouse to freedom, and I follow it into the darkness of my fear with my full attention. Instead of recoil from the aura, I go with it, like it's a message. I center only on my desire to see the truth, and peace dissolves the fear, brightening my mind.

No pain arrives. I bubble with delight. I am free. I look around me and everything is bright, beautiful, crisp, and clear, wafting with love. The world of fear is nowhere. I am in a new world. In gratitude, I thank the migraine for the holy miracle of experiencing a sane world replace insanity.

It's like the first day of kindergarten when you realize there is a whole groovy world happening outside your family and you get to be part of the fun.

As I go about my day, my lesson is the light behind all that my eyes see and colors my world with the presence of another way of seeing everyone and everything. A world free from pain and fear and separation. *"Beyond this world is the world there is a world I want."* It takes my breath away!

How amazing that an experience like a migraine which I have given such value to, as to stop my life and joy in its tracks, could render such complete surrender to divine freedom and beauty. Yum.

CHAPTER ONE HUNDRED THREE

DAY 130

(Lesson 130)

"It is impossible to see two worlds."

(W-pl.130.1)

Today's idea is the flip-switch for our entire experience. Beginning with the course introduction, *"Nothing real can be threatened. Nothing unreal exists. Herein lies the peace of God,"* we have been learning to see this lesson's truth. *"It is impossible to see two worlds."*

It tells us that fidelity to premise is the law of mind, and what we see reflects the premise we choose. Love or fear. From fear, we see a conflicted, competitive, and scary world. From the premise of love, we see a world of happy unity and peace.

It's what quantum physics tell us—there is just this energy field of infinite possibility. How it manifests is determined by the intention of the observer. The mind is always using this field of unlimited possibilities and zeroing in on the dominant choice or thoughts of our attention, making that world real to us. Once we choose the one true option—love—all other options disappear. The strength we need is given the instant the choice is made.

Today, we practice making the choice to see only the world of love, a world that reflects the laws of love and offers peace and joy and oneness in the place of fear, anxiety, and separation. The decision we make today is uncompromising. It is a total commitment.

We cannot hold on to one tiny aspect of our self-concept—the world of specialness and private thoughts and fears. Nor can we keep what we think we love and do not want to lose in making our choice for truth today.

The fear of loss will keep us prisoner to the thought system of fear, obscuring love's presence from our awareness. We no longer want the world of separation, pain, and loss. Today we can make the only choice that can alter our experience of the world. We must give our entire perception to God, without reservation. And as we do, we awaken to heaven—the world that God would have His Son experience in total love, joy, and peace.

I'm driving to work and get stuck in a traffic jam. My mind starts its thing, pretending it knows what's causing gridlock; an accident or road construction—or maybe it's just traffic rubberneckers who can't just keep driving and keep the flow going. When it starts in on how I'll be late to work, and what story I'll tell to stay out of trouble, and I realized the fear stories for what they are.

I start laughing. "Who's impeding the flow, Danét? Sheesh, I'm making a world of fear and judgment right now, in the seeming privacy of my car. It's hilarious." Humor is an instant release into reality. I call my lesson to mind, *"It is impossible to see two worlds. Let me accept the strength God offers me and see no value in this world, that I may find my freedom and deliverance."*

My inner traffic jam of judgment and fear releases and I lean back and trust divine flow. I let myself feel the flow of living love within me. I go with it, letting my awareness drop out of my head and into that vital energy within. Feeling the life force drawing my attention inward and expanding out in love. I am in the eternal peace of this present moment, calm and joyous.

For a few minutes, I forget everything else. Gridlock has become my altar to love's world, and its flow, my meditation. I'm in another world entirely from a moment before. *"It is impossible to see two worlds."* I imagine love flowing from my heart out to the whole jam of brothers. This is the simplicity of salvation, right here, right now. This is the moment of pure presence! Love eclipses all other possibilities.

CHAPTER ONE HUNDRED FOUR

DAY 131

(Lesson 131)

"No one can fail who seeks to reach the truth."

(W-pI.131.1)

No one can fail who seeks to reach the truth." No one can fail. Seeking the truth of who we are is as natural to the amnesiac as breathing is to the body. That's us. Amnesiac. We have forgotten who we are. That's why we're seeking. To remember the truth.

No matter what our story in this dream is, deep within our mind we know something is off. We are haunted by an incessant restlessness—a quest for recollection of the truth. And once we realize it, there is no turning back.

Our purpose in life *is* to know the truth of what we are. And until we recognize the truth of Self in union with Creator and all creation, the restlessness is unceasing.

From nearly the first moment I started reading *A Course in Miracles*, I felt a subtle, soothing recognition, a calming of my condition of restlessness—a quiet assurance that the search was ending. I felt inexplicably compelled to return to the course and rest in the space in my mind it created. Though my life was still a cluster of conflict and not-good-enough beliefs, recognition of the truth of my Self began to dawn. I had found the path to truth for me.

But there is a difference between knowing the path and walking the path. The practice with each lesson is the way we walk the path to truth.

Just after Parker was born, my faith wavered. I'd left the Vision Center, as I wanted more time to devote myself to motherhood. Motherhood was now my ministry. I thought I had it figured out.

Yet nothing went the way I planned. Things that worked before, failed. With each failure, I tried harder, using the formula that made magic happen before when everything seemed to naturally fall into place. I used prayer to bolster my efforts, while never really letting go to divine will.

The final straw—what stopped me in my tracks, literally—my ankles gave out, shooting with pain, making it all but impossible to "do" anything. I am forced to stop.

I stop trying to figure it out. I stop everything. I give up. I plead with the Divine. "WTF am I doing wrong? I don't know anyone who has tried harder than me. It isn't fair. I want to keep the faith, to trust You. Please help." I take a deep breath and let go.

The words from today's lesson come unbidden. *"No one can fail who seeks to reach the Truth."* Ah, yes. Truth is all I really want. I forgot. It is impossible to solve my seeming problems on the level of the problem.

Like waking from a bad dream, I wake to the light of truth. I want only divine will. To be in divine flow in safety and quiet assurance. I feel amazing. I have awakened from my daze that I am on my own.

The choice for truth is uncompromising. I can't have truth and hold onto my fear at the same time. Truth is all I want, and I feel its energy moving me forward.

As I stand, the pain in my ankles is all but gone. I trust the path before me will be revealed. I realize the perfection of my life curriculum. I look around me with full appreciation for each little thing as a gift from the Divine.

I'm at a new frequency now, anything but love and trust is too dense for my path now. Serendipitous things begin to happen right away—opportunities I couldn't see before naturally unfold a whole new set of amazing adventures in a new town. Truth is my home and I am never alone.

DAY 132

(Lesson 132)

"I loose the world from all I thought it was."

(W-pI.132.1)

Today's lesson is showing us the immense power of our minds. We can loosen the world from all we thought it was because we have the power of creation within our mind—the mind we share with our Creator.

We can loose the world because it is not real. It's merely so as a reflection of the thoughts and beliefs we hold. Separation ideas have gripped our minds by our decision, and it is up to us to loosen the grip.

The lesson says, *"The world is nothing in itself. Your mind must give it meaning. And what you behold upon it are your wishes, acted out so you can look on them and think them real. Perhaps you think you did not make the world, but came unwillingly to what was made already, hardly waiting for your thoughts to give it meaning. Yet in truth you found exactly what you looked for when you came."* Astonishing!

As I read today's lesson, I feel I understand that my daily life is due to the power of my mind, so I can loose my world from what I think it is and see God's world shine through, just as easily as seeing problems. If I loosen the thoughts that stabilize the world of fear, only love remains, because the truth is really my natural state.

I start the day, as usual, having coffee with the Divine, resting in the stillness of present love. I imagine what my day will feel like loosing the world I made; letting go all past identifications, labels, and attached meanings, and place my open future in the hands of God. I invite the Holy Spirit to decide everything for me. The image of my young children, totally present to the newness of life, comes to mind. I take it as a sign I'm ready to go about my day.

My children are my first opportunity to see the choice to let go of the world of my ego and choose another way of seeing. Nobody seems to want to do anything but play video games today. An article I read recently comes to mind about how kids today are becoming video zombies and how we should monitor their play. Thinking of it feels icky. Like on impulse, I try to get the kids to change what they are doing to get rid of the feeling, rather than check in to see where it's really coming from.

I say, "Hey guys, how about we go to a museum or do something educational?" But right as I'm saying it, my lesson flits across my mind. Ha! *Loose the world from what I think it is!* I take a breath and follow it down to my feet on the ground.

I feel my heart beating in my chest and presence myself in now. I loosen the article, the ideas I had aligned with, and the icky feeling allowing myself total presence. I see nothing is wrong. The kids are happy. My mind is open. I see love's world showing me peace and synchronicity.

Cole speaks up, "Mom, we *are* doing something educational, and having fun. You should try it. If you want, I can show you how the game works." I laugh. Of course. Here is reality. Here in this moment, free from judgment, and open in gratitude and curiosity for what I might learn. Here is another world of union, enjoying the simplicity of learning in joy and play. Just what I really want. Simply by loosing the world from what I thought it was.

DAY 133
(Lesson 133)

"I will not value what is valueless."

(W-pl.133.1)

I will not value what is valueless." Sounds simple enough, right? The course reaches us exactly where we believe ourselves to be, and begins there, giving us what we can use practically in our lives.

Today we are learning the real criteria by which to test all things we think we want. If they don't meet this criterion, what we're choosing isn't worth having, because it can only replace what offers more.

Today's lesson is a significant step because every moment we make choices. We've already established that we have only two alternatives from which to choose. Truth or illusion. Love or fear. There is no compromise in what our choice must bring. We can't have just a little illusion and have the awareness of truth in our mind. Each decision we make brings us everything or nothing.

Today's criterion distinguishes the valuable from the valueless. (1) If it has temporary value, it is valueless. Temporary value is without value because time cannot determine value since what God gives is eternal. (2) If it takes away from someone else, it is valueless. As we deny their right to it, we have denied our own. This reinforces the false belief that loss can offer gain.

We must learn to question why the choice we make is of value to us. What attracts our mind to it? What purpose does it serve? Every decision is a choice for love or fear. Every single one. We're questioning the very fabric of the ego's hold on the mind, and the ego is sneaky. It's exceedingly suspicious, even vicious, as we bring every decision under this scrutiny.

When Lin and Lucas were teenagers, we needed a new car. Two options immediately show up. A client who is buying a new car has a well running Subaru she wants to talk to me about. I tell her I'd get back with her.

A friend at a dealership can get me a deal on a bright red Thunderbird. Instantly, I get a gut sense not to go down that road. I bypass it. I want the shiny red car. I've earned it, haven't I? Plus, some mean girls at Lin's school have been teasing her and I want her to show up driving the T-bird.

We need a car, but rather than trust my yummy-stat, gut feeling that says wait for the decision where everyone wins, I go with my ego. Within a month, Lin is rear-ended while driving the T-bird. She isn't physically hurt, but the car is totaled. She feels terrible. I feel awful.

Immediately, I am reminded of my initial gut-guidance I'd ignored. The red T-bird is like a cosmic red flag inviting me to check the motivation for my choices by today's criterion. I smile as today's lesson floods into my mind. *"I will not value what is valueless."*

I chuckle as I review my choices by today's criteria. I wanted something that didn't last. I was attracted to the car as a status symbol, meaning someone would lose for me to gain. I wasn't trusting Lin to handle her own life and happiness. I was cheating her, and myself of my faith in her.

It's like the whole purpose of buying the T-bird was to see I was choosing the valueless over the valuable; temporary gratification over peace of mind, joy, trust, and, well, everything. By asking for nothing, I got nothing. I forgive myself and choose again.

I call my client. She still has the Subaru. In fact, she wants to trade it for therapy. I feel a delighted, peaceful sense of rightness. Everyone wins.

DAY 134

(Lesson 134)

"Let me perceive forgiveness as it is."
(W-pI.134.1)

Isn't it wonderful to see forgiveness from a whole new place. It's not that we have to *do* anything, merely let the false be false, seeking only the true. Forgiveness is not where we see the faults of others and pardon them because we are the bigger person. True forgiveness does not see error in our brother. The reason we make it difficult for ourselves is that we believe that we must overlook the truth.

Understanding that everything that happens in our world is an out-picturing of our own mind, we know that what we think someone has done hasn't happened in truth, but is a projection of error in our mind. When we assign blame and then forgive, it's like a double lie.

First, we believe sin is possible and has occurred, then by pardoning it, we mock the truth of our brother, assigning us both the imprisonment of guilt. The one we blame is actually a mirror, reflecting the error back to us, so we can see it and choose again. Forgiveness lets us appreciate our brother's part in our healing.

Forgiveness is the one illusion that corrects illusions altogether. True forgiveness overlooks the idea of sin entirely and sees directly into the innocence we share as children of the Divine.

I never need to seek out opportunities to practice the idea for the day, because everywhere I go I find the story of me.

When my sister, Dione, relapsed, it hit me like a gut-shot. She'd been sober nearly eighteen months, the longest period in her life. I had it wired up that she was finally "getting it." I had a whole vision of how things would go. Que music: "Sober together, marching hand in hand."

She called, obviously drunk, to tell me she wasn't happy sober, and nothing I could say would change her mind. (Well, certainly not while she's loaded!)

Holding the phone to my chest, I slid to the floor, defeated and afraid for her, tears streaming. When she came into Western Institute, where I worked, she was nearly dead from malnutrition and alcohol poisoning. It's a miracle she lived. I thought it was "the big turning point."

She'd be going back to panhandling for booze—putting herself in all kinds of dangerous situations—like she'd done for the last thirty years. That thought was my flip-switch. Who am I to decide sobriety is better for Dione than what she chooses? *Let me perceive forgiveness as it is.* Instantly, the fog of judgment lifts.

Dione is due my wholehearted honor, love, and faith. I don't know because I only see what I put there. I open my mind and the light comes flooding in. Immense love washes through me and speaks these words, "I love you, Dione. I know the Divine is with you and in you. I honor your choice to find your own way and not mine. I extend my faith and love to go with you wherever your life takes you."

I meant it with my whole heart. I truly could not see a problem with her choice—God's got this. It's not my business. My business is only this—to love with complete abandon and trust.

This holy encounter was the last real exchange I had with Dione, for which I am eternally grateful.

CHAPTER ONE HUNDRED EIGHT
DAY 135
(Lesson 135)

"If I defend myself, I am attacked."
(W-pl.135.1)

With today's lesson, we're not just talking about how we defend ourselves against what we perceive as threatening. What we are looking at is the core belief that we are bodies, fragile, and in need of constant defense. But we are spirit, and it is only from this recognition that we have access to our innate invulnerability.

What struck me as I applied today's lesson, is realizing how many decisions I make still put the "my" first. "My" body, "my" life, "my" safety. If I've learned anything from working with the course, it is that nothing is actually "mine." I am the temporary steward for all things as divine flow moves them through my so-called life. Whoa! It's so powerful to see this "my" orientation for what it is—a defense against the truth.

"My" is the antithesis of wholeness. It's where the ego makes its home, perpetuating a false belief about who I am, keeping illusion real in my mind.

The ego is so sneaky and seductive. It will use spiritual language to coerce me into thinking that I am turning my life over to God, while still believing I am not what God created.

In working with today's lesson, I see how I sometimes use my spiritual practice as a balm—trying to use true ideas to fix or improve my circumstances—without really releasing the false reality I still believe to be true. The course calls this "trying to bring truth to illusions." It is actually an attack on the truth.

Today's lesson lays it out in a clear criterion by which to see the pattern of defense as it arises and choose again. It's like an ego bull-shit detector.

I am defending illusion whenever *[I] attempt to plan the future, activate the past, or attempt to organize the present as [I] wish.* Shit man! Isn't that our whole operating system in this world?

By using this criterion, we can see where the false story is covering the portal of grace available in each moment.

It's fun to see how each lesson practice influences the way my day unfolds. After my yummy morning in prayer, meditating on the lesson and reading the course, I notice the shift in my energy when I leave that setting and my mind anticipates the day ahead.

I'm in a mind-watching mode, so I'm able to see the antics my mind gets up to and I pay attention. I'm scheduled to meet with an AA sponsee later. Aargh. I think, "All she ever wants to do is be in problems." This is like a trigger to see how I engage in "self-initiated" planning. I play her life story over in my mind, preparing "helpful" responses to the areas of conflict I anticipate she'll bring up, based on what has happened in our past encounters. I even think how I'll point this out to her.

In a flash, my lesson comes to mind. I burst out laughing! It's so obvious. I see how I'm planning the future, activating the past, and attempting to organize the present as I choose. I'm defending myself from present openness, attacking myself and her with fear and judgment by attempting to anticipate our meeting. It's just fear of the unknown. What it tells me is a lie.

I know when I am open to the present moment, there is nothing to fear. I am given what I need. I release my antics as I repeat the lesson idea, *"If I defend myself, I am attacked."* I feel a burst of joy as my heart opens. How can I know the purpose of our meeting?

Only the present moment can unveil that gift. Now, I am ready to meet with my friend. Now is my portal to be a conduit for truth. Only now.

CHAPTER ONE HUNDRED NINE

DAY 136

(Lesson 136)

"Sickness is a defense against the truth."

(W-pI.136.1)

Today's lesson tells us that, contrary to popular belief, sickness is not an accident. It says, *"Like all defenses, it is an insane device for self-deception."* It is a decision we have made to defend against the truth. The body seems to be proof that we are vulnerable, fragile, and weak, in need of constant defense against unforeseen forces which could attack at any time. All our attempts to fend off sickness by physical means reinforce the belief that the body is who we are, separating us further from recognizing the truth.

Sickness is a sign that we made the decision to experience fear and now it's sent its sentinels. Once recognized, we can choose again.

When I broke my back, I felt ashamed. I wanted to fix the problem and get away from it as quickly as possible. I sought outside answers and, consequently, I accepted the diagnosis the "professionals" gave me of osteoporosis. I let myself slip into the sleep of feeling vulnerable and victimized, attacking myself, and forgetting the truth I know—I am not a body. I was in a lonely hell of self-doubt.

Whenever I feel I am alone in anything, I have mistaken myself for my fearful thoughts, and my thinking has become more apparent to me than the reality of my being.

Finally, realizing this, I let my mind sink down beneath body thoughts into the simple feeling of being. I see how the belief in sickness makes my mind contract around body thoughts as they appear in my mind, which blinds me to the awareness of my invulnerable Self as love. I forgive.

I rest in in the peace forgiveness brings. From this stillness I am able to look at my body situation as an image before me, playing out on the vast screen of my open mind, which remains untarnished by the play. I question what would get me out of seeing myself as broken.

Tears sting my eyes as I realize my "painful body" is a defense against fulfilling my purpose as the light of the world. I see how I have used this "legit" sickness to hide out—to resist the force of divine light propelling my life forward to only God knows where. I place it all on the altar of true healing.

I see that my attempts to give my situation to the Divine previously failed because I had an agenda I wouldn't see past. I wanted a pain-free body.

My lesson brings me back home to what I truly want—the truth—to accept the truth of what I am and let my mind be healed. Words from today's lesson arrive like a song in answer to my willingness, *"I have forgotten what I really am, for I mistook my body for myself. Sickness is a defense against the truth. But I am not a body. And my mind cannot attack. So, I cannot be sick."*

For an instant, I give up my agenda to have a pain-free body. I look past my seeming problem, seeking only the truth. I let go of the identity that houses problems. I surrender all that I believe myself to be, and in that space I allow the truth to dawn in my mind. I feel an immediate and total release of the pain in my body in a flash of light—the truth is searing through me. I say, *"Sickness is a defense against the truth. I will accept the truth of what I am, and let my mind be wholly healed today."* It is the portal that lifts me above the battleground play in the screen. I rest in the Divine quiet of truth.

CHAPTER ONE HUNDRED TEN

DAY 137

(Lesson 137)

"When I am healed I am not healed alone."

(W-pl.137.1)

Sickness is isolation. It feels personal. It is the definition of aloneness. It fences us off from others and from our Self. The course tells us that atonement is a lesson in sharing. When I am healed—when I accept correction for the errors in my mind—it affects the whole mind we share. So every time any of us chooses the truth, we all benefit.

I first experienced this wholeness-healing with alcoholism. Alcoholism is like the posterchild for teaching today's idea to those of us who swore to take our secrets and shame to the grave, rather than ask for help.

As much as we try to convince ourselves we are only hurting ourselves, sickness impacts everyone in our life, separating us from them, and from the love we are. Alcoholism brought me to my knees. To a place where I no longer cared about my precious story of me.

Emerging from my private hell, feeling hopeless and alone, I stepped into the rooms of Alcoholics Anonymous. I laid myself bare, surrendering my secrets, my fears, and shame. It was a trust fall into the arms of the unknown.

I gave my faith to a Higher Power I could see only in the shining eyes of the faces of the strangers who I came to know as brother, sister, comrade, friend. Through joining, I surrendered my will to Divine Will, in union with my brothers, and I was set free.

The grace of this initial experience witnesses to today's lesson, *"When I am healed I am not healed alone."* The decision for healing sends ripples throughout the whole-mind we share—reaching each mind open and willing to be healed. We might not even see the affect in another up close and personal.

I'm in the waiting area while my car is being worked on, when a woman comes up to me and says, "Hi. It's Danét, right? We met while waiting in the doctor's office a while back. My whole attitude toward healing changed that day, and I have wished a hundred times I had gotten your phone number to share with you the miracles that came out of our connecting that day."

I recall the occurrence immediately. A warm rush of love flows as I remember and once again join with her. We met at the orthopedic office. During our wait, we began talking about how frightening it had been to find out that our broken bones were because of osteoporosis—old people's disease—the downward slope.

But neither of us wanted to stay in that thought pattern with each other. We instantly recognized the availability of a higher conversation. One about healing and how every seeming problem, as physical as it may appear, is a spiritual message making its way to us to find and accept a spiritual solution. It didn't surprise me that of all the people in the waiting room we would find ourselves sitting next to each other—two open hearts, willing to see the truth—willing to receive healing.

I really hadn't given it much thought since that encounter, as I have come to expect miracles as a natural expression of love and joining. I am committed to being the face for love—seeing each encounter as holy. Healing defies all the laws the world obeys. It demonstrates that illusions cannot prevail against the truth. It is a portal of grace honoring the oneness we share.

As I apply today's lesson, I think of all the people believing in weakness because of a diagnosis of osteoporosis. I accept the truth for all of us, in gratitude. I offer healing where it is, in the mind. *"When I am healed I am not healed alone."* By refusing to accept illness as my reality and reaching for the truth, I get to be a miracle worker. A healer. I let healing be through me, giving as I'm receiving, extending it to all, banishing sickness from our whole mind.

CHAPTER ONE HUNDRED ELEVEN
DAY 138
(Lesson 138)

"Heaven is the decision I must make."
(W-pI.138.1)

Heaven, it turns out, is not some place "good people" go after death. *"Heaven is the decision I must make."* Heaven is a state of mind. A decision to be as God created me—the Christ Light that shines the way home for all to see. Heaven is being the face of love; it is living in the joy of true being—seeing everyone and all situations through the eyes of love.

We decided for Heaven, and it shifted the axis of reality as we know it. It is a decision without another alternative. Heaven is our zero point of reference for life now, and whatever doesn't fit into it has to go!

We make the decision for Heaven, and it takes care of a lot of bullshit choices that used to hook us up. I mean, what could be so important as to make us close our heart and put ourselves in hell? Something happening on the political screen? Is judging the negative comment our partner made worth the price of peace—of heaven? Is any little preference or grievance? Really?

I relish in this feeling of living in heaven during my morning time with God, certain no thing can rock me out of this gifted bliss. My phone rings. It is my sister, Renelle. My mother has been in a car accident. It's serious. She's been rushed to the hospital.

I feel a gripping in my heart area—fear, worry. My lesson comes instantly as I pause and place my hand on my heart. *"Heaven is the decision I must make."* The grip loosens as love's safety opens my heart in trust. My mind slips behind the incident story and settles into the peace that passeth understanding. I reach out to my mother's mind, deciding for heaven and the peace of God.

I feel guided to drive to Utah and be with her. It's snowing and the roads are icy. I feel my muscles tensing as the visibility diminishes. An unbidden thought emerges which brings total relaxation. I am at home in Heaven, driving on the wings of angels.

When I arrive at the hospital, they're wheeling my mother into surgery. Our eyes meet with a knowing smile. She says, "I felt you coming. I heard your prayer. I feel your love." We are already in heaven. I have no concern about the surgery.

While I wait, my mind rests in today's idea. *"Heaven is the decision I must make. I make it now and will not change my mind, because it is the only thing I want."* It so simple. I feel its frequency lifting and rippling out. I'm inspired to join with a mother sitting with her daughter who has been in a coma for two months. We talk about holding a heaven-state-of-mind. We weep tears of joy, trusting the Divine in union with each other.

When my mother is wheeled back into the room, we pray in gratitude for perfect healing. Like miracles have it, my mother is placed in the room next to the mother and daughter. With a knowing nod, we silently agree to a constant vigil for heaven and the peace of God. A peaceful glow flows from our circle of love and trust. It seems to impact everyone. A conflict at the nurse's station quietly settles as the nurse comes in to attend to my mother. Everyone is blessed with the holiness of our one decision for heaven, no matter what.

Every instant of every day we are given another chance. The goal is clearly stated. Decide for heaven. Period. It is the decision that ends the game of choices and unites us with the eternal love we are, infusing our lives with its gifts.

DAY 139

(Lesson 139)

"I will accept Atonement for myself."
(W-pl.139.1)

Accepting atonement is accepting total correction of our thinking, healing the split and banishing separation from our minds. We are still and always as love created us. And nothing we have misidentified ourselves as—bodies, personalities, thoughts, feelings, actions, or events—have altered or left a mark on our divine Self.

The atonement principle is love. The atonement is an act of love. It is the correction of all errors or lacks of love, which, because of what we are in truth, we will ultimately all accept. It's just a matter of time because time and matter were made for this purpose. And it is for this purpose we are seemingly here, to love, joyously extending what we are in union with all creation.

I followed a single phrase of truth as I headed down the path of spiritual seeking. "Know Thy Self!" The idea rang true deep within, beneath what I thought myself to be. Each step was an act of faith, stepping into the seeming unknown. Those faith steps, which began with an external search, ultimately u-turned, leading me inward to the light of my being. The curriculum and application of the course unveil a path somehow familiar, in which I take sure-footed steps to the truth—I am love, created by love.

Today's lesson, like yesterday's, is uncompromising. Once the decision to accept Atonement for ourselves is made, there was no going back. The path is set. Errors in the form of judgment and fear surface to be forgiven. Sure, we doze off into unconsciousness, get caught up in temporary problem insanity and choose unnecessarily delays in healing, but once the path is set, those states become intolerable in a New York minute.

No matter what my ego gets up to, beneath it all, I never totally forget I have seen the face of love in my own heart. I cannot deny that I am love.

With today's lesson we simply accept that something within us knows the truth. Despite the stories, the ego spins in this illusion of separation, we are as God created us. That's the game changer. Life now becomes a happy game, played with joy and love and unity. I love this, *"I will accept Atonement for myself. For I remain as God created me."* It's so simple. I am as God created me, and what God created cannot be altered. Period.

My morning practice begins with trusting I *do* know my Self. I pose the first question, "Who am I?" I let my mind slip beneath the thoughts, feelings, and sensations that make up "me" and into the awareness deep within, allowing the ripples to move through my being from the stillness of this innate awareness of uncompromising love. Here, deep within the mind of love, I know who I am.

I pose the questions from the lesson. *"Who is the doubter? What is it he doubts? Whom does he question? Who can answer him?"* In this quiet recognition of Self, all doubt has ceased. Ha! Only the ego questions—but I am not that. I see the ego's game for what it is, a ploy to get me to question love, to doubt my Self, my brother—life itself. Tears flow freely, released to a grand recognition that the false can touch me not—and never has in truth. I let myself dissolve into the grandeur of God's love. I accept atonement for myself for I remain as God created me.

I open my eyes and look around me. The boys have come in and joined me. They are sitting on pillows next to me, their eyes closed. They've lit a candle. All the world is but a reflection of the love I am—creation extended. It takes my breath away in gratitude and joy.

DAY 140
(Lesson 140)

"Only salvation can be said to cure."
(W-pI.140.1)

Salvation is a promise, made by God, that you would find your way to Him at last. It cannot but be kept" (W-pII.2.1.1). That's awesome! Right? The deal is that God is always with us, and as we accept Atonement for ourselves, we change our mind about the source of our identity and we are lifted into our right mind.

This is what salvation is. It simply means the correction or undoing of the mistaken belief in separation. It means we quit resisting love. We quit looking for answers *in* the problem and bring the entire illusion of problems to the Source, where healing can be found—in mind—the mind which is One with God.

It's crazy how the lessons show up each day like they are currently being written to address the specific circumstances in my life. Like today's. I have been plagued with cold symptoms for a week or more. I've been trying to tell myself that sickness is a defense against the truth, treating the symptoms, and hoping it'll go away.

It's like ego raised the stakes. Looks like I have bronchitis. Now I'm sitting in the doctor's office waiting for her to return after taking cultures. I notice the icy flash of shame flow through my veins when the doc tells me how bad it's gotten. I literally can't breathe. Hell, I haven't felt like I could breathe for days.

Aha! This is fear. I see how this fear has given the effect in my lungs of not being able to breathe. Getting air becomes the only focus, distracting me from realizing the power of my mind. The thought comes, "When I want truth more than I want to breathe, breathing will take care of itself." Like a flip-switch, today's lesson flashes in my mind, *"Only salvation can be said to cure. Speak to me, Father, that I may be healed."*

Now it is the only prayer of my heart. I reflect on how I have been caught up in treating the symptoms, giving the power of my mind to the belief there is creative power in matter that can affect me. There isn't. The body is neutral. It takes direction from the mind. I am responsible for seeing that the error is in my mind and accepting the source of healing—the atonement.

Correction can only happen where the error occurred. I bring it into the stillness for release. I let my mind slip back behind the sleep scene with the doc, my symptoms, and all sensations in my body, seeing them as one illusion of false identity. Softening into peace, my mind relaxes. My muscles untense, my lungs open. I let truth breathe me. Each breath warms me. Love flows through my veins, till love is the only focus. I am the heartbeat. I am the breath of love. I am whole, immersed in holiness.

It is a turning point. I feel like I'm awake for the first time in days. My mind has been righted. I have denied the power of illusion to hurt me. *"The mind that brings illusions to the truth is really changed. There is no change but this."*

When I feel body discomfort, that's a sign I am falling asleep and dreaming a lie. I use those signs now to remember my conviction to the truth. *"Only salvation can be said to cure."*

REVIEW IV: DAYS 141–150
(Lessons 121–140)

I love this fourth review segment. It is a period of readiness which prepares us for the next stage of our curriculum. In gratitude we invite these new instructions into our minds. It is an invitation from the Divine into a very intimate joining and rest. It feels just right—timely. Keep it simple. With this review we're adding a sponsoring thought—a central theme which unifies each step in our review: *"My mind holds only what I think with God."*

This idea is like a portal for alignment with the truth. We're asked to clear our mind of unnecessary debris—the unforgiving thoughts which we've squirreled away to dark corners of our mind, concealing them from ourselves, and just be willing to hold nothing back from the light of awareness. It opens our field of awareness in which to experience that our mind and God's are one.

Our unforgiving thoughts aren't always immediately apparent. They can be like sneaky little spiders. But here's a clue. Anything lacking love—problems and trying to fix them, self-initiated plans, fears, regrets, worry, hate, or anger, are all equally false and are cluttering up our mind-space, interfering with recognizing our minds are one with God. For five minutes first thing, we zero in on the central theme which unifies each step in the review we undertake.

Because our minds hold only what we think with God, our self-deceptions can't hold. They cannot take the place of truth and will dissolve through our willingness to let our minds be healed.

The format for this review is thus:

We begin the day devoting our minds to the freedom this review can bring. We open our minds to this single thought, *"My mind holds only what I think with God,"* and let all other thoughts slip from our minds.

The instructions say, *"Five minutes with this thought will be enough to set the day along the lines which God appointed, and to place His Mind in charge of all the thoughts you will receive that day."*

Incredible, right? Five minutes. It really doesn't seem to be too much to ask, to guarantee that God's Mind will be in charge of all our thoughts throughout the day. I mean, I've done such a bang-up job of things myself, right? *"My mind holds only what I think with God."* It thumps in my chest like a heartbeat. *"My mind holds only what I think with God."*

After our five-minute devotion, we review the two ideas for the day, close our eyes and say them to ourselves, owning them as ours and letting God's meaning shine in our minds.

Throughout the day, hourly, we bring to mind our central theme and repeat the two lesson ideas for that day, letting them settle, each is bringing a gift for us.

Take a few minutes to jot down your experience; the gifts, the forgetfulness, inspirations, or actions you are prompted to take. You are learning to trust the Divine is speaking to you and through you. Enjoy.

NOTES

NOTES

NOTES

NOTES

NOTES

DAY 151
(Lesson 151)

"All things are echoes of the Voice for God."

(W-pI.151.1)

As I read the lesson, I am filled with thoughts about recent events in a Florida nightclub known for its welcoming atmosphere of intersectionality. People come to be who they are and find acceptance, comfort, and unity.

A few nights ago, a lone, confused individual with hate in his heart, opened fire in the nightclub killing fifty human beings. Opinions of judgments and of outrage fill the airwaves. Perhaps this individual thought killing the perceived object of his hate was the way to irradiate the pain he felt inside.

But isn't that what we do every time we judge our brother—a mini crucifixion of sorts—for both of us? That's the best the ego has to offer. It wears a million disguises to cloak its judgments so we won't see the damage we are causing to the children of love.

But blessedly, I see another thing is happening as well. From the wreckage a phoenix rises. From all corners of the globe, the hand of love reaches out. I see the blinding light of reality cracking open the collective heart like the break of a new dawn in the whole-mind we share—a call for love deep within the heart of humankind. A reaching out and drawing together, suspending our former prejudices, and comfort zones.

What is it in us that rises up, extending love and comfort, if not the echo of the Voice for God within us?

Love is the way we walk in gratitude at times like this. Thousands are giving blood for the victims. Tens of thousands are holding vigils for peace and forgiveness. In times of crises like these, the truth in us is given the freedom to lead. We forget our petty self and let the Christ in us shine through.

We forget our defensive, stingy self and reach out—we clean wounds, we carry water, give blood, offer our homes for temporary lodging. We give the shirt off our back. Deep within, we know our brother is our Self. At our heart, we know *"All things are echoes of the Voice for God."*

The echo reverberating in so many hearts creates laser focus for me. I'm looking into the heart of everyone that crosses my path. "This is my brother showing me the truth of my Self." Why wouldn't I love her with all my heart? I want to see, to catch your eye and let my smile express Christ love. I want to share my gratitude for each encounter. I'll give you the shirt off my back. If you need it, that is why I am wearing it.

Each day and every encounter, the Voice of Love is calling us to hear and extend. But it is impossible to hear in an atmosphere of judgment. Judgment is a delusion that we know what we are incapable of knowing in this realm of perception. It renders us deaf to hearing the truth we must hear from our brother to accept forgiveness and forgive.

The lesson says, *"Refrain from judging, not because it is a right to be withheld from you. You cannot judge."* We can believe the ego's lies and false witnesses, disguised as a complete picture. But we always know that something's off. We feel the fragment of falsehood in our mind. Something's not right. We can't truly judge, for we cannot judge truly.

Honestly, we never have all the information, past, present, and future, by which to judge. Deep within each of us, a true heart beats the echo of the Voice for God. By practicing being still an instant and listening for the truth, we fine-tune to the Divine Heartbeat present in all things—the *echo of the Voice for God* and learn of Its presence in all things.

CHAPTER ONE HUNDRED SIXTEEN

DAY 152

(Lesson 152)

"The power of decision is my own."

(W-pl.152.1)

With today's lesson we must get clear on one thing; our world experience, be it suffering, failure, loss, threat, conflict, or peace, harmony, acceptance, joy, love, and union, comes from our decision alone. We must accept responsibility for it all—our thoughts, feelings, sensations, relationships, and events. The course tells us nothing happens to us but by our choice.

"I am responsible for what I see. I choose the feelings I would experience, and I decide upon the goal I would achieve. And everything that seems to happen to me I ask for and receive as I have asked" (T-21.III).

I am responsible for what I see and experience. Suffering is a choice. Happiness, hate, worry, sickness, health. Each decision, no matter how seemingly small, is ultimately a decision for truth or illusion. It's uncompromising. Choosing one blocks the possibility of the other from our awareness. Love or fear, pain or joy, judgment or freedom, each decision brings an experience.

Each decision is uncompromising, all or nothing. Only the truth is true and nothing but the truth is true. Only perception sees variables. And perception is not a fact. Today we decide for the truth alone, declaring, *"The power of decision is my own. This day I will accept myself as what my Father's Will created me to be."*

Today's idea is at the heart of transformation in my life. It was a single decision I made that changed the course of my life entirely—deciding to keep an appointment with God first thing every morning, come hell or high water.

In over thirty years, I have never questioned the validity of that decision, nor considered not doing it. When my mentor, Betty, suggested I set an appointment with God first thing in the morning and keep it, I experienced something powerful move deep within and without hesitation, I said, "Yes." It was the first real decision I remember making in my life.

Every so-called decision prior was based in fear and subject to influence. But something in me recognized the holiness and power of this decision to begin my day with the Divine. It was a decision without an alternative. I sensed its magnitude even as I prayed I would have the courage to honor it. I decided without question and, doing so, it came easily. It was a pure act of faith. Little did I know what I was signing up for. My whole belief system around God had to go. It didn't fit in the room with the holiness of my decision.

Early each morning I awake with a delicious feeling of eagerness to meet myself anew—to see what God sees. To dump my fears on the altar of this sacred space and let myself be renewed. Here, I know I am love, loved, and loving. This decision was my first real act of self-love. It is undeniable witness to the power of decision being mine. *"The power of decision is my own. This day I will accept myself as what my Father's Will created me to be."*

From the decision for truth, to accept our station as co-creators of the universe, a new dimension of experience opens up. By our decision, the world is made. As we take responsibility for the magnificent power that resides with us as Children of God, we banish the idea of "victim" from our experience. We have the power to change everything. Right now. Hallelujah!

DAY 153

(Lesson 153)

"In my defenselessness my safety lies."

(W-pl.153.1)

Practicing today's lesson proves itself out. We say yes to truth and accept our place amongst the ministers of God, and today's lesson reads like a blueprint. It says salvation is the happy game. I love that. It's like the instructions are laid out right before me.

We cannot defend the ego identity and play the happy game. I like to keep it simple. Don't blame, complain, or explain. That's the ego's game. These are defenses that reinforce attack in my mind. *"In my defenselessness my safety lies."* Whenever we are defending, we are saying that a thing outside of us has the power. We are placing our faith and our power in something outside of us to hurt us.

We have the power of the universe behind every decision we make, so if we choose defense, we have already attacked our state of mind.

Defensiveness is a deadly game, like blinders shutting us off from seeing with the eyes of love. It blocks the awareness of the love we are from our mind, placing it in a state of unreality characterized by terror so complete it must be covered over with layers of stories of tolerability to make it bearable.

Truth needs no defense. It stands untarnished by belief or false ideas we made up. When we defend, we only defend illusions. But in defenselessness, we access the strength of Christ in us, which we learn to rely on instead. Defenselessness changes life entirely. What is it I defend against? Everything is me.

Defenselessness is aligning with salvation. It is the shift away from being a character in the dream world, to recognizing that I am the dreamer of the dream.

Today I do what the lesson suggests and make a game of it. Right away I notice a sort of prep-conversation in my mind for an anticipated meeting with a friend, later in the day. I laugh, "Hey, girl, already pre-defending? Open your heart, spread the joy!"

I want to be available to be a conscious giving and receiving channel for divine union. My meeting with her begins with her asking me why I hadn't called her until yesterday. My heart speeds up, tightening and creating an invisible barrier between us. Defensiveness.

It's fun to notice, I have a choice. I take a breath and smile. On the outbreath I silently choose into my lesson, *"In my defenselessness my safety lies,"* opening my heart, joy spilling off my lips as I say, "I'm so happy to see you, Breda," and draw her into a warm embrace. I recognize her call for love, and it is to that which I respond.

From defenselessness, I happily join with her, extending love, and she responds in kind—the issue forgiven in the blink of an eye. I'm not surprised when she shares a miracle she experienced in a conversation she had with her partner, where she quit defending and just listened to what he was saying. Dedicated to see innocence where she had blamed before.

Sharing this space opened by defenselessness frees us to be faithful to our essential nature. And joy is the result. It is a choice. The decision is uncompromising. Sleep or awake.

DAY 154

(Lesson 154)

"I am among the ministers of God."

(W-pI.154.1)

My first few years with *A Course in Miracles* were dynamic with practicing the principles. I was teaching every day with clients, facilitating workshops, and doing individual and group counseling. And the course naturally became part of it, as I practiced it in my own life. Also, a lot of the staff got into the course, and we had lively conversations about meaning and application. I thought I understood what being a minister of God was. I felt like one.

I also felt I had an example to set—something about that idea haunted me. What is the difference between being an example and setting one? Ego. I am grateful for this haunting question because it kept me watching my mind and trying to be sincere in my practice. It required me to show up every day and question my motives.

Ultimately, the question answered itself as I reinforced my commitment to be the message and let the Divine move through me in thought, word, feelings, and action. The days I felt aligned and honest multiplied. I began to see you are me, and that I needed to give the Word—the happy news of forgiveness, healing, and wholeness, for me to receive the Word of God and know my Self. I felt the practice and my life reflected it.

But years later, all this understanding came into question. When we moved to Albuquerque, I wasn't "teaching" in any classic way. I had moments of what felt like vibrant recognition, but without the context and setting for teaching, I felt insecure as to my ministry.

I love how the Divine works in my life. Having spent years unlearning most of what I taught myself through my practice with the course, I knew it's value. In this new setting, I followed Cole and Parker's lead for learning and didn't enroll them in the school system.

Turns out, there's a name for child-led learning—unschooling. Perfect! But as we began to network with other unschooling families, I felt separate from all the gossipy moms—better than. I didn't like it. I knew I was misinterpreting, defending against union—justifying withdrawal. I needed to turn the dial. I asked to see it differently.

At the next gathering, while reading a book called "Outliers," with a group of unschooling moms and kids, the part about ten thousand hours of practicing triggered something in me.

I'd not been practicing being a minister of God as an unschooling mom. No wonder I feel separate from them. I'm experiencing what I am giving—judgment. If I am not true to my ministry, how can I expect to see the truth in these moms?

Every situation, no matter how seemingly mundane, is the perfect environment to be the message—to be and speak only the truth of what I am. It's a eureka moment! Today's lesson appears like a flashing light in my mind. *"You are appointed now, and yet you wait to give the messages you have received."* So, what am I waiting for? There is no future happiness. The decision for heaven is now.

I silently make my declaration, *"I am among the ministers of God, and I am grateful that I have the means by which to recognize that I am free."* And just like that, I sign on the invisible line. I am a minister of God, and that is why I am here. Period. I am giddy. The barrier I'd placed between us dissolves.

I look around the classroom of my life—my ministry. From the light beam of love bursting from my awareness, I catch the eye of each mom, rising in love with her. The group metamorphoses before me. As self-proclaimed unschooling families, we are willing to see things differently—inviting life's mysteries to teach and learn. Together, we are trusting our children, ourselves, and each other. From this clean slate, I begin a genuine conversation.

CHAPTER ONE HUNDRED NINETEEN

DAY 155

(Lesson 155)

"I will step back and let Him lead the way."

(W-pl.155.1)

"There is a way of living in the world that is not here, although it seems to be. You do not change appearance, though you smile more frequently. Your forehead is serene; your eyes are quiet. And the ones who walk the world as you do recognize their own. Yet those who have not yet perceived the way will recognize you also, and believe that you are like them, as you were before."

(W-pII.155.1.1–3)

All roads ultimately lead to the awareness of our Divine Self—one with God. We have chosen the direct path of awakening. The road of fear, guilt, deprivation, and despair lead nowhere. They step back, as we allow the truth in us to come forth. We step back and let Christ in us step forth.

We let truth use our lips, our hearts, our hands, and feet. We're led to the next right thing say or do, one holy encounter at a time. What's so compelling about this lesson is that it seems to take place in the same old world. But we aren't engaging and getting tangled up in it anymore. A light goes before us. We are a bridge for those who are confused and suffering, even though they might not even realize how much they are suffering.

I have an appointment with my aesthetician today. As I get ready to go, I feel the shadow of the old shame arise whenever I needed to see a specialist—silly proof of my failure or weakness.

Breathing in recognition, I let gratitude step forth now, disbanding the shadow. Love is the way I walk in gratitude. I step back and let love lead the way. Light goes before me, clarifying my path. It's fun. I just be my Self! Joy is my default setting offering a light that leads others out of the dream, just as others have done for me.

When I walk in, the gals in the front office rise from their seats at the front desk, anticipating the hugs and joy we will exchange. I've been here often in the past few months and light has been left in my wake. Our union is holy ground. One gal says, "We're just waiting for you to come and get our fix of yumminess for today." I love it!

Another gal says, "I want to show you something." In her office she has little post-it notes scattered around the room with things she'd heard me say in conversation. "If it doesn't feel yummy, you're off the mark—turn the dial." "Love is always the answer." "Be happy, first. What's the downside?" "Everything goes my way!"—Stuff I say all the time.

It's the most natural thing in the world for me. I love. I am happy. I am a spark of joy. It's why I'm here. My presence invites the Self we share to step forward, shaping our encounter.

No encounter is by chance. It doesn't matter what the context on the world stage of our life is. The goal is God. The purpose of the encounter reveals itself as we step back from the context—work, doctor's visit, or party. We're here to be a light of truth—to see our brother as he really is—divine.

We're here to represent the truth—to be a message of peace—the eye of light in the storm of darkness and confusion. We need not worry about what to say because we trust it will be the right thing—we step back and let the Voice for Truth step forward.

CHAPTER ONE HUNDRED TWENTY
DAY 156
(Lesson 156)

"I walk with God in perfect holiness."

(W-pI.156.1)

Today's lesson reads like divine poetry. Reading it and taking the words to heart resonates with the magnificence we are within. It is one of my favorite lessons. I return to it and read it often—like a love letter to myself.

Who we are has not left the mind and heart which created us—all that we are is this Holy God-stuff. We cannot leave our Source. In truth, we walk with God in perfect holiness. The question today's lesson is asking us to pay attention to is, "Am I walking in the light of this truth about myself and in reverence to all creation as the same big-ass love?"

Or am I walking with a heavy heart filled with guilt and worry motivating my choices? Who walks with me? Is it ego or God? Is it holiness or sin/guilt sponsoring my choice? We walk with the state of mind we choose. And most of the time we make that choice unconsciously.

That's why today's lesson is so powerful. It says we should ask this question a thousand times a day until doubt has ended and peace has been reestablished! The ego mind can get real sneaky with its "good for me" disguises. Like, you should . . . you ought to . . . this would help . . . If I don't check in and honestly ask, "Who walks with me in this choice?" I can be off and running and actually distracting myself from seeing they are motivated by a belief in lack.

Here's the thing though, without fail, every single time I pause and ask, I zero back to what I really want and who I really am. Joy and love. Period.

Here's an example of the sneaky "good for me" interference my mind gets up to. I'm just brushing my teeth a few minutes ago, and I notice a pressing thought, "I've got to get my yoga session in." Seems innocent, right?

A pressing thought is different than being inspired into action naturally. It comes from a belief in loss. Luckily I've got today's lesson in my mind, so I notice the texture of this idea around my yoga practice. I pause and ask, "Who walks with me?" It's guilt that is pressing me toward my yoga practice this morning. "If I miss my practice this morning, I'll feel shitty about it later."

That is not what I want to accompany me in my yoga practice. I step back, and holiness naturally steps forth in response. In gratitude I say, *"I walk with God in perfect holiness,"* and begin my yoga session.

Yoga is holy ground. It is a devotion which unites my will with Divine Will, igniting the inner fire of miracle-mindedness. It is an expression of love, allowing my inner being to express through my body. Yoga is embracing the inner light with each posture and extending it with each movement.

I let holiness move me, relaxing into the natural ease that comes when resistance is let go. Like my morning coffee with the Divine anchors my mind it the truth of what I am as God created me—love. Yoga, when practiced from holiness, sets the stage for miracle-minded action throughout the day.

After yoga, I open the sliding doors and step out on the back patio, breathing in the crisp morning air. The sun is rising, and the sky is luminous in pink and coral hues in an infinite sky of silence—melding with my inner-state. Each heartbeat, like a butterfly's wing, sends ripples of creation, altering the scene ever-so-slightly. *"I walk with God in perfect holiness. I light the world; I light my mind and all minds which God created one with me."*

DAY 157

(Lesson 157)

"Into His Presence would I enter now."

(W-pI.157.1)

Today we are invited into a direct experience of heaven—the Holy Instant, where time and form are temporarily forgotten and eternal joy indelibly alters the way we see. The term "His" is referring to the Christ consciousness, our Divine Self, one with God.

"Presence" is recognizing we live in God. The Christ in us has never left. As we leave the world of time and enter through heaven's door, our minds are lit with eternal love, so it alters the way we see and interact when we return to the world of time.

"Today we will embark upon a course you have not dreamed of. But the Holy One, the Giver of the happy dreams of life, Translator of perception into truth, the holy Guide to Heaven given you, has dreamed for you this journey which you make and start today, with the experience this day holds out to you to be your own."

These are the thoughts I take to heart in trust as I enter my morning session with God. I surrender into the sacred, in reverence for this holy entry, *"Into His Presence would I enter now."* It's like a Divine portal, transporting me to oneness, dissolving into the stillness, peace extending forever.

My inner pilot light is alive, awareness pulsating life itself. It sparkles with a trillion individual stars dissolving into the infinite sky of Holiness Itself. It is the Face of the Divine I recognize. Each sparking star, my Christ brothers, blending as one Face of Love. I am each star in the endless sky of love—bursting with indescribable joy and beauty, profoundly familiar. I am the experience—experiencing itself—the Home of Love and the fullness of eternal Now.

As I return to my person-self, the soundtrack of the Holy Instant plays in the background of my life. It changes the way I look at everyone and everything. It is as if everything is backlit with love, drawing my heart open. I want to share this experience of love I feel. I can't imagine what could move me from the center of joy which gives life to my world around me. Careful what you ask for, eh?

The wind is fierce today. When I get out of my car in a parking lot, my car door flies open dinging the car next to me. Shit! I'm just looking to see if it's left a mark when a guy jumps out and starts yelling. Holy crap, I can feel his breath on my face! He's calling me names and accusing me of doing it deliberately. My heart is racing, sending a rush of adrenaline through my body. Shit. I'm nearly shaking being so close to this fear and rage. I want to run or defend.

But, here's the thing. It's my mind. My brother is expressing the shame trapped in my belief in sin. I force a deep breath and let him talk, while silently inviting Spirit, *"Into His Presence would I enter now."* I see my brother's desperate call for love and recognize my own. I apologize, lightly touching his arm and looking directly into his eyes with the love I want and bless him with holiness. He stops yelling, and though it is apparent he can't receive right then, I do. What's more, I have a profound sense that this miracle will wait until he is ready.

It takes a few minutes for my body to calm down, but my heart is open. I naturally smile and the restless energy scatters in giggles of joy. Ha! This time, I remember to laugh at the absurdity of judgment and fear. I am buoyant with joy and gratitude, feeling totally blessed.

DAY 158

(Lesson 158)

"Today I learn to give as I receive."

(W-pl.158.1)

Today's lesson is saying that we already have within us the knowledge of truth, of our creation as given us by God and that we *will* have the experience of realization—the revelation of all knowledge and truth.

What we are concerned with in our curriculum is the waking up part. And the way we do that is by giving everyone what we want. Peace and happiness. Easy-peasy. Right?

Ultimately, we realize what we always want is what we really already have as children of God. *"Today we learn to give as we receive."* We're letting the veil be lifted from our eyes and see the light of Christ love in union with our own.

We practice today's idea with every encounter given us today. Not one encounter is random. Each has been planned perfectly for our awakening. To recognizing the truth of who we are, who our brother is, and our true relationship with God.

Today, we determine not to entertain judgments, victimhood, or try to figure stuff out. We look past the person and situation to the light within. This is our ministry. We are learning to give as we receive.

I think about sobriety. The first order of business is, I don't entertain thoughts about drinking. Period. I have no business there. Once I decided for sobriety, I simply don't go down avenues in my mind where drinking is an option.

Because I want sobriety like breath, I learned swiftly to look on everyone in AA meetings as brothers in sobriety, instead of suffering alcoholics. I have a clear intent to know the truth of what I am and to see that reflected in those around me.

So, when someone starts spewing about their sickness, I look beyond it, holding them in the light of sobriety. It feels wonderful, and that's the confirmation. I love them instantly.

I use sobriety as an example because it's easy to follow the logic of why the sober alcoholic has no business romancing ideas of drinking, right?

It's the same with everything. Tough, I admit, my mind can get up to some pretty confusing and layered justifications to get me to deny the simplicity of salvation.

Like the phone call from my sister this morning. She starts by asking me what my schedule is on an upcoming weekend. Immediately I feel defensive—I am being set up. Why doesn't she just ask for what she wants? But rather than give what I have received, I throw it back on her. I say, "Why do you want to know?" Make her take responsibility.

It feels shitty. I can feel the tightening of my heart in a defensive, accusatory squeeze, so I know I'm off the mark. I back-peddle and tell her I'll call her back. I need to be still a minute and listen for the truth. I let my mind go quiet and open my heart.

Today's lesson is the perfect flip-switch. *"Today I learn to give as I have received."* What do I want? Love. Acceptance. Generosity of spirit. I want to see her, myself and the situation with Christ's vision. I step back and invite divinity to step forth. Instantly, I forgive.

I ring her back. I cop to my dishonesty and share how I let judgment confuse our previous exchange. I tell her I would love to get together when she comes to town. I do. Our new encounter is alive with the miracles. *Today, I learn to give as I have received.*

DAY 159

(Lesson 159)

"I give the miracles I have received."

(W-pI.159.1)

Today I had a beautiful holy encounter at a gathering. A gal I've seen before but never talked to approaches me. She asks if she can ask me something. Of course. She says, "Have you accepted Jesus Christ as your personal lord and savior?" I chuckle, "Why do you ask?"

"It's the way you talk with such certainty that you are being guided in everything you do," she says. "I've heard you say that you look for the Christ light in everyone. So, being born again, myself . . ." "Ah," I say. "Yes, I try to look for the Christ—the spark of love, which is our true nature, in everyone I meet or think of. Love is my ministry."

"But are you a born-again Christian?" she asks. "I accepted Jesus Christ as my lord and savior on February third of last year. But I don't think I feel it like you do." Ha! She's looking for a meeting place to accept that she and I are one. I tell her that no, I'm not a born-again Christian, in the traditional sense.

I say, "I accept Christ as my savior, just like I accept you as my savior. How I see you is how I see myself. When I see your innocence and perfection and remember my own. Like Jesus did and held the light for us to follow." She says, "So you don't call yourself a Christian?"

I tell her I'm not into labels—that labels tend to separate, and I am looking to join. I say, "For me, it is a matter of trust. I believe anyone I meet already has Christ within them and our meeting is a holy encounter—a chance for a miracle. Like you and me right now. It's no accident that we are having this conversation." I get it. The message comes through me as I speak, I receive and give the miracle simultaneously.

It's funny because a few years ago I had a similar encounter and it went entirely differently. This guy asked me if I had accepted Jesus as my personal lord and savior. I got defensive and tried to convince him that he was seeing it all wrong. That Jesus didn't want us to put him on a pedestal, but to be like him. I got up on my self-righteous-high-horse and missed the chance to join, completely.

We both left the encounter frustrated and disconnected. I think of him now, calling his face to mind, forgiving our mis-encounter of past and join with him, in present love, blessing him in gratitude for his holiness and mine. *"Christ's vision is the bridge between the worlds. And in its power can you safely trust to carry you from this world into one made holy by forgiveness."*

How we experience the miracles that will transform our perception is to give the miracle we would have. We already have them, they were given by God through our Holy mind, where we awaken the Vision of Christ within. Once glimpsed, we are inspired and naturally desire to share the attributes of heaven we have glimpsed.

We intuitively realize this is how we bring forth the full realization of the truth within us and transform the world. If I want peace, I give peace. If I want joy, I am joyous, it radiates from me and draws others into joy. We must give to know that we have received.

This is the law of mind. What I give is given to myself. Love gives unto itself. Whatever it is that we seem to be missing, be it love, safety, peace, abundance, forgiveness—this is what we give. Our giving unveils the miracle we have obscured from our awareness, and we experience its presence in our lives.

DAY 160

(Lesson 160)

"I am at home. Fear is the stranger here."

(W-pl.160.1)

I am at home. Fear is the stranger here." Fear is like a madman that sneaks into our mind and starts coloring everything black. The stranger is the ego; the part of our mind that's always trying to convince us we're something we are not. It's like living with a bitchy, judgmental stranger. But it's in our head.

I used to always say, "If someone said the things I say to myself to me, I wouldn't put up with it. I'd walk away out of self-preservation, as an act of love." Really? Like that wasn't exactly what *I* was doing?

As I learned to watch my mind carefully, I realized there *is* a stranger saying horrible things to me. And I believed it was myself. It is the voice of fear and hatred in my mind, and it was all about my unworthiness. Fear is a liar. So why listen to it? Why pay it any attention? Because I invited it. And in by listening to it and believing its lies, I mistook it for myself. I had a habit of going to it for counsel. It was old-familiar. Yuck!

The sweet thing is, through the mind-training, we learn to listen beneath the noise of this imposter. To lean in close to our heart and listen to the ever-present whisper of another voice. This voice speaks to us in loving tones. It reminds us of our holy worthiness as a child of God. It is gentle and loving, generous and forgiving. It speaks of our innocence, our natural lovability.

It reminds us what seems to be the other, is brother, innocent and one with me. It is honest. This is the voice of our true Self—the truth within our own mind. We feel it in our heart.

Once we recognize our true voice, there's no going back—not for long. Fear is not in control of our mind. It relies on our consent. It is a matter of what we want and only what we want. We want God. We want to know our Self. We want to love. We want joy and happiness as our home. We are tuning in, engaging with this True Voice. The Voice of Love—of God. We are at home. Fear is the stranger here.

We don't let the stranger take up residence for long anymore. Fear and love cannot occupy the same place at same time. It takes earnest willingness to think with love—no matter what. We're practicing wholeheartedness.

My tolerance for the shitty voice, for discomfort, is super low. I can tell by the way I feel—icky! When I doze off and the stranger steps in, joy leaves. Period. That's the flip-switch. Love is my home; fear is the stranger here.

I am committed to joy. I like feeling good. Loving feels good. So, it takes little for me to realize I've missed the mark and zero back into God. Love—this is home. Fear is not.

When fear tries to take up residence, I simply get quiet and listen to the awareness of love, whispering softly of my innocence and beauty. I think of God and the love that we are. I anchor in the stillness, letting the awareness of love fill my being with truth, allowing all things to be exactly as they are. I shift from icky to yummy. From pain to joy.

God *is* with us. There is *nothing* to fear. Love is what we are. *"This is my home. Here I belong and will not leave because a madman says I must."*

DAY 161

(Lesson 161)

"Give me your blessing, holy Son of God."
(W-pI.161.1)

Today we take a stand against our anger, letting fear dissolve as we make room for only love. We stand with the Christ in us and bless and allow blessing. The exercises for today give us a chance to experience a transformation in consciousness from specifics to unified or abstract vision—Christ vision.

The holy spirit uses what we give over, translates sin to holiness and serves it back to us in its purified form. The forms, bodies, and circumstance in our day become the gateway to a state beyond form, a way of seeing from the awareness of abstract truth, which is our one mind. Our holiness looks beyond form, unveiling a magnificent tapestry of one-life.

The political scene right now is fertile ground for my lesson practice today. It is an election year, and neither of the top candidates is, well, what I want to put my vote behind. It's a topic ready-made for my high horse.

Lin and I are listening to a broadcast with the female candidate, who could likely be the first female and the next president, and I've got that righteous, angry buzz going. It's like a virus running through my veins. I can't keep it inside.

I discharge it with my words. "She isn't representing women. She isn't even representing the American people. She is representing big corporate money. She's totally contradicting what she said just months ago. She's a damn smart con artist, just like he is, but with a different coat of colors!"

Righteous judgment projected out only makes me feel small, separate, and out of my integrity. Shitty! Now, I feel personally affronted by this woman. I want her to be something different as a woman representing me. My heart tightens into a little rock.

My energy is pulled in on itself, separating me from her and from Lin, who seems unaffected. In fact, she's in support of this woman being president.

Lin calmly turns toward me. In her eyes, I see my innocent, forgiven self. I receive her blessing.

She shares how she recognizes there have been inconsistencies in the woman's position, but she sees this as an ability to adapt to the needs of the people. Lin sees her strong points. Go figure.

Lin is the voice of reason—and for me, an angel of mercy. Her calm invites me to look within and get honest. Why am I feeling threatened? Who is the self that feels threatened? I think of how the course says everything I see is a witness to the thought system I want to be true. That every brother has the power to release me if I choose. Ha! That's my flip-switch.

I let my mind go quiet and my heart still. I am willing to see this differently. I engage my lesson, looking back at the woman on the screen. Silently I say, *"Give me your blessing, holy Son of God. I would behold you with the eyes of Christ and see my perfect sinlessness in you."* I slide off my high-horse and into the awareness of love. My heart opens. I realize I've been making up a political drama where my true-identity is under attack. Activating into anger at nothing—a silly crazy dream. And poof! It's gone.

Sanity has returned. Now, I let the Christ in me interpret for me and look straight into the heart she and I share. It's like she transforms before eyes. I see her light, her innocence, and the strength of God in her. I forgive her what she never did, along with myself. Dang! I'm honestly grateful to her now. The encounter has been transformed to holiness. Lin sits smiling next to me and takes my hand.

DAY 162

(Lesson 162)

"I am as God created me."

(W-pI.162.1)

I am as God created me." This, in case you're asking, is the word of God. The lesson tells us that this single thought, held firmly in our mind, would save the world. Imagine. Remember that the world we see is nothing more than a reflection of our cherished thoughts. How many are, *"I am as God created me?"*

Truth and illusion simply cannot occupy the same space. Practicing today's idea teaches us to think with God—to recognize our divinity, inviting Christ vision. The light dawns, and we are filled with a genuine desire to extend that light and blessing.

Reminding ourselves, "We are as God created us," is a practice to commit to habit. If I'm experiencing a disturbance to my peace of mind, this is the zero point! I say, "Wait a minute. *I am as God created me.* So, what's the problem?" It is an instant portal to truth and the peace of God.

Meditating on *"I am as God created me,"* I let it fill my mind, dissolving all other thoughts about what I am, and my life is. And in the pristine stillness, I am filled with overwhelming love. Joy radiates from the center of my being like rays of light emanating from a star. I rest in the delicious freedom from which all manifest life arises. I am given one directive to go forth. *"I am as God created me. Be that!"*

As I rise, I feel inspired to take a road trip in my new little IQ car as a sort of emissary for the Word of God. I am the message. My state of being the call to others to recognize our shared identity as love. I feel a power and presence so grand that considering not going seems ridiculous. I put myself in the hands of the Divine with no firm plan on where to go or what to do, only today's lesson at the helm.

But as I put the key in the ignition, fear creeps in. What awaits me on the unknown open road? I place my hand on my heart. The fear dislodges and dissolves—forgiven, as I recall my mission statement: I am as God created me! I am ready. I take out a marker and write *"I am as God created me,"* on the rear-view mirror and start my car.

About an hour into my trip, rain downpours in waves. It feels like my little car is in a storm at sea. Shit. My breath is shallow—fear. I don't want to get washed off the road. The next breath I take is deep, reaching into the space of freedom beyond form.

From the corner of my eye, in bold letters, the Holy One speaks from my rearview mirror, *"I am as God created me."* Like the eye of the storm, I breathe it deeply, feeling the presence and power of my identity. I am completely safe and loved. There is nothing to fear. God is with me.

And no shit! Like two seconds later, I am surrounded by semi-trucks on all sides. It's like the parting of the red sea! The path before me clears, and my trucker angels usher me through the rain till the sun breaks through.

The entire trip is blessed with this certainty. I intuitively know where to go, who to talk to, and what to do. As an emissary of love each encounter is all encounters with my holy Self as God created us one.

CHAPTER ONE HUNDRED TWENTY-SEVEN

DAY 163

(Lesson 163)

"There is no death. The Son of God is free."
(W-pI.162.1)

Today we look meticulously at what death really is—the mental construct of separation. So, we're not talking about the eventual termination of the body.

Each time we look on a brother or on our lives with a lack of love, we block the awareness of love's presence. That is the death script. Death is merely an idea in the mind opposite to love, and life eternal. We're looking at all the ways this death idea takes countless forms we may not recognize as death thoughts—fear, loss, anger, competition, depression or weakness are all death's prison. Each grievance is a jailer of both our brother and ourselves.

Life is love everlasting. Today we look past judgments to life beyond. To what we still cherish more than life eternal. We don't have to look far. We see it in every glitch to our love/joy matrix. So, what'll it be? Death or life eternal—joy, happiness, peace, and love for all creation? All or nothing. It's one or the other. Period. So be honest. Are we ready to let death be banished in all its forms?

Funny how these lessons show up at the perfect time. Or, as I like to say, "Is it odd or is it God?" As I've mentioned before, I had a reoccurring death script that reared its ugly head a lot while I lived in Albuquerque.

One morning, while visiting Santa Fe, a neighboring town of Albuquerque, with my sister Lyn, today's lesson shows up. The day before, we checked out the yummy artist community in Santa Fe and I'd been comparing its loveliness with what I thought was missing in Albuquerque. These comparisons cast a gray hue over everything—separating me from feeling the Divine alive in each moment.

It's sneaky, the way death ideas hang out in my mind. Like saying how I don't like Albuquerque. I miss Vegas. That was my story and I was sticking to it! What makes it all the more comical, is that while in Albuquerque, I experienced an astounding abundance of miracles and holy relationships!

The thing is, with this death script of dissatisfaction imbedded beneath the surface, they'd been clouded over waiting to be grokked fully. "I don't like Albuquerque." So, it's like all the yummy stuff gets sequestered to the waiting room when death thoughts occupy my mind. Miracles can only be seen in light. It's like I get temporary amnesia of my "real" life brilliant with miracles. This death idea robs me of access to the present glorious moments where I love what *is*—exactly as it is.

So, Lyn and I are having this conversation. She's like the clear mirror reflecting what I really want to see. I'm telling my Albuquerque death story, and she calls me back to today's lesson. *"There is no death. The Son of God is free."* And boo-yah! I see it all clearly like I never have before.

I laugh. "Ha! My story on Albuquerque is death. There is no death. I renounce it now. I take my stand with life, with love. I love Albuquerque, right now this minute, all past and future moments, I love."

And just like that, I am alive with love for Albuquerque, and all the yummy miracles and experiences are vibrant in my mind.

DAY 164

(Lesson 164)

"Now are we one with Him Who is our Source."

(W-pl.164.1)

Today, we practice the Holy Instant. We are ready. We enter our holy mind and *"open a curtain in [our] practicing"* today. We review all the things we think we want and recognize them as *"trifling treasures"* and let them go. We just let them slip from our attention, leaving *"a clean and open space within our mind where Christ can come, and offer [us] the treasure of salvation."* This is today's practice.

We pull back the curtain of the story, and open to life eternal, the present moment—the presence of God. *"Now we are one with Him Who is our Source."* We stand in pristine truth with what actually is, and fantasies slip away. It's not an "altered" state. It is actually the unaltered state. It is mind awake. It is holy. It is simply being awake to what is, and nothing else.

Today's lesson shows up one day while I'm at a training as a rebirth practitioner. Rebirthing is a therapeutic technique using conscious connected breath to bring up fearful thoughts and memories we've suppressed and release them through the breath while holding love thoughts in our mind.

One exercise is a cold-water rebirth. It's done in a mountain stream still laced with snow. It's f**king cold—which is hell, in my book. The idea behind this cold-water rebirth is to clear the death-script or body-identity script. Hell yes!

So, I'm in this icy water, and I can hardly breathe. I choose my lesson as my love thought and I declare it as I tiptoe into the mountain stream, reaching to know my oneness with my Creator. *"Now we are one with Him who is our Source."*

My body betrays my desire, contracting, shivering, making me gasp. Everything in me resists being here—being present. I reach for my little willingness. It is enough. I lay my body down and emerge myself in the icy water, following my breath as instructed—in and out in a connected circle. In and out, silently repeating my lesson with each cycle of breath. It is the circle of life. I give myself to the icy water, the eternal moment, life itself, and surrender completely to the impossible.

I abandon myself to the inevitable and let myself receive, leaning into my faith in the Divine to deliver me from the impossible to infinite possibility. My little willingness is a portal to amazing freedom beyond my body, where I locate my divine self. And though I still fully know of the body's agony, I rest my mind in awareness beyond the body. Now, there is only the breath of life, in and out, carrying me into this incredible state of present peace—the ocean of infinite Divine Oneness.

And no shit! I'm warm! It's incredible. The water literally warms around me. I am the water—*"one with Him Who is our Source."* It's a holy instant of eternal peace and present truth. Warmth surrounds me in the arms of divine love. And I am that. I am part of the divine flow, eternally sourced by love—*"One with Him Who is our Source."*

DAY 165

(Lesson 165)

"Let not my mind deny the Thought of God."
(W-pl.165.1)

It is now we must change our mind, stop denying the Thought of God that gives us life, and hold to what we really want in truth. When we want only truth, we have it. It is already ours. When we stop denying the thought of God, we realize it is already in our mind.

I like to keep it simple. Think of God! Have you ever tried to hold a grievance and the Thought of God simultaneously? It doesn't work. Think of God and joy is present, peace and calm assurance are present. We show up. We ask for heaven. We think of God. His certainty suffices.

The instant we no longer deny it by believing illusions, truth comes quietly into our mind, awakening what lay sleeping. The groovy thing about the mind-training is that each day and lesson builds on the next and our minds are slowly changed.

We begin to let go of what we thought was real as we have an experience of reality beyond our beliefs. We start to see all the forms of separation for what they really are—a defense against recognizing our eternal union with God. And we open our minds to the truth we are in heaven now and never left.

Maybe you can relate to this. I'm doing the lessons religiously, and I have these brilliant experiences of release. But then I absentmindedly start running my life again, and some seeming catastrophe happens, and I'm right back trying to fix something and control the outcome.

Today's lesson shows up in the nick of time on the second day of a weekend workshop we're doing at the Vision Center. The previous day, one participant is fixated on a recent breakup and can't focus on the workshop or reason she'd signed up for it. I want her to get onboard. I've got plans for how the workshop is supposed to go.

To keep these plans, I take her aside, on break, trying to squeeze her problem out so my solution can fit. My split focus messes with the flow of the workshop. I can feel it—the off-ness, the lack of synchronistic flow I'd come to count on throughout these workshops. But my mind is not available for the truth. I've got an agenda.

It's a restless night, and I wake even earlier than usual to the gentle tap of the Divine. I release myself and my workshop problem to the stillness and feel freedom's wings rise beneath me. I rest in the holiness of eternal love and peace. My eyes open and light on my open course book. Today's lesson practically jumps at me, like the big cosmic ha! *Let not my mind deny the Thought of God.*

I hadn't been thinking about God, only my agenda throughout yesterday's workshop. I call my participant to mind and place her in His hands. God's certainty suffices. I trust God to give all that is needed. I want only heaven for myself and the workshop participants. I exhale the control thoughts and breath in love's presence and the perfect outcome already in play.

My agenda for the workshop is replaced by trust. I reenter the workshop, with only God in my mind, in total trust. What's wild (miracle) is it's like the participant's mind is changed along with mine, the breakup all but forgotten. The workshop becomes a playground—a celebration in heaven.

CHAPTER ONE HUNDRED THIRTY

DAY 166

(Lesson 166)

"I am entrusted with the gifts of God."

(W-pI.166.1)

We think we know what will make us happy, what we need to happen or acquire to fulfill us, or at least dull the sense of absence, lack, fear, and scarcity we believe to be the truth of our lives. We are wrong. This we know too, for when we have achieved the desired, it doesn't satisfy—not for long. The drive for acquisition itself keeps us from letting the stillness show us it is unnecessary.

The stillness is surrounding and permeating us, infusing everything with life and the gifts of happiness as we realize our Self as God created us.

I grew up in a religious family. Ours was the "true church." There were expectations. Ha-ha. I wasn't a true believer. I tried to be. I felt too hungry, too needy, for the sacrifices required to make the grade. I tried to be good, kind, nice—do right. I always felt there was some secret I was supposed to know but didn't.

Prayers were canned and empty. I tried to live to the story I was given as a child. That story failed me. I became a pretender, and I felt like a fraud to my family. I couldn't seem to find the God of my childhood. I turned away in self-preservation. It was a relief. It was more honest.

Concurrently, like a whisper deep inside, I had a sense there was another God. One that loved me. One that wasn't making black marks on my record of life every time I got mad at my sister or didn't clean my room.

It was a secret haven unearned by me. My prayers with this God weren't like the ones I learned from church and family—the right way to pray, to show the proper respect and solicit notice.

These prayers were wordless and sort of slipped up behind me and held me in a feeling of safety at times when life around me was terrifying and hopeless. It's not like I was consciously aware of this at the time and knew I had this place to turn. It was just there, when everything else failed, as it always did.

Failure seemed to be the one constant in the story of me—when I believed I was alone. But something else kept my heart beating, kept me going. Like just out of my conscious reach, a whisper beckoned me to stop, quit looking without and turn within. The touch of Christ. I recognize it now—always present, always available—waiting for me. Always, entrusting me with the gifts of God.

Perhaps that's how it is for all of us. When our story life fails us, the façade cracks and the search for true happiness begins.

That's just what today's lesson is saying. We walk the world of lies, frightened and alone, believing there is a world where God is not, while all the love and joy we seek are already in us. Today, we turn around and realize what is already ours. We just need to unfold our arms, open our hearts, and accept. And the whole storehouse becomes available for us to give as we receive.

God's trust in us is total. Our will, in union with His, guarantees we will give these gifts where they are needed. We are learning to trust God's trust in us. We have faith that His touch becomes the touch of miracles we bring to the world. So really, what's the downside of trusting that if God entrusted us with His gifts, and it is His will that we bring them to the world, we must be worthy of them? We *become the living proof of what Christ's touch can offer everyone.*

DAY 167

(Lesson 167)

"There is one life, and that I share with God."

(W-pI.167.1)

Let's backtrack a minute and reflect on when we began the curriculum: Some guy pulls in front of us on the freeway and it feels personal. We actually think he did something to us. We believe that he is the cause of our upset.

As we get further into the mind-training: The guy pulls in front of us, and we feel upset, but we know we have a choice. We know that how we feel, and perceive a situation is totally up to us. We can literally choose to love the guy, feel generously open to let him in front of us, and give ourselves the gift of forgiveness, love, and generosity. And often, we do it. Because it feels good. Because we love ourselves and our brother who is one with us.

Now, at this stage: we know we're on the freeway to bring love and harmony, forgiveness and light. The other guy is us.

I love this stage of the mind-training. Our frequency is higher, lighter. We walk in faith that comes from the peace, joy, and miracles we have experienced. We have glimpsed the truth—recognizing that God is life, and we are part of that One Life—cut from the same cloth. We are developing trust. We're at a new level of accountability. We have decided for heaven.

When we doze off, and dream of sorrow, pain, and suffering, an alarm sounds in our mind, waking us quietly to the truth. We take responsibility for our minds because we have seen that our mind determines our experience.

Problems are the indicator to change our mind and choose with life instead of death, with the truth over illusion. We are choosing to be the face of love—the light in the darkness. To be happy and represent Him who sent us. To see the world through our holiness. See every encounter as holy.

It's about being awake to what's happening in our mind and taking responsibility for how we see and feel, and what we are offering to the world as a result. It's about being awake to now!

Today's lesson is saying we can use that realization to see where we are still dreaming separation/death. Like with this thing with my silly back. The instant I quit trying to figure out what happened, why it happened to me, and woke up to the alarm showing me that I had chosen to dream I am separate and on my own, I was back at choice. I choose life, the life I share with God. False ideas just can't hold form in the frequency of love. Now, I am awake to life—as love. God has my back!

Like the other day at the hospital. My phone starts ringing, and the ringtone is this awesome song by Jordan Smith, "Stand in the Light." The nurses attending ask me about it. In response, I play the song again and we all listen together. It's like we enter this prayer state together, just letting it wash over us.

We all want to stand in the light of the truth of who we are! We all have tears in our eyes, sharing something we each know deep within. I don't shy away from sharing truth in whatever way it's served up at the moment because I know it comes from the one life we share with God.

We open the door and play the song again, letting the light sing its melody out into the world. It's awesome! It's why I am at the hospital.

CHAPTER ONE HUNDRED THIRTY-TWO

DAY 168

(Lesson 168)

"Your grace is given me. I claim it now."

(W-pI.168.1)

Today is a day of conscious communication with God. It is not so much the words we use but a recognition of our divinity as God created us. We are looking at the ever-present grace which calls us to the memory of Him and His love for us.

What most of us have done with prayer is to bring our problems to God and ask for His will for us. But what we are learning through the mind-training is to let go of what we think we want, the interpretation we have placed on life, and enter God's frequency—into the peace and stillness where we can have an experience of His love, surety, safety, and joy.

Today, we are invited to claim God's grace, by acknowledging it is ours. An awesome thing happens when we dedicate time to get familiar with the stillness. We begin to realize that God is always communicating with us. It's just been covered over by the ruckus of our ego mind. But when we feel behind that to the stillness all around and in us, we feel His presence. That's communion.

My experience is that God's grace is always operating behind the scenes of my life, magnetically pulling the good, the true, the loving.

Here's an example of God's grace powerfully handling a situation. It's one of those times when Parker goes missing. We're at the skate park. Parker is about five at the time. Life is all about the adventure for Parker. He is fearless and is always bending the rules of time and space to accommodate his adventurous spirit.

Like skateboarding. We lived near the pro-park in Vegas. Parker loves doing tricks he sees the pros do, skating alongside them in the rotation, dropping into giant cement bowls and skating out. And that's the last time I'd seen him. I don't see him come out. I ask if anyone has seen him come out. No one has.

You can't see inside the bowl from the outside, only from the top. Time passes. As I walk over to the big bowl, my heartbeat speeds up. What if he's just laying at the bottom? Skaters are dropping in and skating out. I get to the top of the bowl and breathe in silent prayer, recalling my lesson, *"Your grace is given me. I claim it now."* Peace settles over me, assuring me everything will be all right. I look down in the bowl. He isn't there.

I notice an interesting dynamic. Although my mind starts spinning stories of potential catastrophe, my heart is calm. I ask the skaters at the bowl if they remember seeing him. Of course, they had. But none knew what happen to him. I whisper a silent prayer of gratitude for the certainty of grace I feel within. Which isn't like me.

In times like this, my prayers tend toward panic pleading, convinced of my fears and wanting God to do something about it—to fix things for me. Instead, I feel His grace with me—a powerful feeling that God already has this, and everything is truly okay.

There is a tap on my arm, bringing me out of my reverie. It's Parker. He's been helping a little kid learn to kick-flip on the sidewalk just outside the park. We do the happy dance of celebration for the grace that makes all things right.

DAY 169

(Lesson169)

"By grace I live. By grace I am released."

(W-pl.169.1)

Our ongoing forgiveness is how we clear the altar of our mind and prepare for grace to be known to us. Grace, the lesson tells us, is not learned, but is beyond learning, yet the aim of all our learning here. It comes to the mind that prepares itself for acceptance.

That is what we have been doing with our curriculum—clearing the false, preparing for the true. It is grace to leave the world an instant and communicate with God. With each holy instant where we enter the stillness and commune with God, we acknowledge His grace *is* ours.

So, as we venture back out into the world of seeming fear and loneliness, we bring our awareness of grace with us. We become the reflection of grace which lays the ground for miracles. We come to realize that we are living in the flow of grace, and we see the witness to it in every aspect of our lives. We live in a state reverence where the undercurrent is peace. God is.

I have a lovely experience of grace at the bank while waiting to talk to an account manager. In the waiting area with me are a young couple and an elderly couple. The elderly couple sits close, hands held. They frequently look fondly into each other's eyes. They are present. Their love is deep, constant, trusting, knowing. It exudes from them like a magnetic pull of contentment. The grace of God apparent.

The young couple is anxiously waiting to find out if they are approved for the loan for a new home. They're restless. Apparently, they had seen a loan officer and fear has taken up residency. Their conversation is disconnected. The wife, talking incessantly. The husband, aloof, plays a game on his phone, ignoring her anxiety. The wife tears up but tries to put on a brave face.

I give her a warm smile and a Kleenex, wearing the face of love I am, remembering and forgiving a self I once was in her. A silent prayer ticks in my heart, *"In grace I live. In grace I am released. In grace I give. In grace I will release."* I encircle the couple in my prayer, loving and blessing.

A minute later, the senior couple smile at each other and stand up. The older man sits next to the young man and strikes up a conversation. The older woman sits next to the young one. She takes her hand and strokes it gently. The young woman leans in, lets her tears spill and receives. I hear the wise man telling the young man of his gratitude for each and every day with his wife.

The women look up and listen, as I am. He says loan or no loan, he still has everything because he and his wife have each other. His wife speaks next. "We've been married for almost fifty years. Every day we tell each other we love and appreciate the other. That is what really matters. Everything else comes and goes." The young couple nod and smile at each other, clearly receiving this grace.

A minute later my name is called. As I walk past, I notice the young husband has taken his wife's hands in his. I hear him say, "Honey, no matter what, it's going to be okay. We have each other." Grace.

DAY 170

(Lesson 170)

"There is no cruelty in God and none in me."

(W-pI.170.1)

Today we address attack and defense from the place where we can finally lay the whole idea to rest. We've acknowledged that if we defend, we are attacked, and in our defenselessness, our safety lies, but today we are being asked to look at how we have made a false god of attack to keep ourselves safe.

We are looking at the premise on which the idea stands. It is fear. We think we are attacking what we believe will harm us, and that will keep us safe, forgetting attack originated within our own mind. We then project it on to the one to be attacked, effectively separating us from seeing our own responsibility for it. This makes attack seem justified—even loving to ourselves.

What we've done is give attack and cruelty the attributes of love. So actual love seems like a threat to us. This belief that "cruelty keeps us safe" becomes a false god in our mind that we don't want to question, believing it protects. And this gets projected onto our belief in what God is.

I love how this lesson comes up right now. Because we have said, we take our stand with God—with love. But are we still believing that certain things or people are wrong and that we need to defend against them in some way? Because all attack is an intent to hurt and that's cruelty. Be honest. Because right now we can be completely free from cruelty forever or keep believing there is something outside of us that can affect our peace of mind. Our choice.

I've had a particularly sticky place in my mind where I kept this idea tucked away, which is brought to the light with today lesson. When I see people treating their children with disrespect, I have this impulse to shame the mother or father into seeing that they are wrong.

So, today I'm at the grocery store, and a mother is shaming her child for crying and making a scene. I imagine walking up to her and saying something. You know, to rescue the child. I've done it before. Nobody gets saved there.

But, like groovy grace, my lesson flashes in my mind. *"There is no cruelty in God and none in me."* It's like a wave, and I'm released to a new dimension. I know what truly helps. I forgive my confusion that cruelty is love, grateful to see the error in my mind. I bless mother and child. I've been them both.

When I go to check-out, guess who's ahead of me in line? Yep. I'm astounded by the feeling of overwhelming love I have for this mother who has offered me release. The scene before me now, as I watch the mother and child, is filled with light—the Madonna and Christ child.

Suddenly, the child drops the mother's purse and starts crying. Mom and I both bend to pick it up. As we do, our eyes meet. Love and gratitude spill from my eyes, my mind washed clean of cruelty. Holiness is all I see. The child has stopped crying and is intently watching us. For the rest of the time in line, this mother and I talk about the gift of motherhood and how it is the best job in the world!

CHAPTER ONE HUNDRED THIRTY-FIVE

REVIEW V: DAYS 171–180

(Lessons 151–170)

Today begins the fifth review period in the curriculum. The introduction to the review invites us to intensify our practice. Let this review be one where we claim our hallowed identity, our wholeness now complete, as God established it. The thought which is to proceed and follow each of the two lessons we review is the ultimate truth of what we are as children of love. It is: *"God is but Love, and therefore so am I."*

The instructions say, *"This time we are ready to give more effort and more time to what we undertake. We recognize we are preparing for another phase of understanding. We would take this step completely, that we may go on again more certain, more sincere, with faith upheld more surely."*

Let's take an honest inquiry. How active is the mind-training in our moment to moment life? Are we basically practicing in earnest in the morning but unconscious of the lesson much of the day? Are we feeling divinity in what we are thinking, aligned with thoughts of God—with love, and making choices from that divinity? This review period is the chance to stayed tuned to God always—to experience ongoing Divine flow in every aspect of our lives. Our devotion is our gift of gratitude to God and the mind that gave this divine curriculum to us.

This is the prayer we repeat each morning throughout this review, which sets the day along the course love would have us go.

> *Steady our feet, our Father. Let our doubts be quiet and our holy minds be still and speak to us. We have no words to give to You. We would but listen to Your Word, and make it ours. Lead our practicing as does a father lead a little child along a way he does not understand. Yet does he follow, sure that he is safe because his father leads the way for him.*
>
> *So do we bring our practicing to You. And if we stumble, You will raise us up. If we forget the way, we count upon Your sure remembering. We wander off, but You will not forget to call us back. Quicken our footsteps now, that we may walk more certainly and quickly unto You. And we accept the Word You offer us to unify our practicing, as we review the thoughts that You have given us. (W-pI.V.2–3)*

This is an exciting time of deepening our resolve to remain aware of the love we are, created by Love.

You might want to make notes to refer to when the mind gets foggy. Write about the instances you forget and then remember. The experience of grace our surrender brings. Let this review work in you and through you, deepening your communion with Divinity.

NOTES

NOTES

NOTES

NOTES

NOTES

DAY 181
(Lesson 181)

"I trust my brothers, who are one with me."

(W-pl.181.1)

Today's lesson, *"I trust my brothers, who are one with me,"* we seek for innocence and nothing else. For the longest time I didn't trust myself as a mother, and of course, that played out in my life, in heartbreaking ways, such that I felt my children were better off without me. In my forgiveness of this false idea of myself, I surrendered motherhood, my children, and my future to the Divine. A kind of reformatting took place without my even realizing it.

Early one morning, after a long run in the woods in Ft. Lewis, Washington, where I was stationed during Desert Storm, I realized something had shifted in my mind where it came to trust. The sun was just peaking up over the horizon, casting rainbows across the beautiful green. I think of my children back in Utah with their father and know I am forgiven.

I realize I feel worthy of the grace I live each day—faith in God's plan for salvation—in myself, and my brothers. My children come to mind, and I pray, "I'd like the chance to experience myself a mom again. I trust I can honor that stewardship now—and to forgive when I get it wrong."

Little did I know the miracle activated that dawn. Within months, my tour of duty ended. Lin and Lucas came back to live with me, and I'm trusting Spirit is guiding me as a mom.

Today, I think of motherhood as my holy temple where forgiveness set me free and opened mind to an experience of reality in glorious, expansive, freedom and indescribable love.

Flash forward ten years. I now have Cole and Parker. I use my mind-training to stay true to this miracle called motherhood—forgiving mistakes and returning my mind to the Holy Spirit. The glitch happens around my relationship with Lar, and his with the boys. I feel powerless.

I resist taking responsibility for it. I blame and judge Lar. With my focus is on his imagined sins, my radar is on high alert, gathering evidence to justify my perception. I'd watch when he'd go into a room where the boys are and I'd decide he's just looking for something they are doing wrong so he can bully them to do things his way. I saw him as not having faith in the boys to live their lives and work out their values for themselves. This projection is excruciating, I know that ultimately the lack of trust is in myself.

This day, I want Christ vision more than I want to be right about my story. I realize today's lesson can undo this belief entirely if I will let it. I set my intent to see his sinlessness, to be present, refusing to let past interpretations or future goals to intrude on my recognition of innocence in myself and Lar.

Lar is in the game room gaming with the boys when I walk in. I feel the shadow of my trust-lack story and fill my mind with the words from the lesson *"It is not this that I would look upon. I trust my brother, who is one with me."* I gasp, suddenly awake to a forgiven scene before me. They're all sitting together at the computers, laughing and enjoying each other. Perfectly innocent.

Love shines brightly in the union of father and sons. I see only innocence and joy. I feel free and innocent too. The mistrust story seems ridiculous to me now. This moment is brand new. I am one with Lar and the boys, filled with gratitude and trust. Absolutely!

DAY 182

(Lesson 182)

"I will be still an instant and go home."

(W-pI.182.1)

All my life I had this feeling that something was not quite right with the world—or was it me? Turns out this feeling, what Morpheus from *The Matrix* calls "a splinter in the mind" seems to be hardwired in our human psyche. I think it is true for all of us, until we go home. It's just that we distract ourselves from it with self-improvements and future goals. You recognize it, don't you? You've known it along.

Today's lesson is telling us to stop and answer its call. To *"be still an instant and go home."* It's saying that there is a memory deep within us, which is totally home for us. It is a place of pure comfort, safety, protection, and love that can't be found in form.

The lesson says that this feeling that something is off is the Christ child within us. She comes to us defenseless, purely innocent, calling us back home to our true Self. Nothing but this return will satisfy. And we are lost until we are willing to be still an instant, leave the noisy world we made, and go home.

Practicing today's lesson profoundly altered my state of being and subsequently the way I saw my place in the world. I noticed an ache right around my heart. It had been there all along, but I had been distracting from it. It's just I'd been resisting taking the plunge into the unknown.

Now I pay attention. During my quiet time with God, the feeling intensified—a profound longing deep within me. I apply the lesson, *"I will be still an instant and go home,"* And I let go. My hand touches my heart, and I feel the innocent child of defenselessness within. She is like a magnetic pull into a memory I can almost touch—freedom, presence, love, and total peace. It's the most natural state ever. I'm completely immersed. I am the experiencer and the experience. I am home.

It happens in an instant, not after long hours of meditation. It is an instant of pure intent. I am my holiness. I whisper, "The search is over. I am home." My paradigm has been altered. I realize my home is my Self in God, and I will return again and again until I no longer leave.

No matter what is happening in my so-called life, deep within there is a stillness that cannot be disturbed. This is my home. There's not this yummy home I feel in my quiet time with God and this less yummy world I step into each day. Home is my Self. There's not me and the other. The other is my Self.

The experience has a rippling effect in my life that softens my interactions in the world. The boys and I are at a craft fair with the unschoolers when we hear a crash. Frantic commotion breaks into the harmonic atmosphere. Someone has knocked over a display down the hall from where we are.

Parents are checking with kids to find the culprit. Usually, I'd be concerned about how I'm being seen by other parents, but peculiarly, my mind doesn't even go there. I don't try to fix. I don't even see a problem, just folks being folks.

As we approach the crash site, a father is talking to the two boys that knocked into the display. I see an appeal for help and healing and extend love where upset has erupted. I see their holiness and simply mop up spilled paint.

The display belongs to a Downs-girl, who is readjusting her paintings. Our eyes meet. Her eyes twinkle with the joy of sharing. She's not upset in the least. Her smile is off the charts. I see home in her face—her light, healing the world. Joy is home.

DAY 183

(Lesson 183)

"I call upon God's Name and on my own."

(W-pI.183.1)

Calling upon God's name is claiming who we are in truth. God is our surname. When we call upon His name, it literally raises our vibration to a state of divine love, which alters our perception of what is going on around us. *"Repeat the Name of God, and call upon your Self, Whose Name is His. Repeat His Name, and all the tiny, nameless things on earth slip into right perspective."*

Whether we call it God, Love, the Divine, the Universe, Allah, Buddha, or Infinite Possibility is not what matters. It is the pure intent to know the truth which raises our frequency to Divinity and recalibrates our perceptions, opening our vision to see through the eyes of love. Calling upon God's name opens a channel where we can receive guidance for whatever arises in our lives.

With today's practice we lay down all the false god's in our world we've thought to make us happy and replace them with the one thing we really want—our Self in God. We begin the day with God filling our whole mind.

We call upon God's name as our own and place it at the forefront of our mind and use it like a mantra throughout the day. When we are with anyone, it is our first response. We might be having a conversation, maybe listening to problems or worries, but from the stillness of our mind we are invoking God. We are holding God's frequency from our inner altar and inviting our brother to join us here.

It totally works too. During an unschooling activity, we moms are sitting together knitting, and a juicy gossip session ensues. A family who was central to our group activities has detached from the group without explanation. There are a lot of accusations being thrown around about disloyalty. Promises for planned future events that wouldn't be kept. Assumptions and blame.

I hop on the bandwagon, saying, "Cole went out of his way to teach them how to make boppers last week, and they were supposed to practice on Saturday." My energy becomes heavy and contracted. I feel shitty before the first sentence of blame has left my lips. My heart is tight. Just as I'm judging the whole gossip-clan as the culprit. I stop.— my lesson at the ready. *"I call upon God's Name and on my own."*

Ah, forgiveness opportunity. I turn within and silently invoke the Divine. I instantly feel present, released from judgment and gossip. The name of God is the only word I want to flow from my lips. A wave of appreciation flows through me. I see our request for healing, bypassing the blame and seeming loss of our friends, and straight into the love we share. I share my gratitude with the group for the wealth of happy experiences we shared with each other and this family.

Looking with innocent eyes in the faces of my friends, I acknowledge our oneness in God, feeling His presence surrounding us in peace. It's like everyone catches the wave, and the most beautiful thing happens. It's like the previous conversation never took place and everyone shifts to sharing about happy moments we've shared.

Some of the children join the conversation, talking about how funny and clever the boys from the family could be, what fun they've had, and that they'll be missed. *"I call upon God's Name and on my own."* And He has answered.

DAY 184

(Lesson 184)

"The name of God is my inheritance."

(W-pl.184.1)

Until we recognize our inheritance, whole and united with all living things, living and breathing in God, we label and separate with space. No wonder we feel unsatisfied, each part of our lives is missing something—it's meaning and purpose. But we do it with everything.

In fact, we're trained to recognize labels and symbols from the minute we are born. We learn to separate things that make up our world into mine and yours. We're compulsive about labeling and setting apart.

We encounter something wondrous and rather than let its mystery speak to us about what is unknown to us, we try to fit it into a known category. "There! I've named it. Got this! Wrestled it to the ground and pinned my meaning on it!" It gives us a false sense that we're in control. But it never fills the longing for completion, wholeness, joy.

Yet the invitation is there each moment to enter the mystery that can't be labeled. Today's lesson is saying that this vast mystery behind the scenes includes the scenes, and it is our inheritance as the holy child of God. We claim it by recognizing it is already ours, we're the Divine's kids, after all.

With today's lesson occupying my mind, I am determined to experience my wholeness, beyond the limits of symbols that separate, as I set out toward the French Quarter in New Orleans. I reach St. Charles Street as musicians seemingly out of the ether form a jazz band and begin to play.

First, a lone saxophone starts playing a love song for all longing hearts. I'm filled with love. Like it is divinely choreographed, he is joined by a violinist, a trumpet player, then drummer and guitarist, each adding their gift, creating music together.

I realize some mystical calling beckons them to give their gift. I naturally start swaying with the small group gathering. I'm filled with awe at the perfect synchronicity of all the elements coming together—like it is scripted by the hand of God—the music, the vibrant joy of the band playing off one another, and the crowd swaying in sync.

This darling man of color makes his way through the crowd until he is right in front of the band. He must be 100 years young. He lifts his arms as if holding an instrument, his fingers moving up and down before him, his cheeks puffing in and out, playing what appears to be an invisible saxophone. He is bringing *his* music.

In fact, we all are, our hearts full and extending, connecting everything, lifting and unified. As I look around, I see everyone is bathed in this simmering joy. No one is out of place—this is just a natural unfolding.

Divine buzz unifies us in one purpose—joy. Nothing is out of order, each of us playing our part in this heavenly concerto. I let my music rip through and hum appreciation and joy.

Today's lesson fills my mind, beating to the rhythm of unity. *"The Name of God is my inheritance!"* Everything and everyone *is* the Divine. This is my music. The bounty of my inheritance is in me and all around me. Today, I have eyes to see and ears to hear. *"The Name of God is my inheritance."*

DAY 185

(Lesson 185)

"I want the peace of God."

(W-pl.185.1)

Today's lesson asks for sincere honesty because choosing the peace of God is an uncompromising decision. It asks, *"Is this what I would have, in place of Heaven and the peace of God?"*

It's a "come to Jesus" question. Where have we been saying we want the peace of God when our actions show us we have other goals we prefer more? If the peace of God is already ours, it can only be our denial of it that keeps us from experiencing His peace now. We say we want the peace of God, but we're still seduced by distraction, guilt, or blame or fixated on future happiness. The list is infinite. Because the peace of God is uncompromising. It handles everything.

Be honest. If you truly, deeply felt the peace of God always, would anything you're concerned with now be a problem? Would you still be trying to find happiness outside yourself? No! Seeking ends in the peace of God. It is the alpha and omega for handling our attachment to goals in the world of form because we have returned to the only thing we really want—the peace of God.

I was always saying I want the peace of God, but what I wanted was relief from the ego's murderous attacks on my state of being. But as I worked with the lessons, forgiving and choosing peace instead of stories of woe, I became more peaceful overall, and I more easily choose peace when conflicts arise in situations with others.

But when it came to mistakes within myself, I'd want a do-over. I'd tell myself, "I'm on my way." Here's the thing: "being on my way" is putting the peace of God off as a future goal. I was judging my acceptance according to *my* worthiness criteria. The peace of God is beyond criteria and my worthiness is established by God. The peace of God is beyond time and space. It is the decision for eternity now. I want the peace of God. Period.

It's always wild to me, the catalyst moments where I crack open my defenses and give myself to God.

During a session of hot yoga, I realize the criteria I have set between myself and the eternal peace of God. At the beginning of the practice, I set today's lesson as my intention. *"I want the peace of God."* I'm flowing along, feeling peaceful, and then BAM! I can't get into a difficult pose, and it breaks me. I try harder—like my life depends on "getting this right." It's like my life force is squeezed into the furrow in my brow.

Totally off balance, I fall, tears of defeat coming in waves. I lay on my mat utterly surrendered and remember my lesson. *"I want the peace of God."* I pray, "I don't care about the stupid pose. I don't want to care about what doesn't matter anymore. I just want the peace of God." I let the tears fall.

I am release, and the peace of God is there, all-encompassing and complete. Yoga pose and body goals forgotten. *"I want the peace of God"*—everything else drops away. I am present and whole, in a state of imperturbable tranquility—the eye of the storm. I am free—transcendent in perfect peace.

The peace of God has always been with us—the everlasting arms of the Divine—the wind beneath our wings. It is the air we breathe with our Creator.

DAY 186
(Lesson 186)

"Salvation of the world depends on me."
(W-pI.186.1)

The salvation of the world depends on me? That's impossible for the small self to comprehend, yes? Thank God, we're not doing it. We offer our willingness and the Holy Spirit within our mind makes all the arrangements, so our part feel just right for us.

I joined Lar for a business trip to Richland, Washington. We arrive at our hotel and join the other guests waiting to check in. A visibly upset woman frantically rushes up to the front desk, oblivious to the rest of us waiting in line.

"Has a call come for me, yet?" she says, her voice cracking. "No. Nothing yet." I notice a tear trickling down her face as she turns away, head bowed. I want to help, but how?

We check in and settle into our room, all the while her image haunts me. I think of my lesson, *"Salvation of the world depends on me."* Is there something I am to do? How can I be truly helpful? Oh yeah, I fulfill my function. I forgive my perception of the woman in need, allowing holiness to fill my mind and reinterpret for me. The image of the sad and frantic woman dissolves, transforming in the light of forgiveness, and I see her glowing in vivid light. It is from my holiness I look again at the image and I just let it be what it is.

I trust her and the Divine.

There is a beautiful courtyard through the sliding doors of our room. I grab my *ACIM* book and sit on a bench near the waterfall. I soften my eyes and appreciate the beauty all around me and bask in the Divine.

I open my book to today's lesson and feel a deep trust in Divine flow. If I am meant to do something, I will be shown. I close my eyes and pray, "Thank you, God. I accept my role in the salvation of the world. Forgiveness is love, the way in which I fulfill my function. What is not love does not exist. I deny the denial of truth."

Right then my course book drops from my lap onto the ground. As I lean to pick it up, I nearly bump heads with the woman from the lobby, reaching to catch the book as she sees it fall.

She has been sitting, unbeknownst to me, across the courtyard, observing me. She says, "I hope you don't mind. I saw you praying, and I felt it was also for me. Do you mind if I sit with you a while?" Wow. The salvation of the world does depend on me. Sobering. Awesome!

The salvation of the world depends on each of us forgiving and returning our minds to love. As I forgive, situations and their purpose directly right themselves in my mind and the path before me becomes clear.

DAY 187

(Lesson 187)

"I bless the world because I bless myself."

(W-pI.187.1)

Nothing in the dream of form is real in and of itself. We give everything all the meaning it has for us. What's real is the love which inspires right thinking and action. Today's lesson is asking us to go within to the holy altar of the love we are and look upon the innocence and purity of our identity as God created us. This is how we bless ourselves.

We then look out from this pure mind and bless the world with that same love, innocence, and purity. We offer everyone the lilies of forgiveness from the altar within us. We receive as we give, dispelling the belief that giving is sacrifice.

I love the image of infinite lilies of forgiveness laid upon the altar within, which we take one by one and give in each interaction, seeing the holiness we share. It might take the form of a loving thought, a helping hand, a smile, a moment of our time, but it is the Holy Spirit in our mind inspiring each. Each is a blessing will return the blessing we give, in infinite supply.

This morning, having coffee with friends from last night's *A Course in Miracles* gathering, today's lesson is abundant in my mind. *"I bless the world because I bless myself."* I look about me and see holiness shining in their faces.

Across from us in the coffee shop, a brotherhood of senior men is joined in laughter and community. When we started meeting here, I saw the chance for a holy encounter with these guys and introduced myself. I see the spark in their eyes, I honor them, extending love, hugs, and joy. It's like we've made this silent agreement with each other, where illusion is dispelled and only love remains.

We greet with hugs and the café becomes the holy ground where truth reigns.

I flash on a conversation with my mentor, Betty, back in the day when I first started working with these ideas. I was basically arguing for my limitations, saying, "It's hard to stay in a state of love, forgiveness, and joy. No one cares. People are basically unconscious and selfish. They don't really want peace. They don't care about forgiving false beliefs and living in integrity to love and unity."

She laughs and says, "Kid, that's your world, not mine." I say, "If everyone was like you, Betty, it would be so much easier." She says, "Kid, It's all about your state of mind. You see what you want to see. You got to be what you want to see first. Then you give and keep giving it without reservation, even when you think it's not working. One day you will look around you and see that everyone in your life is like me. And better—you'll see they are like you."

I look around me now and I see abundance everywhere. The world is waking to the truth all around me. I smile, and the world returns my joy. I see the light in my brother's eye, each time I pause and remember she and I are one. The peace of God surrounds me and all the world. *"I bless the world because I bless myself."*

CHAPTER ONE HUNDRED FORTY-THREE

DAY 188

(Lesson 188)

"The peace of God is shining in me now."
(W-pI.188.1)

The lesson begins with a compelling question. *"Why wait for Heaven?"* The light is in us, now, always. Recognizing this is enlightenment. Today we leave the past and all we believe about the world behind and go deep within and let our thoughts rise to heaven.

> *Sit quietly and close your eyes. The light within you is sufficient. It alone has power to give the gift of sight to you. Exclude the outer world, and let your thoughts fly to the peace within. They know the way. For honest thoughts, untainted by the dream of worldly things outside yourself, become the holy messengers of God Himself.* (W-pI.188.10.6)

Once we recognize this light, it goes with us. We're like lighthouses constantly abeam; the peace of God shining, extending from our hearts for all to see and recognize their own. We bring renewal and vision and leave a blessing that remains with them forever.

Today's lesson, in the nick of time, brings a miracle for me. Fear had gripped my heart, drawing a veil of darkness over my psyche. Lin has just come back to live with me, after living with her father for several years. I walk on eggshells—afraid I'll say or do something that might alienate her from me.

Then out of the blue, this opportunity to do an empowerment training together presents itself. We go for it. It seems like a great way to work through old wounds and start fresh. The training begins with a feedback session. I hear people giving Lin feedback, and it breaks my heart.

This shifts my focus from myself to spending my mental space in Lin's training. By the second day I worry that the training is entirely the wrong thing. But Lin insists on continuing. Apparently, she's having her own experience. Go figure.

The last day we are given a "stretch" assignment. Lin's is a metaphor of the caterpillar and butterfly. She creates a cocoon with butcher paper. On it, she writes her negative beliefs about herself, and the hurts she's received from others. She encases herself inside. She stays in that cocoon long into the day. It's agonizing. Why doesn't she come out? I'm in hell—my own cocoon of ego.

It's that thought that calls me to return home, *"Why wait for Heaven? The light is in me now. The peace of God is shining in me now."* I close my eyes and release everything. Ting! Like a Zen bell, my mind fills with pristine light, peace settling my mind. I take my first full breath of the day, breathing the peace acknowledged and extended it.

I open my eyes in gratitude. I trust Lin. I trust the Divine. This is *my* training. It is why I am here. The peace of God came with me and shines bright and clear showing me my trust in Lin, myself, and God. Heaven is here, now.

Moments later, Lin busts through the cocoon of paper! She leaps into the air with pink butterfly wings on her back, her arms outstretched, her heart wide-open, dancing in joy for all to see. The crowd goes wild! One by one, we join the dance of light and joy. I see Lin truly. She is light as Spirit. She's tremendous—the sun and sunbeam—the peace of God shining in her and through her, and all of us as one.

CHAPTER ONE HUNDRED FORTY-FOUR

DAY 189

(Lesson 189)

"I feel the Love of God within me now."
(W-pI.189.1)

Today's lesson practice is the way to the inner sanctuary of God's love. As we feel the love of God within us, we know our identity is only love. We realize a new way of being in the world, our purpose laid before us.

Our exercises for today: be still and empty our mind of every preconceived idea, and open completely to the experience of God's love. We are reminded that the power of decision is ours, and we will see accordingly. It asks, *"What would you see? The choice is given you. But learn and do not let your mind forget this law of seeing: You will look upon that which you feel within."* The choice is ours.

The "law of seeing" drops the whole of responsibility for happiness right in our lap. If we're seeing shitty politicians and a hopeless America, feeling the world is mistreating us, it is coming from within us. These are the effects of the ego thought system. Recognizing this and choosing with the Holy Spirit is forgiveness. As we see everyone as forgiven, we feel it within as the Christ love we are. The deal is, that whatever we want to see, we will see. The world and everyone in it will always reflect our inner state of being. Why not go directly for the love of God!

Today's practice is a grounding force. I make a habit of going within, feeling the love of God rising within me so I know who I am and remember my function before each counseling session with clients.

I take a few minutes and try to empty my mind of everything—my personal life, the business at the Vision Center, the previous clients, and the one I'll be seeing next. I want to see them the way Spirit sees them and not my ego, ensuring that the session will be given over to the Real Therapist, the Holy Spirit in my mind.

This day, I am to meet with the father of a client who has gone off to follow the Grateful Dead. I hear him in the lobby, angrily pressing to see me. A feeling of being in trouble, so familiar from childhood, comes up. My heart races—my mind seeking defense. This is a block which must be forgiven, now, if I am to feel God's love and let Spirit handle the session.

I close my eyes and empty my mind of falsehood. He comes in and I motion for him to take a seat while I prepare. My mind is filled with one thought only, *"I feel the Love of God within me now."* Love rises within and calm assurance fills my mind, expanding and extending.

I open my eyes and across from me this father sits with tears in his eyes. He's fondling a friendship bracelet his daughter had given me, to give to him, before she left. It had been on my desk. It says, "I love you, Dad," in beads.

This man, who was angry minutes before, says, "Thank you for showing me what it is you do before I had a chance to make a fool of myself. I started calming down in spite of myself. And then I saw the bracelet. Will you let my daughter know I give my blessing for her tour with the Grateful Dead when you hear from her?" Miracle!

DAY 190

(Lesson 190)

"I choose the joy of God instead of pain."

(W-pI.190.1)

Today we are making a cardinal choice to remember that we are spirit and not a body. When we experience pain whether physically or psychologically, we are called to forgive. Pain is wrong perception. That is all. The dream of separation *is* painful. Recognizing this, we choose again.

No matter the extent of the pain we perceive or the form it takes, it is still the dream of separation. We are not a character in the dream, but the dreamer. As long as I am making the pain real, I am identifying myself with separation.

Breaking my back, the immediate and ongoing pain, and the subsequent diagnosis of osteoporosis, was a total blow for me. At first, I was in denial, thinking I'd rest up, then muscle through, as always. But when the pain persisted, I felt ashamed. "What the fuck? What am I doing wrong? Why am I doing this to myself? It must be some deep-seeded guilt coming to the surface—proof I really believe the dream I am a body, vulnerable and alone."

I tried to forgive. Every day I practiced lesson 136, "*I accept the truth of what I am and let my mind be wholly healed today.*" I'd look at the guilt and place it on the altar for the Holy Spirit. But the more I analyzed the darkness, the more fear and pain I experienced.

It was practicing today's lesson where I finally made the shift. *"I choose the joy of God instead of pain."* "Oh, my God. I have had pain on the altar where only God's joy will awaken me to the truth beyond my body." It is a present decision for joy—for truth—now. The dark cloud of confusion and pain lifts instantly and only my love for God and feeling God's love fills the altar of my mind. Instantly, I feel the difference. I am infused with energy, bubbling with delight—free at last.

I know it is a turning point and can't wait to apply it in everything I do. I have physical therapy today—a perfect training ground. At the therapy center, they speak the language of pain as a diagnostic tool and reference point for healing.

I know joy is the reference point for healing. Today's lesson is alive in me as I walk through the door. I greet my therapist with a smile. He says, "On a scale of one to ten, what is your level of pain?" I place my hand on my heart, checking within first, before I answer. I am filled with the joy of God, and I literally feel no pain!

I say, "I feel amazing. I've decided to choose the joy of love instead of pain. I'd like to use a different diagnostic tool going forward. I want joy and happiness to determine my progress and healing, not pain."

A big smile spreads across his face, and he says, "You know, a lot of super-athletes use that technique, mind over matter, to push to a new level of excellence. I'm all for it." Our relationship shifts to a higher frequency and I feel light and free while I do my physical therapy. The whole atmosphere is infused with lightheartedness and cheer. Joy is therapy.

DAY 191

(Lesson 191)

"I am the holy Son of God Himself."

(W-pI.191.1)

In accepting today's idea, *"I am the holy Son of God Himself,"* as our only identity, we quit playing the game of death, and we set our Self and the whole Sonship free to live in immortality. The lesson talks about viewing the world as a game we've been playing, where we see ourselves as vulnerable, afraid, in pain and trying to get something outside of us to make us happy.

Today, we accept the truth of our identity, *"I am the holy Son of God Himself."* One mind in God. We are the rays of the One Sun that sees itself reflected there. Where are we viewing from? Ego or the holy Son of God Himself?

Yesterday, a friend died by suicide. We were scheduled to get together today. She texted me the night before to cancel. She said, "I can't forgive. I've been thinking about it, and I just can't do it. I am too hopeless, too much of a victim to change, and the pain every day is too much. But thank you for loving me."

I try to call her back—talk her off the ledge. No answer. I check myself. I feel powerless to help and angry she won't accept help. It hits me. This is the ego game at its finest—the dream of victimhood, hopeless, in unbearable pain, where death seems the only way out.

I'm caught up in false empathy, believing the dream that we are bodies, and wanting to fix the effect rather than look at the cause, which is the belief that we are separate from the Source that heals.

I turn within, bringing the delusion of vulnerability to the altar of my mind and forgive. I hold Maggie in my mind filled with the light of awareness and release her to the Holy Spirit we share and feel the love of God. I bless her with the love I am as the Holy Son of God, understanding we are as one. I feel love surrounding and shining in and through us—the light of God's grace. I ask if there is anything I should do and wait for guidance.

During my quiet time with the Divine, I receive a phone call that she has died by suicide. Odd, I rarely bring my phone into my yummy room. The lesson is fresh and alive in me when my friend Shar calls. Though the news is disheartening, I'm not really surprised. I see the game of death played out to its natural conclusion.

Beyond it, I see the Holy Child of God, known in the dream as Maggie, a light in the mind of Sonship. I bless her even now and thank her for her holiness. Shar and I talk about the perfect synchronicity of this lesson showing up just now. We join in the surety of this pure and holy statement from the lesson: *"I am the holy Son of God Himself. I cannot suffer, cannot be in pain; I cannot suffer loss, nor fail to do all that salvation asks."*

I hold this idea in the center of my mind and heart as the phone calls come in—friends feeling devastated, angry, grieving, and distraught. With each, I forgive. If a word of comfort is needed, I am given what to say. In my mind the message is one: *"We are the Holy Son of God Himself."*

DAY 192

(Lesson 192)

"I have a function God would have me fill."
(W-pl.192.1)

Today we are saying, "Yes, I am the one. I have a function of forgiveness God would have me fill. I accept it and fulfill it, now." The lesson says, *"Creation cannot even be conceived of in the world. It has no meaning here."* Creation is our function in heaven. But here, forgiveness is the closest thing to creation we have. Fulfilling our function of forgiveness lets us think with God, which reflects creation here. And those images reflect a happy dream.

It can feel daunting to think of taking 100 percent responsibility for our minds—to catch the lies we tell ourselves and see that if we're was experiencing conflict, selfishness, hurt, loss, worry, and anger in the world, we put it there, forgive, and let it go.

But we don't actually need to concern ourselves with anything but this experience, right now. Built within our human framework is the portal to reality. It is in the way we feel at any given moment.

I keep it simple. Yummy or icky? I call it my yummy-stat. Love feels yummy—right. Fear feels icky—wrong. If I feel icky, I am seeing something that is not there. The remedy is to forgive and ask to see it differently.

Each time I release the energy the belief holds, I feel free. Little by little, it becomes a natural habit. There are even holy instants where we experience a profound shift and realize we can stay free.

Visiting my mother at her B&B is one of these times. My mother and I rarely have time alone when I come to visit because she is the hostess to beat all hostesses and she's busy with other guests.

But this day we have a free hour just to ourselves. She starts telling me her end-of-the-world story, with disasters soon to happen, earthquakes, famine, and evil. How she knows God wants her to prepare a healing center for when it all goes down. She tells me of a friend's revelation experience, "who'd been on the other side of the veil."

Like I give a shit about some friend that had a near-death experience. As she talks, I think, "You know, Mother, this is probably the one hour we will have to spend with each other this year, and you're talking to me about doomsday fantasies, and crazy visionaries." Yuck! My judgment nearly chokes me. I stop. Today's lesson fills my mind, *"I have a function God would have me fill."*

These thoughts follow, "You know, Danét, this might be the only hour you have to spend with your mother this year. Are you going to judge her and rob yourself of the union you could be experiencing with her right now? She is holding out her heart to you. Will you give her yours?"

Thank God! I forgive us both for *my* fantasies. Instantly my viewpoint changes to love. I finally see her. She's like a kid showing me a caterpillar she's just found. Bright-eyed, generous, joyously sharing. An instant shift from dread to joy.

Forgiveness releases me and I gratefully zero in. I receive her loving presence, joining with her. She's giving me herself, her greatest gift. Beliefs dissolve in the light of forgiveness's love. I recognize the language of love from her and receive gratefully. I accept her wholeness and know my Self.

The world I see is a forgiven world. A happy dream where I am awake, forgiving, loving, and blessing. Sure, shit still comes up, I glitch on stuck beliefs, wish something differed from it is, but I know the truth. I do not forget that this is a dream and *"I have a function God would have me fill."*

DAY 193

(Lesson 193)

"All things are lessons God would have me learn."

(W-pI.193.1)

"All things are lessons God would have me learn." And all lessons are really the same lesson: *"Forgive and see this differently."* Atonement is the divine correction built right into our human program. Every single situation is ready made for our return to love and happiness. Our willingness to forget so we can remember, lets us take our hands off the wheel and let the Divine lead.

We say everything happens for a reason or there are no accidents. And then we run around trying to control or change situations to make them happen differently.

Nothing could have happened differently.

Whatever is showing up in our life is reflecting our thought system. If it's not love and supreme happiness, we're seeing illusion. It's a forgiveness lesson. Period. When shit shows up in our lives, the natural/ego tendency is to project it outward—to blame, complain or explain—to distance ourselves from it.

Once we take responsibility, we can *"Forgive, and see it differently."* We are here to heal our minds from fear to love. *Everything* that happens is *for* us. It is the perfect happening for us to heal our mind.

Take for instance my relationship with my sister Renelle back in the day. With problem after problem, she'd call me for a listening ear or ask my advice. It seemed like the same ol' same ol' and nothing changed.

Often when I'd see her name come up on caller ID, my heart would clench and I'd ignore the call, immediately resisting. I felt suspicious of her motives. I felt she wanted something from me *I* couldn't give her.

I'm actively applying my lesson when the phone rings and I see her number on the caller ID. I smile. It makes perfect sense. Renelle is my lesson to forgive and see this differently. I answer, and while she talks, I pray. *"All things are lessons God would have me learn, take my resistance, and show me what You would have me learn."*

Clear as if she were standing right next to me, I hear the Holy Spirit in Betty's voice, "Forgive kid. Forgive, and you will see this differently." "Forgive what?" I say. "I'm not holding anything on Renelle." "Kid, you've got to forgive your own mind, to see this differently. This is your dream."

Eureka! This has nothing to do with Renelle. It is my own belief in scarcity, lack, and feeling separate and alone." Instantly I forgive, grateful for this lesson and Renelle as savior, sister in Christ.

It seems as if Renelle changes too. Now she talks, and I listen. I share her call for love and healing. She trusts me with her Self. An act of pure love. And, no surprise here, I trust her too, for the first time. In fact, I can't remember a reason not to trust. I adore Renelle. She is my mighty companion in awakening.

We learn to trust everything. We see that everything is *for* us. Every resistance or conflict is the call to awaken. We're grateful for whatever shows up because we realize it is bringing us home. *"All things are lessons God would have me learn."*

DAY 194

(Lesson 194)

"I place the future in the Hands of God."

(W-pl.194.1)

We've been practicing forgiveness, realizing we see only the past and letting it go. Today we are releasing the so called "future," placing it in God's hands.

We grow up believing in a timeline where the present is squeezed between the past and the future, right? We learn to decide based on the time sequence. We drag our faulty interpretations from the past into our plans. So, we're not available for the miracle that lives within each moment. When we feel a stab of anger or fear, we are realizing it's a forgiveness lesson. We are learning to pause, forgive, and wait for guidance.

Imagine what our lives would be like if we truly believed that our future was wholly and entirely in the loving hands of the Divine, who wants only supreme happiness for us. It handles everything, right?

Would you be worried about what your finances, or the cruel thing someone said five years ago? Anxiety, fear, and guilt would literally disappear. Seriously, if you knew for sure God was handling everything, so you'd be fantastically happy all the time, wouldn't apprehension and worry disappear? Would we take the risk of self-initiated plans when our perfect happiness is guaranteed by trusting God?

When we decided on unschooling the boys, it was scary. Unlike homeschool, where you choose an academic curriculum as a guideline, unschooling is about trusting your children's choices for what they want to learn, when, and through what medium.

It is then stepping back and letting them learn from their own experience—to teach only if asked something specific from them. As parents, we support their choices and desires and try to help them realize them. We expose them to new experiences and ideas, then take our hands off and let them decide for themselves.

If you ask me, unschooling is as much for parents as the children. It requires total trust in God, in His children, and in life. It requires, that as parents, we take a back seat, and let our children drive their education. Letting their choices do the teaching. Awesome in theory, right? Wholly aligned with the undoing of my ego through my *A Course in Miracles* curriculum. So, perfect for me. I loved it!

It was like my own personal classroom for practicing today's lesson—every day. Ok, I didn't always love it. Sometimes my fear about the unknown future would temporarily paralyze me, and I'd give into the temptation to try to steer the children in some way that I thought would relieve my anxiety.

It's one of those days. Cole and Parker are playing video games and jumping on the trampoline all day. It's the third day in a row they don't want to go out. I feel anxiety building. Thoughts about being a good parent, fears and worry about their future blast my mind.

But rather than address these directly, forgive and place the future in the hands of God, I try to control their actions to change the way I feel. I suggest we go to Explora, this groovy science activity place where kids experiment and learn about physics and science-y stuff. The boys are usually all for it. This day? No.

Finally, Cole says, "What going on mom? Why is it so important to you?" And that's my flip-switch. Cole sent the responsibility for my experience right back to me, and I remember my lesson. *"I place the future in the hands of God."* I pray, "I let go and let God. I trust you've got this. I'm placing the future in Your Hands." The shift is immediate. I am calm. I trust. God is with me. I hop on the tramp and jump with the boys. Joy is what's happening, now.

DAY 195

(Lesson 195)

"Love is the way I walk in gratitude."

(W-pI.195.1)

Today we are learning to think of gratitude in place of anger, malice, and revenge or any form of otherness. We are making the other, our brother in love. Comparison seems built into our idea of gratitude. For instance, we're grateful we've been able to stay sober—so many others have gone back to drinking. We're thankful our relationship has improved—saying how bad it was before. We feel grateful for our food—so many are starving.

It's like we're scared shitless to stand in our own light as deserving, grateful for what we are.

"God has cared for us, and calls us Son. Can there be more than this?" Gratitude is a way where we honor the dignity of our brother. We develop a new capacity to accept and love them wholeheartedly, just as they are, releasing all comparison from our mind. Their part is essential to the perfection of God's plan for happiness for us.

Resisting anything is resisting God, resisting love. *"Love is the way [we] walk in gratitude."* When we see all the amazing things that others have in their lives, rather than compare ourselves, get jealous, think it's not fair, or wish it could be ours, we thank our brother for his gift of sight.

I recall a turning point with today's idea during a conversation with Betty. I'm telling her how grateful I am for sobriety—for this amazing chance to remake myself, to undo my old programming, and have a clean slate. Compulsively, I bring up others in the program, judging how they don't appreciate what they've got.

I say, "I can't believe people in the program with years of sobriety can still be so angry and miserable." Betty bypasses my comments entirely and says, "How does that judgment feel? These guys are your teachers. And they are in *your* life for a reason." Shit!

I defend, "I don't want what they have." She says, "How do you know, you can't see them as they are. You see only your judgment, and you are making them fit that picture." This pisses me off. She continues, "The question to ask yourself is why you're bothering yourself with them. Why your gratitude is contingent on comparisons. That's where you'll get your answer."

I feel the spark of truth in what she says. I pause and look within. I see why I'm bothered. I see my belief in separation. They must be guilty so I can be innocent. Suddenly I recall today's lesson, *"Love is the way I walk in gratitude."*

I realize I have projected my fear of love onto these brothers—the part that refuses to forgive and see things differently. Why judge rather than appreciate? Aren't my brothers my Self? In that instant of realization, I'm filled with gratitude for these same individuals that used to bother me.

I love them for reflecting the barriers to love's awareness in my mind, and I forgive them for what they never really did. I'm suddenly filled with love for these guys—I want to hug them and say thank you. They are my saviors.

Love includes everything. When we see we are love and our brother is too, we're grateful for everyone and every situation as the perfect happening. Gratitude is love's way of directing our path—it is how we let God's love expand our heart and gather everyone in. Gratitude touches that soft spot within us where our real Self resides.

CHAPTER ONE HUNDRED FIFTY-ONE

DAY 196

(Lesson 196)

"It can be but myself I crucify."

(W-pl.196.1)

Everything we see and every thought we hold reflects what we believe about who we are. *"It can be but myself I crucify."* Only my Self can set me free.

I'm at the airport waiting for a flight when I meet my guru for practicing today's lesson. I'm sitting next to this darling elderly man with an aura of peace about him. We'd just begun to visit with each other when I'm suddenly distracted by a loud voice at the counter.

A man, dressed in a business suit, is at the gate counter demanding that he be upgraded to first class. The attendant pleasantly tells him that it is a full flight, so there will be no upgrades and to please take a seat. He raises his voice, "Look again. There must be a mistake. I simply cannot travel in coach."

He's leaning over the counter now, looking at the computer. She tells him to take a seat or she'll have to call security, and she picks up the phone. Now, he's yelling, "Not until I get my upgrade! Call your supervisor. I want my upgrade!"

Everyone is staring. I'm thinking, "What an asshole!" It seems everyone agrees with me too, whispering and shifting in their seats.

Everyone, that is, except the serene dude next to me. What?

I turn to him and say, "Can you believe this guy?" His response is golden. "No. I do not believe anything that could disturb my peace of mind." Wow!

Instant flip-switch! This is my lesson. *"It can be but myself I crucify."* I realize I was afraid and using judgment and self-righteousness to project it away from me. Which literally blocks awareness of love and peace.

Instantly, I take total responsibility for the projection, silently thanking this guy at the counter for reflecting my belief in vulnerability. How simple—how glorious to forgive. I am filled with love and join my guru in peace. I look again at my brother at the counter, and see his call for love, and bless him.

I turn to my new guru friend and thank him for his peace and example. He says, "At my age, I'm not interested in believing in anything. I am at peace. That's all I need." I tell him I've just experienced a miracle due to his present peace, shifting my perception 360 degrees. A knowing smile spreads across his face.

Every single person and situation in our lives reflects our own thought about ourselves. This guru reflects my healed mind. When we are willing to take 100 percent responsibility for how we see everything, every person, place, and experience, we are free.

The thing the ego dreads the most is salvation. Seeing it dispels the myth. A little willingness and we go home to the truth. This instant! *"For what would seem to need a thousand years can easily be done in just one instant by the grace of God."* Through our willingness and the grace of God, we can step back from fear and make advance to God, resurrecting the memory of our True Self in our mind.

DAY 197

(Lesson 197)

"It can be but my gratitude I earn."

(W-pI.197.1)

I love the yummy feeling I get when I give something to someone, my heart expands and takes in the whole world. Don't you? It feels incredible, right? We feel blessed as we give, whether it be love, forgiveness, or something monetary. Yes? That's where the gratitude is. It opens us up, and we feel expanded, united. Giving is the gift to ourselves.

The gift is in the giving. It's just when we attach an outcome, a right response, or a need for appreciation from the recipient, that we sidestep the real gift we have already received. We cheat ourselves by thinking it must be validated by another. It's actually an attack on giving—on ourselves and them. When we attach an agenda, we rob ourselves from the gratitude of an open-heart.

Here's an example. A young mother and her young son moved in next door to us. They had been there only a month when her electricity went out. I saw her at the mailbox one day. She was shy. With her head down, in almost a whisper she asks, "Umm, do you have electricity?" I say, "Yes. You don't?" Turning to walk away, she mumbles, "I thought so. Couldn't pay the bill." I touch her arm and ask, "Wait, can I help?" She shakes her head, and says, "No, we'll be fine," and keeps walking.

I can't get her off my mind. She's struggling to make ends meets. I know how that feels. I think about the little boy and how alone they must feel. I want to help. That evening I knock on her door and ask if maybe the little boy can come over to play. "No thanks. We've got someplace to be right now," she says, while she pulls a shirt down over her son's head, which looks to be a couple of sizes too small. Damn. I'm just trying to help. I say, "Well, maybe another day." She doesn't reply.

I go home feeling frustrated. Why can't this mom just accept a little help? Which brings my lesson to mind and I realize my agenda. I had an expectation this mother would appreciate my efforts and accept my help. As much as I did want to help, I wanted to be seen as a hero. I wanted something *from* her! And I'm sure she could feel it.

My lesson fills my mind. *"It can only be my gratitude I earn."* I forgive her for not responding to my way of helping, grateful to see the error in my mind. I utter a prayer of thanks to her for the gift of awareness. I release us both from the prison in my mind and open to trust. Another realization comes. I had been pitying this mother and child, rather than seeing their light as perfect children of God. Wow!

I forgive myself, with gratitude in my heart, holding mom and son in the light of God's care. I place us all in the hands of God. "If there is something You want me to do. It will be clear and I'll do it."

As I'm leaving the house the next morning for work, I notice a box of clothes Lucas had worn when he was younger, set aside to go to Goodwill. I smile. I know what to do. I pick up the box, and on the way to work, I place it on the little family's doorstep, with love and gratitude.

My heart is full, gratitude is abundant in my heart. *"It is but my gratitude I earn."* I can't lose.

CHAPTER ONE HUNDRED FIFTY-THREE
DAY 198
(Lesson 198)

"Only my condemnation injures me."
(W-pI.198.1)

Today's lesson is for us to take responsibility for what we feel. Do we feel gratitude or injury? *"Only my condemnation injures me. Only my forgiveness sets me free."* We can only feel injured if we believe in condemnation.

No one can hurt us unless we hold attack in our mind. Nothing outside of us can disturb our peace. Today's lesson is a further step in accountability. We are being asked to recognize that if we blame anyone for anything, we have chosen to move away from peace and happiness, thinking condemnation will give us something we want more.

A few years ago, I was facilitating *A Course in Miracles* group. A woman who'd recently joined the group said she channeled a higher being from another planet and placed her interpretation on the section we were reading. I redirected her back to the course, saying here we are letting the course speak for itself.

Apparently, she felt offended, and had begun a small campaign against me. I only found out over coffee with my friend Tom, a member of the *ACIM* group, a few days later. As he tells me the story, I notice the old familiar feeling of wanting to defend—to explain—blame. But thankfully, I have my training.

Today's lesson is fresh in my mind. I note the feelings, recognize them as the illusion of condemnation, and forgive, restoring my mind to peace. I'm smiling, hand on heart, as I do my internal process.

Tom's hand goes to his heart too. He says, "We're forgiving and blessing her, right?" I say, "It's today's lesson practice, *"Only my condemnation injures me. Only my forgiveness sets me free."* We bless her with the freedom, born in our oneness, and know that we cannot be attacked. And feel the truth of it deep within.

This inspires Tom to share about his relationship with his mother. He says he'd been withholding his love from her for over twenty years because of something she had said, and that it had colored everything between them since.

With tears in his eyes, he says, "I just realized I felt justified in seeing her through the eyes of condemnation because I was hurt. Now I see how bogus my attitude toward my mom has been, and how much I have cheated us both. I've thought I condemned my mom, but I have really condemned myself. I feel like I just released us both, right now."

I swear the entire coffee shop was lit with the brilliant light of the miracle forgiveness unleashes.

Often when we talk now, he shares stories of how this fundamental shift transformed his relationship with his parents, and of the beautiful changes that have happened in their relationship through his forgiveness. *"Only my condemnation injures me. Only my forgiveness sets me free."*

DAY 199

(Lesson 199)

"I am not a body. I am free."
(W-pI.199.1)

Do we still see our body as our self? Have we indeed released the belief we are a body? When seeing our Self as a body, we automatically start putting up defenses for its safety and protection, it's contentment, well-being, and happiness. It's like we're always trying to outrun the inevitable decline and death, right? So, the body's comfort becomes our primary goal.

But now, we are seeing that freedom and peace take place in our mind. We're seeing that allowing the body to be used by the Holy Spirit in the service of God's plan for happiness, just might be a more stable goal.

So, we've begun to see the unreality of the body. But here's where it gets tricky. Any "have-to" beliefs about the body—take supplements, eat a certain way, exercise, etc.—is thinking we're a body. Everything must be given over. Have we given our body to the care of our Guide, or are we still making decisions about its care based on false beliefs?

The actions could look exactly the same—one is playing god, the other listening to His voice within.

That split is what today's lesson is helping us heal. *"I am not a body. I am free. I hear the Voice that God has given me, and it is only this my mind obeys."* Living from Spirit's purpose takes abundant trust. The choice is simple. Do we want to be imprisoned in the body, or free to experience our boundless joy and fulfill our purpose as the light of the world?

It's like my experience with my back, right? Who would have thought this would be such a powerful experience of awakening for me? Duh, my Self. I always prided myself on my physical fitness. Good word, right? Pride. Sneaky. A clue.

The course tells us the ego uses the body for pride, pleasure, and attack. So, it is here great lessons in forgiveness and body dis-identification became my playground. As long as I was thinking, "Shit, I broke myself." I was identified as being a body, limited and determined to get fixed.

Once I declare my innocence and release my body-self to the truth of what I am as spirit, I am free. I am able to give my mind, including my body's care over the Holy Spirit. My real purpose for the experience with my back is revealed in the miracles I receive and bring to every encounter. Who knew I was to be an emissary for light and joy to the medical world, one doc-brother at a time?

As a communication device for spirit, this body becomes a vehicle in which I bring an undivided goal of freedom.

Can't you just feel the momentum of healing through our curriculum? It's like we're being swept up in the flow of love's purpose in the world. We are bringers of salvation. Who could resist its pull?

We are given these words to hold in the center of our mind as a beacon for others to see the light and be drawn in. *"I am not a body. I am free. I hear the Voice that God has given me, and it is only this my mind obeys."* We hold the truth for everyone till they see it for themselves. In our freedom, we carry freedom as our gift.

DAY 200

(Lesson 200)

"There is no peace except the peace of God."

(W-pI.200.1)

Today's lesson concludes Part I of the workbook with a lesson that bring a singular experience of complete peace. The peace of God. It only requires we release all other goals.

We want to be very honest with ourselves today. Where do we still look for peace and happiness "out there"? Do we still think that special someone will make us happy? Do we think if only this one thing would change?

If there were only a worthy candidate in the presidential election coming up, that I could put my vote behind, instead of two crooks? *You* probably haven't had that thought. But *I* have. The peace of God is the bridge everyone must cross. These candidates, America, the world, my brothers, need my faith, not my judgment. We need trust in the Holy Spirit we share, in only what is real—the peace of God.

I'd be amiss if I didn't talk about "special relationships" here, because they are often our hold out, the thing in this world that promises peace and happiness, which we choose over the peace of God. It's one of the hardest areas to "let go and let God."

It could be with our children or even a pet. But often, it is the romantic love donkey which we pin the happiness tail on. We have a seemingly universal belief that a "special" someone will bring us happiness, and we can rest. It's a silent contract to not look at the fine print within, where we would recognize its faulty premise, which is fear. Right?

Instead, we look to the bold Prince Charming story promising us the world. It says the search for love would be over and we would be at peace. But it never happens. Not long term. So, we blame the relationship or Mr. Not Prince Charming.

The ego's sleight of hand is to keep us from looking within—the only place where we can find the peace we seek.

If you have come this far in the mind-training, you know. But here's what I love. The Holy Spirit works with us from right where we are. If we are in a "special relationship" where we have expectation of the other for our happiness, we simply offer our relationship to the Holy Spirit for reinterpretation. We see where we can forgive the false ideas, and we are glad and grateful for the awakening to our true Self and our partner as one.

I met my husband, Lar, on the heels of deciding I was done with romantic relationships. The peace of God was it for me. I gave all relationships, past, present, and future, to the Divine, asking they be used to serve the goal of bringing peace to every mind. I was in love with God, and I couldn't imagine how being in partnership could add anything to that.

So, when I met Lar and we felt an instant connection, I wasn't seeking anything. Uniformly, we felt an incredible force drawing us together, at this moment in time for its purpose. We talked about *A Course in Miracles*, and I wasn't surprised to learn that he was a student.

We discussed how a holy relationship mirrors our relationship with God, and we chose in, right that instant.

Crazy, I've never thought of our relationship as special, even in the hot and passionate beginning. Not when we have gone through challenges and released them to forgiveness. We know forgiveness is the key to happiness. And we've been through some shit.

Whoever has been saner at the time of the struggle, just holds the truth of the love we are, until the other is ready to remember. It's in God's hands. *"There is no peace except the peace of God. And I am glad and thankful that it is so."* Gratitude is our touchstone. The peace of God the soundtrack.

REVIEW VI: DAYS 201–220
(Lessons 181–200)

Today begins our sixth review period, which will conclude Part I of the workbook. Here we are given the central theme with which we start and end our day and each practice period: *"I am not a body. I am free. For I am still as God created me."*

These last twenty review lessons are structured to facilitate dis-identifying with being a body and reclaiming our Self as spirit. Each of the twenty review lessons begins and ends with this central idea.

We repeat the idea, and let it fill our mind. Then we review the idea for the day and related thoughts and let them open our minds to reality. When idle thoughts arise, we catch them and refuse to let them intrude upon our holy mind.

We're training our mind to stop extraneous thoughts in their tracks, deny their hold on us, and let each go. They're just thoughts.

The key is to, *"Permit no idle thought to go unchallenged."* When we notice one arise, we note it and say, *"This thought I do not want."* We don't hop on its train and let it take us for a ride. We let it pass, replacing it with the idea for the day, and return to peace.

The more we do it, the fewer thoughts bother us. Until ultimately, we are resting in the peaceful state of God's love. At this point in the mind-training, we realize all the lessons are leading us to one place—home to our Self as God created us.

Each idea we review contains the whole curriculum if it is understood, accepted, and applied to what happens throughout the day. That's an amazing promise, right?

Whatever we think of, how we feel or experience another, comes from what we believe we are. And if we are as God created us, then we are spirit. Spirit doesn't attack or feel pain. Spirit moves as loving trust. We trust our brothers because their inner guide is the same Holy Spirit within our mind.

The Holy Spirit is always guiding us back to our identity as spirit. Whatever is happening is the perfect classroom where we can forgive and remember the truth. We remember that our home is the stillness—the quiet calm within, where we find perfect rest and timeless peace—not the body.

Reality is whole. It is the unity beyond all forms. Oneness is truth. We're a hologram of oneness—each containing the whole. We're learning to look at the beliefs we adopted as part of our earthly inheritance and to forgive them. This opens our mind so our true heritage can awaken within us. It is God.

Have fun with this and take notes. We bless as a natural extension of our identity in God. It is as simple as being as we are—love—and following its lead.

NOTES

NOTES

NOTES

NOTES

NOTES

CHAPTER ONE HUNDRED FIFTY-SEVEN
PART II: INTRODUCTION

The introduction to Part II is sublime. Just reading it raises our frequency such that we feel joined in Divine purpose. It speaks directly to the Self we are as God created us, trusting us to rise above the ego and enter the still and holy space in our minds where Self and God commune.

Part II of the workbook contain the prayer lessons. Oh, my love, they're so beautiful. They are transforming in and of themselves. Each has the potential to completely release us and transport us to Divinity. We approach each with reverence and the honor due God's holy children.

As we read this introduction, we recognize we are entering holy ground, uniting us in prayer and thanksgiving as we step forward together, for this final trek of our year given over to the Divine.

Part II. Introduction (W-pII.in.1–11)

Words will mean little now. We use them but as guides on which we do not now depend. For now, we seek direct experience of truth alone. The lessons that remain are merely introductions to the times in which we leave the world of pain, and go to enter peace. Now we begin to reach the goal this course has set, and find the end toward which our practicing was always geared.

Now we attempt to let the exercise be merely a beginning. For we wait in quiet expectation for our God and Father. He has promised He will take the final step Himself. And we are sure His promises are kept. We have come far along the road, and now we wait for Him. We will continue spending time with Him each morning and at night, as long as makes us happy. We will not consider time a matter of duration now. We use as much as we will need for the result that we desire. Nor will we forget our hourly remembrance in between, calling to God when we have need of Him as we are tempted to forget our goal.

We will continue with a central thought for all the days to come, and we will use that thought to introduce our times of rest, and calm our minds at need. Yet we will not content ourselves with simple practicing in the remaining holy instants which conclude the year that we have given God. We say some simple words of welcome, and expect our Father to reveal Himself, as He has promised. We have called on Him, and He has promised that His Son will not remain unanswered when he calls His Name.

Now do we come to Him with but His Word upon our minds and hearts, and wait for Him to take the step to us that He has told us, through His Voice, He would not fail to take when we invited Him. He has not left His Son in all his madness, nor betrayed his trust in Him. Has not His faithfulness earned Him the invitation that He seeks to make us happy? We will offer it, and it will be accepted. So our times with Him will now be spent. We say the words of invitation that His Voice suggests, and then we wait for Him to come to us.

Now is the time of prophesy fulfilled. Now are all ancient promises upheld and fully kept. No step remains for time to separate from its accomplishment. For now we cannot fail. Sit silently and wait upon your Father. He has willed to come to you when you have recognized it is your will He do so. And you could have never come this far unless you saw, however dimly, that it is your will.

I am so close to you we cannot fail. Father, we give these holy times to You, in gratitude to Him Who taught us how to leave the world of sorrow in exchange for its replacement, given us by You. We look not backward now. We look ahead, and fix our eyes upon the journey's end. Accept these little gifts of thanks from us, as through Christ's vision we behold a world beyond the one we made, and take that world to be the full replacement of our own.

And now we wait in silence, unafraid and certain of Your coming. We have sought to find our way by following the Guide You sent to us. We did not know the way, but You did not forget us. And we know that You will not forget us now. We ask but that Your ancient promises be kept which are Your Will to keep. We will with You in asking this. The Father and the Son, Whose holy Will created all that is, can fail in nothing. In this certainty, we undertake these last few steps to You, and rest in confidence upon Your Love, which will not fail the Son who calls to You.

And so we start upon the final part of this one holy year, which we have spent together in the search for truth and God, Who is its one Creator. We have found the way He chose for us and made the choice to follow it as He would have us go. His Hand has held us up. His Thoughts have lit the darkness of our minds. His Love has called to us unceasingly since time began.

We had a wish that God would fail to have the Son whom He created for Himself. We wanted God to change Himself, and be what we would make of Him. And we believed that our insane desires were the truth. Now we are glad that this is all undone, and we no longer think illusions true. The memory of God is shimmering across the wide horizons of our minds. A moment more, and it will rise again. A moment more, and we who are God's Sons are safely home, where He would have us be.

Now is the need for practice almost done. For in this final section, we will come to understand that we need only call to God, and all temptations disappear. Instead of words, we need but feel His Love. Instead of prayers, we need but call His Name. Instead of judging, we need but be still and let all things be healed. We will accept the way God's plan will end, as we received the way it started. Now it is complete. This year has brought us to eternity.

One further use for words we still retain. From time to time, instructions on a theme of special relevance will intersperse our daily lessons and the periods of wordless, deep experience which should come afterwards. These special thoughts should be reviewed each day, each one of them to be continued till the next is given you. They should be slowly read and thought about a little while, preceding one of the holy and blessed instants in the day. We give the first of these instructions now.

DAY 221

(Lesson 221)

"Peace to my mind. Let all my thoughts be still."

(W-pII.221)

"Father, I come to You today to seek the peace that You alone can give. I come in silence. In the quiet of my heart, the deep recesses of my mind, I wait and listen for Your Voice. My Father, speak to me today. I come to hear Your Voice in silence and in certainty and love, sure You will hear my call and answer me."

(W-pII.221.1)

Today we begin Part II of the workbook. The goal of our curriculum is to totally retrain our minds from separation to oneness. Part I taught us to watch our minds, recognize the ego's false identity, forgive falsehood, and choose to let truth replace the error in our mind.

We have been undoing fear's thought system and letting love's thought system rise within us and take the lead. We are developing the habit of engaging with God, of listening to the Voice for God consistently, so that it naturally becomes our first response to temptation of any kind.

The instructions are now leading us into a direct experience with God. These are prayer lessons. They are designed to help us stay accordantly on the path of truth we have chosen, such that our thoughts and actions are in service of miracles.

The first time through the lessons, arriving at this stage, I made the mistake of feeling guilty because of how often I still wavered, got caught in the ego's games and forgot my training. Then in a moment of clarity, I realized that guilt is the trigger finger back into the ego's game of doubt.

The instructions for going forward bypass ego interference, straight to the part of our mind that knows the truth. We are merely remembering what we displaced. In this realization, we're able to lean back, and practice in trust. We welcome God in quiet expectation and let the experience of His Divine Love fill us, setting each day in Its service.

Our first central theme is forgiveness, which is the crucial step to cross the bridge back home.

I experience true intimacy with today's lesson. *"Peace to my mind. Let all my thoughts be still."* In the center of my mind is a single point of light which expands as I say today's prayer.

I feel lifted from body-identity and into a state of pure light. Divine radiance vibrating as my Self—a deep all-encompassing peace—penetrating and full. Pulsing through and all around is a magnificent force, a love so glorious and joyous—a state of absolute inclusion. There is no me. Only this love.

I'm given a beautiful image, a vast golden pathway lighting the way of heaven, ever present and impossible to miss. I know it has always been there and that I am walking on it. It is as though the mist is confusion which lifts and disappears as I walk the light-way.

I see everything is in its forgiving light. I witness to love everywhere and in everyone. My Self is part of a brilliant and magnetic beacon of light and love. Divine content gives new meaning and purpose, unifying the whole.

Returning to the awareness of my body, I am present to this golden pathway interwoven in the world my eyes see—a golden pathway of a forgiven world, laid before me. Finally, I know my path is set—a blessed holy instant of recognition. This peace has never left me, and with it, the certainty of accepting the atonement for myself.

DAY 222

(Lesson 222)

"God is with me. I live and move in Him."
(W-pII.222)

*"Father, we have no words except Your Name upon our lips and in our minds,
as we come quietly into Your Presence now, and ask to rest with You in peace a while."*
(W-pII.222.2)

Today's lesson perfectly describes the way I want to experience my life 24/7. The ideas that take us into our prayer state literally raise our vibration to the frequency of truth.

God is with me. He is my Source of life, the life within, the air I breathe, the food by which I am sustained, the water which renews and cleanses me. He is my home, wherein I live and move; the Spirit which directs my actions, offers me Its Thoughts; and guarantees my safety from all pain. He covers me with kindness and with care, and holds in love the Son He shines upon, who also shines on Him. How still is he who knows the truth of what He speaks today.

It's a whole new level of the idea we learned earlier in our curriculum. *"God is in everything I see."* It totally invites us into an experience of God being everything, blessing and purifying for our joy and union. Right? Can you feel it? Our Home is with us, holding us in surety, safety, and peace.

We're getting an experience that Home is a constant state of being. Anytime we feel vulnerable to forces outside ourselves we remember, *God is with me and I live and move in Him.*

My resistance to Albuquerque was a continual classroom of forgiveness. I felt disconnected from my spiritual center. I'd show up for my time with God—awesome. But mostly, I didn't feel divine. I'd have peaceful meditations, but they didn't seem to inform my daily life.

Wasn't New Mexico supposed to be some sort of spiritual vortex? I felt like I was walking in quicksand and it was pulling me under. I couldn't see beyond the feeling of stuck-ness I was experiencing. Those I met didn't feel like a "good fit" for me, which justified my withdrawal.

Luckily (Divinely), it didn't take long before I was absolutely sick of myself, and finally surrendered into reality. *"God is my life. I live and move in Him."*

Thank God I had my training. One morning I'd simply had enough and came with open heart and mind—Ready to be honest with myself and God about what I was up to. I cop to full responsibility. I see the pattern I set forth with the first thought of disappointment which went unchecked.

The fog of evidence rolled in distorting my perception, making it impossible to see that my life is divinely orchestrated for the highest possible good for me. I was in unreality—and nothing could satisfy me there. It was one unforgiving thought, that something should be different than it is, which spun the dial, denying truth, and projecting a world of victimhood.

Seeing it, owning it, and, in gratitude, forgiving and releasing it happen simultaneously. The fog lifts and I remember I am not this pretend version of me. I am God's holy child and joy is my birthright. I proclaim today's lesson. *"God is with me. I live and move in Him."* Gratitude washes over me, releasing my pent-up joy!

I read the lesson aloud, reinforcing my decision. Just for good measure, I write it in marker on the mirror in our entryway to remind myself *God is with me. He is my Source of life.*

It becomes my mantra for weeks to come. Each day before we venture out, I look into my eyes in the mirror and remind myself, *"God is with me. I live and move in Him,"* letting His presence infuse me with trust and vision. It brings new opportunities and friendships, which had been invisible to me just days before.

CHAPTER ONE HUNDRED SIXTY

DAY 223

(Lesson 223)

"God is my life. I have no life but His."

(W-pII.223)

"Our Father, let us see the face of Christ instead of our mistakes. For we who are Your holy Son are sinless. We would look upon our sinlessness, for guilt proclaims that we are not Your Son. And we would not forget You longer. We are lonely here, and long for Heaven, where we are at home. Today we would return. Our Name is Yours, and we acknowledge that we are Your Son."

(W-pII.223.2)

The curriculum is designed to systematically undo all our false associations, so the truth, which is still in our minds, can dawn. We review the central theme: forgiveness prior to each day's lesson, and forgiveness's meaning sinks deep within our minds informing the way we approach the lesson.

It prepares our mind to accept the lesson ideas wholeheartedly and make the prayer our own, entering into communion with God. Here, we accept instruction in how to utilize the lesson throughout our day. We're really starting to live our lives from our state of being, and not from reacting to our environment.

At age fifteen, Parker decided to try public school, after being unschooled for years. I wanted to be supportive, and trust that the same guide for my happiness lives and breathes within Parker, guiding and directing his choices as well.

Still, all the reasons we'd decided against traditional school rush back into my mind. Judgments about the education system institutionalizing students, training them out of their own creative thinking and learning, fears about the competitive nature of the grading system, and the competition for status and popularity, made me feel in conflict about supporting Parker's choice.

I try to get above the fears, to lean into the trust I had in Parker and the Divine. But as he takes the entrance tests and gets feedback about his strengths and weakness, I feel defensive and over-protective. I fear he'd feel outcast, be teased or bullied.

I knew none of these thoughts and fears were helpful and try to forgive as they surface, while putting on a supportive face. Notice this whole trying theme? That's what the ego does. It tells us to try, so we won't look at the falsehood we're making real for ourselves.

One day, while dropping Parker at school, I'm saying what we always say, "Have a yummy day, and remember who you are," and I just stop in mid-sentence. *"Remember who you are . . ."* Oh, my God, remember who *I* am. It's like I plucked myself out of the movie I'd been pretending and dropped myself back into the producer's chair. This is my life—the life I share with God. My response to Parker's life is my classroom.

I park my car, and, right there in the parking lot, change my mind completely. I let every fear and judgment I'd been pushing aside into the light of awareness and lay them one by one before the altar of truth to be forgiven and let go.

This is what's so cool about the mind-training. I am intimately infused with a true alternative the instant I quit trying and accept that reality is not mine to decide—but God's.

Instantly, I can see through the cloud of falseness to the light within, and the true ideas transform my thinking. Today's lesson moves through me like lightning. *"I was mistaken when I thought I lived apart from God. God is my life. I have no life but His."*

I look around me and everything shimmers with light—I let love change my sight. I watch students entering the building, clusters of friends talking and laughing and where I saw error before, I see joining.

This is my life. My life with God.

DAY 224

(Lesson 224)

"God is my Father, and He loves His Son."

(W-pII.224)

"My Name, O Father, still is known to You. I have forgotten It, and do not know where I am going, who I am, or what it is I do. Remind me, Father, now, for I am weary of the world I see. Reveal what You would have me see instead."

(W-pII.224.2)

These lessons in Part II of the workbook are beautifully deepening. Their purpose is to facilitate a direct experience of God. They teach us the language of truth and how to speak with truth by first recognizing our identity as God's holy child. Like, *"My true Identity is so secure, so lofty, sinless, glorious and great, wholly beneficent and free from guilt, that Heaven looks to It to give it light. It lights the world as well."* Today's lesson is inviting us to enter into the stillness and let our mind open, feeling our vibration lifting to the speed of light, fanning our little spark into a brilliant glowing light of love.

It always blows my mind how easily I can doze off and start dreaming up problems and solutions to them. Just recently I caught myself in one of these spells.

Since we moved back to Vegas, Cole and Parker haven't yet found their niche. I make it my business to help (unsolicited by them). I encourage them to get involved in some interest groups, like a meet-up group and just see if it sparks joy.

It seems innocent enough, yeah? But my motives are suspect. I can tell by the way I feel. I check myself and let awareness shine. I see how I have made myself feel responsible for how things work out for them. I've got my control mitts in their business and God's business, and not my own.

Today's lesson is perfect. *"God is my Father, and He loves His Son."* Of, course. There is no place where God's love losses its effectiveness, and my self-importance needs to fill in the gap!

I start laughing. "Thank You." I forgive and leave their business in His hands. The answer as to what to do is staring me right in the face. *"Do nothing, then, and let forgiveness show you what to do, through Him Who is your Guide, your Savior and Protector, strong in hope, and certain of your ultimate success"* (W-pII.1.5). Grateful for the awareness, I trust that if there is a part for me to play, my Guide will let me know.

Next thing I know, the boys start a new business making e-juice for the vaping community. They invite me to join them for a vape conference. It's awesome watching them network, making friends, and contributing knowledge and experience. I witness a gorgeous flow of connection and community. (They couldn't find their niche, my ass.)

It is a blessed witness to trusting God's love for His Son, played out before me, through forgiving eyes. My true identity *is* the gift I bring to our relationship. Of course, the boys want to share their lives with me—want my presence to join them in their adventures. *"This is reality, and only this. This is illusion's end. It is the truth."*

CHAPTER ONE HUNDRED SIXTY-TWO
DAY 225
(Lesson 225)

"God is my Father, and His Son loves Him."

(W-pII.225.1)

"Father, I must return Your Love for me, for giving and receiving are the same, and You have given all Your Love to me. I must return it, for I want it mine in full awareness, blazing in my mind and keeping it within its kindly light, inviolate, beloved, with fear behind and only peace ahead. How still the way Your loving Son is led along to you!"

(W-pII.225.1.1–7)

Today's lesson full circles yesterday's idea. My Father loves me and naturally I love Him. Love is what we are—our Divine DNA. Holding this love in our mind tethers us to our truth identity as God's loving Son. Love is creation—the real we bring to every encounter.

Our prayer today serves as a way we enter into an experience with God and our relationship with Him. It is the only thing we're truly interested in. Everything that happens now reflects this relationship. Our Father has given His love to us, and the way the we accept it fully is by then extending it to everyone and everything. That is our part in completing the cycle of giving and receiving.

Every lesson is speaking to the part of our minds that remembers the truth. So when we run up against areas in our lives where we feel conflicted, upset, or afraid, we simply remember we have a Guide who holds the truth for us, and the way is open. We simply return our minds to the stillness, to our relationship with God.

The day I graduated from my physical therapy, my therapist, while running his final diagnostic tests on my progress, is smiling from ear to ear and says, "Your progress really is a miracle. You're a miracle. You told me when we started together that we were in the presence of a miracle. I wouldn't have believed it if I hadn't experienced it myself."

He asks if he can use my case for review with his board of directors. He says, "It shows how important our attitude is. I've documented our conversations and you're proof that maintaining a positive state of mind is pivotal to the patient's progress."

He asks me to give a statement for the camera. I say, "I simply accepted the truth of what I am, which is already healed and whole within my mind, and had faith my body would follow the direction of my state of mind, which is love."

This experience exemplifies today's lesson, *"I love my Father and He loves me,"* reflecting how giving and receiving are the same. I witness to the power of God's love and mine by holding it in my full awareness, letting it blaze in my mind as a light for others to join the open way with me. I hold to the truth, no matter what. I refuse to engage in illusions, regardless of seeming physical evidence. I invite these healers into the truth with me. And they witness to miracles with me. *"I love my Father and He loves me."*

CHAPTER ONE HUNDRED SIXTY-THREE
DAY 226
(Lesson 226)

"My home awaits me. I will hasten there."
(W-pll.226.1)

"Father, my home awaits my glad return. Your Arms are open, and I hear Your Voice. What need have I to linger in a place of vain desires and of shattered dreams, when Heaven can so easily be mine?"
(W-pll.226.2.1–3)

This lesson reminds us that everything we want or need for supreme happiness and everlasting peace is right here, this instant, awaiting our acceptance. We're done waiting for special circumstance, recognition, people, places, and things to change.

We make a decision and hasten home. We trust-fall into the arms of the Divine. We leave the world of story problems behind. We don't waste an instant in recognizing our home—our oneness with God.

Since what we see with our eyes is a projection of the idea of separation, it's really no big thing to give up all we value in this world. As mere projections, we lose nothing but confusion about who we are, when we make the choice to change our mind about the purpose of everything.

Today we leave it all behind and go home. When we go home to God, everything goes with us because there is nothing outside of us. Our state of being is home. The choice is ours.

I love living in new environments. I've moved around a lot in my life. I love the adventure of it. The one unmistakable thing I've learned is that wherever I go, I take myself with me. What's more, the relationship I have with myself is what determines the type of adventure I have.

Back in the day, hastening looked like running away from circumstances or relationships where I felt trapped. The thing is, after the honeymoon of running away, the same fears that produced the problems in the first place were right there, within my thought system, waiting for me.

What has been so fun about the mind-training is that it goes with me wherever I go too. And what was once running from, changed to running toward. The very things where I'd misplaced value or been afraid to face are the classroom where I forgive my purpose and accept the purpose of atonement.

A deep, abiding sense of belonging and joy is what I now recognize as my Home. Things and circumstances are more like the backbeat to the rhythm of eternal love in the center of my being—my Home. I am whole—everything is part of that whole. Now, I take my Home with me on my adventures.

When we moved back to Vegas, the buzz of adventure vibrated through us. Cole, Parker, and I left in the quiet of night, a caravan of love-cars on the open road. We used walkie-talkies to stay in sync. I decide I'll send favorite quotes from the course over the airwaves.

I start with my lesson for the day, *"My home awaits me. I will hasten there."* As I speak the words, I'm humbled at how different this move is from another many years ago when I left in the dead of night, afraid, and alone.

I hear some static, then laughing, and Cole comes back laughing, "You got a jet pack we don't know about?" Parker says, "Dude, Mom's saying home is where the heart is. It's your course lesson, right Mom?

Yep! I love how our lives are steeped in *ACIM* love.

Our Being is Home. Everything is a chance to hasten home to the recognition of love's presence, which, in turn, lights the world in a warm glow. Even when shit hits the fan, I feel a tickle of excitement, knowing truth is wiping the sleep from of my eyes, waking me to my Self.

DAY 227

(Lesson 227)

"This is my holy instant of release."

(W-pII.227.1)

"Father, it is today that I am free, because my will is Yours. I thought to make another will. Yet nothing that I thought apart from You exists. And I am free because I was mistaken, and did not affect my own reality at all by my illusions. Now I give them up, and lay them down before the feet of truth, to be removed forever from my mind. This is my holy instant of release. Father, I know my will is one with Yours."

(W-pII.227.1.1–7)

This moment, Now! This is our holy instant of release. It is in the instant we quit deceiving ourselves that being free takes hard work, or that happiness lies somewhere in the future.

There is no future. Now, is God's will for happiness for us fulfilled. The only reason we are not wholly joyous, free from any concerns, is because of this belief. But we're just mistaken. Simple as that. Our mistakes have never even touched the truth! We are released this instant by our decision. Our total freedom is in realizing that our will *is* God's.

A place where I have had a tendency to imprison myself is in my relationship with Lin. She often appears unhappy. I don't like it. I want her to be happy. I want her to see things differently. I want her to surrender her judgments that cause her pain and forgive.

I want her to quit identifying with struggle, determined to see the world as against her, and life as an uphill battle that she must push against and fight. I'd think my way is better for her. I think she should want to lead with joy, to expect miracles, and see everything is ultimately for her highest good. I want her to see that if what's happening doesn't spark joy, it is unreal, and to forgive it.

What's so funny about that is how blatantly it reflects my own experience. I'm pushing against rather than forgiving and accepting, right? I'm putting true relationship off, until Lin "gets it."

When I'm in this place, dreaming something should be different than it is, I am not seeing Lin because only my Self, as love, can see. Judgment and fear are blind. I am blinded to the truth and only truth can truly join.

The entire façade disassembles one day, while practicing today's lesson, *"This is my holy instant of release."* I catch my thought-train mid-judgment when Lin is passionately sharing a twitter feed about intersectionality with me. As the thought, "I wish you could just relax and accept things just as they are," surfaces in my mind, my hand goes to my heart.

"Wait, I'm mistaken. This is not my true will. What is this for?" The "wish" judgment crumbles. I breath in the stillness, letting everything else go. I accept Lin just as she is.

Looking at her through the eyes of my release, Lin is luminous—ignited with the fire of love in action. Tears sting my eyes as realize we share the same desire to see love reign. Instantly, I love Lin's way, her passion for justice and equality.

The immediacy of true intimacy I feel with Lin is overwhelming. Now I listen to Lin through her radiance. What I notice as she reads the twitter feed is remarkable, behind the words she speaks is the message of inclusion. I feel her quest for union and outreach of love. I receive her blessing of awareness and connection. *"This is my holy instant of release."*

DAY 228

(Lesson 228)

"God has condemned me not. No more do I."

(W-pII.228.1)

"Father, I was mistaken in myself, because I failed to realize the Source from which I came. I have not left that Source to enter in a body and to die. My holiness remains a part of me, as I am part of You. And my mistakes about myself are dreams. I let them go today. And I stand ready to receive Your Word alone for what I really am."

(W-pII.228.2.1–6)

Today we end the reign of condemnation. We are taking God's word for what we are and laying our mistaken identity at the feet of truth. We have been forgiven, and now we forgive, and accept our holiness.

We let the memory of our holiness fill our minds. Now, what we extend to our brothers is sourced by the Divine wisdom of our true identity.

Condemnation is like looking at the world through a tiny peep hole and believing what we see is the whole world. Then we try to make sense of the speck we see, determined it's all we have to work with. Forgiveness is like stepping back from the peephole and swinging the door wide open. And what we behold is the beauty and glory of creation. *"The memory of God is shimmering across the wide horizons of our minds"* (W-pII.in.9.7.5).

The ego-self is hardwired for condemnation. It is the sleight of hand the ego uses to shrink our perception to littleness. It only takes a holy instant of complete willingness to see, and the balls we've been juggling drop, revealing truth's clarity.

Right in the middle of berating myself for letting petty bullshit derail me from my commitment to see the world through my holiness, I see today's lesson shining bright.

It's like I see the cosmic joke of condemnation and bust up laughing. In this belief, there are two of me. One in the world, subject to its drama, and the one I experience in these incredible holy instances with God.

In brilliant clarity, I realize only one of them is true. And I know her. In fact, I love her. She is free, innocent, untainted by last night's dream. That instant, theory became experience. I made a decision for the One, with no other, banishing the false self as an option from my mind.

I'm at my annual sister's retreat. One of the sisters appears to be over-medicating. We sisters, under the guise of concern, gather in the courtyard to condemn—I mean, discuss strategy. So, naturally, we're doing this behind the sister's back. Clue.

I can feel self-righteousness rising like acid in my throat, and, automatically, I shame myself as judgy and insincere, privately condemning us all to the illusion of mistaken identity. Blessedly, I catch what I'm up to. "Hey, wait a minute. I am not this. The truth is blocked from my awareness by condemnation. I forgive." My eyes soften, my mind quiets, and today's lesson speaks gently, *God has condemned me not. No more do I.*

A little shake of my head and the mist of confused identity clears. It's so potent and pure, all else is gone. Innocence rises like the morning sun, refreshing my memory with the truth. I turn back to my sisters, I see the love that unites us. And now I bring a miracle, healing condemnation for all of us. Let's just talk with her.

DAY 229

(Lesson 229)

"Love, Which created me, is what I am."

(W-pII.229.1)

"Father, my thanks to You for what I am; for keeping my Identity untouched and sinless, in the midst of all the thoughts of sin my foolish mind made up. And thanks to You for saving me from them. Amen."

(W-pII.229.2.1–3)

Today's idea is perfect to complete this section on forgiveness. Love is what we are. And forgiveness is ultimately releasing our mistaken belief we are something else—leaving this one perfect thought—*"Love, Which created me, is what I am."* We did not create ourselves. Love did. Hallelujah! The search is over.

Silly us. Turns out, *we are* what we were searching for. *"Love, Which created me, is what I am,"* is the alpha and omega, the premise which sees the world forgiven—where we live the happy dream of miracles.

It redefines life completely. There's really nowhere to go and nothing to do, but to be what we are. It's like waking from a bad dream, to see the sun rising, casting a shimmer of joy across the horizon of our lives.

I feel the fullness of love during my morning coffee with the Divine, my heart beating alliance with God. Light fills me, infusing my cells and lighting the way before me. No past. No future. I am divinely present. It's not something happening to me. It is the absence of something else. It is pure being—one with all that is. God is. I am. Love being itself!

I get a phone call from an old friend. She's calling to remember who she is in truth. She comes by way of a story where she's trapped in a relationship falsehood. Behind her words I feel the call for love. She's come in search of the light, trusting I am the lighthouse which leads her back home.

She's crying as she begins her story. "I just found out I've been living a lie these past two years. The man I've been living with is married. How could I not have known? I'm such an idiot." Rather than sign on to her story of pain, I say, "Tell me what you love about this man."

Her voice is soft and reverent when she speaks again. "He sees me. He knows just what to say when I get off the rails and doesn't think I'm nuts. He's thoughtful and generous. I've never felt so loved and accepted. Honestly, we live in a harmony I've never known before. I guess that's why this hurts so much. It's been wonderful."

I say, "Sounds like a holy relationship. What happened?" She says, "Divorce papers arrived yesterday."

I say, "Perfect. What's the problem?"

She says, "I feel like a fool. I didn't even think to ask him if he's married. Why would I. He's been living with me for two years. I ask, "Did his marriage affect the relationship before the divorce papers arrived?" She says, "Of course not. Everything was perfect."

I ask, "What happened when the papers arrived?" She says, "He took me in his arms and said, 'Darling, we've been living our own lives. It's just a formality." I say, "What's the problem?" She says, "I feel stupid."

"Ah," I say, "Silly ego. Could any of this change who you are, and the love you've shared?" She says, "No." Long pause, then, "Oh, I see what you are getting at. Stupidity is not who I am. Love is." I say, "I think my job's done here."

Love is this holy instant of pure responsibility. That's why we're the light of the world. In truth, there is no darkness in us. Only light. Only love. That is our ministry. We can no longer pretend that there is some story worthy of delay. The love which created us, shines the way before us. Our job is to be unwavering in our extension of love. Uncompromisingly clear that there is no answer but love.

DAY 230

(Lesson 230)

"Now will I seek and find the peace of God."

(W-pII.230.1)

"Father, I seek the peace You gave as mine in my creation. What was given then must be here now, for my creation was apart from time, and still remains beyond all change. The peace in which Your Son was born into Your Mind is shining there unchanged. I am as You created me. I need but call on You to find the peace You gave. It is Your Will that gave it to Your Son."

(W-pII.230.2.1–8)

Peace. Behind every goal I've had in my life there have been the deeper reasons I wanted them. Things as everyday as enough money to pay the bills, to building a career I enjoyed, to being in a loving relationship, have ultimately been a quest for the peace of God. It was through the active application of the mind-training that I became aware of what my true goal was. The awareness of continual and ever-present peace abiding quietly within me came gradually, but profoundly.

One day while sitting on a lawn chair, watching the boys ride bikes around our little cul-de-sac, I realize I'm deeply content, safe, and totally at peace. It seems it's always been that way. As I watch them play, I realize peace is my natural abode. Nothing in this dream world can take it from me. Here I abide. Joy bubbles within and I giggle uncontrollably—so completely free from worry of any kind.

Then CRASH! Parker, trying to jump a curb, goes down. "Seriously," I say aloud, looking at the sky, as I jump up and rush to see if he's hurt. He's laying immobile, splayed on the pavement. My mind races with fearful thoughts. But simultaneously, my lesson whispers, *"Now I seek and find the peace of God."*

Peace, like soft tentacles reaches into every cell of my being and I know everything is fine.

As I kneel next to Parker, he turns his head toward me and hangs his tongue out the side of his mouth. He's playing possum! "Fooled ja," he says, and hops back on his bike. I flop back on the lawn laughing at the silliness of concern when peace is holding me in safe eternally.

Cole and Parker circle past—carefree, alive, innocent. They reflect the happy news of today's lesson. *"In peace I was created. And in peace do I remain."*

Peace is what we are. It is only by denying our identity as love that we deny our peace. *"It is not given me to change my Self,"* only to return to recognition of the truth of what I am as God created us. In that realization nothing outside of us can harm or disturb us.

Nothing actually needs to change or be different. We have a new assuredness we can't really lose our way; peace goes with us.

When we start to bother ourselves with fear or worry, just pause and find the peace of God already resting within, answering our call to the present peace of God.

Sure, we forget and lose our way at times, but deep within we know peace never really leaves us. The call to awaken has been activated and beckons our return. It takes but an instant to stop and return to sanity, where we know we are home, resting in the peace of God.

DAY 231

(Lesson 231)

"Father, I will but to remember You."

(W-pII.231.1)

"What can I seek for, Father, but Your Love? Perhaps I think I seek for something else; a something I have called by many names. Yet is Your Love the only thing I seek, or ever sought. For there is nothing else that I could ever really want to find. Let me remember You. What else could I desire but the truth about myself?"

(W-pII.231.1.1–6)

Today we begin a new theme of special relevance: *"What is Salvation?"* It says, Salvation is a promise, made by God, that we will find our way back to Him. This promise is our true will—it resides within us as a yearning that calls us Home. We've displaced this yearning toward all kinds of false gods along the way.

It shows up as wishing and hoping for the perfect thing, person, lucky break, or set of circumstances that will bring us happiness. And it seems it's only when all these false promises fail us that we turn within and listen to our true will—to what the Voice of Love wills.

That's today's lesson. We want one thing—to remember God and know God's love. *"Father, I will but to remember You."* What we truly will is to remember our divinity and feel the love of God beating our hearts.

I was taught as a child that salvation was granted by someone outside myself, after I suffered, paid penance, and confessed to the appropriate authority figure. Salvation and crucifixion were tied together.

I never really got how a God who loved us could set up his "special" son to suffer and die. That's not love. I believed that God was outside of myself and that I was basically waiting for Him to wave a forgiveness wand if I could just get the formula right. Never did.

I tried to be good, follow the rules, be nice. I felt like I was always playing catch-up—guilty and unworthy from the moment I woke up in the morning. Yuck. Then I had this cool experience around age ten.

I'm on my knees praying-by-numbers, as usual. I'm thinking how impossible it is to be good enough to earn God's love, and just give up, and say. "Forget it. This doesn't work. I'd rather be a bad girl who feels good about herself than a good girl who can never make it."

Suddenly, I felt a surge of peaceful okay-ness, a feeling of utter peace—like warm water flowing through my veins. I was not alone after all, but part of this okay-ness that just is. I felt loved—God's love—asking nothing from me.

This experience did not match the God of my religion—which ultimately I abandoned out of self-preservation. This was my first experience of what salvation is. The simple truth that God is love and I am part of that.

I'd all but forgotten the aforementioned experience as the serial adventures of my ego spun my world into darkness, shame, and despair. But it was this experience of okay-ness, of not being alone, but part of something loving and magnificent that I didn't need to earn, was present from the moment I began *A Course in Miracles*.

Contemplating today's lesson, resting in God's love, I'm delighted for the return of this childhood experience as a present memory of recognition in eternal holy instant I experience now. Nothing true is ever lost—in fact, loss is impossible.

The memory of God is in each holy instant we're willing to see the world and ourselves differently. The mind-training is now anchored in our operating system. Any disturbance to our state of peace and something clicks in our mind—to stop and choose again. *"Father, I will but to remember You."*

DAY 232

(Lesson 232)

"Be in my mind, my Father, through the day."

(W-pII.232.1)

"Be in my mind, my Father, when I wake, and shine on me throughout the day today. Let every minute be a time in which I dwell with You. And let me not forget my hourly thanksgiving that You have remained with me, and always will be there to hear my call to You and answer me. As evening comes, let all my thoughts be still of You and of Your Love. And let me sleep sure of my safety, certain of Your care, and happily aware I am Your Son."

(W-pII.232.1.1–5)

Isn't today's prayer the best! It is a perfect guide to a happy day. It's is the prayer of our heart which places us in a state of readiness for the day along the lines Divinity has set. We're practicing the end of fear today, which is what all our planning and worry serves, yes? Awesome right. In fear's place we place our faith in God, and by extension each brother we encounter and our Self. It is pure joy!

I got called for active duty when Desert Storm began. Boy, was I conflicted. War was the last thing I wanted to put my stamp on. I was in the Reserves, and it was my duty to go. When the call came, it's like I could see my fear/ego sending out its minions, bombarding me with thoughts of unfairness, and looking for a loophole.

Thank God for my mind-training—I see the temptation to feel unfairly treated is way beyond the temptation stage. Before talking with anyone and confusing myself further, I go within and give the whole thing to the Divine, asking for guidance. "God, I don't know what to do here. How can I possibly show up for this? It seems like the opposite of the love and happiness path I have chosen. What is the purpose? And what would You have me do?"

The Holy Spirit (sounding like Betty) says, "Kid, there is no opposite to love, so there is no conflict to your chosen path. Nothing is random. Everything has been designed for you to perfectly fulfill your function. The war is in your own mind, Danét. And it is here you must forgive. Your only function is forgiveness. Where better to fulfill it? Now get on that plane."

I sense my wholeness and love. I am safe, at home in heaven. I am the peace that is needed. I am the love that heals the idea of war. I step all the way in and answer the call.

As I'm gathering my gear to go to Fort Douglas for deployment, I ask for a beacon to help me remember my purpose at all times. I grab my course book and open to today's lesson. *"Be in my mind, my Father, through the day."* Perfect!! I am a love badass and peace is my ministry! Here's this prayer designed especially for me! I write the prayer on a post-it.

I say it as I board the plane and every morning of my tour of duty. It's my go-to anytime I start feeling frustrated with what the military is doing. And if you've ever dealt with the military, you know you can always find a reason to feel frustrated if that is what you are looking for.

I couldn't have a better classroom for seeing how deeply ingrained victimhood and judgment are in my psyche. With each realization, pause, and forgiveness, I realized a higher reason for being there. Today's lesson served as a constant vigil with the Divine—my blessing for peace and love in a seemingly opposite construct—war.

I look back on these six months fondly, as a truly holy time in my life where I felt the Divine in my mind reflected everywhere; guiding me to teach peace and love while I counseled soldiers and we returned them safely home—each encounter truly holy.

DAY 233

(Lesson 233)

"I give my life to God to guide today."

(W-pII.233.1)

"Father, I give You all my thoughts today. I would have none of mine. In place of them, give me Your Own. I give You all my acts as well, that I may do Your Will instead of seeking goals which cannot be obtained, and wasting time in vain imaginings. Today I come to You. I will step back and merely follow You. Be You the Guide, and I the follower who questions not the wisdom of the Infinite, nor Love whose tenderness I cannot comprehend, but which is yet Your perfect gift to me."

(W-pII.233.1.1–5)

Today's lesson and prayer is a touchstone reminding us to tune our frequency to God, spending quiet time with Him, giving our mind over totally to His will for happiness for us. *"God is my life. I have no life but His"* (W-pII.223.1). If we're not supremely happy, we've let ego beliefs hijack our mind. Giving our life to God to guide, means withdrawing our attention from private thoughts and placing it on the Divine.

As I recite today's prayer, it takes me back to when Lin and Lucas first came back to live with me full time, and I was trying to "be a good mom." I was doing my best, but I didn't feel authentic or joyful. I had every reason to be happy. I'd wanted this so badly. I wanted to feel worthy of this gift.

I was a peaceful warrior until they came back to live with me—then boom! I'm overwrought with doubt and fear. Daily, I'd pray to be a good mom and start fresh. I was mired in the dream, confused about the cause of my problem which is the choice for guilt in my mind, reflected now in my mom-story. I kept thinking if I could do "good enough" I'd suddenly feel competent. From the guilt construct, I was always trying to qualify.

I knew I wasn't in my right-mind, but I felt desperate to fix the mom-story so I'd feel better. I did all the right actions, but kids know. Motherhood is a wake-up call. All I wanted was another chance at motherhood and now I was faced with my utter incompetence. I broke, thinking, "I really don't know the thing I am or how to be in the world."

Finally, I pause. In that instant I see my way free, with today's lesson, *"I give my life to God to guide today."* I drop into emptiness of my mind and feel my sanity. I am not this. I am as God created me—guilt and love cannot coexist. "Yeah. I'm totally incompetent. I've got cause and effect upside-down. I've been trying to behave myself into an experience of forgiveness. Of course, life brought witnesses reflecting my guilt belief back to me. Gratefully, the guilt is my mind and it is here it can be released.

I forgive. I drop all pretense I know anything or what being a mother is. Tears flow freely as release washes over me. I pick up my book and read today's lesson, holding each thought in my heart as my own. *"I give my life to God to guide today."* *"Father, I give all my thoughts to You. I would have none of my own."*

A new confidence settles in my heart—God is with me. His Love is my perfect example—my guide to presence with my children—I've got my perfect role model. I give all my thoughts and actions to Him. In innocence and trust I step back and follow Him. It is His wisdom I lean toward, His strength I rely on. In my willingness to forgive my mom-story, I am given the gift of motherhood—love!

DAY 234

(Lesson 234)

"Father, today I am Your Son again."

(W-pII.234.1)

*"We thank You, Father, that we cannot lose the memory of You and of Your Love.
We recognize our safety, and give thanks for all the gifts You have bestowed
on us, for all the loving help we have received, for Your eternal patience,
and the Word which You have given us that we are saved."*

(W-pII.234.2.1–2.)

It's funny—I mean perfect—that today's lesson shows up right now. Since Cole and Parker moved out last month, I've been fixated on where Lar and I are relocating and how I will get everything accomplished this month. We're downsizing to create our new "empty-nesting" home. We need to be looking at houses and actually moving in by the end of the month.

But next week I'm supposed to be with my darling Mama, assisting with her physical well-being, which I want to do. I love these extended times with her, where we share love for the Divine and our devotion to living in joy and peace.

The thing is, as soon as I get back, Lar and I have a long-awaited return trip to New Orleans, the city we where we fell in love, scheduled. I've been feeling a bit overwhelmed, to say the least. I watch how my mind wants to make time constraints real—to make or alter plans in the dream to diminish my discomfort. I see how my attention gets pulled into scheduling details and away from trust.

Today's lesson reminds me to stay awake to the truth—to forgive the impulse to activate past learning and attempt to organize the present or make self-initiated plans. I laugh—thank God there is another way.

Sinking into today's lesson, *"Father, today I am Your Son again,"* I zero my attention on the truth of what I am as God created me—love. *"Father, today I am Your Son again."* I open my mind to God. Deep contentment and incredible Love wash over me and fill me with trust. I let my energy and attention go toward that trust.

I have everything I need. I am sourced from the powerful magnetic flow that is my identity, and everything organizes around my happiness and success, according to Divine will. I feel confident, aligned in purpose for each occurrence that happens. *"Father, today I am Your Son again."* I am remembering that God is with me. He is Source in all circumstances. I am tuned to the frequency of joy—trusting the flow.

I'm feeling buoyant with adventure when the phone rings. It's my friend Shar who is a real estate agent and an *A Course in Miracles* student. She calls with several listings for homes in the area we want to live. We can start viewing them tomorrow. She brings an ease and confidence which makes it fun and easy to trust the process.

My sister and mother call firming up plans with her. I get a confirmation email that everything is set for New Orleans. Everything falls into place when my focus is on divinity. It's incredible to see this holy connection cannot be un-connected. We are God's Son—we are God's love.

DAY 235

(Lesson 235)

"God in His mercy wills that I be saved."

(W-pII.235.1)

"Father, Your holiness is mine. Your Love created me, and made my sinlessness forever part of You. I have no guilt nor sin in me, for there is none in You."

(W-pII.235.2.1–3)

I need but look upon all things that seem to hurt me, and with perfect certainty assure myself, 'God wills that I be saved from this,' and merely watch them disappear." Could there be a more comforting thought?

This little prayer has seen me through some pretty scary times. Like when Parker went to live with his biological father. He was only ten years old.

This man was the donor when I chose to have children again, and we'd remained friends. So, the boys knew him. Parker had spent some time with him during the summer and became convinced he was supposed to live with him awhile.

Inside I was screaming, "No! Don't go! It won't be like you think. They have an agenda for you. They won't *see* you and honor you. STAY!" I'd see these fear thoughts and forgive as quickly as they surfaced, so I could trust God and Parker.

Holding to my promise to remember my children are not *my* children, but the Children of the Divine, I was committed to supporting Parker to follow his heart and to trust that whatever his experiences brought him, were divinely his life path, and that my love and support were ultimately a part of that.

I released my Parker to the Divine and this man's household. A very different environment than what he was used to. Like opposite in every way.

Parker and I talked daily, and he shared his experiences with me. Some of which were very difficult for him and excruciating for me to hear. I'd actively forgive and extend love. Inside I was riddled with helplessness, feeling powerless and wishing I'd never let him go.

One such morning I lay curled in a fetal position, (what Parker calls the fatal position) and give it all to God. "Dear God, I feel as though my heart is being ripped out. I am afraid of losing Parker. I am afraid that Parker will lose himself. I fear that his innocent, loving Self will be stomped on—that his bright smiling heart and personality will be squished into a form too small for him. I know that these fears are strangling my trust and faith—please help."

Suddenly, I realize the decision for victimhood in my mind. I calm immediately, and one thought fills my mind. *"God in His mercy wills that I be saved."* I grab my book and read the lesson, each word sinking deep and out across the spirit-waves. *"I need but look upon what seems to hurt and in perfect certainty I assure myself, 'God wills that I be saved from this,' and merely watch it disappear."*

Peace like warm water flows through my veins—God's unquestionable love and healing flooding into every cell of my body. Holding Parker in my mind, I read on. *"I need but keep in mind my Father's Will for me is only happiness, to find that only happiness has come to me. And I need but remember that God's Love surrounds His Son and keeps his sinlessness forever perfect, to be sure that I am saved and safe forever in His Arms. I am the Child He loves. And I am saved because God's mercy wills it so."*

Oh, my God! We are at home in God, perfectly safe. I feel Parker with me. I trust.

The next time I talk with Parker, he says, "Mom, there's so much fear and fighting. They don't even realize what they're doing. I'm glad I'm here. They need the love. I just bless them in my heart to want to be happy." Damn. I love that kid.

It's only a week later when Parker feels complete and chooses to return home.

DAY 236

(Lesson 236)

"I rule my mind, which I alone must rule."

(W-pII.236.1)

"Father, my mind is open to Your Thoughts, and closed today to every thought but Yours. I rule my mind, and offer it to You. Accept my gift, for it is Yours to me."

(W-pII.236.2.1–3)

This is such a powerful lesson. Before I began the mind-training with *A Course in Miracles*, I mostly felt powerless over my thoughts and feelings, always reacting to my environment, trying to predict the future and avoid the pitfalls.

But one of the first things I noticed as I began watching my mind is that whatever I focused on became bigger in my reality. And I was always thinking about my problems and how to fix or avoid them.

One of the biggest aha moments for me early in my training was seeing how I was orienting myself around survival and being a single mom. I was always struggling, afraid there wouldn't be enough, afraid I wouldn't be able to take care of my children, and that they wouldn't have what they needed for a happy life.

One day during a bout of mental gymnastics with expenses in my life, I stopped and mentally placed what I was experiencing before me as if on an altar to look at honestly with spirit. My breathing was constricted. There was a tight band across my forehead. I felt weak and powerless, frightened and alone. Suddenly I realized the *"I"* noticing was separate from the experience, from my thoughts and feelings.

Also, I could see how I felt was a result of the way I was thinking. I realized, there's another way to look at this. The "I" could make another choice. To see a different purpose for the situation, though I had no idea what that would be.

Ultimately, I realized the only choice I need to make is to see with the Holy Spirit. Instantly I felt more peaceful. These fearful ideas are reflections of past fears. Not present moment awareness. By focusing on the awareness of my thoughts rather than the particular subject matter, I realized they are just thoughts. I give them the meaning and experience I choose.

If the past is gone, there is nothing to fear, and I forgive the illusion of a past-projected-future. The relief was palpable. *"I rule my mind, which I alone must rule."* I am responsible. I choose the experience I want to have and everything that happens I ask for and receive in kind.

An explosion of joy released from my constricted heart and I felt a sense of freedom. I had intellectually understood the principle behind our thoughts create our reality, but this was my first clear experience of being the ruler of my own mind.

I felt excited and so grateful for the awareness. I noticed that as I focused on the gratitude and joy I was feeling, other thoughts of things in my life that I was grateful for started flooding into my mind. "I get to be a mom. I have the most delightful kids. I like my job."

I thought of goofing around with the kids just the night before, and we were totally immersed in laughter and fun—no problems in sight. What had changed? Only my focus. I rule my mind—love instead of fear.

DAY 237

(Lesson 237)

"Now would I be as God created me."

(W-pII.237.1)

"Christ is my eyes today, and He the ears that listen to the Voice for God today.
Father, I come to You through Him Who is Your Son, and my true Self as well. Amen."

(W-pII.237.2.1–3)

The lessons we are doing right now come under the theme idea, "What is Salvation?" It's the daily practice of being our True Self (Christ) as God created us, which not only saves us from the dirge of the ego identity, but as we radiate our light, we become a beacon calling all minds to remember the Christ within which we all share as One. In this way we are the salvation of the world.

Today's lesson, *"Now would I be as God created me,"* is a declaration of being. We're saying we let the past be gone and leave the future in the hands of God. We're at home as the Self God created us, and it is from here we intersect with the world of our experience. Remember that the ego speaks first and loudest. That's why being still an instant when the impulse to react is so crucial. So we can choose again what we would *be* in the situation—the love that we are.

The thing that ensures the best possible chance of living from our right-mind, happy love, light, wholeness, and peace, is the way we start our day. We decide. The mind-training teaches us exactly how. Our lessons now are speaking directly to the Christ within us. Today's is asking us to rise up and stand as the light.

The prayer is like the launch pad for the day: *"Christ is my eyes today, and He the ears that hears the Voice for God today."* Joining with our Source, *"Father, I come to You through Him Who is Your Son, and my true Self as well. Amen."* We are acknowledging that we have our being as Christ—our One Self, as God created us.

When I first started to notice that the mind-training was becoming a habit, I started seeing the simplicity of living in divine flow and the lesson would just be in my mind.

Like I'd be running errands, picking up dry-cleaning, grocery shopping, using today's idea as a mantra while I drive. *"Now would I be as God created me."* Then before I get out of the car at each destination, I'd automatically get quiet and feel into my identity as love, as a set-point from which to move into the experience before me.

One such day comes to mind. The weather was bleak, grey, and foggy. As I walk from the car into the dry-cleaners, I feel like I am a light cutting through the fog. I'm smiling and beaming love, and out of the corner of my eye, I notice an elderly woman tentatively making her way through the parking lot.

I walk over, offer my arm, and begin walking next to her. I have a sense of expanding God's certainty of safety and comfort as we silently walked side by side through the parking lot and up to the shop next to the dry cleaners. As we depart ways, she releases my arm and says, "You're an angel."

Back at my car, I find I've locked the keys in it. I feel panic beginning to rise. But instantly I remember, *"Now would I be as God created me."* I call Cole, and straight away he brings my spare key. He is my angel. Circle of love!

CHAPTER ONE HUNDRED SEVENTY-FIVE

DAY 238

(Lesson 238)

"On my decision all salvation rests."

(W-pII.238.1)

"Father, Your trust in me has been so great, I must be worthy. You created me, and know me as I am. And yet You placed Your Son's salvation in my hands, and let it rest on my decision. I must be beloved of You indeed. And I must be steadfast in holiness as well, that You would give Your Son to me in certainty that he is safe Who still is part of You, and yet is mine, because He is my Self."

(W-pII.238.1.1–5)

Today's lesson is another way of acknowledging our Oneness as God created us and extending it to everyone and everything. It is a way of saying, "I accept atonement for myself," which the course tells us is the sole responsibility of the miracle worker. It is the recognition that the power of decision rests with us.

As we identify with the love of God within our mind and heart, the Holy Spirit, our Christ identity, we transform each experience of seeming separation into one of healing and wholeness. Every decision we make determines the fate of the world in our experience. How we choose to see those we encounter as either the other (separation) or our brother (wholeness) changes our experience of the situation entirely.

Like the other day, I stopped by the clubhouse in our new community. I noticed I had a subtle sense of unease as I walked about. There were clusters of people gathered in conversation. I noticed how my ego mind was interpreting the situation. It seemed to me that they were closed groups, having private conversations from which I am excluded—a mirror of my private thoughts of exclusion.

This interpretation makes me feel apprehensive and alone, saying things like, "I don't know anyone. I'm not part of." It makes me feel invisible, unimportant, afraid—icky. Noticing I don't like the way I feel is my flip-switch to recognize the call for love within me. *"On my decision all salvation rests,"* rings in my mind. I decide.

I change my mind about how I am seeing. Taking a breath, I enter into the still center of my mind, tuning into the love and joy of my true Self. I press pause on my interpretation, and zero in on love's. *"On my decision all salvation rests."* I take responsibility for being the light of love and joy.

I approach a group of women and introduce myself. "I came to meet my new best friends." The response is overwhelmingly open and inviting. We exchange phone numbers and they tell me what they love about the community, inviting me right into the fold—yummy!

The power of choice is a primary theme throughout the course. It is the only power we have in this world. It's really only one decision we have to make: truth or illusion (nothing). God or the ego (edging God out). Love or fear (false evidence appearing real).

We are the One. Quite literally, *on my decision all salvation rests.*

DAY 239

(Lesson 239)

"The glory of my Father is my own."

(W-pII.239.1)

*"We thank you, Father, for the light that shines forever in us.
And we honor it, because You share it with us. We are one, united in
this light and one with You, at peace with all creation and ourselves."*

(W-pII.239.2.1–3)

Coffee shops are like church for me. I love checking out the congregation that comes and goes and gathers together for joining. What makes it remarkable, is that, like all aspects of my life, it is the perfect training ground for recognizing my holiness and applying the lesson ideas.

Today's idea, *"The glory of my Father is my own,"* calls to mind a time when I'm to meet a friend at Starbucks. I go early and take a seat. I'm happy to wait and practice my lesson, looking around at the glory of God in everyone and seeing that it is mine too. I'm greeting people as they pass and silently thanking each person and blessing them with the holiness we share as One Love.

So, instead of feeling like a loner, sitting by myself, I'm in full glory, shining my light. I'm smiling and saying, "Hi, and have a yummy day," and I feel glorious. I feel that Divine glory in myself and see it in everyone around me. I'm joyous, serene, and bright—a light of joy, peace, and love.

I notice a teenaged boy sitting alone at a corner table. My first thought is that he seems withdrawn and sad. But I correct myself, remembering my lesson. "Wait, that is my evaluation. Is that how I would see myself? No." As if he hears me, he looks up and directly at me.

I say a silent, "Thank you for your holy light, for it is mine." He tips his coffee cup to me. I feel his spark of light the moment he looks up too. A few minutes later, he looks directly at me again, this time with a big smile.

Next thing I know, the boy is walking toward me. He sits down across from me and says, "I feel like I know you. Are you a friend of my mom's?" Though I wasn't familiar with his mother, a connection had been made of a shared identity in love which drew us together. We talk until my friend shows up.

"Let not the truth about ourselves be hidden by a false humility."

Had I listened to my first (ego) reaction to this boy—he's a sad and lonely kid—I'd have missed all that glory. No connection can be made between what is false. Only the truth can be truly shared. The truth comes innocently into view when we have eyes to see. *"The glory of my Father is my own."*

DAY 240

(Lesson 240)

"Fear is not justified in any form."

(W-pII.240.1)

"How foolish are our fears! Would You allow Your Son to suffer? Give us faith today to recognize Your Son, and set him free. Let us forgive him in Your Name, that we may understand his holiness, and feel the love for him which is Your Own as well."

(W-pII.240.2.1–3)

This is a perfect lesson for me to share about right now. *"Fear is never justified in any form."* Now, I have returned my mind to my one identity as love, Sourced by Divine love. (Hindsight is 20/20.)

My trip to India was enlightening. But not for the reason one might think. The flights were long, and I let fear creep into my mind. It started with anticipating the long flights. Remember that lesson, *"I am at home. Fear is the stranger here?"*

Well, that's just what I did. I invited the stranger in. Seemingly innocently, I prepared for the future pain in my back I would experience throughout the twenty plus hours I would be on the airplane. Such began my defense against the truth; the stranger's campaign against my wholeness as love.

I packed my pillow and fear in my carry on and pushed snooze on my awareness of joy, temporarily dis-identifying with the truth, that I am love, the holy child of God Himself, invulnerable to pain and suffering and fear. The flight proved it all out for me too.

When I get to the hotel, I read my lesson and turn within. Today's lesson, *"Fear is not justified in any form,"* begins; *"Fear is deception."* Bingo! I had been in a fog of deception and could not see my Self. It says, *"It attests that you have seen yourself as you could never be."* Once I placed my faith in fear, that impossible reality that pain is real and must be mitigated by fear, a different world spun out before me. A world of suffering and a campaign for "symptom removal" as proof of healing, began.

Remembering the truth through today's lesson invites me to look again at what I was experiencing and ask if this is what I would have instead of peace, of joy, adventure, and fun. I laugh out loud. Laughter is such a yummy release. With it I let go of fear's story of pain, becoming present with the love I am and the adventure before me. Happiness swoops in and fills the space occupied by fear just a moment before.

The India culture is rich with devotion and I let myself fall in love with everyone I encounter, "Namaste." We dip in Ganga River and meditate in caves. Fear is never justified in any form.

Turns out enlightenment is presence, here and now, as love and happiness!

DAY 241

(Lesson 241)

"This holy instant is salvation come."

(W-pII.241.1)

"We have forgiven one another now, and so we come at last to You again. Father, Your Son, who never left, returns to Heaven and his home. How glad are we to have our sanity restored to us, and to remember that we all are one."

(W-pII.241.2.1–2)

We enter into the quiet of our hearts, into the presence of the Divine, we leave everything we thought we were before this present holy instant behind. We wait in quiet expectation for the truth to come.

The holy instant is not a moment in time. It is the eternal instant beyond time that unites us with our Self, our Source, and all creation. It is the decision to be the love that God created us as and let that whole-mind heal our perception within time and space.

Here's an example from the other day, when choosing a holy instant and seeing the situation from love, really altered the energy in the room.

Lar had gone to meet a new heart doctor. When he returns, he's visibly upset. I ask him how the appointment went and he tells me he didn't see the doctor. That he'd waited for an hour and a half. He says the staff was inconsiderate and incompetent. How he got increasingly angry until finally, he felt justified in leaving.

I have one of those out of body experiences as I listen to him. My body's impulse was to judge Lar, to think there's a better way of dealing with it than what he's doing. But I catch the contraction as the thought forms and stop. "That's not what's happening. Accept and love or deny and close your heart. Your choice!"

"This holy instant is salvation come! This is our holy relationship. This is our call for love." I sit next to him, silently blessing with the holiness we share, and thanking him for showing me the conflict in my mind.

I take his hand, stroke his neck, and say, "I love you." It's like grace floods the room with light and ease.

In a holy instant, conflict dissolves, not just from my mind, but his as well. His face is serene. Love is. We were bathed in holiness, and joy practically burst from me. A few minutes later and with no further discussion, Lar turns to me and says, "I think I'll make an appointment with another doctor."

Practicing the holy instant teaches us that the eternal love we share is present, each and every instant. This instant, the world can change. A holy instant where the darkened world of separation is reset to oneness. And we are set free to love and be the presence of hope and love in every encounter. The portal of grace is always open.

DAY 242

(Lesson 242)

"This day is God's. It is my gift to Him."

(W-pII.242.1)

*"And so we give today to You. We come with wholly open minds.
We do not ask for anything that we may think we want. Give us what You
would have received by us. You know all our desires and our wants. And You
will give us everything we need in helping us to find the way to You."*

(W-pII.242.2.1–6)

The idea is that every day and each moment is God's. How we use it is our gift to Him. When I am not distracted by pretending that I am somehow distanced or separate from God, His love is right there, present within me.

The gift of the mind-training is that by our decision and willingness we are training our minds to the ever-present awareness of our union with God.

First thing each day, I zero in on that foundational idea that there is only love. I approach my coffee date with the Divine with reverence as I enter holy ground. It is as if I never believed I was separate, or that God was somewhere off in the distance or the past or future, but right here, right now—that is the holy instant.

What's become habitual as I wake, before my bare feet hit the ground, I remember God is, therefore I am. I feel the love of God rising within me and remember God is love, creating me like itself. I give my eyes and ears and hands and feet to the service of Christ love.

I'd like to say I remember each day all day, that I am because God is, and that my life is the heartbeat of His love, but I forget. I dream up scenarios of past pain and lack and fears of future ones. The groovy thing about developing the habit of engaging with God, is that when I'm off, it doesn't take much for it to be intolerable, and I happily surrender into peace and return to love.

When the boys were young and we were doing the unschooling thing, I remember a day where the poignancy of today's lesson struck home solid. We were at the space museum. Cole is questioning everything that the guide is telling us. He'd been studying quantum theory on his own and keeps asking questions of the woman who's doing the tour. She doesn't have the answers.

Several of the mothers say things like, "Just listen or go outside. Don't make a scene." They're looking at me like they want me to do something. I get pissed. "Isn't unschooling all about questioning everything, and learning based on what one discovers as true for themselves?" From my defensive perspective, those mothers suddenly look like enemies. I feel all mother-bear-like. Aargh.

I'd zero my focus on supporting Cole—and being right. I'm not feeling joy. This isn't about Cole. He's happily doing Cole. Clearly, not asking for or needing me to intervene. Feeling the tightness in my gut, I know my perception is skewed. That was my flip-switch.

I step aside and take a moment to myself and God. I turn within to feel the prayer rising in my heart—today's lesson, *"This day is God's. It is my gift to Him."* I surrender. I see I was giving the situation the negative meaning it had for me and ask to see only what God would have me see. All defensiveness slips from me and I feel great trust in Cole, the guide, the mothers, and myself. Peace. It's as if the scene totally changes, in the blink of an eye.

DAY 243

(Lesson 243)

"Today I will judge nothing that occurs."
(W-pII.243.1)

"Father, today I leave creation free to be itself. I honor all its parts,
in which I am included. We are one because each part contains
Your memory, and truth must shine in all of us as one."
(W-pII.243.2.1–3)

Today I will judge nothing that occurs." It's fun to watch what the ego-mind does with a lesson like today's. The first sneaky thought is, "Easier said than done." My ego is making its case for laziness—for rightness—for repeating yesterday's movie dubbed over the new, fresh aliveness of this moment.

But we don't have to let it take hold. We can choose to be present—that's the mind-training. We watch what our mind gets up to and choose to see it differently—letting Christ vision show us something new—we let love do the seeing.

Funny thing, we simply can't look with love and judge at the same moment. They feel completely different, right? That's the clue and the flip-switch. One feels wonderful, and the other awful. Judgment is the way the ego validates itself.

That's why as we start watching our minds, we see we have a constant commentary about everything. "I like this. I don't like that. Look at what that person is wearing. What she said. How he looks. What they must be like . . ." Judging keeps us from being open to what is present now.

As I look over the movie of my life, it's not so much the events, or even the people involved that draw me to remember. It is the feeling I had during those moments that fill me with the sense of what my life is really about.

Like yesterday, I spent much of the day in the French Quarter in New Orleans. I start out with the idea for today fresh on my mind. *"Today I will judge nothing that occurs."* I want to be experiencing everything brand new and be open to whatever happens exactly as it is. I decide to walk to Café du Monde for chicory coffee and beignets. Yum.

I am hoping for sunshine but am greeted with a gray and drizzly atmosphere as I step outside. I notice the feeling of disappointment begin to occupy my mind as I greet the door guys and head out, squelching the impulse to declare my disappointment and get them to align with me. But, remembering my goal for the day, I let the idea that sunshine was preferable slip from my mind as I open to what's actually happening. Instantly, I feel my heart open wide and notice the drizzle is warm on my skin. I happily dance skip in the rain.

I never make it to Café du Monde. I end up making friends with a couple of gals from Canada visiting New Orleans for the first time. They ask about my experience with this amazing city. I share how I love the energy—like you can feel the creativity, like a living heart beating as you walk through the quarter.

Musicians play on street corners, artists are setting up easels, palm readers and psychics are all around us. One gal has her palm read, the other buys from a local artist.

As we say goodbye, they thank me, saying what a ray of sunshine I am. I smile as I skip on. I got my sunshine after all. A judgment-free mind is sunshine and joy.

DAY 244

(Lesson 244)

"I am in danger nowhere in the world."

(W-pII.244.1)

"Your Son is safe wherever he may be, for You are there with him. He need but call upon Your Name, and he will recollect his safety and Your Love, for they are one. How can he fear or doubt or fail to know he cannot suffer, be endangered, or experience unhappiness, when he belongs to You, beloved and loving, in the safety of Your Fatherly embrace?"

(W-pII.244.1.1–3)

As I started watching my mind through the mind-training, I began noticed that when I'm thinking of God's love, when I'm feeling gratitude and open to the present moment, fears that I have been disturbing myself with naturally slip from my mind. It's ongoing forgiveness of the false to allow the awareness of the truth to dawn.

Eventually, I came to realize that if I put God first, my identity as love first, happiness bubbles up from within. I feel safe and secure. From this state, trust comes easily. It is only when I use my past or some external "expert" as a point of reference, that I feel afraid. When I remember to keep counsel with my inner guide, miracles happen. I feel swept up in the joyous flow of life itself.

I am reminded of when I was in India. I was in the public market, and I had lost my companions. One moment they were in front of me and the next, I couldn't find them. I felt anxiety starting to rise, and immediately I started praying, using today's lesson. *"I am in danger nowhere in the world."* Instantly, I am reminded I am God's holy child and I'm on a divine adventure. I am safe no matter where I am because God is with me.

Right then an Indian woman approaches me and bows, "Namaste." I love that. I feel her blessing me with her holiness and reminding me of mine. She points to an alley just around the corner of the next shop which is just beyond my vision. I say, "Namaste," following where she pointed. I'm back in adventure mode, bowing "Namaste" with everyone I meet, so serene and okay I nearly bump into my sister as I turn the corner.

We are in no danger, the love of God is but instant's pause, and we are home. There is nothing to fear. We are never alone because we are part of God and divine love is what we are. Trust will handle every problem now.

DAY 245

(Lesson 245)

"Your peace is with me, Father. I am safe."

(W-pII.245.1)

"Your peace surrounds me, Father. Where I go, Your peace goes there with me. It sheds its light on everyone I meet. I bring it to the desolate and lonely and afraid. I give Your peace to those who suffer pain, or grieve for loss, or think they are bereft of hope and happiness. Send them to me, my Father. Let me bring Your peace with me. For I would save Your Son, as is Your Will, that I may come to recognize my Self."

(W-pII.245.1.1–8)

I read through today's lesson and instantly the feeling of transformation and joy floods my mind with a memory. The prayer from today's lesson was a great source of comfort during my tour of duty with Desert Storm. And now as I revisit it, it feels like coming home.

It was our first leave weekend since being called to active duty at the beginning of Desert Storm, and there was talk of us going overseas. I had tons of resistance thoughts flooding my mind. I'd feel guilty and selfish, untrusting and afraid. I wanted to "buck up" and be brave, but I had what felt like bees fluttering around in my heart area.

I turned to my course lesson and ran a hot bath. I read over the lesson and let tears flow. *"Your peace is with me, Father. I am safe."* As I continued reading the prayer, it felt like warm water was seeping down from the top of my head and bathing me in comfort and peace. I sank into the bath and let the prayer bless me, my situation with the military, the situation with war and peace and everyone and everything. I let the bath be the arms of the Divine that day—the eternal peace I needed extending beyond time and circumstance, wrapping me in total comfort.

A new idea of what "being called to active duty" meant came to mind with the words from today's lesson, *"Where I go, Your peace goes there with me. It sheds its light on everyone I meet. I bring it to the desolate and lonely and afraid. I give Your peace to those who suffer pain, or grieve for loss, or think they are bereft of hope and happiness."*

I open my eyes with the recognition that location doesn't matter. Wherever I go, God's peace goes with me. I am perfect for the task at hand. Out loud I say with glee, "Oh yes! I am the light of the world. Let me bring peace and light and joy into this dark idea of war." Talk about a total flip!

The rest of my tour I had innumerable opportunities to be the presence of peace, to shine light in dark fearful corners of soldier's minds who were deploying and returning.

Daily we have the same chance to feel this peace and safety and comfort. The more we do it the more it becomes our comfort zone. It's what we are practicing today. The peace of God resides within us at all times and in all circumstances. Will we trust it? Are we willing to let go of what we think we need and settle into this eternal peace and trust?

The best way to experience peace I know of, is to offer it to another, whether in thought or action. When we see the other as our Self, we join in this peace. The mind can only hold one thought at a time. If we're thinking of love, fear is gone. If we're thinking peace, conflict cannot stay. If we're thinking of bringing our light to another, we are no longer alone. We are the center of peace and from that center, conflict dissolves.

CHAPTER ONE HUNDRED EIGHTY-THREE
DAY 246
(Lesson 246)

"To love my Father is to love His Son."
(W-pII.246.1)

"I will accept the way You choose for me to come to You, my Father. For in that will I succeed, because it is Your Will. And I would recognize that what You will is what I will as well, and only that. And so I choose to love Your Son. Amen."
(W-pII.246.2.1–4)

To love God is to love His Son. That means each and every single being. Period. The course teaches us oneness through our relationship with others. We are all one love. But that's too abstract for the human mind to grasp. So, we are given the people and circumstances in our lives as steppingstones which lead to the goal of recognizing God and our Self in everyone.

Today's practice is all about loving where we want to judge or be afraid. Anytime we are feeling unloving about another, we do not see the truth. We say we love God, but then we reject the person next to us based on our opinion of their looks, race, sex, or other distinctions. Distinctions are always ego-based thoughts—separation devices by design.

We are learning to look past appearances or distinctions to the light within each other which unites us. The lesson says, *"Let me not think that I can find the way to God if I have hatred in my heart."* So, if I am saying I love God, I want only to know God's will for me. Then, a few minutes later some news about Trump's presidential decisions pops up on my feed and I get angry or feel deflated or fearful for the future, I am countering my previous statement that I want to feel God's love with me all the time, right? That's the red flag to pause, forgive my reaction, and choose to look again with the eyes of Christ love.

The thing is, there is nowhere God is not! So, my brother is already part of me by the way I hold him in my mind. Will it be holy or judgmental? My perception is not reality. It's my opinion. Right? So why not release the auto-ego-response of separation, and stretch out the true desire of my heart to surround the upsetting situations with the light we share as one whole child of God?

It takes practice, sure. Lots of practice. But mostly it takes willingness to see things differently. Do we want to be right or happy?

I bring up the Trump thing because changing my mind from fear to love about him, and what constitutes the "proper person" for president of the United States (like I know, ha-ha) is a classic example of where I feel justified in withholding love from a brother. I can find all the evidence I want to validate my judgments.

But the thing I can't deny is that it doesn't feel good. It feels icky. I don't feel God. That's my flip-switch. Trump being president is not better or worse than his not being president. I choose to remember that he is my brother, a holy child of God. I judge, not because of Trump, but to separate myself from my fear.

Once I have identified that this is fear, I know the remedy is love. Big love! The love unveiled by forgiveness. And that is just what I do with Trump. I hold him in my mind as a brother, just like me, innocent, forgive him for what he never did in truth, letting my judging thoughts fade away. I see how he was just like me, God's kid. Peace settles over me. After all, that's all I really want.

DAY 247

(Lesson 247)

"Without forgiveness I will still be blind."

(W-pII.247.1)

"So would I look on everyone today. My brothers are Your Sons. Your Fatherhood created them, and gave them all to me as part of You, and my own Self as well. Today I honor You through them, and thus I hope this day to recognize my Self."

(W-pII.247.2.1–4)

Today we are looking, again, at how our belief about our identity gets projected through our perception onto the world we see. But remember perception is not a fact. It is useful only to validate what we want to believe.

The lesson starts out talking about sin. The course tells us that sin is a lack of love. It says sin is the symbol of attack. Attack is an ego device used to reinforce the separation. Forgiveness is the willingness to see the situation, person, and reality differently—to see there is no sin, only a belief in lack.

We are recognizing that whatever we have not forgiven blinds us to the truth. When we're using the body's eyes, we're looking at the world of appearances—separated out by names and labels through the eyes of judgment. "This one I like and this one I wish were different . . ." What we are seeing is an illusion, blinding us to the truth within and all around us. We are attacking reality by wishing things would be different. They're not. Why not accept the actuality of what is happening now? Here, now is the presence of love, the power of divine creation.

Sin is wanting something to be different than it is. For me that's hell. Whenever I feel unhappy, without exception, it is because I'm thinking something should be different than it is. I want something outside of me to change so I can feel better. That is a prison. The world we see is the projection of our thoughts, so it is only in our thinking that we can affect change. We can choose to think of God and see through eyes of love.

Forgiveness is the key to happiness and offers everything we need. By opening my mind and releasing my preconceived ideas (judgments) and allowing the Spirit to flood my mind with truth, I see something different. Until I do, I am blind.

One week I am in Salt Lake hanging out with my kids. Cole and I are driving around the city, and I'm telling stories about when the city had been my stomping grounds. I notice a couple of things. First, much of what I'm recounting to him, the embarrassments and difficulties I went through, simply don't have any charge. They're stories I'm no longer tethered to by remorse or guilt. In fact, we're laughing like hyenas!

Second, I see that it was the perfect happening for my life at the time. The things that made me wince to think about before, I shared with laughter and understanding. The shame-story becomes a unifying story that brings joy and acceptance. That is forgiveness.

Forgiveness works beyond time and space. When I am ready to see, with forgiveness and love, and circumstances arrange themselves to meet me where I am right now. It's the same whether it was fifteen minutes or a lifetime ago. That's how miracles collapse time, bringing us into present love and joy.

DAY 248

(Lesson 248)

"Whatever suffers is not part of me."

(W-pII.248.1)

*"Father, my ancient love for You returns, and lets me love Your Son again as well.
Father, I am as You created me. Now is Your Love remembered,
and my own. Now do I understand that they are one."*

(W-pII.248.2.1–4)

I'm so happy about today's lesson. It's something I've been dedicatedly practicing over this past year in a new way. I thought I knew what the lesson meant. I am as God created me, which is the fabric of love, and what isn't love, is not part of what I am in truth. But I still thought I needed to do something about a perceived problem.

What I have come to realized is that's not my job. Correction comes by noticing the error in my mind and allowing the truth or Holy Spirit in my mind to reinterpret it for me.

I recall the impact of today's lesson from years ago when my sister, Dione, died by suicide. I was looking for a way of accepting her choice to end her physical life. I was trying to deal with the grief and guilt I felt for being so detached—for not really trying to connect with her in a meaningful way for years. Now she's gone. As phone calls, conversations, and accusations circulated within the family, I felt a deep sense of suffering in our family.

On the third day after her death, I landed on today's lesson. *"Whatever suffers is not part of me."* For the first time I saw the perfect artistry of the wording. It isn't saying, "If I'm suffering, I'm doing it wrong," like I had interpreted it previously.

It's saying whatever suffers, grieves, or feels guilty is not part of who I am as God created me. It is a story of ego identity. It is showing me how easily I slip from my steady place of peace, joy, and love, and into the pool of ego-body identification. I think of how minutes before I heard the news, I was meditating and thinking only of God and His love—whole, loving, and filled with peace.

But, it's like there was this irresistible pull to feel shitty about Dione's death—like a responsibility to an idea— like paying homage to death and suffering.

In gratitude, I'm aware, "Ah! That's not me. Love which created me is what I am." Immediately, I'm at peace with everything. I'm okay with her death—even the family gossiping. Freed from the idea that I "should" have done something to prevent it. I honor Dione as a holy child of love. The Divine's got this!

The lesson says, *"I have disowned the truth. Now let me be as faithful in disowning falsity. Whatever suffers is not part of me. What grieves is not myself. What is in pain is but illusion in my mind. What dies was never living in reality, and did but mock the truth about myself."* What we are is eternal life itself. That is how God created us.

Today's lesson isn't asking us to deny what we're feeling as bodies and persons in this world, but only to realize that it does not define or change what God created—which is pure love, light, spirit. It is asking us merely to notice and remind ourselves of the truth.

DAY 249

(Lesson 249)

"Forgiveness ends all suffering and loss."

(W-pII.249.1)

"Father, we would return our minds to You. We have betrayed them, held them in a vice of bitterness, and frightened them with thoughts of violence and death. Now would we rest again in You, as You created us."

(W-pII.249.2.1–3)

"*F*orgiveness paints a picture of a world where suffering is over, loss becomes impossible and anger makes no sense. Attack is gone, and madness has an end."* Wow, right? Much better picture than the bloody ones where no one wins that we dream up when we feel wronged, yes?

Forgiveness is the end of suffering and loss. I am living proof.

Six months ago, Lar was diagnosed with stage-4 cancer. Talk about a witness to the truth of this lesson. We met cancer face to face, forgiving all previous ideas we held about it and accepting it just as it is. This is what's happening, now.

It doesn't even occur to us to resist—to want it not to be happening. It is what it is. What I'm interested in is being fully present as the love I am for each and every aspect of this experience with Lar—to be the light that heals through the surgeries and recoveries, the immunotherapy infusions, the laughter and tears. It has been incredible just being present with each other—deepening our holy relationship. Lar would like his hair back . . . but other than that, we wouldn't have missed a moment of this precious holy acceptance experience.

The prayer from today's lesson is key. *"Father, we would return our minds to You."* It's love, right? *"Attack is gone, and madness has an end."* Yay! Forgiveness is really about not holding on to anything. We let all things be just as they are and wrap our love around it.

Forgiveness is not dredging up grievance stories and how we've risen above them. Like, "Oh, she was such a bitch to me that time . . . but I forgive her." No, forgiveness is the end of the story. We release all rights to victimhood. We and our brother are one. We see the past is gone and each brand-new moment is innocent, and we, too, are born again each moment until we decide once and for all to release the dream of death from our minds. Life is and we are that life.

In some circles we actually lead with our "woundology." It is the ego's attempt to mimic union. You've been through, or are going through, a similar difficulty as I am. I feel close to you. But are we joined? The course tells us only love can truly join.

It's a tricky business to spend gratuitous time discussing hardships, relating, and bonding. It gives the ego free reign to teach us what we are not. We are not our suffering, our pain, our fear. What is not love is not real. Without forgiveness we are imprisoned by wound identity, trapped in falsehood.

Happiness is what is left when suffering identity is let go. It's crucial we see our invulnerability as children of love. Love and suffering cannot reside together. One must go. Love, being what we are in truth, is the only real choice.

DAY 250

(Lesson 250)

"Let me not see myself as limited."

(W-pII.250.1)

"He is Your Son, my Father. And today I would behold his gentleness instead of my illusions. He is what I am, and as I see him so I see myself. Today I would see truly, that this day I may at last identify with him."

(W-pII.250.2.1–4)

Our lessons now are about staying in the ground of our being. Because what we believe we are is what we automatically project onto everyone else. So, if I feel weak and limited, fearful or angry, that is what I am going to believe you are also. But when I am in touch with my essence as pure love, I feel joyous, I feel open and loving toward others. These prayer lessons are cleaning up areas of disconnect in our minds. The places where we still feel limited.

Haven't you noticed that when you're supremely happy, you naturally feel generous and open to seeing the goodness in people? Or when compassion expands our hearts in some seeming crisis, and we no longer see differences like color, age, sex, or race—we are focused on being truly helpful. It feels amazing, right?!

God is the impossibility of limitation.

Daily, through our lesson practice, we come with open hearts and minds to experience our oneness with the Source of limitlessness within us. This is our point of creativity. It has nothing to do with what role we play, what our little selves can or cannot do. It is about opening ourselves to be part of the majesty of creation and trusting it to unfold according to God's plan.

If I'm thinking about pure joy, peace, and limitless release, I'm not thinking about problems. Period. We cannot hold opposing thoughts at the same time. We can't hold illusion and truth in our minds simultaneously.

My Albuquerque adventure served as a preeminent classroom in forgiveness for me. I'm reminded of an unschooling outing where, feeling in the funk of disappointment yet again, I see how I limit my options for happiness. I can feel my heart closing.

Feeling imprisoned by my limitations, I look about me and see my judgment pattern like a dense film over everyone and everything, distorting my perception. I begin practicing today's lesson, silently saying, *"Let me not see myself [or you] as limited,"* to each of the unschooling moms in my midst and feel the tightness in my chest release.

It takes only an instant to release limitation from my mind. I'm instantly free and happy. You'd think I wouldn't waste a second on judging, when pure joy is so readily available. These women are my sisterhood of joy. Hello.

I hear laughter coming from the children over at the picnic tables. We, moms, check it out. Cole who is about 11 at the time, is teaching the other kids how to make wallets out of duct tape. They're adding more creative ideas. Blessed love family. There was nowhere I would rather be than right here, right now.

DAY 251

(Lesson 251)

"I am in need of nothing but the truth."

(W-pII.251.1)

"And for that peace, our Father, we give thanks. What we denied ourselves
You have restored, and only that is what we really want."

(W-pII.251.2.1–2)

Today we begin a new theme through which we look at the next section of lessons. *"What is Sin?"* The course tells us that sin is lack of love. Which makes sense since love is what we are. If we are seeing without it, then what we are seeing must be illusion. If we are seeing, thinking, or acting lovelessly, we aren't sane.

The yummy thing about our relationship with the Divine is that sanity is always just a brother away from us. Wherever we're not feeling loving, that's our guide back home to truth. The course says that whoever is saner at the time a conflict happens can hold the truth for both of us.

But what if both are confused and feeling a lack of love at the time? Here's where our training sees us through. The holiness we share knows the truth. We turn to it. Love is all inclusive and seeks only to extend and unite.

Today's lesson starts with a statement familiar to all of us. *"I sought for many things, and found despair."* When we realize this, it is a turning point. It invites us to turn within to a deeper Source—to seek the truth. This becomes our single goal. As we continue to return to this one goal to recognize the truth, all seeming needs are handled, cravings slip away, aligning us with God's will for happiness for us.

Let's not confuse our little truth with The Truth. Thinking we deserve certain facts or disclosures due to the nature of our relationships. This is usually what passes for truth in this dream. Truth is what we are. It can only be given and received from this recognition. If we think we need "truth" facts, we're looking for lies. The only fact that is real is, God is.

Let me give an example of what I mean.

A few years ago, frustrated with my husband, I let a story about it form in my private mind. I thought he was secretive and dishonest with me. I felt disrespected and alone.

In recognizing my predicament, I bring it to my coffee date with God. I say, "I think I need Lar to be honest, to be open about his feelings, so there can be real understanding and communication between us. I need him to want a more spiritual connection for our communication." Today's lesson, like a beacon of light, comes as I'm saying I need, need, need . . . *"I am in need of nothing but the truth."*

Holy relief! I apply today's lesson, revealing myself on the altar of truth. I have not been honest. I've been secretive, blaming, and judgmental, not sharing my fears, and seeking the truth *with* him. In my private thoughts I believed needed *him* to do something different for me to be happy. That's why I hadn't talked to him, right?

Seeing my lack of love, my withholding, I realize the only thing separating me from happiness in our relationship is the love *I'm* not giving. I zero to the love which is always constant—the truth! I am love!

Whew! Boy, give an unforgiving thought a little reign, and it's off and running. With truth now my only goal, I can't wait to clear things with Lar. That's our holy relationship! The opportunity comes immediately.

We talk long into the night, blowing through fears that had arisen, and with each our connection deepens—we let go and fearlessly bring everything to the altar of our holy relationship—till our hearts are beating as one heart. Love, as always, works its alchemy, like a blazing light of truth burning through and healing. Together, we let love settle every one of them.

CHAPTER ONE HUNDRED EIGHTY-NINE

DAY 252

(Lesson 252)

"The Son of God is my Identity."

(W-pII.252.1)

*"Father, You know my true Identity. Reveal It now to me who am Your Son,
that I may waken to the truth in You, and know that Heaven is restored to me."*

(W-pII.252.2.1–2)

I was just on the phone with a dear friend, and we were just talking about this lesson! Well, not this lesson exactly, but the idea of moving in our lives from our true identity as love. We were talking about doctor appointments and how initially we think we are going to see them for what they can do for us.

But what we are really doing, whether it be doctor visits, hanging out with friends, or grocery shopping, is we are bringing miracles—we are the light that dispels the shadows of a fractured world. Because of what we are in truth.

The lesson says, *"My Self is holy beyond all the thoughts of holiness of which I now conceive."* In other words, my grandest vision of my worth and yours is but a ripple in the ocean of light, compared to the brilliance fullness of what we are as God created us.

But it brings to mind a recent visit with our New Orleans friends. One evening over dinner, the energy of light and love seems to be flowing through us like a symphony, connecting us in an amazing conversation I never expected.

Chris and I have a lot in common, with similarly constructed personas. We're both quick with wit and feel fun is our birthright. We had also both invested a lot of time and energy in our bodies, proud of how fit and badass we were. Then the impossible happened. I broke my back, and Chris got a brain injury.

As we talk, I notice there are many times where we could have bonded over the disappointment, loss of self, daily pain, or fear of what might happen in the future. But we make a different choice.

We chose to remain grounded in our true identity as joy and see that Self reflected back. I see Chris's holiness as my own. While we talk, I feel incredibly blessed. A quiet certainty fills the space surrounding us, that everything, past, present, and future, is the perfect condition for healing our minds and sharing our hearts.

We share about acceptance and how precious it was to love each thing that happens and rejoice in it. We share about the transformation of mind by refusing to operate from a feeling of being limited; but in identifying with something bigger—the mystery and perfection of things unseen, but known, and the peace and relaxation of trusting life. Chris is Christ—my one Self.

That is what today's lesson is about. We are accepting our true identity as pure, unlimited love—holy because we are God's children, and holiness is our love DNA.

DAY 253

(Lesson 253)

"My Self is ruler of the universe."

(W-pII.253.1)

"You are the Self Whom You created Son, creating like Yourself and One with You. My Self, which rules the universe, is but Your Will in perfect union with my own, which can but offer glad assent to Yours, that it may be extended to itself."

(W-pII.253.2.1–2)

Wow! Can we step up to what today's lesson is inviting us to? Hell, yeah! We're ready to shed the ego skin and step up as our Self. All of our mind-training has prepared us. We have been releasing our self-concepts and accepting our Self as the Divine Child, Loving, joyous, and free, with the power of God behind every thought we have and action we take.

We can use it for miscreation and the result is fear, worry, problems, and unhappiness. Or we can create by divine law, for which we are designed. It simply requires that we stay in the frequency of the joy, of the love which created us. Whenever we feel our frequency getting dense, we imagine a lack, a problem, a hurt, or an unfairness, this is the sign to pause and tune back in.

The way we see the world is how the world is for us. It is impossible that anything come to us unbidden by us. What we believe, is what we see. We are the ruler of the universe of our own making.

As we accept the truth of our identity as the Self, holy child of God, the universe we live in changes. We realize we already have everything we need for whatever arises each moment, and the great rays of light and holiness that radiate from the Christ within all of us is making it all happen. Miracles naturally flow from us as an extension of our will aligned with God's.

As I started seeing how my life really was reflecting my state of mind, it was easy to see that if I felt frightened or worried, events reflected it back to me; one of my children would get hurt, or my bank would overdraft, or someone I wanted to like me would reject me. But as I began changing my view to see with love, my world changed too. I changed.

I recall a day I was late for a staff meeting. I had been sweating it out, fearing I'd be in trouble then flip-switching using today's lesson, the entire drive to the institute.

My palms are sweating, my heart beating so loudly I'm sure everyone can hear it when I slipped into the room. Sure enough, before I can take a seat, the Doc in charge says, "You're late. We have to round on this patient before she discharges today, and you're her case manager. We can't be expected . . ."

Spontaneously, I interrupt, "No, you can't. But I have been preparing for this. Sorry I'm late." A miracle took over. I don't go into a victim story and make excuses. I see my universe reflects the dominate thoughts I want.

As I talk, calm flows through and from me. The lesson is alive in me, speaking the truth of my Self through the words needed to handle the situation. My tardiness issue dissolved, as I spoke about a support group I had just recently learned about which I would connect the patient with. I hadn't planned to discharge her to this support group—prior to that moment, I hadn't connected the two—Not until I was in my right mind, creating from my true Self.

My life manta is, "Everything goes my way!" It's like, *"My Self is ruler of the universe,"* in Danét speak. I finally understand what I mean.

CHAPTER ONE HUNDRED NINETY-ONE
DAY 254
(Lesson 254)

"Let every voice but God's be still in me."

(W-pII.254.1)

"Father, today I would but hear Your Voice. In deepest silence, I would come to You, to hear Your Voice and receive Your Word. I have no prayer but this: I come to You to ask You for the truth. And truth is but Your Will, which I would share with You today."

(W-pII.254.1.1–5)

Today we decide voice for God, for love, be the only one we hear, and the only thing we teach. We set our goal as we begin our day, centering our being in the silence within, using today's prayer. We want only the truth to guide our life.

I often use this prayer in morning quiet time with God. It is like a portal that instantly transports me to the holy space between my thoughts, where I can reside, listening to the stillness, and feeling God's love and joy within me, blessing my life with certainty and peace. It is a blessed way to launch my day and letting my petty me-preferences drop.

As we give ourselves to the prayer, our "me" thoughts dissolve into the stillness of our open mind. We let the silence permeate our being, and in the stillness, we hear the voice for God. His voice is always speaking His love for us. It's just drowned out by the thousand competing voices demanding more or less of something.

They are voices of needs, problems, gossip, or other stories, and if we're listening to them, we can't hear the voice of God. That's why practices like today's lesson are so important, we learn to recognize the ever-present stillness of love beneath the surface of our insane mind.

As we pay no mind to the voices telling us that something should be different, and that we should do something about it, we leave a space in our mind for God's voice to occupy it. Today we are practicing zeroing in on that single voice—God's voice and listening to His word.

The other day I had lunch with a mighty companion and wonderful friend. I began the day with today's prayer, and I am still basking in the light and simplicity of trusting the Divine. When we greet each other, I see that she's been crying. I notice the urge to ask, "What's wrong?" But I pause, and in the quiet, I hear, "Wait a minute, nothing is wrong. Whatever is happening is always the perfect happening for our awakening to truth."

I look into her eyes and see the light of love shining through. Instead of asking what's wrong, I share with her the light I witness in her, of my joy in our union. How lovely to notice this chance to bless rather than tell stories.

Isn't it crazy how often during the day we have this chance, but we don't pause and ask for the truth? The story of woe feels too juicy to pass up, and we listen to the voice that tells us we have to know the details of the story or add our input. It even tells us that they need us to join them in their pain or anger to feel better, right?

The ego tells us we can connect through stories of woe, fear, and wrongness. But only truth can truly join. If we want something real—something holy to happen in our encounter with another, we must bring it. When we let every voice but God's be still in us, what comes forth is always helpful. We're no longer relying on ourselves alone. Divinity flows through us.

CHAPTER ONE HUNDRED NINETY-TWO
DAY 255
(Lesson 255)

"This day I choose to spend in perfect peace."
(W-pII.255.1)

"And so, my Father, would I pass this day with You. Your Son has not forgotten You.
The peace You gave him still is in his mind, and it is there I choose to spend today."
(W-pII.255.2.1-3)

The key to today's lesson is "I choose." Yes, perfect peace is our home in God, and is available always because God wills we spend our days in perfect peace. Our choice for perfect peace opens our awareness to it. It is already ours. But our decision must be uncompromising. We can't choose problems and perfect peace at the same time.

Today's lesson is inviting us to have faith that if we choose peace, it is ours because we were created in peace. We trust our inherent relationship with Divinity, and our experience will bear witness to this truth.

When we are focused on problems, it creates a chaotic turmoil in our mind.

Perfect peace is the still point, the eye of the storm within our mind, where no illusions touch. As we zero our mind on this one thought of perfect peace, it's like a portal directly to our whole Self, where we are in communion with God.

It's that simple, but requires practice. This is our mind-training. First, we choose to spend the day in perfect peace. That's the ground of our being. So, everything that isn't consistent with love has to go. We set our frequency to God's will for us—which is perfect happiness.

The peace today's lesson is talking about is not situational, though it shows up in the situations in our lives. It is the nature of our relationship with the Divine—perfect peace and happiness are one in the same.

Here's an example. I'd had a long weekend leading a workshop—late nights of uncovering and discovering—forgiving and healing—love and peace. It was blissful, but when it wrapped up, I was tired.

There had been a nagging voice in the back of my mind yammering on about not having any time to myself. I'd push it aside, refocusing on the workshop. But, after the workshop is over, that nag gets traction. I'm putting the workshop space back for next time, and there it is—judging. One unforgiving thought, gone unchecked, spins a story—like it's true or something.

The squash in yummy feelings of the weekend is impossible to miss. I pause and confront what's going on in my head. "It sure would have been nice if the participants would have pitched in after. Don't they realize how taxing it is to be 'on' all weekend?" Yadda, yadda . . . Ha! It's this load of lies that is making me feel tired and frustrated! This is how it happens. Allowing unforgiving thoughts to go unquestioned in my mind, is the path away from the perfect peace that is my birthright. I forgive.

Back in my right mind, I ask, "Isn't it truer I've been infused with energy, inspiration, and miracles? Do I really feel cheated that no one stayed to help? No. I don't!" I laugh.

I'm not waiting for some special, private time for myself. My Self *is* my connection with others. Now, I choose perfect peace!" And instantly it's mine.

DAY 256

(Lesson 256)

"God is the only goal I have today."

(W-pII.256.1)

"And so, our Father, would we come to You in Your appointed way. We have no goal except to hear Your Voice, and find the way Your sacred Word has pointed out to us."

(W-pII.256.2.1–2)

God is not off somewhere outside our Self. The Divine is everything! That's why it's easy for it to be our only goal. That's the essential starting point. Love is the zero point. Love is the frequency which unites us all. Love is God. It is divinity, the creative energy that lets us recognize our brother is one with us. It transcends the barriers of separation where all judgment, fear, and defenses reside, and straight into the heartbeat we all share. It is the goal of God.

The poignancy of today's lesson was captured perfectly for me in a supreme example yesterday. My sister, Lyn, and I spent the morning at the 9/11 memorial at Ground Zero in New York City. The truth of the Divine was impossible to miss. The selfless and heroic acts by everyone in this incredible crisis is overwhelming.

Their holiness and faith in life sprung forth and led decisions and actions, superseding whatever barriers might have been in place prior to this immense call for love. A huge act of forgiveness ensued. People offered everything they had, including their lives, to come to the aid of seeming strangers. They offered their home to those misplaced or wounded physically or emotionally. We gave our money and blood and prayer vigils. And our hearts grew a thousand sizes through it all.

At times like this, the ego loses control of the dream. It can't gain footing when love is the only answer that can help. The call for love is transmitting so powerfully that not a single heart can resist its pull. We all zero in. We set our little self, with its special needs, aside. The call is too compelling. Then we memorialize it. We don't want to forget. We can't.

We meet our Self in these moments, and we love what we see. We love what comes through us. We love how we show up courageously as brave warriors of love and holiness. This is our Self in its purest form. This is the goal of God.

I fall in love with the museum attendant we meet as we enter the building. His transmission to join in love is unmistakable. He says he is a 9/11 survivor and shares his miracle with us.

He was in one of the towers when the first strike happened but had just left the building for an impromptu reason or he would have been right where the plane hit. (Odd, or God?)

The thing about this encounter that is remarkable to me, however, is that this brother recognizes him Self in us. In us, he sees someone who can join with him and share his miracle and gratitude. He is not sharing the story of victims and perpetrators. He's sharing the magical mystery of God. He transmits the blessing of awakening to love.

We're filled with grace as he tells his story of that day, tears flowing freely as we join. The grace of this holy encounter is like a tuning fork for perception as we enter the exhibits. Perfect! How blessedly beautiful it is all put together. A museum of grace, hope, and miracles unfold before my eyes. God is the only goal I have, the only thing I see in the faces and stories, and the only one I receive.

DAY 257

(Lesson 257)

"Let me remember what my purpose is."

(W-pll.257.1)

"Father, forgiveness is Your chosen means for our salvation. Let us not forget today that we have no will but Yours. And thus our purpose must be Yours as well, if we would reach the peace You Will for us."

(W-pll.257.2.1–4)

Today's lesson is a simple instruction to our mind, *"Let me remember what my purpose is."* When I have conflicting goals, my purpose seems split in my mind. My only purpose is the one God gave me. Forgiveness is the way I keep returning my mind to the single goal that renders happiness.

Last week I missed my flight to New York. I thought my purpose was to get to New York at the appointed time to meet up with my sister. I was put on standby for the next flight. It got delayed due to weather. I felt disappointed and guilty—that's my flip-switch to forgive my purpose and let true purpose be revealed.

I close my eyes and center my mind on a single thought, "I am love." I sit for a few moments in the stillness, remembering God, feeling big love rise filling me with light. I dismiss all thoughts I'd been disturbing myself with—my perceived plans and what I thought *should* happen, placing them on the altar of forgiveness within. Peace stills my heart and all ideas that something different *should* be happening dissolve. I looked around me, blessing and sending love vibes.

A few minutes later, a couple of mature, delightful women sit down and start talking with me. "You waiting for a flight to New York?" I say, "Yes." I feel the pull to tell them my story about missing my flight, but I stop myself, shifting back to my yummy space. My yumminess is why they're here after all. I fall in love with these women.

They're from New York City and this is their return trip. They tell me stories of starting in the secretary pools, when there were only certain jobs for women and men, and how they lived and thrived through all the changes and new developments in equal rights over the last half-century.

They share with such joy and presence. They know who they were. They are thoroughly enjoying sharing their histories and who they are now. We share about miracles and how sometimes (like today) it turns out that the very thing you didn't want to happen, ends up reaping unforeseen rewards. Ah, the glory of hidden gifts of present happiness!

DAY 258

(Lesson 258)

"Let me remember that my goal is God."

(W-pII.258.1)

*"Our goal is but to follow in the way that leads to You. We have no goal but this.
What could we want but to remember You? What could we seek but our Identity?"*

(W-pII.258.2.1–4)

Today's lesson is another reinforcement in training minds to remember that God is our only goal. Remembering God is love, which is our true identity, *is* our goal. We are love. We are part of God—of God's whole extension of love. We're training our minds to overlook all senseless aims and remember—to keep coming back home to where we recognize our Self as God created us—as love, as joy, as the light of the world.

What do we have on the inner altar? Do we have God? Do we have love? Or do we have a multitude of conflicting goals, problems, fears, worries, or guilt? We can think with spirit or the ego. And what we fix on our inner altar determines how we see everything, and therefore the experience we have.

Last week while visiting with my sister and her daughter in New York, the glory of today's lesson rang through in an experience at dinner. We arrive after spending a day exploring the yummy spots in the west valley. When we get to the restaurant, I notice I'm bothering myself with back pain, and start looking at the seating to see how comfortable it is. Not a cushy chair in the place!

As we walk to the table, I step inside the lady's room, reminding myself that pain is not what I want on my inner altar and open my heart to the alternative. *"Let me remember that my goal is God."* I centered my mind on love, and on joining. My pain slips to the background as joy takes center presence in my mind. Now I'm ready to be present at dinner.

At the table my niece was crying. Her mother holds her hand, lovingly listening as she tells of the experience that led to this moment. I, too, join in love, holding the goal of God like a beacon to see the truth beyond the story of pain.

The determination to recognize the truth guides our communication, which was deeply emotional and awakening. We are all totally present and engaged and a peaceful awareness opens up to see things differently. Pain forgotten, I engage only in the present moment of love. Past the senseless aim of catering to illusions, and directly at where love can heal and bring a miracle.

After, while we wait for a cab, Lyn apologizes for the uncomfortable seating. I say, "Holy Shit! I didn't feel my back once at dinner. I was pain free. I was fully immersed in seeing the truth with you." We can't join and have a problem at the same time.

By remembering that God is our goal, the light that shines from our inner altar glows. People instantly feel comfortable, safer, invited in.

DAY 259

(Lesson 259)

"Let me remember that there is no sin."

(W-pII.259.1)

*"Father, I would not be insane today. I would not be afraid of love,
nor seek for refuge in its opposite. You are the Source of everything there is.
And everything that is remains with You, and You with it."*

(W-pII.259.2.1–5)

et me remember that there is no sin," is the same as saying, "Let me remember that there is no lack of love in what God created." Love is the DNA of creation and it is not missing anywhere. If we're not feeling joyously in love with life, our interpretations are off the mark. We have mistaken illusion for the truth. But mistakes become vehicles for forgiveness and return to love. So, there's love—even in a situation where we are feeling guilty and afraid. In the presence of love, fear and guilt disappear.

The lesson says, *"Sin is the only thought that makes the goal of God seem unattainable."* As long as we hold onto anything we think we need, that is not what God created, we are blind to the complete joy of God's whole gift to us. We're doing it!

If I am experiencing some lack of love in any situation or with anyone, it is only because I am not bringing it! I am responsible to make the shift. No one, nor any circumstance can give it to me. I must align singly with love. My experiences will reflect the premise I choose. *"Fidelity to premises is a law of mind"* (W-pII.6.11). The law is uncompromising. Love or fear? Everything I experience, I have asked for.

Which is awesome! If I feel a lack of love, I have forgiveness at the ready, to restore my awareness of the love. There is no meeting place for love and grievances. If I am holding on to feeling wronged, I cannot know my right-mind—my whole mind as love.

Sometimes it's the simple moments of clarity that really strike a lesson home for us. I'm at a coffee shop having a lovely conversation with the barista and holding up the line. The woman behind me starts making huffing noises, and the thought goes through my mind, "How passive-aggressive!"

But that thought hits me like a gut shot. I shake my head to clear it, and in its place surfaces today's idea, *"Let me remember there is no sin."* Seeing it is my own mind, projecting guilt, I instantly forgive myself, and her for what, in truth, she didn't do.

It brought me so present to my moment by moment practice of recognizing the lack of love is only illusion. The instant I choose to remember love, everything looks different, I feel connected to the woman sharing the line with me. Graced with forgiveness, I smile, thank the barista, and pay for her coffee.

There is no sin in love. We can't have both. We can't have some grievances, fears, and suffering and experience the freedom, safety, and peace inherent in our identity. They have to go.

We must shift from identifying with being a body in a world of opposing wills, to where God is, and our identity is in Him. This changes our will because once we leave the ego world behind, our will is already one with God's. It can't be otherwise. We are part of God. So, everything else is just our little movie of specialness. Our real specialness is in our identity, which unites all creation within it.

CHAPTER ONE HUNDRED NINETY-SEVEN

DAY 260

(Lesson 260)

"Let me remember God created me."

(W-pII.260.1)

"Father, I did not create myself, although in my insanity I thought I did. Yet, as Your Thought, I have not left my Source, remaining part of Who created me. Your Son, my Father, calls on You today. Let me remember You created me. Let me remember my Identity. And let my sinlessness arise again before Christ's vision, through which I would look upon my brothers and myself today."

(W-pII.1.1–6)

Today's lesson invites us to be the living Word of God all day, with everyone we meet and in every situation that arises. God created us whole and complete with all the light and love and peace the world needs, in all circumstances. Our part is to remember that this is our identity. And nothing else is.

We are not our insane stories of ourselves. We are not bodies. We are not the seeming problems our body-minds get up to, but rather, we are the answer. We are spirit, the Holy Child of God, Himself. This is the orientation by which we want to begin each day, zeroed in on the one true thing that cannot be altered, no matter what seems to be happening around us.

Yesterday was another travel day for me, back to New Orleans, where I am now. Traveling is such a wonderful metaphor for where we are locating ourselves. Is it in time and space, or in eternity, with God at the helm?

I love how we're all in this together, in the shared experience of recognizing our brother—or not. I mean you can totally travel alone. Many do. Head down with a silent don't-mess-with-me barrier around them. It's easy to see and a delight to penetrate with love.

For me, yesterday was a fun and miracle-laced day. I began it with the premise of truth. I felt joyous from the moment I woke, reminding myself as I always do that *I am as God created me, complete and healed and whole,* and spending some quiet time in communion with His holy love.

When we get to the airport, Lar is upgraded to first class, and although he offered to let me take the upgrade, I felt sure I should stay exactly where I was. We board early, so I'm seated when the others start boarding. I watch and smile, acknowledging each as the love which created us.

I noticed an elderly woman with an oxygen tank making her way down the aisle. She sits directly across from me. I help her with her bag and ask if she needs anything. She smiles and say, "Thank you. I have everything I need. I always do." I love her instantly and begin our new friendship.

Unapologetically, we launched into a conversation about God. We recognize the Divine kinship we share. We talk about how every moment contains the perfect circumstance for happiness—even if we don't realize it at the time. Like meeting each other and sharing this sacred conversation.

When we remember we are as God created us, we are living in a different frequency than when we forget. When we believe we are bodies in a world competing for a limited supply of everything, that's what our world reflects. But given to the heart of truth, we see that behind the appearances, Divine flow is at work, unveiling this perfect opportunity to recognize Divinity everywhere and in each one we encounter. Making every encounter holy.

DAY 261

(Lesson 261)

"God is my refuge and security."

(W-pII.261.1)

"Let me seek not for idols. I would come, my Father, home to You today. I choose to be as You created me, and find the Son whom You created as my Self."

(W-pII.261.2.1–3)

Today begins a new theme, through which we practice the next ten lessons. It is *"What is the Body?"* I love how it starts because it perfectly describes how it is when we are identified with our body Self. It says, *"The body is a fence the Son of God imagines he has built, to separate parts of his Self from other parts. It is in this fence he thinks he lives, to die as it decays and crumbles."* Right? Graphic.

That's pretty much exactly how it seems—that we are separated, body by body, by the seeming space between us. Here we think we have private thoughts and needs that others don't really understand or care about, nor can hurt. It is the epitome of exclusion.

So first off, we are not bodies. We are spirit. The body senses are the portals through which we experience divinity expressing itself. We just imagine that we built this fence of separation around us—that's the ego's game—exclusion, separateness. Without it's sleight of hand, our obvious inclusion would be undeniable.

The music I hear is not exclusive to my ears alone, it plays for all to appreciate. The buzz of life I feel when our eyes meet or our hand brush against each other's is felt by you in your own way.

Life is generously aways giving. When I breathe the fragrance of a flower or appreciate its beauty, that doesn't diminish it in any way for you when you come along. The secret is to give ourselves fully to what comes and goes, as a part of us, of the one life we share. To fence ourselves off is to believe that separation is safety and that is insane. For we are one.

But like the lesson says, *"For within this fence he thinks that he is safe from love."* Why would any sane being, want to be safe *from* love? That's the key. It's insane. We have it wired up in this world that love can hurt us. Crazy. Love is what we are. It is our life's blood, our connection and our gift.

This morning is total grace. I start my day with the Divine and today's lesson: *"God is my refuge and my security."* It says we behold ourselves where we believe our safety and strength is. So rather than making plans for my body adventures, I give my day to Spirit, reminding myself that God is my strength in which I trust.

I head out spreading the joy, meeting people, and sharing my light. About midday, I notice weariness settling in. Noticing this, I pause and remind myself that I am not this body fencing me off from the joy of my heart. I sit down for some delightful people watching in the French Quarter. Ah, what joy! I'm instantly refueled.

The grace of seeking sustenance where it can be found! In that moment, another Grace comes taxing by on her bike-taxi and asks if I'd like a ride. And off we go promenading down Royal Street.

Along the way she tells me her friend is all into this new spiritual study. Yup. *A Course in Miracles*. I share my experience with her. She's totally intrigued and asks where she can get a copy of the book. When we arrive back at my hotel, I ask her to wait a minute and run to grab the copy I've brought with me.

Inside I write, "For the Grace of God—and yummy friendships you meet along the way." Total inclusion, surety, and joy!

DAY 262

(Lesson 262)

"Let me perceive no differences today."

(W-pII.262.1)

"Father, You have one Son. And it is he that I would look upon today. He is Your one creation. Why should I perceive a thousand forms in what remains as one? Why should I give this one a thousand names, when only one suffices? For Your Son must bear Your Name, for You created him. Let me not see him as a stranger to his Father, nor as stranger to myself. For he is part of me and I part of him, and we are part of You Who are our Source, eternally united in Your Love; eternally the holy Son of God."

(W-pII.262.1.1–8)

Today we reach our hand to another and walk along with her, joining the great crusade of atonement. *"Let me perceive no differences today."* We're looking past the seeming differences the body's eyes perceive and looking from our light to the light shining from everyone and everything. No living thing is without light. And where there is light, darkness disappears.

The lesson says, *"Father, You have one Son. And it is he that I would look upon today. He is Your one creation. Why should I perceive a thousand forms in what remains as one?"* Why indeed? The mind-training is teaching us that once we see the truth in one brother, we can see it in everyone. We simply choose the instruction for today, *"Let me perceive no differences today,"* and start looking for the truth of our Self in whomever we meet or think of.

That's how I start the day, with a spring in my step, joy in my heart and a smile on my face. As I walk to the cathedral to a yoga class, each person I meet along the way, I meet with my purpose for today, to see no differences, but only the Self we share.

Then I meet him. One brother in perfect harmony, willing to join and bless. On another day, I might have passed right by him. He might have looked like a hobo, or panhandler, or someone unsafe. But that is not what I'm looking for. I'm looking with love, expecting to see it in whomever I come upon. So, with today's instruction activating my actions, I stop to bless this brother, and see the holy Son of God.

He's sitting on a window curb. I say, "Good morning," silently blessing him and blessing our oneness. He touches his ears and mouth, as if to say he doesn't hear or speak. I smile and nod a little namaste and walk on.

As I'm passing by, he reaches out and touches my arm. I turn, scrunch on my haunches and look him eye to eye. His eyes are soft, gentle, and penetrating. I feel his love light searing through and blessing me. Namaste indeed! It is a holy communion. He is no stranger to me. He is my Self. We, as one, are the Son our Father loves.

Shit man, one judgment and I could have missed the whole beautiful holy encounter. I love these lessons which guide me to stay true to my one intention for truth!

My eyes are shiny, overflowing with gratitude for the holy recognition with my Self, as I enter my yoga class, which is filled with the Son of Love—my one Self, sitting on yoga mats, with the sun streaming through the cut glass windows of the Caballito cathedral. The perfect flow is majesty—true yoga is a heart state—a devotion to the truth.

CHAPTER TWO HUNDRED

DAY 263

(Lesson 263)

"My holy vision sees all things as pure."

(W-pII.263.1)

*"Father, Your Mind created all that is, Your Spirit entered into it, Your Love gave life to it.
And would I look upon what You created as if it could be made sinful? I would not perceive such
dark and fearful images. A madman's dream is hardly fit to be my choice, instead of all the
loveliness with which You bless creation; all its purity, its joy, and its eternal, quiet home in You."*

(W-pII.263.1.1-1–4)

Today we're looking out from the altar to the truth within, and the world of form is secondary. If you're like me, you've always had a sense that something bigger was happening than what it seems. And that something is felt in the mystery of life that somehow balances itself out, bringing unforeseen miracles and lessons in love.

All of us, at some point, realize there must be a better way to see the world than the combat training which has not made us happy. Into this open heart and mind, another way is unveiled. *"My holy vision sees all thing as pure."* We realize we've had glimpses of it all along which remain in every memory of joy we have ever had. *A Course in Miracles* undoes the past, false program, while opening a portal to let truth come through and express in a life of unity and love.

A couple of years ago I was taking a hot yoga class with a brilliant instructor, Rebecca, who seemed to see into the skeletal structure of an individual and could bring one into alignment with a simple instruction or touch. It seemed each time people would respond with spontaneous acknowledgments like, "Oh, I feel that. OMG. I finally get how I am supposed to feel. Oh, it's so simple, I passed right by it before."

I'm experiencing this one morning in class and today's lesson is center in my mind, so naturally I make the connection.

We flow through vinyasa pose and I have one idea permeating my mind: *"My holy vision sees all things as pure."* I feel joyous and connected. Everyone was at different stages in their yoga practice and I easily see the perfection of our unified whole. Until, that is, I start to struggle with a couple of poses.

Suddenly, I feel alone, insecure, and start to fixate on my body, my ability or inability to do the poses, afraid I wouldn't be able to do the upcoming back-bending poses. Aargh.

When we came to Cobra pose, where you're lying on your tummy and you lift your upper body up from the floor with your heart to the heavens, without using your arms, I start to contract, but, I remember my lesson, *"My holy vision see all things as pure."* I turned my sight within, off my body identity and toward my altar to love.

Everything loosens up. I easily open and lift, higher than ever, my heart open to the universal being all around me. Rebecca had come up behind me and, ever so gently, had placed her hands and love beneath my wings, positioning me into what was possible for me.

That is exactly what our training does for us. We set the instruction from each daily lesson, then apply the lesson as circumstances arise, and it opens us to receive the assistance we need at the time, such that our hearts remain open and we see with love. It positions us to see that it *is* possible to *see all things as pure, through our holy vision.*

DAY 264
(Lesson 264)

"I am surrounded by the Love of God."
(W-pII.264.1)

"Father, you stand before me and behind, beside me, in the place I see myself, and everywhere I go, You are in all the things I look upon, the sounds I hear, and every hand that reaches for my own. In You time disappears, and place becomes a meaningless belief. For what surrounds Your Son and keeps him safe is Love itself. There is no Source but this, and nothing is that does not share its holiness; that stands beyond Your one creation, or without the Love which holds all things within itself. Father, Your son is like Yourself. We come to You in Your Own Name today, to be at peace within Your everlasting Love."
(W-pII.264.1.1–6)

Oh my God, I love today's prayer! It is everything I want all my prayers to say! Right? It covers every aspect of life and everything is already complete in it. It is a prayer worthy to commit to memory as the breath of life. Breathing the heartbeat of God's love in every breath we take and returning our love and trust to Him with each exhale.

Today's lesson holds a precious significance to me. It was my "go-to" prayer the first year Randi and Lucas came back to live with me. On my own, I tended toward being fearful I would do something wrong—mess them up somehow. I wanted them to like me, forgive me for the years apart, understand my reasons.

Often, I would hear the Voice for God (sounding like Betty) reminding me that how they feel about me is none of my business, but loving them purely without any intent for a return *is* my business. I would remind myself, "I am not alone. I couldn't be. God is with me. I am surrounded by His love. His love is in these children and in me, and that's our identity. And whatever we face today is just God dressed in different disguises."

Somedays this prayer was my only oasis in the turbulence of my self-doubting mind. I would begin repeating the prayer, *"Father, You stand before me and behind, beside me, and in the place I see myself, and everywhere I go, You are in all the things I look upon, the sounds I hear, and every hand that reaches for my own . . ."* and about here, I could release my self-doubt, I could feel the Divine surrounding me and moving through me.

Lucas, at around eleven years old, wasn't sleeping through the night. When I ask him why, he says, "I just can't sleep. I don't know why." I suggest falling asleep reading a book or putting on meditation music. But I sense there's more to the situation than perhaps either of us realize.

One night, I ask Lucas if he'd like to pray with me and ask for a peaceful sleep. He does. I begin, "Dear God, Lucas has had difficulty sleeping. Be in charge of his sleep and dreams, that he might be at peace and awaken refreshed and filled with a joyous spirit for the day ahead."

Lucas pipes in, "And God, please bless the children in Bosnia, who no longer have homes, or don't know where their parents are, or have nothing to eat. I've tried to think of how I can help, but I think it's up to You. Thanks God." And he drifts right off to sleep.

He had been carrying that burden and didn't even realize it. But given the context to release it back where help can truly be had, in his innocence he saw his burden, the way home, and released it. Immediately, I think of today's lesson prayer and utter it in gratitude.

DAY 265

(Lesson 265)

"Creation's gentleness is all I see."

(W-pII.265.1)

"In quiet would I look upon the world, which but reflect Your Thoughts, and mine as well. Let me remember that they are the same, and I will see creation's gentleness."

(W-pII.265.2.1–2)

The boys and I created a freedom garden in a big square in our back yard as one of our unschooling projects. Two things about that experience come to mind. First is that we planted these little vegetable seedlings in a place that got equal sunshine and shade every day. We watered them and checked for growth every day, encouraging them to grow, telling them how much we wanted them and how grateful we were to have them in our family. Within a couple of days, the first little green sprouts arrived.

I suspect what we are seeing are weeds. I warn the boys that it's very likely they're weeds, as it's too soon to see any of the vegetables. Parker says, "They have the same right to be here as the tomatoes, don't they?" We agree. Parker bends down, putting his face right next to the little green sprout. He says, "Hey, even if we didn't plant you, we want you, and love you."

Several other sprouts like the first come up within the week. I was raised with farming, and my past programing told me to get rid of the weeds or they would grow rampant and choke out the vegetables' chances for growing big and strong.

But the thing was, Parker had started this welcoming blessing, and no one wanted to go against it. So, we let them grow. With each one that came up, we blessed and welcomed it. Only a sparse few of the vegetables ever came up.

But what we had was a true freedom garden, filled with wild plants and wildflowers blooming. What wanted to grow, we let grow. And we watched curiously for what would come up next. What we saw was *"Creation's gentleness"* bloom before our eyes.

At the same period of time we had a trampoline in the back yard and the boys would jump and do tricks for hours. The neighbor lady, who was deaf and mute, would stand at the fence, thumping on it and shaking her fist angrily at the boys while they jumped.

We tried to communicate with her, but she'd walk away as we approached. At first, we laughed and joked about it, distancing ourselves from what we didn't understand. But creation's gentleness was all I wanted to see, so I prayed for another way of seeing this woman, other than the frustrated and confused way I felt.

One day she enters through our back fence with a broom, shaking it at the boys. I'm watching from the kitchen window and walk out, trying to communicate with her. She throws her hands in the air and leaves the way she came. The boys and I discuss it and say a prayer, asking to see our neighbor through the eyes of love, to understand what she needed or wanted.

The next morning, I looked out in the back yard to see what the boys were up to, the usual ruckus of them jumping and playing had gone quiet. What I see is creation's gentleness communicating.

Parker is on Cole's shoulders and they're at the fence. They were talking to the lady and her husband. Everyone was smiling, and Cole was signing his own sign language.

Parker was holding a bouquet of the weed flowers from the garden, which he gives to our new friend. Tears of joy sprang to my eyes. *Miracles naturally occur as expressions of love.* Creation's gentleness is a universal communicator which reflects back in a beautiful holy encounter.

DAY 266

(Lesson 266)

"My holy Self abides in you, God's Son."

(W-pII.266.1)

"Father, You gave me all Your Sons, to be my saviors and my counselors in sight; the bearers of Your holy Voice to me. In them are You reflected, and in them does Christ look back upon me from my Self. Let not Your Son forget Your holy Name. Let not Your Son forget his holy Source. Let not Your Son forget his Name is Yours."

(W-pII.266.1.1–5)

Today, we want to really recognize that the one before us, or that person we keep thinking of, is truly our savior. What message are we receiving? She is our counselor, speaking God's holy voice to us. What are we hearing? If it isn't love, it's a chance to look at our thinking and forgive our misperceptions.

If you've ever had a super awesome relationship with a counselor or mentor, you know that feeling, like you can go to them with anything, and they will offer higher wisdom and brings a miracle. I think of Betty—the holiest of mentors. She not only saw through my bullshit, but she always reminded me that whatever problem I was having, the error was in my perception, not in the situation.

In the early days with her, I felt she was discounting the seriousness of the messes I would get myself into, and the unfairness of the players in my world. She'd listen. But then she'd always turn it back on me. Funny, it never kept me from going to her for guidance, nor from taking her guidance and applying it as she suggested; first to my perception of myself, and then to the situation that was bothering me. The truth is just too compelling and drew me back time and time again. That's love for ya!

One time in particular comes to mind. It wasn't long after I had begun working with the course, but I hadn't developed the habit of automatically applying the lesson to whatever happened. In this circumstance, it's me as "therapist." That label came with preconceived ideas about being wise and helping clients change for the better.

I was struggling with seeing a particular client as anything but a guilty manipulator. I knew this perspective wasn't useful, so I talked to Betty about it. She brushed past my problem and asked me how I felt about *myself* when I was thinking of or working with this client.

Myself? I wanted to say, "I'm innocent in all this. She's the one is taking advantage of my time and trying to manipulate the sessions so that she doesn't have to do any honest work."

Instantly, I see the answer, and, keeping the focus on myself, I realize I feel inadequate. I thought if I were a better counselor, I could get the client to see things differently. I realize I was accusing us both of the same thing—dishonesty and manipulation. I was judging that I was justified, due to our roles, and she was not. Wow. Who's doing what?

Filled with gratitude I see the meaning of today's lesson *"My holy Self abides in you, God's Son."* My "client" is my counselor and savior. She is my holy self.

The next time I see this client, I see her innocence and my own. In the light of true joining, our encounter is holy and we both experience transformation. It changed the way I did therapy.

With each client, I started first with reminding myself that I am always looking at myself, or my holy Self, and turning the session over to the Divine. I wasn't always successful and often I had to forgive us both for mis-attempts the ego got up to, but those were just as precious a counsel, forgiving and guiding me back to the truth we share as one Self, the holy child of God.

CHAPTER TWO HUNDRED FOUR

DAY 267

(Lesson 267)

"My heart is beating in the peace of God."

(W-pII.267.1)

*"Let me attend Your Answer, not my own. Father, my heart is beating in the peace
the Heart of Love created. It is there and only there that I can be at home."*

(W-pII.267.2.1–3)

Today's lesson text is like a credo of truth for miracle workers, for you and me. I begin the day with this holy remembrance, laid out in the words and meaning of the lesson, holding it in my heart and mind, directing my sight.

In my quiet time with God, I direct my awareness wide open and feel my heartbeat move my breath. *"My heart is beating in the peace of God,"* breathing the fullness of amazing love, filling my awareness, expanding, and bringing in all the world breathing with me.

Peace fills my being, my heart expanding with each breath, flooding my body with the purpose of forgiveness—everyone and everything are welcome here. Joy and gratitude and a quiet anticipation for the day rest in my heart. My purpose is to be a bringer of light, of joy, of peace, of the love we are as one.

I'm in Savannah, and it is like the garden of Eden all around me. While Lyn and I sit on her deck overlooking her courtyard, it's like the plants are raising their hearts to us and the waterfall whispers of compassion and love. I feel the alive presence of God's love which this lesson opens within us. Every living thing sings the chorus of God's love and holiness pervading my experiencing.

Next up in the day is yoga. We do sun salutations, which feel like a natural extension of my lesson practice. The lesson itself is a salutation to the truth and the practice of moving through life in peace and joy. Instead of focusing on doing the posture correctly, synchronizing my breath with the movement, I let my intention direct my practice. *"My heart is beating in the peace of God,"* is the center of my being, the movement is whole, as the entire class is in unison.

Each heartbeat is bringing peace, each breath infusing us with strength. Tears of gratitude stream from my eyes, and I see the fountain in the garden in my mind, knowing it is all God.

It is a day of grace. Everyone we meet expands my joy. I share my Self unabashedly, joining in moments small and extended. Today's lesson is living and breathing in me, in each heartbeat. I feel every being, every flower, car, kitty, bird, or breeze is blessing me with holiness, and I bless all creation right back.

It's the miracle mindset we embark on the day with, using the words from the lesson as our credo:

I am a messenger of God, directed by His Voice, sustained by Him in love, and held forever quiet and at peace within His loving Arms. Each heartbeat calls His Name, and every one is answered by His Voice, assuring me I am at home in Him.

DAY 268

(Lesson 268)

"Let all things be exactly as they are."

(W-pII.268.1)

"Let me not be Your critic, Lord, today, and judge against You. Let me not attempt to interfere with Your creation, and distort it into sickly forms. Let me be willing to withdraw my wishes from its unity, and thus let it be as You created it. For thus will I be able, too, to recognize my Self as You created me. In Love was I created, and in Love will I remain forever. What can frighten me, when I let all things be exactly as they are?"

(W-pII.268.1.1–6)

Today's lesson is talking about reality; creation as it really is, as God created it. Reality as love, which created it to be. It is about letting our perception be exactly as they are but recognizing we've overlaid our meaning, from past assessments and present judgments. It is about letting go of our meaning, to let divinity show us reality as it is.

A few years ago, I was ministering weddings for a little chapel on the strip. The day had been fun. I cofacilitated with an Austin Powers impersonator in a crazy unconventional ceremony, followed by a very traditional wedding with bridesmaids and ushers and the works, carefully preplanned by the wedding party. I was in high spirits as the evening came to a close.

As I'm about to take my leave, this couple comes stumbling in without an appointment. Which wasn't uncommon. But they had been drinking, and I feel my energy droop. I feel compelled to counsel them to think twice about their decision and come back when they're sober—if indeed they still want to get married. Besides, they're going to keep me later than I planned, and I want to get home to my family.

It's standard practice to meet briefly with the couple to check their license and decide what type of ceremony they're looking for—if they have their own vows, traditional ones or something special. I feel put out—and I haven't even talked to the couple yet! All this will take time—time, I don't want to give.

It's impossible to not notice the barrage of negative thoughts flooding my mind and destroying my yummy peace of mind. With my hand on the knob, just before entering the room where the couple waits, I stop. "This won't do! I've got to get my shit right!" I turn and step into the Ladies for a brief counsel of my own. I kneel by the commode.

Instantly, I'm reminded of other times I've knelt before the porcelain god in a similar way, drunk, desperate, and alone. Gratitude for the grace of sobriety fills me with love and joy, my judgments laid aside. Who could be better to bless this couple than me? I ask to see only what love would have me see.

Today's lesson sings in my heart and mind. *"Let all things be exactly as they are"* as I join the couple waiting for me. Love has called and I answer. It is asking me to bring my greatest gift—my whole and holy presence.

With eyes cleared from judgment, I join the couple where they sit there writing their vows to each other on the back of some programs left by the previous wedding party. I see the love they feel for each other. I join them here, in love and union.

Grace blessed us all that night. Everything exactly as it is—supreme happiness.

CHAPTER TWO HUNDRED SIX
DAY 269
(Lesson 269)

"My sight goes forth to look upon Christ's face."
(W-pII.269.1)

"I ask Your blessing on my sight today. It is the means which You have chosen to become the way to show me my mistakes, and look beyond them. It is given me to find a new perception through the Guide You gave to me, and through His lessons to surpass perception and return to truth. I ask for the illusion which transcends all those I made. Today I choose to see a world forgiven, in which everyone shows me the face of Christ, and teaches me that what I look upon belongs to me; that nothing is, except Your holy Son."
(W-pII.269.1.1–5)

Today's lesson is the practice of awakened seeing. We are instructing our mind to see with the Holy Spirit, which is our Self. We're aware of mistaken perception that filters through and look beyond them to the face of Christ—at presence of love, which is true reality.

Haven't you noticed how when you're really happy for no reason, everything you see feels touched with the soft light of love? We don't want anything foreign to that state of bliss to intrude upon that holy instant, right? It feels yummy to desire nothing more than to look upon the face of everyone, like looking at a sunrise or children sleeping, where we're joined with the majesty of what we behold.

The way we feel is the litmus test. It tells us if we've gone deep enough—if we've been honest—if we have surrendered false goals for the single purpose of truth.

I'm walking around a part of town unfamiliar to me, looking for an office in some strip mall. Google tells me it was right in front of me, but I don't see it. I need help. The only person I see available, whom I could possibly ask, I nearly discount.

She's sitting on a curb inside the complex, with a shopping cart she holds onto with one hand. She's apparently having a conversation with an invisible (to me) someone. I sum her up in a flash, "Talking to herself—crazy. Unwashed, with a shopping cart full of possessions—homeless."

I have enough experience with noticing that my ego speaks first, judging what it is afraid of, to recognize it when it happens. Everything that is unknown to the ego is a threat. So, it starts categorizing and bullying me to ignore what is before me so that I won't realize it's a possible blessing, a miracle, or a holy encounter. That way, it can maintain control of my mind.

But because I recognize it, I can see it for what it is, and I realize that what it is telling me is not the truth. And I choose again. That's my mind-training. It happens in a flash. In an instant I'm walking right toward her with the reverence due a child of love. My heart is full, eager to bless and receive blessing. With curiosity and joy, I approach her and ask if I could join her for a moment.

She looks up at me and smiles, quiets, and pats the pavement next to her. In that instant, I feel I know her. Hers is the face of Christ. "Ah, you are my Self," I think, and sit. Neither of us say a word. We sit in pure presence for a long moment. I feel she is teaching me with her presence, and I take it in in gratitude. After a few minutes, I rise, bow a little namaste, and turn toward the strip mall buildings.

Yup! You guessed it. On the building, right in front of me, are the numbers of the address I'm looking for, bold and beautifully displayed.

DAY 270
(Lesson 270)

"I will not use the body's eyes today."

(W-pII.270.1)

"Father, Christ's vision is Your gift to me, and it has power to translate all that the body's eyes behold into the sight of a forgiven world. How glorious and gracious is this world! Yet how much more will I perceive in it than sight can give. The world forgiven signifies Your Son acknowledges his Father, lets his dreams be brought to truth, and waits expectantly the one remaining instant more of time which ends forever, as Your memory returns to him. And now his will is one with Yours. His function now is but Your Own, and every thought except Your Own is gone."

(W-pII.270.1.1–5)

Today is the final lesson in the *"What is the Body?"* section. And once again, our lesson today is on sight. The course teaches us that our body's eyes don't actually see. They report images from our mind. Our mind-training is teaching us to quit trusting what they report.

But rather, we rely on an internal experience of recognizing the light of truth beyond the physical, which shines in every aspect of creation. We are no longer focused on the sharp edges of the world around us that make up the fences of separation. We a looking with love through the lens of a unified whole.

Here's an example from a day in sync with today's idea a couple weeks ago. I had a bunch of errands to run before setting off on my travels for three weeks. I start my day, as I always do—with God. Knowing I have a big day before me, I center deeply on the prayer from today's lesson, imprinting it in my heart and mind.

I haven't left the house before my ego starts yammering on about the to-do list it wants my day to be about. "You need to get vitamins, confirm with the cat-sitter angel . . ." And that's my flip-switch. I pause, letting my mind fill with the gratitude, thinking of how, right when we need it, Jessyca, pet lover extraordinaire, shows up in our lives. *"I will not use the body's eyes today,"* I say as I picked up my list, reminding myself to trust that whatever arises, God is with me and my Guide's got this.

The so-called to-do list shifts in my mind—from what *I* needed to do for *me* to places and people I get to shine my light.

Whole Foods is first on my new list. As usual, a minister of health approaches me and asks if I need anything, tapping me on the shoulder. As I turn and look into his aqua-blue eyes, I see his holiness, his pure intent to be truly helpful. It is a pause in time—a holy encounter. We smile in through the pause. I thank him, and I'm about to say I'm familiar with this section of the store, so I don't really need his help.

But in that pause, I see our union. I say, "Now that you're here, yes. That's what I came for. Your yummy smile and awesome attitude. I've already got my vitamins." He joins my frequency, saying, "I know just what you mean. It's these chance meeting with people that make me love my job." I say, "That's our real profession behind every job, right? To leave a little joy in our wake. So, thank you." I give him a little namaste, which he returns. A holy encounter.

DAY 271

(Lesson 271)

"Christ's is the vision I will use today."

(W-pII.272.1)

"Father, Christ's vision is the way to You. What He beholds invites Your memory to be restored to me. And this I choose, to be what I would look upon today."

(W-pII.271.2.1–3)

This is such a perfect lesson for me today. *"Christ's is the vision I will use today."* We trust we will be shown the way to interpret with love.

We're having our annual sister's retreat right now. Yesterday while we were catching up with each other and sharing the highlights of this past year in our lives, one sister brings up an event between two of the other sisters' that took place via family email.

She recounts it as one sister seemingly attacking the other, twisting facts in such a way so as to diminish this sister in the family's perception. This competitive dynamic between these two sisters has been going on for years. It's just that the family forum seems to heighten (or as I see it, bring to light what forgiveness offers us) this conflict display.

The sister, bringing it up at the sister's retreat, stood up for the attacked sister in a no-nonsense, this-abuse-needs-to-be-confronted type of way, also in the family email forum. The sister who was the apparent target of the attacks expresses in our gathering that she didn't feel supported by any of the siblings except this one who spoke up on her behalf in the public forum.

This causes me to pause. At the time, I feel impressed to not add to the fray of disillusionment, knowing that attack is not justified in any form. I chose to send her a private email thanking her for her expression of love, citing examples from both our personal encounters and particularly sharing my gratitude for the incredible service of Christ love she extends with our mother, as her primary caregiver. It was a holy encounter, awash with forgiveness. So, for me it was past—forgotten.

But now this sister says she needs public support in proportion to the attack she felt was wielded against her. I'm thinking of how the course tells us that if a brother asks something from us, to recognize what does not matter, and do it because it doesn't matter. That if we have no investment in anything in this world, we can teach each other where our treasure is by our inner relinquishment of investment in the unreal.

I choose to see the Christ in her. And leave the past behind. I listen with love while she speaks, asking the Divine intently to see her with Christ vision and respond in a way that is truly helpful. I silently blessed her and forgive the misperception for all of us.

I know this situation with my sisters isn't a problem, but a misperception. When I run into a problem, and I attempt to empathize through the story of attack the other is telling. When I do, no matter which side I come down on, I am disconnecting from my Christ Self and cannot see the truth. The truth is that we are one in Christ. And attack is not possible in love.

Last night my sister who had expressed she hadn't felt supported, comes to me. She shares about an insight from her meditation telling me that God showed her that in wanting our support to look a certain way, she was not trusting God's support in her. That her divinity was all the support she needed to be aware of. Then, she thanked me for seeing it in her when she couldn't herself. Miracle.

DAY 272

(Lesson 272)

"How can illusion satisfy God's Son?"

(W-pII.272.1)

"Father, the truth belongs to me. My home is set in Heaven by Your Will and mine. Can dreams content me? Can illusions bring me happiness? What but Your memory can satisfy Your Son? I will accept no less than what you have given me. I am surrounded by Your Love, forever still, forever gentle and forever safe. God's Son must be as You created him.

(W-pII.272.1.1–7)

Today we ask ourselves an honest question. *"How can illusion satisfy God's Son?"* The mind that lives in illusion—the ego mind—cannot answer it. Sure, it jumps in and starts telling us things we need to be satisfied, incessantly. It tells us we need more, to be better, to strive, and to sacrifice to be happy. That what we are right now is not enough.

But even when we get the important thing or recognition we fought for and won; do we really feel satisfied? No. Sure, we might feel happy, even elated when we get what we wanted, even proud, perhaps superior, but satisfied? We hardly get a breather before it starts up again. The ego doesn't know what satisfaction is. It is the antithesis of satisfaction.

Satisfaction is fulfillment. Deep within, we know the truth—happiness is in each present moment devoid of ego conditions. And it is only this which can content us. Only our wholeness satisfies.

I swear, it's the simple moments that illuminate the transformation these lessons have had on my mind. My experience one day with a Reese's candy brought this one home to me. It so powerfully impacted me, I dubbed it the Reese's syndrome.

When the freedom to eat what I wanted was no longer controlled by my parents, Reese's chocolates became a favorite comfort food for me. Honestly, it was ridiculous. I could bite into a Reese's, and for a minute, my problems couldn't touch me. That is until the guilt for eating them became the next problem. But, where Reese's were concerned, I suffered from euphoric recall. When I thought about them, I recalled only the taste and the delicious reprieve from my overanxious self.

Well into the mind-training, problems were *my* problem. I was having moments of serene okay-ness, even in situations where I'd felt inadequate before. I was experiencing true joy and real satisfaction.

It was the holidays and I was swept up in the dream that illusions can satisfy. Feeling weighted with responsibilities as Santa and mom and family provider, I was making the story of the holidays more important than the truth.

One day after shopping every toy store in Salt Lake for the popular action figure Lucas wanted, I stopped home to drop off the Santa presents I'd gotten for the kids, to secretly store them away for the blessed day. As I'm picking up my keys, I notice a bowl of Reese's chocolates. I pick one up, feeling anticipation as I unwrap the Reese's and put it into my mouth.

As bite into the chocolate, letting the taste sit on my tongue, dripping down the sides and melting slowly and sliding down my throat, I notice something has changed. The emptiness and burden of my false self, which I had used eating Reese's to fill, was no longer there. Just the habit.

Only the truth, remembering who I am and my home in the Divine can really satisfy me now. I wrap my arms around myself and thank God for the tremendous release . . . I am satisfied here, now—happy and fulfilled.

DAY 273

(Lesson 273)

"The stillness of the peace of God is mine."

(W-pII.273.1)

"Father, Your peace is mine. What need have I to fear that anything can rob me of what You would have me keep? I cannot lose Your gifts to me. And so the peace You gave Your Son is with me still, in quietness and in my own eternal love for You."

(W-pII.273.2.1–4)

Perhaps we are ready for a day of undisturbed tranquility." I remember my first encounter with today's idea, my immediate thought was, "I wish I could have a day of undisturbed tranquility, but I can't imagine how I could. I disturb myself constantly with problems." I was at a place where I knew that the cause of my problems was in my mind and not whatever context it showed up in: money problems, work dynamics, body issues, or other people. But I still had the habit disturbing myself when things didn't seem to "go my way."

I come to this lesson, and it says exactly what I want in the deepest part of my heart, *"a day of undisturbed tranquility."* It speaks directly to me in the place I believe I am, which felt incredibly personal and intimate. Like it knows me and understands—and had an answer for me. It says, *"If this is not yet feasible, we are content and even more than satisfied to learn how such a day can be achieved."* It gives me clear instruction as to what I can do. *"If we give way to disturbance, let us learn how to dismiss it and return to peace."*

I direct my mind. *"We need but tell our minds, with certainty,"* and that word certainty shifts something inside me. "Oh," I realize. "I have wished, like it was not in my power to *decide* to live in undisturbed peace." And right there I make the decision for the stillness of the peace of God. It tells me exactly the instruction that would be my flip-switch if I start disturbing myself again.

I tell my mind with certainty, *"The stillness of the peace of God is mine, and nothing can intrude upon the peace that God Himself has given to His Son."*

That decision opens a portal to serene tranquility, and I am certain it's up to me, that I can have a day, a life, of undisturbed peace. God's presence is with me. As the day goes on, I see it everywhere and in each choice I am given to make—how crucial watching my mind is, and how easily I still get lazy and allow disturbing thoughts to go unchecked and unforgiven.

Later in the day, I'm at the grocery store and one of my pet-peeve disturbances occurs. A child is crying, and I knee-jerk interpret the mother as shaming the child into being quiet. I judge her embarrassment of the commotion her son was causing.

I feel the tightening in my chest and I catch myself. I pause and applied the lesson, instructing my mind with certainty, *"The stillness of the peace of God is mine, and nothing can intrude upon the peace that God Himself has given to His Son."*

An amazing thing happens. I'm at peace with the situation. I extend my peaceful glow, surrounding mom and child in peace. No shit, the babe quiets. The mom and I exchange smiles of knowing and union.

The stillness of the peace of God is always just beneath the surface, resting undisturbed by the mind-body dance, in the stillness that is God forever one with us. We can't screw it up. We can only delay recognition.

CHAPTER TWO HUNDRED ELEVEN

DAY 274

(Lesson 274)

"Today belongs to Love. Let me not fear."

(W-pII.274.1)

"Father, today I would let all things be as You created them, and give Your Son the honor due his sinlessness; the love of brother to his brother and his Friend. Through this I am redeemed. Through this as well the truth will enter where illusions were, light will replace all darkness, and Your Son will know he is a You created him."

(W-pII.274.1.1–3)

T*oday belongs to love."* Doesn't it though? Love is God. Love is you and love is me. Love is creation. Love is the Christ we share, eternally unchanged by the fearful dreams we entertain for an instant before we remember our Self. It is the Divine breath we breathe that moves the elements, wholeheartedly synchronizing the beating of our hearts.

The second part of today's lesson, *"Let me not fear,"* allows us to bring our experience into alignment with the first. We make our declaration that we will let all things be as Love created them and honor our Self and everyone we meet as innately innocent, untouched by fear's dreams of false identity.

We are dedicating ourselves to a day of living love. The lesson acts like a mission statement for the day. When we start with this wholehearted commitment to let the day belong to love, trusting rather than planning, it's beautiful. It's literally like love marches before us, making clear our path and shining a light on where to go, who to talk to, and what to say. When we encounter resistance, whether internally or as an obstacle before us, it's like love whispers gently, "Not that way. Turn here. Forgive that need. Trust this instead."

Here's an example. I thought I had a day of shopping ahead of me, I needed groceries. I had lists for Whole Foods, Sprouts, Smith's, and Costco. So, as far as timeframe goes, my day was pretty much already spent before I left the house. As I get in the car, habitually I tune into God, give the directive from my lesson. "This day is Yours my Love, let me not fear when obstacles arise, but trust."

Turns out, I never even pull out my list. As I enter to Costco, an elderly guy, toting a legal pad of list items, approaches me. "Can you help me? I don't know where to start. It's overwhelming, the size of this place. I have no idea where to find anything. My wife usually does the shopping." He pauses, looking down for a moment. I join his pause in reverence.

His eyes are shiny as he raises his face to mine with a gentle smile. My heart breaks open at this delicious holy encounter. The innocence and love wafting from this brother shines the light of a thousand stars. He says, "The drugstore is about the extent of my shopping usually. Now I have this list." I say, "Looks about like my list today. Why don't we shop together?" It's perfect.

As we shop, he shares of his wife's passing. Their present love is all over him. I feel so blessed. He tells me the list is hers. She left it with a note telling him to go to Costco for the things he needs. While we picked up items, he shares about his life partner of fifty-two years.

How she loved to shop, and how when they'd bring the groceries from the car together, she'd be like a little kid excited about new finds and the people she met along the way. I thought of my mother and the child-like joy she encounters life with—and also myself. My heart is bursting by now—full of gratitude as we part. In the check-out line, I thank him. He smiles knowingly and nods.

CHAPTER TWO HUNDRED TWELVE

DAY 275

(Lesson 275)

"God's healing Voice protects all things today."
(W-pII.275.1)

"Your healing Voice protects all things today, and so I leave all things to You. I need be anxious over nothing. For Your Voice will tell me what to do and where to go; to whom to speak and what to say to him, what thoughts to think; what words to give the world. The safety that I bring is given me. Father, Your Voice protects all things through me."
(W-pII.275.2.1–4)

Today's lesson says this is the time when we will seek and hear and learn and understand. That's some promise, yes? All of our practicing has prepared us. We are ready. This is the time we join the great crusade of healing, guided by God's healing voice, which protects our wholeness and all things in His healing love.

We have the presence of God empowering our understanding and moving us in the way of love set forth before us. Today, we quit attending to the voice of illusion, which speaks for separateness and specialness, and attend to only what can serve the whole. Today is the day confusion ends. But the decision is ours.

When the opportunity to move to Vegas finally came, I was conflicted. My life was rich with making Albuquerque my home by my decision to love, instead of resist. Which, as you know, was my first reaction to Albuquerque, and its inhabitants.

Now, I was surrounded by mighty companions of love: the deep and intimate relationships built through joining during the unschooling years, my *A Course in Miracles* and AA friends, the love-adopted kids that Cole and Parker brought home to live and heal with us a while. My heart was full. Still, I felt the perfection of the call back to Vegas.

Even as we left Vegas, nine years before, I felt a quiet knowing that my mission here was not complete. I've shared in these pages, many of the lessons and miracles that lead to understanding my purpose for being in Albuquerque. Forgiving what I thought it was, led me into the subtle vistas of guidance I learned to trust; listening intently for God's healing voice, feeling His protection and care, unfolding a deeper level of understanding given by my mind-training.

Albuquerque became the ground for opening the next level of what I saw as my heart-training; consistently attending to God's voice. Through love, I gave myself over to my present ministry, and the results were miraculous.

When I felt conflict begin to rise within me, I easily turned within, attending to God within my heart and listening as His love beat my heart. I realize that the battle within was between my illusory self, and the purpose of Self, which is for all. I realize, "I don't know why now the Vegas move was happening, or what the future brings. I can't. Now is the only moment where I can hear the voice for God."

Today's lesson appears in my mind, and I open my course book and read the lesson. I understand. New meaning had been given between the words, which I was now prepared to live. Joy fills my heart and I know all my mighty companions, and all things, go with me, protected eternally through God's healing voice, through me. So, off to Vegas I went, companions and healing in tow within my heart.

CHAPTER TWO HUNDRED THIRTEEN
DAY 276

(Lesson 276)

"The Word of God is given me to speak."

(W-pII.276.1)

*"Father, Your Word is mine. And it is this that I would speak
to all my brothers, who are given me to cherish as my
own, as I am loved and blessed and saved by You."*

(W-pII.276.2.1–2)

I want to speak the word of God in whatever situation arises—asking for the words that will convey the message which will reach the heart of those before me. I want to resonate at the frequency of the love of God and be the voice His word has given, *"My Son is pure and holy as Myself."*

I recall a day when I experienced, profoundly, that I am given the words to speak. I was facilitating a group for healing around food and weight falsehoods. I taught that Self love was ultimately the only answer. We began with finding loving acceptance with the body and food illusions we believed, and not making them wrong, but being willing to see that it is not the truth of what we are.

Each session I asked to speak God's word, before the gathering, and the trust in my relationship with the Divine. I knew that I didn't have the answer but trusted that the answer could come through the divine within me.

A gal we'll call Ashley, resisted. Her go-to response for whatever came up was, "I can't do that." Or, "that doesn't work for me." We'd been meeting for weeks, and she remained resistant.

This day, she's using her usual responses, and others in the group are trying to help. They share ways they remind themselves that their cravings for food or feelings of guilt aren't the truth. How they turn within, reminding themselves that love is what they are, or, if they can't, they reach out to another member to be the voice for love for them. Impatience and frustration filter into the group as Ashley blocks each suggestion, finally saying "You don't understand, I don't deserve to love myself. I'm too far gone. Please quit talking to me."

I'm praying silently like mad, "Dude, you gotta help me. How can I be truly helpful in the face of such resistance? I have no idea what to say or do. Please speak through me." Suddenly, I see Ashley as my younger self. I recall the moment I realized God loved me and I was that love, by bringing an image to my mind of holding my son, Lucas, as a babe—the feeling of wholeness and of the connection between God, myself and Lucas and the incredible love and innocence that flowed through me. Words come.

I ask Ashley, "Is anyone worthy of your love?" She responds indignantly, "Yes. My daughter. She is only three, and she's innocent and deserves everything. She's better than me."

"Yet," I continue, "she is entrusted to you. Certainly, you must have the love necessary for the job. Where do you think that comes from?" The shift in Ashley's demeanor is immediate. I press on. "Is it possible that the same innocence, love, and purity in your daughter is also the essence of who you are, but just covered over with these repetitive affirmations of self-rejection you've been telling yourself for years?"

"When you need it, for your daughter, it naturally comes forth from you, yes? Where else would the tender loving care you show her come from, but from your true identity as pure and innocent love? Is it possible for you to conceive that, like your daughter, you are still as you were created, not the false beliefs you have been identifying as yourself?"

Ashley bursts into tears. "I see it. Oh, my God. I see it!" Miracle!

CHAPTER TWO HUNDRED FOURTEEN

DAY 277

(Lesson 277)

"Let me not bind Your Son with laws I made."

(W-pII.277.1)

"Your Son is free, my Father. Let me not imagine I have bound him with the laws I made to rule the body. He is not subject to any laws I made by which I try to make the body more secure. He is not changed by what is changeable. He is not slave to any laws of time. He is as You created him, because he knows no law except the law of love."

(W-pII.277.1.1–6)

Today's lesson is a prayer. *"Let me not bind Your Son with laws I made."* We need to be clear that the Son of God is you, and me, in our pure unadulterated Self, pure and holy as God created us. The term Son is a way of reminding us that the entire Sonship is a holographic whole. As the Son of God, we are free.

But when we add laws we made—laws of separation, lack, attack, competition and comparisons, and blame—we become the slave to them. We're talking about laws of the body as a creative agent, subject to disease and death. We're talking about the laws of economics, politics, and moral judgments on who is right and who is not.

We bind ourselves, and our brother, whenever see an error and then try to "fix" it ourselves. Every time we take issue with another, judging what they do or say, we are binding our minds to the dream of separation and its laws, making miracles temporarily unavailable to us. We interpret with fear what was merely a request for love.

I love this because I am always free. I might choose to bind my consciousness, valuing blame or pain for a bit, but the instant I am willing, I easily see it is as call for love.

Remember the other day I talked about my sister not feeling supported by me? That moment of apprehension I felt in aligning with her, was a chance to either bind us both with laws of family dynamics, blame, and acquiesce or see the Christ in her, my sisters, and my Self. This choice frees us to trust the truth to find a resolution that would result in a peaceful and happy outcome.

The temptation to try to make her understand my perspective pulled at me. To help her see things differently, right? But that's the trap, see? The second I think she needs something, I am binding us both to laws of personhood. What I want to do is free her from the laws I made, not reinforce them in both of us.

I want to see her as the savior she is. I do. I am grateful. In reality, we are already free and whole. We are spirit. By remembering the truth, I realize I need do nothing. She needs nothing. The Holy Spirit is in her mind and mine as one. Forgiveness offers everything I want. *"Let me not bind the Son of God with laws I made."*

The call for love in the face of this hurt, fear, and misunderstanding becomes instantly evident. "She is the holy Christ, whose identity is mine. Love is what we are. Through our shared identity, the power and presence of God are with us." That's what lit my mind, allowing the purpose of true communication to unfold for all of us.

Love wants to join. It proved itself out with consistency for the rest of the sister's retreat. A new level of acceptance of a higher law, the law of love, guided our time together. Once we see that our "imprisonments" are calls for love, we're in the frequency of miracles.

CHAPTER TWO HUNDRED FIFTEEN
DAY 278
(Lesson 278)

"If I am bound, my Father is not free."
(W-pll.278.1)

"Father, I ask for nothing but the truth. I have had many foolish thoughts about myself and my creation, and have brought a dream of fear into my mind. Today, I would not dream. I choose the way to You instead of madness and instead of fear. For truth is safe, and only love is sure."
(W-pll.278.2.1–4)

This lesson is humbling. It asks for a level of accountability that reaches beyond belief, and into the heart of truth. The section of lessons we are doing right now is about recognizing that Christ is the Self we are in truth. Whatever beliefs we hold that interfere with the recognition of the love we are, is fear. Fear shows up as laws of limitation and imprisons our thinking and therefore our experiences to the thought system we are identifying with as real for us.

When I was working at a neuropsychiatric institution, one of the rotations was in the locked ward. My first reaction to being there was fear. Crazy scares. I felt such resistance, I figured it must be a part of my mind I had denied. So I listed myself as someone who could be called when a patient needed one-on-one care.

Whenever I got the call to come in, I'd prepare myself by praying to see the Christ in this being and forgive the fears that arise represented my repressed thought system. These calls often came for the night shift.

A call comes in late one night for a patient who is dying of a terminal illness. And how I remember it is that although she had a psychiatric diagnosis, her transfer to our facility had to do with insurance coverage. She didn't want to be there. She was considered by staff to be, and I quote, "A cantankerous old bat."

No one wanted to spend time with her. She yelled and threw things and basically rejected all attempts at kindness or assistance. It seemed she didn't sleep much, but made demands, then rejected efforts by staff to meet them.

So, when I get the call, her reputation proceeding, I feel, I admit, afraid. Resistance wafted over me. But I say yes and prepare to spend the night with her. I pray fervently for peace. For a way of seeing her that heals us both. I pray to love her, while also praying that maybe this might be the night she sleeps.

When I enter her room, she immediately demands I leave, knocking the glass of water off her bedside table with her arm. I pick it up and leave. I'm shaking as I fill a plastic pitcher with water, imagining that if I feel so frightened and attacked, she must be feeling just as tortured inside.

Maybe I could calm her fears in some way. I pray to find that way. I pick up a small plastic tub and fill it with warm soapy water and a washcloth and reenter her room. Though it's dark, she lay there still. Perhaps asleep after all? I send a blessing of love and peace from my heart to hers and pull up a chair at the foot of her bed, bringing the tub of warm water with me.

I pull back the covers to reveal dry, swollen, and scaly feet. I begin bathing her feet, peace washing over me. Softly I hum, then quietly sing "Amazing Grace." This beautiful angelic voice joins me. "Amazing Grace" rises from within this woman as she sings full and rich, while I bathe her feet. It's beautiful. It's heaven.

I swear the room was bathed in a soft glow as she drifts off to sleep. "God is. This is everything," I weep in gratitude. I kiss her holy forehead as I leave to go home, irreversibly changed forever. The next afternoon when I return to work, she's gone. She had passed in the early hours that morning.

DAY 279

(Lesson 279)

"Creation's freedom promises my own."

(W-pII.279.1)

"I will accept Your promises today, and give my faith to them. My Father loves the Son Whom He created as His Own. Would You withhold the gifts You gave to me?"

(W-pII.279.2.1–3)

Today's lesson is inviting us to live in faith, trusting that the promise of freedom, given in our creation, is ours now. We've all felt ourselves free. When we are present to what is, love fills our being with the mystery of what the thinking mind cannot grasp.

For me, today's lesson is all about being present. When I am present, the stories I dream up about myself don't exist. I'm being with you. Our exchange of love overrides story telling. The newness of this moment refreshes and enlivens. Something creative is happening, and I want to be part of it. Heart takes the lead. The truth of what we are as God's creation comes forth, expressing through us.

So that's the thing, right? We can't think storylines and be present at the same time. Presence is being. What we need is given. Presence is freedom. This moment now is free. The past cannot intrude upon it—we have to make a choice to let it, which is dreaming. The thing I love is that in each present moment, I am always enough. You are enough. And what is happening is just fine the way it is. In fact, it's kinda magical.

What causes discomfort is when I start bothering myself with ideas from past or future fantasies. Oh, sure, at the time I believe them relevant, but in the stillness of my heart, I know. I've drug them in from the past to mitigate the brightness of love's presence—they show me I'm identified as a body-person, separate from you.

I admit it. I get scared. I resist. I doze off and dream that there is some kind of problem that needs my attention when what I need to see gets too close, sometimes. I'm free to do that, but it doesn't feel so yummy. That's the flip-switch.

Here's an example. Recently l joined a community writer's club. When I arrived, I sought out the chairperson I had been corresponding with by email and introduced myself. She welcomed me and introduced me around, telling me of the participants various accomplishments, publications, and rewards.

It seemed each had a long history of successes as writers of fiction, novels, and even a couple had published text-books that were being used nationwide. At first, I felt excited, inspired, even a little in awe.

But as questions came my way, I started to feel a little small in comparison. My mind told me these weren't my peeps. No one was writing spiritual stuff. (Like I knew). But that temptation didn't stick.

Even as these thoughts and feelings of separation tempt me to withdraw, I recognize their unreality. I share a silent chuckle with spirit as I'm reminded of today's lesson. *"Creation's freedom promises my own,"* and open my heart to full presence.

I remember what it says in today's lesson, that the end of dreams is promised me because God's love is what I am. I am the presence of God's love in the world. Instantly I feel one with the alive creativity that surrounds me.

CHAPTER TWO HUNDRED SEVENTEEN
DAY 280
(Lesson 280)

"What limits can I lay upon God's Son?"

(W-pII.280.1)

*"Today let me give honor to Your Son, for thus alone I find the way to You.
Father, I lay no limits on the Son You love and You created limitless. The honor
that I give to him is Yours, and what is Yours belongs to me as well."*

(W-pII.280.2.1–3)

Okay, so we're considering these lesson ideas and practices from the perspective that we are Christ, the whole and holy Son of God, whom God created limitless and free. Today we're asked to honestly consider whether it is possible that Christ could be limited by dreams of judgment we design to enhance the specialness of our self-concept.

Love encompasses all creation—totally free and totally limitless. Right? So, we have to consider also if it is possible that the God of Love could have actually left room for something else to intrude upon the holy heart in which we have our being. Doesn't sound reasonable does it?

No one has left God's mind except in illusions. We have such propensity to diagnose problems, to find fault, then try to fix it—to see ourselves as special, superior, or inferior. We make comparisons and lay judgments and limits, then make up solutions within the context of the laws of limitation, while maintaining that we are trying to help—and we can almost believe it is true. It's like a knee-jerk reaction to anything that feels uncomfortable. That discomfort though is the flip-switch to pause, recognize we are investing in the false and choose again.

I remember it totally hit me one day. I was teaching a small class of "first time offenders" about chemical dependency and the disease concept. A guy in the class, Aaron, keeps throwing up resistance. I'd seen it before—a lot. It's the nature of the addictive mind to protect its laws and maintain its fertile ground. So, I'm not really paying attention to what he was saying. I already know, right? I'm more or less brushing him off with quick, canned answers.

Then he says something that brings me present and causes me to pause. He says, "Can I ask you a personal question?" I say, "Sure, you can ask." He says—and this is what stopped me in mid-judgment—he asks, "Will you answer honestly?" I realize right then that I had not spent a truly honest moment with the class—with my brothers.

I'd judged them based on the reason they were here, and slipped them into neat little categories, I was trained to help accordingly. I was in business with my ego, and I could not see the face of Christ before me. That was my flip-switch. I pause and look again, seeing the faces of these beautiful beings for the first time. I pull up a chair and joined the small group.

"Okay, Aaron, what's your question?" He says, "Do you see yourself as superior to us?" I feel the heat start to rise to my face, and shame chills course through my veins. "Yes," I admit. Holy shit! I *have* been seeing myself as better. Which is different than the part of me that has this awesome knowledge to impart about addiction and treatment.

"I have been distancing myself from you all, rather than joining. And you saw it, Aaron. Thank you for your courage in witnessing for me."

Honesty changed the texture of the class to one of honor and true learning. By my taking responsibility for my projections and forgiving, the invitation for honesty was established. We met each other with the honor due to the holy Son of God. Miracle.

CHAPTER TWO HUNDRED EIGHTEEN
DAY 281
(Lesson 281)

"I can be hurt by nothing but my thoughts."

(W-pII.281.1)

"Father, Your Son is perfect. When I think that I am hurt in any way, it is because I have forgotten who I am, and that I am as You created me. Your Thoughts can only bring me happiness. If ever I am sad or hurt or ill, I have forgotten what You think, and put my little meaningless ideas in place of where Your Thoughts belong, and where they are. I can be hurt by nothing but my thoughts. The Thoughts I think with You can only bless. The Thoughts I think with You alone are true."

(W-pII.281.1.1–7)

Today we begin a new theme from which we consider the next ten lessons. That theme is *"What is the Holy Spirit?"* The Holy Spirit is the part of our minds that knows the truth. It is the correction for all the errors we have accepted into our minds. It is the part of our mind that holds the truth for us, while also seeing the illusions we've used to deny the truth, which is that we are love.

The Holy Spirit acts like a mediator between illusions and the truth. The Holy Spirit is the sanity in our mind which transforms when we have allowed insanity to enter.

Whenever I think something should be different than it is, when I am upset, or my peace has been disturbed in any way, my part is to recognize the feeling is not what I am, and take responsibility for it. Then be willing to see it differently through the eyes of love. The Holy Spirit is this different way, already in my mind, bridging the gap between illusions and reality.

Today's lesson, *"I can be hurt by nothing but my thoughts,"* is really speaking to the incredible power of our minds. Remember we are the thought of God's love extending eternally. We have the same creative power as God. Everything is an idea. My thoughts make up the whole of my reality.

So, if I am feeling hurt, it must come from my own thoughts. Only I have the power to hurt me. The responsibility is mine. If I'm thinking with the Holy Spirit, I feel peaceful and love directs my responses. Whenever I am hurt or sad or resistant, I am reacting to the thoughts in my mind that I have projected, but not taken responsibility for—my own unforgiving thoughts. Forgiveness sees that the thoughts that hurt are not true, leaving space for the truth to enter.

The first time I came to today's lesson, I was struggling to know myself, my role as a single mom, going to college while working full time to provide for my children. My schedule felt taxing and I often felt overwhelmed by it all. Struggle and overwhelm were my constant companions. I'd have moments of clarity and release, but they weren't sustainable.

The day I came to this lesson, I'd hardly given myself time in my schedule to really consider it, I thought I had so many things to do before getting the kids up.

But I kept my date with God as I promised I would. I let my mind still into the idea that God is with me, and let love fill my being. As I read the lesson, I began to cry. *"I can be hurt by nothing but my thoughts."* "Oh my God, I am hurting myself. I have been thinking it's all up to me. I am deciding for all this worry and fear and overwhelm!" I felt blessed compassion and cried harder.

Then a thought seemingly out of the blue came into my mind. "Think love." This became my go-to for every glitch in my mommy-matrix, and ultimately my life.

CHAPTER TWO HUNDRED NINETEEN

DAY 282

(Lesson 282)

"I will not be afraid of love today."

(W-pII.282.1)

*"Father, Your Name is Love and so is mine. Such is the truth.
And can the truth be changed by merely giving it another name?
The name of fear is simply a mistake. Let me not be afraid of truth today."*

(W-pII.282.2.1–5)

will not be afraid of love today." This is our choice for truth. It is the single decision to be as we truly are—already in relationship with everyone and everything. Today's lesson is about deciding to unite in love with each being and every experience that arises in our day. Love is union.

It is about dedicating all our thought to union. Not just with our brothers and sisters but with *all* things. Love is what heals this world of perception.

I used to be super selective about what I allowed into my mind—avoiding all the horrific news drama, selecting environments that nurture and celebrated rather than competitive, winner/loser ones. It seemed like a good thing. A loving thing. Seems reasonable enough, right?

The awesome thing about becoming miracle-minded is that I became aware that this selectivity was showing me the separation still permeating my mind. The thing about truth is that it needs no defense.

Love stands, shining bright. It permeates and heals. And nothing can actually stand against it. When it looks like something is in the way of love, it is only a reflection of my fear of totality. It's like the ego's last-ditch effort to get me to favor specialness over the magnitude that is my One Self, and includes all.

It is an incredible thing to realize that by allowing all things to be as they are, excluding nothing from love, but rather joining through allowing, it makes it holy. I don't need to protect myself from anyone or anything.

Love sifts out the false, making union possible. It makes all the difference in the world. If it's in front of me, or in my thoughts, it is mine to make holy by loving. It is an awesome practice to think union with everyone and everything that arises. My heart must lead my mind to make this possible.

I've been traveling for nearly a month. I love what I experience, because I can't predict ahead of time, and the poignancy of making the choice to join in love or pass by (which is fear) seems obvious.

The guy next to me at the coffee bar, will he be my present love, or a cog in the coffee shop machine, unseen by me and excluded in my love for my Self? The fat lady with too big a suitcase to go in the overhead on the plane—will she be a pain in the ass, or will I join her in holiness and a solution for her burden.

What about the weather, an unpredictable force I can resist or love exactly as it is. It is my joining with what is, that makes it holy. Sometimes it's easiest to practice with strangers, to see that no one is excluded in holiness.

A couple evenings ago, we went to a fundraising event for the rape-crisis center. The topic itself can raise a flag of separation between victims and perpetrators. So, keeping the decision for union in my mind, where this topic is concerned, was no small feat.

The focus seemed heavily weighted toward punishing perpetrators and protecting victims. The temptation to feel justified in judging the perpetrator, to not join but to withhold love, was tangible. But one thing kept running through my mind. *"I will not be afraid of love today,"* and realized this incredible universal call for love permeating the room. One heart beating love.

257

DAY 283

(Lesson 283)

"My true identity abides in You."

(W-pII.283.1)

"Father, I made an image of myself, and it is this I call the Son of God. Yet is creation as it always was, for Your creation is unchangeable. Let me not worship idols. I am he my Father loves. My holiness remains the light of Heaven and the Love of God. Is not what is beloved of You secure? Is not the light of Heaven infinite? Is not Your Son my true identity, when You created everything that is?"

(W-pII.283.1.1–7)

Yesterday we said that relationship is union, uniting lovingly with everything, allowing all into our hearts. Today's lesson falls perfectly in line with this. Our true identity is our union with the Source of union and all that really is. Love needs no protection. And only what love created is real. So, with forgiveness, we are merely stopping the reign of separation.

Today's lesson is reminding us that our true identity stands untouched by what we made, because of what it is. It is our relationship with God that makes us what we are. It is our identity and the love of God extended that gives us life.

It is the holiness of our identity that breathes life into all that we join with here. The idols we make cannot touch the truth. They were made to separate us from it. The body is the idol that we made to represent our Self. But even as we believe this to be true, there is this almost haunting and undeniable awareness that we are more. Its pull is compelling.

That's why the grand question throughout the ages is, "What am I?" The course tells us that in truth we, of course, do know. It is only the mind of separation that asks.

We are learning to return our minds to the stillness beyond questioning. In that stillness, a memory comes. It doesn't come in form, but in an experience of love—of God—of Self. It cannot be captured and kept for future use. Love cannot be used. True relationship cannot be used. Love is now and our identity is beyond time and place but permeates and encompasses all time and place.

In Savannah a couple of weeks ago, while in yoga class I had one of those experiences where I'm experiencing my body as outside of my Self. My mind is completely still. And it's like I'm watching my body take instruction and move accordingly, with no involvement from my mind. I'd given over my body struggle and surrendered to a higher authority—and what it creates is beautiful.

Suddenly, we move into a difficult posture, and a thought that brings me crashing back into my body identity. "I don't think I can do this posture." Just like that, I've dis-identified with the truth. The shift was so obvious, forgiveness comes easily.

I am not my body identity. This was surely true, as my body moved easily as love, but judgment brought contraction and discomfort. I give up the posture, the judgment, and my body, repeating today's idea in gratitude, *"My true identity abides in my God,"* and rest in savasana.

I love this metaphor. Savasana is also called corpse pose, but its aim is being fully awake. Savasana is like forgiveness. As I lay there, I'm fully awake to the awareness of love, to my identity in God.

I think of how this is all I need do with all these corpse poses of false identity, or idols, made to separate; let them be as they are, while I am surrendered to love. I just allow my awake state to assimilate my asana practice of forgiveness.

DAY 284

(Lesson 284)

"I can elect to change all thoughts that hurt."

(W-pII.2841)

*"Father, what You have given cannot hurt, so grief and pain must be impossible.
Let me not fail to trust in You today, accepting but the joyous
as Your gifts; accepting but the joyous as the truth."*

(W-pII.284.2.1–2)

Today's lesson describes exactly what happens with the mind-training of *A Course in Miracles*. We can elect to change any thought. The thoughts we want to change obviously are those that hurt. Imagine pain and grief and suffering as completely off the table of experience. Yummy, right?

But we've all had experiences throughout this course of lessons where we've had a total change of heart. And what once hurt like the dickens, now warms our hearts because an ancient hate has become a present love. "Elect" is the key word here, isn't it? When we elect to change thoughts that hurt to ones that forgive, they become a present love. The choice rests with us.

You've all heard about the nemesis relationship I created with my sister Keri. In fact, you're probably sick of it. I am. Which is why I elected to change every thought I had about her from ones that hurt to forgiving thoughts that showed me what I had rejected in myself and blamed on her.

Let me be clear about this. Keri did nothing. In fact, I'm sure she's unaware I had her in this role of nemesis. I needed a bad guy for all my failures to measure up to my perfect ideal. She, being better at almost everything than me, fit that bill. Thanks, Keri.

What I had to forgive were the projections of guilt I'd named "hurts from Keri." I had to forgive my interpretations that saw her as separate from me and see that she is my perfect Self. I let love tell me the truth. Love said she is Christ, just as I am.

The countless times she has shown up as an example for practices with the lessons has left me with only deep appreciation for her holiness, which has shown me my own. Thank you, Keri. You are my One Self.

Adopting this lesson in electing to change all thoughts about Keri that hurt, resulted in my seeing the gift she has given me to experience the Christ we share, and the holiness which lets me bless instead of blame.

It's a transferable blueprint for all the things not of God, which I have believed were true about my life and the people in it. By recognizing first that I can elect to change my thoughts at any instant, and therefore change my relationship with my life, everything changed, an incredible power arose in me that let me see that I truly am not a victim of what I see, but the maker.

I can elect to love, to embrace, and to join rather than feel victimized, hurt, or grieved about what was never real anyway. To see that suffering of any kind is but a dream and pain is impossible, let's me choose to change the constraints put on me by my body-identity, to wholehearted presence to the love I am, beyond bodies and their constraints. With love there is always union. And in union there is no pain or suffering, no loss or grief. In this present moment, I elect a holy instant to witness to the truth. Please join me here, now, in love.

CHAPTER TWO HUNDRED TWENTY-TWO

DAY 285

(Lesson 285)

"My holiness shines bright and clear today."

(W-pII.285.1)

*"Father, my holiness is Yours. Let me rejoice in it, and through forgiveness
be restored to sanity. Your Son is still as You created him. My holiness is part
of me, and also part of You. And what can alter Holiness Itself?"*

(W-pII.285.2.1–4)

This is such an awesome lesson. We get specific instructions to give our minds for happiness, the instant we wake. So often in the past, we wake up already worried for the day; filled with fear and apprehension and anxiety. But we're no longer wholly insane.

We make a choice for sanity as we wake now. We wake in joy! First, we remember that wherever we are, there holiness is. So, we tune to our holiness frequency—love—God's frequency—which is joy and happiness.

Naturally, we expect the happy things of God to come to us. We ask them to come through the holiness of our shared identity in God. Holiness naturally shines bright and clear. From this clear view, hurt and loss, pain and suffering make no sense. Insanity is dismissed in the sanity of our holiness as love and joy.

I started this practice years ago when I read about the path of unconditional happiness and absolutely knew it was the path of my heart.

The basic idea is that love is what we are, and being love, we keep our hearts open, no matter what! The feeling is pure joy—the Divine flow of present happiness. It is this joy in which we realize our state of heaven here on earth. For me it is a call to action—a call to forgive the insanity of joylessness immediately.

Practicing this change of mind, this trust in my innate holiness has not always been easy, but it is always effective. God wills only happiness for me and the way that becomes possible in every situation is by electing to change thoughts that hurt, which allows *"my holiness [to shine] bright and clear."* When we are thinking about holiness, we are allowing the love part of our mind to shine through, to bless and heal.

Here's an example. I'm feeling all openhearted, forgiving, blessing, and loving everyone I see on my way to work. The barista, the guy driving slowly in the car in front of me, the girl singing to a rap song next to me at the stop light—rap music.

I stopped by the bank to get a little cash, only to find out I'm overdrawn. My heart sinks. I want to accuse the bank attendant of, I don't know, something—anything rather than feel this defeated feeling, which seemed incredible in the face of how I was feeling just two seconds ago. I keep telling myself, "Don't close your heart. Don't close your heart," and it isn't working. But, that's my flip-switch.

I call today's lesson to mind. *"My holiness shines bright and clear today,"* and repeat it like a prayer. And boom! My heart bursts open, forgiving banking altogether, it's radiance shining brightly through my smile. Laughing, I see the craziness that money or lack or anything situational could actually alter my true state of being.

My heart is open as the attendant asks if I'd like to take a look at my account together. Rather than feel ashamed, I feel blessed. I'm here to join in joy, no matter what! Turns out, I'd made a miscalculation. In a matter of minutes, we squared it away, becoming fast friends.

DAY 286
(Lesson 286)

"The hush of Heaven holds my heart today."

(W-pII.286.1)

"Father, how still today! How quietly so all things fall in place! This is the day that has been chosen as the time in which I come to understand the lesson that there is no need that I do anything. In You is every choice already made. In You has every conflict been resolved. In You is everything I ever hope to find already given me. Your peace is mine. My heart is quiet, and my mind at rest. Your Love is Heaven and Your Love is mine."

(W-pII.286.1.1–8)

Isn't this prayer beautiful? It feels like heaven, doesn't it? The hush of heaven is here, now. It is in the center of our being. It is the stillness of now; the quiet beat of our heart. The hush of heaven is that still center of our being, in this holy instant, that is our Self as God created us.

To experience it, all we need to do is to stop believing stories of problems and future happiness and get totally present. This present moment is totally ours. Listening in stillness is peace, and from it all things fall quietly in place.

Each present moment holds the hush of heaven. We are learning to live from this still center within. It requires we give up trying to control the dream—we stop thinking we have control. In us, is every choice already made, and every conflict been resolved. The only control is the choice for truth.

We choose this moment's presence. One choice to think with love or regurgitate yesterday's fear. What is showing up in our lives was put there long ago and the return home to heaven was placed there with it. We're like this magnetic center of love which draws all things into alignment with love's purpose.

On the plane coming home from my trip yesterday, I made a list of appointments that needed to be made, and things that needed to be done to square the household away, after being gone for nearly a month. I closed my notebook and settled into the stillness, listening to the hush of heaven beating my heart, trusting that what needed to be handled will fall into place.

As day breaks this morning, the sun shines from my heart, lighting the world with joy. As always, I begin in the wee hours with God—the hush of heaven permeating all creation of which I am a part.

As the day proceeds, my phone rings periodically, appointments are made, and the household business simply falls into place, while I easily stay present to each moment. What needs to be handled is handled by Divine flow. I'm keen to the hush of heaven holding my heart and I move to its melody in total trust. One of the calls is for an appointment this afternoon.

As I enter the facility, I hardly close the door behind me, and staff friends gather to greet me, happy to see me and wanting to join. It's a hug-fest! Each blesses me, telling me they miss the yumminess, the joy, the light, I bring with me. Holy encounters—the hush of heaven holding our hearts today.

How'd I get so lucky? Of course, there's days I throw a wrench in the works and have to start again at ground zero. But the thing is, I do. I pause and remember the truth and keep my heart open. That's the miracle of choosing to love above all else. All things flow perfectly from this present moment where reality is—where the hush of heaven holds our hearts eternally.

DAY 287

(Lesson 287)

"You are my goal, my Father. Only You."

(W-pII.287.1)

"You are my goal, my Father. What but You could I desire to have? What way but that which leads to You could I desire to walk? And what except the memory of You could signify to me the end of dreams and futile substitutions for the truth? You are my only goal. Your Son would be as You created him. What way but this could I expect to recognize my Self, and be at one with my Identity?"

(W-pII.287.2.1–7)

I contemplate today's lesson, and it feels absolutely true to me. The only thing I want is God—to be present with God's love as my own Self in each and every moment. It is the experience of present happiness. It has never left me, sourcing me with joy even in situations where I doze off and forget, thinking I can look for happiness somewhere else. It takes but a holy instant, and I return to the experience of perfect peace and happiness of Divine love.

I love the way the lesson walks us back from our lofty (albeit true) goal and makes sure we've gathered up all the sneaky little worldly substitutes we still might have tucked away.

First off, if we look at all the goals we've ever had, wasn't the reason behind each the belief that when achieved it would bring us happiness and peace? We look closely at our goals to the underlying reason for them. The reason is we want to be happy. We want to be at peace. We want to give up the fight and rest.

We want connection and love. We ask honestly, isn't it possible that even in these, it is God we are trying to connect with? We're using the questions from the lesson today to look at all the goals we have invested our hope for happiness in, forgiving, and moving past them to the real goal—God.

I entered this writer's anthology competition for the writer's community in Vegas last year. When I learned about the competition, I felt inspired to enter. I saw it as an opportunity for me to join in an active way, as a writer, in a community of writers.

But then I started feeling silly about it, and nearly brushed it off as something frivolous, a goal unworthy of my attention. As I looked more deeply at my apprehension, I saw that I was afraid I would start fixating on the outcome, hoping my story got picked for the anthology, setting the stage of happiness or disappointment based on something outside myself. Why go there?

I talk to my writer sister, Lyn, the next day, telling her about the process in my mind. She laughs. "So, what if you are apprehensive? That's what we do, when we put ourselves out there. You have special tools to deal with whatever comes up when it arises. That's your thing! You'll deal with whatever comes up because you know what your real goal is." Ah, the voice for God . . .

Truth be told, I didn't even think about the outcome after that. I felt complete with in doing my part. What would have been my goal in the past—recognition or validation of some sort—had been replaced by Heaven. When someone asked me if I'd heard anything, I said I figured the participants that were chosen, and had been contacted, and that was that.

So, imagine my surprise when I got an email a couple of weeks ago asking me to sign a release for publication. It was a yummy surprise, yes. But I already had my goal, deep within and spread throughout my life. God is my goal. My only one. What a beautiful lesson in trusting the goal of God.

DAY 288

(Lesson 288)

"Let me forget my brother's past today."

(W-pII.288.1)

"This is the thought that leads the way to You, and brings me to my goal. I cannot come to You without my brother. And to know my Source, I first must recognize what You created one with me. My brother's is the hand that leads me on the way to You. His sins are in the past along with mine, and I am saved because the past is gone. Let me not cherish it within my heart, or I will lose the way to walk to You. My brother is my savior. Let me not attack the savior You have given me. But let me honor him who bears Your Name, and so remember that It is my own."

(W-pII.288.1.1–9)

Today's lesson is one of those come-to-Jesus lessons. *"Let me forget my brother's past today."* Who am I holding hostage to their past? Who am I still seeing outside of heaven, now? I cannot abide in the wholeness of God or in heaven and abide in separation at the same time. My brother must come with me. I must see your holiness to recognize my own.

This lesson is so powerful, because the last thing we spiritual types want to believe is that our salvation depends on those we judge as not giving a shit, or at least not as spiritual as us. Right? Remember, the Son of God is one. So, we've got to gather up all those we've split off from ourselves, in the arms of love to remember our wholeness—our identity as God's kid. The past *is* gone! Why drag it into now when heaven waits our release.

How I see you *is* how I see myself. Letting the story of the past go and looking only to the Christ in you—to the holiness we share—*is* the way I see the light of Christ is also mine.

The course tells us that forgiving is forgetting. As we see our brother as the holy Son of God along with us, we let the story of his past go, leaving only the love that has been shared within our mind. As long as I am holding you hostage to something you did or didn't do in the past, I hold myself there too, because I am upholding the belief in sin in my own mind.

Forgiveness is total. It is uncompromising. All or nothing.

I love that this lesson is coming up right now. We all have someone in our lives we don't see as heaven-abiding. In fact, we might even think our judgment of him keeps us safe in some way.

Enter Trump—stage right! I bring it up now because he is such an easy target for my self-righteous unforgiveness. For me, he represents justification for seeing unworthiness in a brother. I mean he's a fear-monger, for God's sake! Fear is always the dream the past is real, now. I choose to wake, forgive, and bring my brother into the heaven of my peaceful mind.

I know the image I held of Trump is not the truth. It's coming from unforgiving thoughts I have not forgotten. So, into this fertile ground the Holy Spirit bring my savior. Thank you, Trump.

The charge I had around his presidency fizzles and dies. And so it is with each and every one of us. You are my savior. Only when I cherish your holiness as your identity, am I in touch with my own. When I forget your past, I can forget my own. I cannot see myself any higher than I see you. You are my One Self. Holiness is not a sliding scale. It is the essence of the Son of Love itself.

DAY 289

(Lesson 289)

"The past is over. It can touch me not."

(W-pII.289.1)

"Father, let me not look upon a past that is not there. For You have offered me Your Own replacement, in a present world the past has left untouched and free of sin. Here is the end of guilt. And here am I made ready for Your final step. Shall I demand that You wait longer for Your Son to find the loveliness You planned to be the end of all his dreams and all his pain?"

(W-pII.289.2.1–4)

Forgiveness lets us leave the past behind. But we have to let it be done. Most of us would agree that, in theory, we believe that the past is over, but we don't act like it, do we? Too often we bring it along with us like it's our favorite pet, taking it everywhere with us.

Like one of those little tea-cup dogs, we dress the past up and let it ride in our purse. Everything has to be contrived to maintain its comfort, lest it snaps and bites. It yips incessantly if not fed on demand, wants special attention at inopportune times, demands we avoid things and people that frighten it, lest it lose control of its bladder. It barks and makes a scene if it doesn't get its way. Hell, it's more like we're *it's* pet!

But the past is actually nowhere. The ego lives in memory-mind. Once we engage the past, it runs the show—we've stepped away from reality, which is now—and dozed off into dreamland. And it's usually a shitty dream. It's 100 percent unnecessary.

The present moment contains everything we need for each moment. In fact, it is the only time that does, because it is the only time the portal to eternity is open, allowing divinity to flow through freely, unhindered—in its light we see clearly what's now.

A thing I like to do is to set moments like going from one setting to the next—stoplights, getting onto elevators, or entering another room—as reminders to presence myself in the now.

I get onto the elevator at a building I hope is the right address for where I need to drop off some papers. It isn't. But that, it turns out, isn't the real reason I'm here, getting into the elevator, right now.

I step inside the elevator and softened my eyes, letting everything but now slip to the background of my mind and feel the pulse of life, of divinity flowing through my veins and breath. A little self-conscious, I open my eyes and look to see if anyone else is in the elevator with me.

There is. Someone I know. Her name is Trish. She'd been in a group with me when I first started doing counseling. She'd left the group after a confrontation encounter with me, and never came back. I'd felt unresolved afterward but couldn't get her to return my calls. I worried I'd been unfair. I had planned to apologize but she never showed up again.

Immediately, I feel the past unresolved guilt tighten my gut. Recalling today's idea, I release the contraction, becoming totally present now. As our eyes meet, Trish blurts out, "I can't believe it's you. I feel terrible about that group session, and how I ran. I blamed you. I was just thinking about, wanting to make amends, and here you are!" "Is it odd or is it God?" I say. "I feel I, too, owe you an amends." I take her hands and say, "Dude, this is so perfect. The past is gone. We're here and totally good with each other now, yes? I'm so happy to see you now. Got a few minutes for coffee?" A brand-new dimension opens right there in the elevator and onto coffee and a holy friendship we share to this day. Easy-peasy.

DAY 290

(Lesson 290)

"My present happiness is all I see."

(W-pII.290.1)

"With this resolve I come to You, and ask Your strength to hold me up today, while I but seek to do Your Will. You cannot fail to hear me, Father. What I ask have You already given me. And I am sure that I will see my happiness today."

(W-pII.290.2.1–4)

Happiness is in us and all around us, in each present moment. It's what's left when the past and future attachments have gone from our minds. In fact, the only thing that keeps us from seeing and experiencing our present happiness is our thinking.

If we weren't dragging the past along with us and projecting it all over the loveliness of the present moment, the magnitude of joy would make us want to dance and play and sing and join. We know it's true too. We watch children playing, without a care in the world, and envy their carefree, spontaneous joy.

The course pretty much says the whole drama dream we call our lives, is due to a tiny mad idea that we're separate from our source of happiness, where we forgot to laugh.

We just keep replaying it over and over like one of those crazy YouTube videos that go viral, because you just can't believe that girl did that crazy thing, so you just keep replaying it. It's like we get stuck watching that replay. But the replay isn't us, is it? We're just addicted to watching the replay.

Within each present moment we need but realize we are not there, in the world of thought, but here, in the love that makes the replay possible. We are the love-being enjoying the show. That's our present happiness.

Years ago, I decided for present happiness as my divine path, determined to keep my heart open, no matter what. Sheesh man. In the beginning it seemed almost impossible.

Cole and Parker were little when I began this yummy trek. They were like my own personal gurus for joy. Everyday I'd suffer a glitch in my happiness matrix. Here are these amazing beings of pure joy and just being with them was my happy place.

But then I'd start to notice I'm bothering myself with supposed tos and what ifs. Looking closely at the thoughts in my mind for the cause, I realized what I call the parenting script. Like a mind-parasite trying to manage my mom-life, and that was serious shit. The burden of the parenting script set a contingency on my happiness. It monitored me based on its rules.

But I also experienced beautiful glimpses of awakening to myself as love, and moments when I experienced God outright, as well as the tranquil groove of Divine flow in my life. So, the glitch was easy to see. But the shift? Not so much.

One day, Cole, dressed in his Batman attire (as usual), and Parker, suited up as Spider-Man, ask me to play superheroes with them. Now this seems like an easy enough request, right? Fun, in fact. I'd done it before. But often, I let the parenting script convince me I had mom duties that were more important. (Like laundry trumps fun! Shit!)

This time, I feel the glitch and know its bullshit. I see I'm actually a little scared of the untethered joy of present play with the boys. Like if I unleash it all, there'd be no going back! Mom-script takes that shit seriously! Play time in my childhood play had been twisted up with chores, and the fear of getting in trouble for shirking responsibilities.

Ha! The past is gone! In a holy instant I see it—shining the light of awareness on its nothingness. It's like magic! I strap on my Wonder Woman cape and start laughing and singing, "Nana, nana, nana, nana, Batman, Batman." The boys don't miss a beat in joining. Joy is superhero energy—present happiness and play.

DAY 291
(Lesson 291)

"This is a day of stillness and of peace."

(W-pll.291.1)

"This day my mind is quiet, to receive the Thoughts You offer me. And I accept what come from You, instead of from myself. I do not know the way to You. But You are wholly certain. Father, guide Your Son along the quiet path that leads to You. Let my forgiveness be complete, and let the memory of You return to me."

(W-pll.291.2.1–6)

Today we begin a new theme of special relevance from which we consider these next ten lessons: *"What is the Real World?"* The real world can only be seen through forgiving eyes. It looks on now and nothing else. That's what makes it real. It is the love aspect of this world we live in.

It is this world cleansed by forgiveness and seen through the eyes of innocence. It is this world when present happiness is all we see. It is the world, in union with itself, united by our love. The real world is what *is*, and has always been, in and all around us. It resides at the frequency of life, of creation, of joy, of truth, of love.

It's just that when we're operating from the premise of fear, from the desperate dream of separation, our frequency is too dense to see it. We're focused on fixing yesterday's problems and worrying about how were going to get that happiness we think we're missing. Forgiveness wakes us up from that dream and raised our vibration to the frequency of reality—where we recognize our identity as love—that you and I are one. It's like the light switches on Christ's vision and we see that God is, indeed, in everything we see.

Last year, the boys moved from our family home. The day the boys moved was bonkers. (Best laid plans . . .) We'd booked a U-Haul a week in advance, to be picked up at first light the day of, to get everything loaded so they could drive to Utah and unload by nightfall.

But the night before we were supposed to pick it up, U-Haul calls and says they won't have a truck available until the afternoon at the earliest. I want to be pissed. It seems legit. Like being the righteous victim of their error would somehow mitigate the lack of control I feel in the situation. Damn. I see it immediately and laugh at the folly of it, releasing it to divinity, and myself to present peace. Nothing is actually wrong.

Now I can listen to the guy on the call. I am present. I can hear the apprehension in the guy's voice. This call isn't easy for him. This is a time for joining. He is my brother, and what I need is what he needs. We talk options and strategy. A plan develops, and we're all set with a truck from another location.

The next morning the new location calls to say that the truck they were expecting to come in, had gotten held up on the road. I have to laugh. It just so happened that today's lesson had landed in my heart that morning. *"This is a day of stillness and of peace."* Life's sense of humor alive and well!

Taking it all in happy stride, we make a game of moving everything into position to load the truck when it arrives and having a blast. Cole makes a joke about not breaking down the pool table because he might be sleeping on it tonight. It's yummy. We simply surrendered our agenda in the name of peace. From the stillness of acceptance of life exactly as it is, joy and happy fun ruled the day and the moving event in peace. And before long they were off!

DAY 292

(Lesson 292)

"A happy outcome to all things is sure."

(W-pII.292.1)

*"We thank you, Father, for Your guarantee of only happy outcomes in the end. Help
us not interfere, and so delay the happy ending You have promised us for every
problem that we can perceive; for every trial we think we still must meet."*

(W-pII.291.2.1–2)

I don't know about you, but even the first time I read this lesson, I felt Divinity reach from beyond the words and spark the joy in my heart. My body relaxed, my mind got quiet and I breathed the promise, deep into my soul. Joy's peace breathing through my being. Take a breath. A happy outcome to all things is sure.

Look at these first few lines in the lesson, *"God's promises make no exceptions."* Feel your mind relax? We are part of God. Exceptions aren't. *"He guarantees that only joy can be the final outcome found for everything."* Of course He does. What is not joy, is not part of Him—and so it is not real.

Seeing this is forgiveness's gift. So, being of God, a happy outcome is guaranteed. Yes, we can use our free will to make up whatever experience we want in the dream of separation from our Source. We can struggle in fear's dreamland of danger and doom, sequencing time, until we earn, or fight, our way to a hoped-for pleasant outcome, on the bloody backs of pretend enemies, for as long as we see fit.

But it's a shitty dream at best, yes? What a bore. Present happiness is here, now, if we but choose to look beyond the dream and see with innocence from the eyes of love.

When we're spending our days trying to make something work out the way we think will eventually make us happy, we miss the entire present happiness already here, right now, just beneath the surface of our agendas.

Case in point. My broken-back gift. It's been remarkable to see how this forgiveness lesson has played out on the pages of this book, in real time, as I have accepted that I am not this body, this back, this pain. Miraculously, I see the so-called problem holds within it the answer to all that I had denied. My fit and lovely body was my pride and joy.

Until it broke, I had no reason to question the stronghold I had on keeping it the center of my gravity in this world. I did the lessons, "I am not a body. I am free," and I felt their truth. It seemed my body reflected this awareness.

But I never got beneath the surface of my identity confusion. I didn't question if I would feel so free if suddenly I got cancer, or broke my back, for instance. I didn't think it could happen to me. I thought I was above that kind of vulnerability. I was unaware that this stance was holding me separate from my brothers and my Self.

It has been humbling to see the resistance I have had to surrender, and the determination I've had to fix the problem in order to reestablish my status quo in regard to how I felt about myself. The gift of clarity and true union by loving all of it, exactly as it is, is truly experiencing an identity reality where my body is outside of me with all the other bodies and things of this world.

Nothing is wrong. Pain shows me I have dozed off into temporary amnesia of the truth that remains the foundation of who I am and wakes me up to the choice for now—to the present happiness where I reside beyond the body dynamics of this world. The instant I do, love and joy replace pain and fear. When I am present happiness, joining with whatever is arising—a happy outcome to all things is sure.

DAY 293

(Lesson 293)

"All fear is past and only love is here."

(W-pII.293.1)

"Father, let not Your holy world escape my sight today. Nor let my ears be deaf to all the hymns of gratitude the world is singing underneath the sounds of fear. There is a real world which the present holds safe from all past mistakes. And I would see only this world before my eyes today."

(W-pII.293.2.1–4)

Today we're tuning into now, to only love. The past is gone. It can't touch us. Its source is gone. Why keep suiting up and locating ourselves there, feeling powerless to change anything. We have the power of the Divine now—the past is gone, it's not here *to* change. What is here, now, is present love. Its Source is with us always, already.

Present love is sourcing our very life. What we *can* do, now, is to change the way we are looking at what appears before us. If we get present, right here, in this moment, present love is obvious. Without the taint of past upon it, life looks bright and welcoming and clear. Check it for yourself.

Today's idea is what all this mind-training has gifted us—a quick release from fear, realizing its impossibility in present time. An opening to choose—to see the truth of love now, reflected all around us.

Earlier this morning I'm talking to my daughter, Lin. She's calling because she was in a loop of fear about the state of affairs our nation is facing around healthcare. Her concern is the lack of available care for the majority of citizens if this bill that is being voted on today passes.

In fact, the first thing out of her mouth is, "I think I need a Xanax. The healthcare bill goes to the house today and if it passes, millions of people won't be able to afford insurance or pay for healthcare. I can't believe the lack of compassion one group of elite people can have toward everyone else."

As she shares her concerns and the feeling of total powerlessness she feels to impact the outcome, it's apparent that fear and worry fill her perception and that's all she can see. I silently hold a space for truth to enter while she purges this cloud cover blocking her present love feelings. Within minutes, the density lifts.

After all, that's why she called. The vibratory field shifts, and we're in a different world. Like on a dime, Lin tells me about a call for compassion she witnessed from a talk show host. How, from his innocence, he shared how his newborn child was born with a heart condition. In a heartfelt appeal to his national audience, he asks them to insist on healthcare policies that would allow anyone finding themselves in a situation such as his to be able to get the help they needed—bringing tears to my eyes.

She says she's been doing things like contacting her representative in congress. She's such an activist. She's darling like that. She tells me how she's tweeting to encourage people to get involved, to have a voice and I feel her love energy light up as she's totally present to her own offering to the world, right now today.

Everything has lightened up. She's enlightening the world with the present love already here as she loosened the past fear from her mind. I dig how she does it! Of course I relate it to today's lesson, *"All fear is past and only love is here."* It's so apropos.

DAY 294

(Lesson 294)

"My body is a wholly neutral thing."

(W-pII.294.1)

*"My body, Father, cannot be your Son. And what is not created cannot
be sinful or sinless; neither good nor bad. Let me, then, use this dream to
help Your plan that we awaken from all dreams we made."*

(W-pII.294.2.1–2)

I am a Son of God." Today's lesson it starts with the truth of what we are. It reminds us to start here. We are love—and love is formless—yet, its effects are easily seen and experienced in form. We are light, the light that unites us all. One, with no separate parts.

Still, as long as we dream of separate parts, love, which is beyond bodies, unites us in time or space. We are beyond the body, in truth. But that doesn't mean the body is irrelevant. It is the vehicle through which divinity flows in this world of form.

The body is the vehicle spirit uses to communicate this love through thoughts, words, and acts. Often, a simple smile is just what's needed, and a holy encounter is made. It is a wholly sacred thing.

Identification with our Christ Self naturally places the body in proper alignment as useful when needed. Not to be glorified, nor vilified. It is simply neutral, like the sky is clear of clouds today.

The body also displays our thoughts for us to see, so we can choose to change our mind and think with God. The gratitude I feel for this awareness right now in my life is immense. I'm totally grooving in it.

It's easy to check this out in any moment. Think about the last yummy encounter you had with someone where you were totally present. Where was the body then?

The heart presences us with love when we are present with another. That's what the body is for—to be a communication device for love while we work through the forgiveness mechanisms needed to heal the world we made.

So, it doesn't really matter what's seemingly going on with the body. When we are present and fully engaged, loving, and uniting with whatever shows up in our lives, the body really is a neutral thing. In a way, it's already laid aside, because we are using it for a holy purpose.

When we think our body is us, or at least a part of us, we make it the boss of what we do. "I don't feel well, so I don't want to get together with these people." Or, "I'm too old to play with the kids on the playground." Or, "I've got this back pain, so I can't . . . whatever."

But the body only takes instruction from the mind that sources it. If we source it from past learning, from fear of hurt or pain, we see it as limited, always in need of maintenance to be effective. But sourced from the truth, the body becomes a wholly neutral thing—to be an instrument of service for awakening.

We wake up, and rather than thinking what our body needs, we remember we are love and our purpose is to light the world with joy. Our mind immediately resonates with the heart, where we are available to be of service as we are needed.

CHAPTER TWO HUNDRED THIRTY-TWO
DAY 295

(Lesson 295)

"The Holy Spirit looks through me today."

(W-pII.295.1)

"My Father, Christ has asked a gift of me, and one I give that it be given me. Help me to use the eyes of Christ today, and thus allow the Holy Spirit's Love to bless all things that I may look upon, that His forgiving Love may rest on me."

(W-pII.295.2.1–2)

The Holy Spirit is inseparable from us. Once invited, we realize that we have within us a constant voice of clarity that is always available, by our request. Now, we are increasingly trusting this guidance. We recognize its overwhelming appeal, guiding us to live love's natural way of joining interrelationship with everyone and everything.

Today we let our Christ Self use the eyes we made to see separate things, for our holy sight which sees only the wholeness of love. Our Christ Self sees the truth within and beyond forms, and blesses all things with love, including us.

When I was invited to go to India last fall, the idea was like revisiting an old friend. During my spiritual seeking days, I fell in love with the guru Nisargadatta Maharaj while reading his book, *I Am That*. I wanted to go to India and sit with him, and hopefully be awakened by his presence. I felt the same pull with Mahavatar Babaji, and H. W. L. Poonja (a.k.a., Papaji), the joyous guru who followed in his footsteps. I wanted to walk those footsteps too.

I imagined living a life barren of worldly things but filled with the joy of spirit. Then *A Course in Miracles* came into my life, and my desire for India and gurus left. I began to have a feeling, instead, that the guru was within me, beneath all my ideas of what I believed I was. I knew that the only journey for me now was the journey within, back to the Home I felt present just beyond my mind's grasp but nestled deep within my holy heart. The Christ within is my guru now.

So, when I was invited to go to India, I remembered the place I had imagined through my guru search, feeling blessed to get a chance to visit.

When I arrived, it wasn't anything like the peaceful quiet India of my imagination. In fact, it was completely chaotic. And the noise! Too many sounds to make out anything. I'd never seen so many people in one place. I mean, it kind of blew my mind. I immediately felt timid. How would I find my sister, who had come the week before, amidst the fray?

I pause and let my mind still to the center of my being where I am always home. I let my hearing expand, taking it all in, as one big symphony, until all I could hear was the beating of the heart of life itself.

I softened my eyes and ask the Holy Spirit to look through them and show me my purpose right then, and while in India.

It's incredible. The chaos organized into people all around me working in unison. I see love acknowledging love, respect and reverence for each living thing in equal order. This is Christ vision. I am seeing with the eyes of Christ, which are my own. Peace and certainty that all is, and will be, well, settled in my heart.

From this peace I hear my name called out. I look to see this giant smile of the guide my sister sent for me. Namaste!

DAY 296

(Lesson 296)

"The Holy Spirit speaks through me today."
(W-pII.296.1)

"The Holy Spirit needs my voice today, that all the world my listen to Your Voice, and hear Your Word through me. I am resolved to let You speak through me, for I would use no words but Yours, and have no thoughts which are apart from Yours, for only Yours are true. I would be savior to the world I made. For having damned it I would set it free, that I may find escape, and hear the Word Your holy Voice will speak to me today."
(W-pII.296.1.1–4)

We are trusting the Divine to speak through us today. If we don't plan what to say with those we encounter, or the circumstances for our teaching, what occurs becomes our ministry. Instead of planning what we will say, we listen in silence for the words to come. And in trust, we allow the Holy Spirit to speak through us.

We might not even see how the ideas that come apply, but we trust they are what can best invoke the truth in a way that can be received.

Trust is crucial. The ego is incapable of trust. When we're with someone, sense their call for love, and feel inspired to offer a word or idea, first we realize it is our call for love as well. What comes through is a lesson in love for both of us. We can trust that the desire to join comes from the holiness in us—and we just let it come through. As we do, our trust increases.

My first experiences with letting the Holy Spirit speak through me were while doing counseling. I was lucky. Right away, I realized that when I joined with another, something bigger than us happened. Something magical that blessed us both. I felt like those that were sent to me, came to bring a message. Those messages somehow appeared in my mind as a comment, or assessment, or a coming together of facts, but seen in a different way.

But as I grew into my role as a counselor, my ego started hijacking these encounters, and telling me I knew more than the one in front of me. I began to measure my success off how well people were responding to my counsel. The stranger had taken up residency. Fear had entered.

One day, during a particularly difficult session with a recovery client, I felt like crying, I was so frustrated. I could actually feel the split in my mind. One part was saying, "She's lying," and it backed it up with that popular adage, "How do you know an addict is lying? Her lips are moving."

But the other part, deep within, truly wanted to be helpful. Knowing my attention is currency, I focused wholly within. I hear these words, "Set Danét aside."

I take my client's hands and ask, "Can we take a moment of silence together, please? It seems I have forgotten why I am here." Silently I pray the lesson for today, "Holy Spirit, speak through me. Please hear my call for love. Please use my voice that I might hear your words and be healed."

I'd been talking to this client in recovery platitudes and had not been present with her at all. I see with clarity right then that my presence *is* my gift. Through being present, the Holy Spirit worked through our union, and healing became possible.

Something I've realized over the years is that we can't trade on yesterday's miracle. We can't say, "Okay, I got it. I know what to do the next time." Only the present is alive with miracles that serve this present encounter, which makes it holy through our present holiness.

DAY 297

(Lesson 297)

"Forgiveness is the only gift I give."

(W-pII.297.1)

"Father, how certain are Your ways; how sure their final outcome, and how faithfully is every step in my salvation set already, accomplished by Your grace. Thanks be to You for Your eternal gifts, and thanks to You for my identity."

(W-pII.297.2.1–2)

Today's lesson, *"Forgiveness is the only gift I give,"* cuts through all the bullshit. Every thought, every opinion—the way we hold anything in our mind—creates the relationship we have with it. *"Everything I give, I give to myself. This is salvation's simple formula."* I love the simplicity of that. It leaves no room for misunderstanding.

If I want to be saved from experiencing a lack of love, I must grant you the same. For we *are* in relationship. Creation is relationship. What's *real* to me is the way I hold that relationship in my mind and heart. This creates the world for me. Forgiveness is the only gift worth giving. It restores us back to our natural state of mind in union with God. It is love's gift that erases what we scribbled over the pristine purity that is our one Self, as God created us—love.

Life is union—we are in relationship with everything. I pick up a pencil and there's a relationship. I choose not to pick it up, and that's another type of relationship. We can't get away from it. Relationship—union—is the nature of creation. We chose not to pick up the pencil. That doesn't mean it's not there. I just means we chose a different type of relationship. God created His Son for His joy. That's relationship.

When I realized the simplicity of forgiveness, it changed everything for me. Forgiveness is totally Selfish. It is total Self-care. I can't judge you without feeling the effects of it. I've tried. I have failed. When I realized this, I made a shift in how I looked at everyone.

See, I can't bear feeling like a loser—inadequate, needy, mean, or victimized. When I made the connection between what I judged in another and how it made me feel about myself, I saw the similarities. Ick. But gracefully, I also understood that I could see everything differently. Yum.

The course gave me a context by which it made sense. I already saw the connection. No matter how hard I tried to make you wrong and me right, I ended up feeling shitty. Maybe a little self-righteously victorious for a second, but then I had to face myself as that person that was willing to hurt to win.

I'm still in relationship with you. In fact, you, the enemy I've made of you, require care to keep intact. I have to install the loop of victim and victor in my mind, jailer and jailed. It hijacks the energy alive with joy and squeezes it through the constructs of joylessness. There's no chance of happiness—no chance of knowing my Self as I am, and you as part of me.

Selfishly, I just want to be happy. And damned if I won't do anything to remain in open-hearted joy!

Awesomely, forgiveness is the groovy way we both get what we want. I grant you all that I want for me and let forgiveness erase everything else from my mind. Love shines bright and happy as the sunshine of our soul.

DAY 298

(Lesson 298)

"I love You, Father, and I love Your Son."

(W-pII.298.1)

"Father, I come to You today, because I would not follow any way but Yours. You are beside me. Certain is Your way. And I am grateful for your holy gifts of certain sanctuary, and escape from everything that would obscure my love for God my Father and His holy Son."

(W-pII.298.2.1–5)

I love this beginning line in today's lesson. *"My gratitude permits my love to be accepted without fear."* It has proved itself out to me so many times and in so many ways that it is astounding I ever forget to be grateful first! If it's showing up, it's for me. Period. Thank you.

Whatever it is, is for my highest good. If seen through the eyes of forgiveness, it is impossible to miss. Through forgiveness my holy sight is restored—it literally vaporizes the contraction blocking my awareness of the love I am, you are, and the relationship which unites us as God's holy kid.

What would we need saving from but the mad ideas that we've all placed in front of love's awareness? Love's there anyway. Waiting. Holding the door open. Gratitude lets us see past the artificial values we've placed before the face of love, seeing the gift of holiness encompassing it all, which is our union with Divinity.

Gratitude softens the constructs made to separate us from what we have judged and leaves an open door for forgiveness to enter and dissolve the constructs all together. Say we have this problem with thinking we don't have enough time to get everything done. In that construct, we've limited ourselves, and we can't see the answer to what we think is impossible because we've made an enemy of it.

But love shows a different view. In remembering we're love, we become grateful. Being love, we have dominion over time, and use it for the purpose of joy. This cuts through the to-do list quickly and dissolves all the unnecessary have-to's. Love's joy is complete in each thing we join with in relationship. So it is with every seeming problem; by being grateful for all that appears, we let love shine that different view. It's like, bring it on—right?

The other day I was at the decompression center and just being my yummy light of the world Self. I love these guys. They are my brothers, my Self, my comrades in arms. From the minute I walk in we're hugging and joining. It's cool how it happens. I'm lying next to this new friend on decompression tables. She asks, "Where do you get all your energy? And where can I get some?" I say, "It's pure joy! It's my spiritual way. It makes every experience a gift."

As I get up from the table, my chiropractor approaches, "I thought that was you out here. I could feel your smile clear in the other room." He gives me a big hug. It's today's lesson, right? *I love my Father and I love His Son.*

They say my joy is infectious, and in a way it is. But really, it's just there's not much interfering in the way of love, filtering out what wants to happen. We want to love, to join in joy. And gratitude abounds. So, a place designed around a problem-fixing becomes a haven of love and joy. Gratitude returns us to sanity. And we see that beyond the dream of separate problems is the unity of love.

DAY 299

(Lesson 299)

"Eternal holiness abides in me."

(W-pII.299.1)

"Father, my holiness is not of me. It is not mine to be destroyed by sin. It is not mind to suffer from attack. Illusions can obscure it, but can not put out its radiance, nor dim its light. It stands forever perfect and untouched. In it are all things healed, for they remain as You created them. And I can know my holiness. For Holiness Itself created me, and I can know my Source because it is Your Will that You be known."

(W-pII.299.2.1–7)

The whole point of today's lesson is for us to claim our holiness, once and for all. We are holy, created by Holiness, for God sake! Let's talk about this term holiness a minute, because I think it gets an unfair wrap. Mostly we think of holiness as attached to some kind of sacred person, or even object that holds some magic power unknown to us.

Or, if we've been on the spiritual circuit for a while, we see it as a state to achieve. Yes? But us, holy? Not so much. We kind of think it arrogant to consider ourselves holy. Right?

Then we come to *A Course in Miracles*, and it tells us that holiness abides in us like our blood or breath. It says our holiness blesses the world and envelops everything we see. In fact, it says that there is nothing our holiness cannot do. But if you're like me, it feels almost scary when we first start applying the term to ourselves.

Why is that? Here's my theory. I think we sense the magnitude of how identification with our holiness can change everything. It feels like an awesome responsibility.

When seeing ourselves separate from it, it feels daunting. The ego identity is threatened by the idea of holiness. It can't understand it, nor know it, but it does recognize the threat. It wants us seeing ourselves as separate from our Source, with a separate will, so we won't realize that holiness abides in us.

But we aren't separate from our Source and we don't really have a separate will. Love is whole. Our will and our Father's *are* one in truth. The will of love is holiness. *"Eternal holiness abides in me."* Period. So that's the starting point, the alpha and omega of life through our identity as God created us.

For so much of my life, I looked to others for validation of my worthiness, my okay-ness, my right to be here, to take up space, to breathe the air. Even when validated, acknowledged, even placed on a pedestal for some, I was haunted by the feeling that I was a fraud.

It wasn't that I was misrepresenting myself—the Self I believed was me, it's just that I felt like I had this secret I was keeping from myself, and therefore everyone else. What was it I was refusing to see? What was this thing that needed such protection from anyone, least of all myself, finding out?

With the mind-training, I started to question the validity of the premise from which this feeling came. It seemed it had been with me all my life. My answer came through applying the lessons of *A Course in Miracles*. The answer is today's lesson, *"Eternal holiness abides in me."*

As I began to forgive my self-concept, immense love rose within me. This love felt real. I felt real. The self-doubts that came up in situations I began to see as outside my Self, like a program that I was dismantling, while this feeling that *Love is what I am,* remained intact. Awesome secret!

I'm not a made-up identity, but holy. I fell in love with this idea that holiness abides in me. It wipes away my falsehood in a smooth and joyous swoop. It bequeaths a feeling of being in this world and also a part of Divinity. It lets me have faith in a happy outcome to all things!

CHAPTER TWO HUNDRED THIRTY-SEVEN

DAY 300

(Lesson 300)

"Only an instant does this world endure."

(W-pII.300.1)

"We seek Your holy world today. For we, Your loving Sons, have lost our way a while. But we have listened to Your Voice, and learned exactly what to do to be restored to Heaven and our true Identity. And we give thanks today the world endures but for an instant. We would go beyond that tiny instant to eternity.

(W-pII.300.2.1-5)

Today is the last of our ten days of lessons where we're considering, *"What is the Real World?"* It couldn't be more perfect, because it just takes an instant to change our mind. In an instant we can shift from fear to love, which instantly changes the world we see from a dream to real.

I love the imagery from the lesson, picturing our holy minds like this vast serene blue sky. And this world of story problems we believe are just clouds passing through it, soon to be gone. They ultimately don't even leave a mark on the tranquil peace of our true reality. They're just passing through.

I first came upon this idea of the mind being a clear and pristine sky, and our thoughts being like clouds passing by, many years ago (a lifetime ago). I was doing a kundalini retreat with some very cool yogi types. This is the imagery they gave to us, as a practice while sitting for hours in meditation. Talk about a humbling experience. I sat for excruciating hours, determined to gain enlightenment during the weekend. Yeah, that didn't happen.

What happened was that all I saw were problems. My body hurt from sitting. I was constantly comparing myself to the other participants and what they were getting, that I obviously wasn't. Time was like nails on a chalkboard slow, and I constantly chastised myself for my lack of focus.

What happened was I saw how absolutely restless my mind was. In fact, I felt insane. It's like my whole mind was a big, dark cloud, and the serene sky was some distant memory I couldn't reach. For hours I tried. I sat there, and the only glimmer of awareness I had was I realized that I was waiting for something outside of me to do something for me.

I hoped that my effort would be recognized by some magnificent force outside myself, which would waive its magic wand, tap me on the head, and all my problems would disappear, and I would see God or something otherworldly. Nope. That didn't happen. But what I did see is that separating my salvation's responsibility from being mine, was not going to work.

A Course in Miracles came into my life shortly after that event. It spoke directly to my holy Self already united to the Divine. When I came to today's idea, though the imagery was basically the same, I am different. I am at home, part of the clear and pristine Divine Mind, in which this world passes through like clouds, which, too, are one whole creation.

Today's lesson is a beautiful meditative practice we can use to leave all constructs of self-concepts behind and join the eternally serene vastness of love, letting our stories and problems pass like clouds in the sky.

As we go throughout the day, we want to keep our mind and heart focused on seeing God's world, paying attention to the vast serene sky of our holy mind. When some seeming problem arises, we remind ourselves to take our attention off the cloud-problem and onto the serene Source in which the clouds appear. Then lean back and trust the answer for a happy outcome will be made clear.

DAY 301

(Lesson 301)

"And God Himself shall wipe away all tears."

(W-pll.301.1)

"Father, unless I judge I cannot weep. Nor can I suffer pain, or feel abandoned or unneeded in the world. This is my home because I judge it not, and therefore is it only what You will. Let me today behold it uncondemned, through happy eyes forgiveness has released from all distortion. Let me see Your world instead of mine. And all tears I shed will be forgotten, for their source is gone. Father, I will not judge Your world today."

(W-pll.301.1.1–6)

Today we begin a new topic by which we consider the next ten lessons. It is, *"What is the Second Coming?"* The second coming is what we are bringing about, through our awakening to the truth. I love how the commentary starts. *"God's world is happy."* That's it! God's world is happy. That's the frequency where we realize God's world, right here, right now!

Something wonderful and unexpected happens as we experience the simplicity of salvation, we realize it is the same thing as perfect happiness. It's incredible! Being happy each moment *is* our essential part in God's plan. We realize, with great joy and reverence, how necessary our contribution of being in joy is.

I used to think I needed to do something big, like head up some humanitarian effort to save the children in a third world country, to make a godly impact. And maybe that would be so if this world of pain and suffering were the only option.

But it turns out, that's not the case at all. Turns out, my favorite thing—circulating about in the world as a divine spark of infinite joy, my spark igniting others sparks and together, us lighting the world with joy—is godly impact! That is my contribution. Joy—for the love of God—is the way I bring heaven with me wherever I go.

It's crazy simple and delightful. I'd have never believed it if I hadn't taken the leap of faith to make the happy heaven of now my only goal. That shift in perception is the miracle that lets me be a miracle worker in the world next door. It blows my mind every day. In a whole and holy way, I get to be part of God wiping all tears away.

Joy is what the world is thirsting for and the second they spot a bright shining spark of it, they come running and joyously lap it up.

Here's an example from yesterday. I'm at a meeting and an angry complaint is brought to the table and it's like it sucks all the air out of the room. Instantly the energy is hijacked by ego negativity and spewing out judgments about whose perspective is right. Seemingly at once, all the human hairs start standing on end. Everyone is palpably contracted.

The ego is like a dog with a bone; feelings were hurt, and opinions argued, positions set, and air became too thick to breath.

I call upon the Divine for space, and a healed perception for all concerned and take my breath from its peace.

As the meeting is wrapping up, the chairperson says, "We haven't heard from you, Danét. We can all use a little joy right now." It's like a balloon pops! The air clears before I even say a word!

Spark to spark, we light the world by choosing joy, *"And God Himself will wipe away all tears."* In truth, we want the peace and joy of God, we are magnetized toward it. The thing about choosing to live in God's world—to be the face of joy, no matter what—it leaves an imprint. *"God's world is happy."*

DAY 302

(Lesson 302)

"Where darkness was I look upon the light."

(W-pII.302.1)

"Father, our eyes are opening at last. Your holy world awaits us, as our sight is finally restored and we can see. We thought we suffered. But we had forgot the Son whom You created. Now we see that darkness is our own imagining, and light is there for us to look upon. Christ's vision turns darkness into light, for fear must disappear when love has come. Let me forgive your holy world today, that I may look upon its holiness and understand it but reflects my own."

(W-pII.302.1.1–7)

"*Where darkness was I look upon the light.*" We aren't just feeling around in darkness anymore. We have turned on the light. Our decision for truth is the switch. Our forgiveness keeps the darkness gone. So, we see differently. The light is on. Light dispels darkness.

We turn a light on in a dark room and where did the darkness go? It simply disappears. Is it so hard to imagine that forgiveness is that light switch which awakens our Christ vision, that once we've turned it on, we don't have to wander around in the dark, frightened and alone ever again?

I'm not saying we won't. We all catch ourselves sitting in darkness from time to time, even yet. We catch ourselves judging, blaming, complaining, or feeling sick. Right? But now, we know where the switch is. It is in the stillness of the peace of God. It is in a holy instant where we choose again.

The flip-switch is forgiveness. That light is joy. It is gratitude. It is union. It only takes an instant and we see a different world. You know when you've judged someone and later you found out you were dead wrong about them? It totally feels like a light goes on, right? Love literally makes fear disappear.

Here's an example. A young woman comes to my workshop and according to me, won't participate—that judgment throws a cloak of darkness over everything for me.

The first evening of the workshop she doesn't participate at all, and I'm wondering why she even signed up. I judge her lack of participation as a bad attitude and her withdrawal as counterproductive to the overall group.

Plus, I feel like she's just sitting there judging me. I try to engage her in the discussions, using my best antidotes. But nothing. At most, an occasional slight smile—which I discount. I take it as her trying to appease me and get me off her back. Of course, I don't share that with her, I just let her sit in the dark cloud of judgment I surrounded her in, feeling unfairly judged and superior.

Finally, when we wrap up for the night, she waits behind. I'm oblivious to her presence as I straighten up. Suddenly, I feel a touch on my arm. It's her. I surmise she's going to pull out of the workshop. But she begins to speak; tears in her eyes. At first, I can't understand her, her stutter is so severe. Shit.

I still my mind and heart and focus up. She's actually telling me how grateful she is to be here. She's apologizing for not participating due to her embarrassment over her stutter. Tears fill my eyes as I realize how completely wrong I've been. The joy of being wrong floods my being.

That instant, I see her for the first time. Funny thing too, now I can understand everything she says. I take her hands in mine, knowing that *she's* here for *me*. She is the spark of light here to ignite my darkened mind. I thank her and say her presence is all I need.

DAY 303

(Lesson 303)

"The holy Christ is born in me today."

(W-pII.303.1)

"Your Son is welcome, Father. He has come to save me from the evil self I made. He is the Self that You have given me. He is but what I really am in truth. He is the Son You love above all things. He is my Self as You created me. It is not Christ that can be crucified. Safe in Your Arms let me receive Your Son."

(W-pII.3032.1–7)

We have prepared for this day. We have accepted God's word and welcomed our Selves as God created us. Our practicing has ushered in a time of ending our identity crisis. We have accepted atonement, and today we invite Divinity's angels to witness our acceptance of our true identity as Christ, the child of love. The illusory me is shed as the Christ within emerges.

The sights and sounds of the dream of separation and loneliness disappear in the quiet of our holy Christ mind, welcomed by us today. This is our willingness to let forgiveness rest upon all things leaving only the real.

What's happened for me is I no longer question that who I am impacts the healing of the world. Will I choose union and love in situations that arise? Or self-centered agenda? Honestly, it feels so yummy to accept all things, and join in love and joy, the choice is usually easy. In fact, it's become a habit. I am not attached to how things turn out. That's not my business.

I am more attuned of the subtle shifts in frequency around me. I'm attuned to the calls for love. It's funny, and I'm not sure when the shift happened, but opinions don't matter much to me anymore—least of all my own. I don't care if I look silly or whatever, with my shit-eatin' grin and my yummy attitude. And believe me, it used to mean everything, how I thought you perceived me.

Somehow, I have shifted to a higher authority—love is the ground of my being. And it is from this I take direction. I'm not saying all the time. But, on the whole, I'm simply not comfortable anymore in the world of judgment and separation.

Yesterday, I am on my way to the spa. Spontaneously, I decide to stop for a juice at the juice bar. As I'm leaving, I brush by this the guy coming in. He's a little dazed and confused. I sense a buzz between us, and I know to pause. Now, I'm on a schedule here, right? But what is so cool, is now days, schedules, it's almost like they bend to the will of a holy purpose happening in the present moment.

So, this brush with a dude I recognize as a chance for a holy encounter and engage him. I smile, and a warm smile spreads across his face. He asks what juice I ordered, and a brief and warm conversation ensues. This is the context. Joy and love is the content. It is my attention to present awareness that is the surprising and amazing gift that makes each moment full and alive.

No encounter is by accident. This I have come to realize. Each brings a gift I don't want to miss! We have a brief holy encounter, and I'm on my way.

I trust the sense I have about someone I meet, and I trust the guidance I receive in interacting with them. They are my one Self. It's interesting, learning to trust this intuition. I can't care how it is received. Caring how it is received throws a wrench in the circle of love between us. Joy is the great magnet and vibrating at joy's frequency makes me a safe place for someone to lay their head or chat a while.

CHAPTER TWO HUNDRED FORTY-ONE

DAY 304

(Lesson 304)

"Let not my world obscure the sight of Christ."

(W-pII.304.1)

"You lead me from the darkness to the light; from sin to holiness. Let me forgive, and thus receive salvation for the world. It is Your gift, my Father, given me to offer to Your holy Son, that he may find again the memory of You, and of Your Son as You created him."

(W-pII.304.2.1–3)

Today we are being reminded that perception is a mirror, not a fact. We're always looking at our state of mind, reflected outward. If we see darkness, it is reflecting an error in our mind and nothing else. The restorative is to forgive and give our mind back over to Christ so we can see the situation through the eyes of love. What we look with, is what we look upon.

The choice we make goes with us, whether it be hell or heaven, which means that we are responsible for its care. That's where today's lesson comes in. We don't want to obscure our holy sight with the darkness of past programming. We don't want it to intrude upon the holy sight given us by our Christ self. We actively forgive the instant our peace is disturbed in anyway.

I am so grateful for Trump! I live peacefully undisturbed by much of the drama on the world stage. To say I was surprised to experience this rush of hate, powerlessness, and fear flood into my experience during the recent political campaign for president, is at best an understatement. It stopped me dead in my tracks. Apparently, I have to be hit in the head with a nuclear bomb to realize where I'm still dancing with darkness. What a wake-up call to see how deeply I cherished separation, and the specialness it makes me feel.

The temptation to get on the hate-train and feel righteous and afraid was unbelievable. The projection of fear and the judgments of wrongness, which rose in my perception, blinded me to the truth for a brief time.

The banner against Trump was raised by loving, well-meaning individuals across the planet. Would I take up arms with them? Is this the world I would see in place of God's?

I admit, I leaned in that direction for a bit. But, thank Christ, only to long enough to see it is the road that goes nowhere. It is the road which makes death and danger real. It is not what I am and not where I live.

I forgive, and I ask to be restored to sanity and remember I am Christ, and I can see this differently. Again, and again . . . until all I see is light, and the perfect happening for healing the darkness of our world-mind.

As light floods my mind, my eyes open to another world. Pristine and forgiven of the past dream of fear and danger.

To see the reflection of my state of mind in my perceptions of this new president, broke my heart. A broken heart is a surefire flip-switch—a mighty beam of forgiveness is necessary for peace of mind and world peace too. "He is a child of God. He is my one Self," I heard the still small and mighty voice within say, "Oh, my love, wake to reality."

He *is* me. What would I have him be? The holy Son of God, or the harbinger of hate and hurt? The only way to look at him and the seeming state of affairs in the world is to forgive and call upon Christ vision to show me the truth.

I cannot afford to let my fearful thoughts intrude upon the holy sight I have been gifted. Thank you, God. I choose to be the light that dispels the darkness. For when love is present, fear disappears. Join me.

DAY 305

(Lesson 305)

"There is a peace that Christ bestows on us."

(W-pII.305.1)

"Father, the peace of Christ is given us, because it is Your Will that we be saved. Help us today but to accept Your gift, and judge it not. For it has come to us to save us from our judgment on ourselves."

(W-pII.305.2.1–3)

Today we see clearly, the gift of peace that Christ bestows on us, and hold our experience up to its divine light. I don't know about you, but peace of mind is what I was seeking when I found *A Course in Miracles.*

Peace is the goal for which this course aims. One of the earliest lessons in the workbook is *"I could see peace instead of this."* Through applying the lessons, we learn to forgive our guilt by forgiving others, and peace follows.

Today's lesson is talking about peace that cannot be disturbed—deep and quiet and wholly changeless, a peace in which *"the world contains no counterpart."* This peace is not situational. It is beyond specifics. Where is this peace? This peace is our Christ identity. How do we experience it? How do we attain that state of constancy? It is accomplished in us as we accept our identity is Christ.

I live in a state of deep and quiet peace. It's like the soundtrack to my experience of my life on the world stage where my forgiveness lessons play out. It doesn't change and is not altered by anything that occurs. This peace is beyond occurrences.

Once tuned into this deep and penetrating experience within us, we can always feel it. Even in moments where we get fixated on some aspect of the dream, we can't take it altogether seriously. Because back beyond the characters on the screen, who we are rests undisturbed in this deep abiding peace.

The second I turn my attention toward it, I am home. And the circumstances before me are seen in a different light. The light of love. By my decision, I give my sight to Christ, and the situation looks differently, and present peace accompanies my view.

We start to see that we're never alone and the answer to any situation is always with us. We just move in the direction that feels most peaceful and joyous and things start lining up, and before we know it our circumstance has changed, for we are at peace with all of it.

I had this wondrous experience of recognition one day while dealing with an angry mom. She was upset over something that had happened between our children. She wanted me to punish my son, since she was punishing hers. I'm watching her talk; her face is red, and her hands shake as she waves them while she screams accusatory things about me as a mother.

But it's like it's a mirage. I can see she's not this body of emotional meltdown. I can even see she doesn't, in her heart of hearts, want this encounter to be like this. I feel only compassion for her as I let her have her say, completely unengaged in the drama. I feel only love.

It's wild, because rage is one of those powerful boogiemen I always feared running into. I melt to her call for love and peace wafts from me quieting her energy and calming her heart, without my saying anything.

Suddenly, she stops and stands perfectly still. I take her hands and look into her eyes, appreciating her holiness in union with mine. For a long moment we just gazed into each other's eyes and feel our one heart beating as love. We are in a moment beyond time, in the holy instant of reality.

Right then, the kids come running past us, happy and playing. We laugh, released, and let joy fill our souls.

CHAPTER TWO HUNDRED FORTY-THREE
DAY 306
(Lesson 306)

"The gift of Christ is all I seek today."

(W-pII.306.1)

"And so, our Father, we return to You, remembering we never went away; remembering Your holy gifts to us. In gratitude and thankfulness we come, with empty hands and open hearts and minds, asking but what You give. We cannot make an offering sufficient for Your Son. But in Your Love the gift of Christ is his."

(W-pII.306.2.1–3)

Is the gift of Christ all we want? Today's lesson invites us to enter the real world, right now, today, through remembering our identity is really Christ, God's joyous extension of love. I like the word "seek" because it speaks to me in the place I locate myself regarding the world I see. The lesson reminds me that I am seeking to see with Christ vision, the world of love.

Today's prayer is our invitation to join God, remembering we really never went away. We *are* at home in God. And His holy gifts *are* ours now. As we give them in each interaction with our brother, we recognize that they are ours to give. Full appreciation for our identity as Christ opens our minds and hearts, through which the gifts of Christ can be given and received.

Here's what I have noticed. When my attention is wholly present, I feel the holiness of my Self as a gift of love and joy. I feel one with whatever and whomever I give my attention—my presence. So, no matter the context, it is heaven. My presence is the presence of Christ. This is what allows me to see our unity instead of separate interests.

I was at an event a while ago where the topic was women's rights. There was a lively discussion going on when I slipped into the back of the room. While I observed, I took a pulse of the energy predominate in the room. It wasn't hard. The predominate energy was that of seeking an answer that would serve everyone. It made me think of todays' lesson. *"The gift of Christ is all I seek today."*

The group was having a hard time coming to a consensus as to the next course of action for the group as a whole because the discussion kept derailing into issues of past unfairness. It was an open forum, so anyone could have a voice.

I stand back and think about today's lesson and ask myself if *I* am seeking only the gift of Christ and instantly feel myself expand and open to see what my purpose here could be. I look with love on the field of beautiful beings around me and wait.

Finally, one woman stands and says, "Look, we're just rehashing the problems and we're not getting anywhere. We know what the problems are so let's move forward."

That's my cue. I say, "Yes, I love that. We are here because we know that when we're united, an answer can come that we cannot see alone, right? I want to relinquish any other reason I thought I came here for, so something I haven't seen can be revealed."

Heads are nodding and another woman picks it up from here. "We want to stand united. Let's shift the discussion off of what's wrong and unfair and onto some of the proactive suggestions that have been brought up. We'll pick one that we can start with." In minutes we settled on a course of action we all agreed upon. The gift of Christ lets us see a different world, right now.

DAY 307

(Lesson 307)

"Conflicting wishes cannot be my will."

(W-pII.307.1)

"Father, Your Will is mine, and only that. There is no other will for me to have. Let me not try to make another will, for it is senseless and will cause me pain. Your Will alone can bring me happiness, and only Yours exists. If I would have what only You can give, I must accept Your Will for me, and enter into peace where conflict is impossible, Your Son is one with You in being and in will, and nothing contradicts the holy truth that I remain as You created me."

(W-pII.307.1.1–5)

Our goal today is to live out the lesson prayer. We set our prayer's intention as our single choice today, *"Let me not try to make another will, for it is senseless and will cause me pain."* Can we? Will we? Can we have a different will and be at peace? Knowing that only God's will offers what we want.

My first time round with the lessons, this was one of those come to Jesus lessons for me. **"Conflicting wishes cannot be my will."** "I get it," I think. "God wills and I am part of that." Wait, no, I don't get it. I still think I can live in this eternal now, in peace, and where conflict cannot enter, but keep past learning at the ready for some unforeseen purpose. But, determined to trust the lesson, I do my best.

That little willingness . . . and it's amazing. I felt my *little* will drop from me. Like when a rocket goes in space and the bottom part drops off. I felt I was entering into this silent state and conflict fell away from my mind. As I moved forward in my day, I looked myself in the mirror on my way out the door, reminding myself. *"Conflicting wishes cannot be my will. Let me not try to make another will, for it will only cause me pain."*

So, as it goes with the mind-training, I get the chance to see where my sincerity has wavered pretty quickly. On the way to work I get into a fender bender. My first thought is, "Shit. This is the last thing I need. (Like I know.) I don't have time for this. I need to be at work!" And there it was. Conflict. Thinking something different should have happened.

It's one of those both-persons-responsible fender benders. But see, because of my mind-training, I feel the glitch, somethings off—I've given myself a will apart from God's. I repeat my lesson silently, *"Conflicting wishes cannot be my will,"* while we wait for police.

Now I'm present and strike up a conversation with my comrade, my mind clear, and my heart available for joining. This dude's calm, taking everything in stride. We exchange information, and as it turns out, he's heading to the hospital where I work. He was looking for the address when we collided. We're instant friends. We have a common bond. I invite him to follow me to the hospital. No conflict in sight.

DAY 308

(Lesson 308)

"This instant is the only time there is."

(W-pII.308.1)

"Thanks for this instant, Father. It is now I am redeemed. This instant is the time You have appointed for Your Son's release, and for salvation of the world in him."

(W-pII.308.2.1–3)

We hear now is the only time there is, and "be in the present moment" has become a sort of spiritual lingo. But do we experience the timelessness this lesson is inviting us to recognize? Or do we still think of now as the space of time sandwiched between the past and present? Be honest. The holy instant invites us into the timeless now, the presence of love—of God Himself. The mystery behind the curtain of sequenced time.

We're already here, now. Where else could we be? We can't not be in the present moment. Prove me wrong. Have you ever been anywhere but here, in this instant? Only the mental process travels in time. The lesson says we must elect to reach past time to timelessness. We decide. This instant of decision is the eternal now.

We do it by changing our perception of what time is for. Time is for union. In the holy instant the idea of separation is inconceivable. Christ consciousness is now, with no perimeters.

As long as we are sequencing time as a reference point as to where we are now, we are not electing to reach past time to timelessness. We think, here I am, like this right now, but yesterday I was like that and tomorrow I hope to be this other way. That's the story of me, the story of the separate self. And it takes place on an imaginary continuum. Time is the glue that holds the fearful story of separation together.

This instant is holy. As we enter into a state where conflict cannot come, recognizing our will and God's are one, where is time now? Our union is timeless, and the idea of time disappears, already forgiven.

The course tells that every day should be devoted to miracles. Miracles happen outside of time, that's why miracles collapse time. It's like we shift to a whole new reality, seeing things from a totally different vantage point. We see from love because it is love that changed our perception. As we move into union with Christ consciousness, miracle-mindedness becomes the norm, and the sequencing of time no longer can serve to define us or our lives.

In effect, each day is brand new. We enter into Divine union, giving our so-called timeframe in service of divine order. Trust takes the place of planning. Our day is used for union through our holiness, or Christ Self. The context is the irrelevant. It is to the content (love) which we have elected to spend our day.

Yesterday while waiting for my car at a carwash, the fellow next to me shares about visiting the Holocaust museum with his family. He's present in telling, still feeling how moved and gratifying he found the experience, how blessed he and his family felt. I'm feeling the same as he shares.

I love it how spontaneous he is in joining in this instant—like it's the only time there is! He says he and his family see the experience as an oracle of sorts, reminding them to be grateful for all the little gifts every day brings.

I say, "I get you. I'm feeling that way right now. Thank you." It truly is like we're being held outside of time in this wide amazing gratitude view, and I'm so happy for this moment with him. Like he can read my mind, he says, "Gratitude is my number one priority. When I'm grateful, I'm happy."

DAY 309

(Lesson 309)

"I will not fear to look within today."

(W-pII.309.1)

"The step I take today, my Father, is my sure release from idle dreams of sin. Your altar stands serene and undefiled. It is the holy altar to my Self, and there I find my true Identity."

(W-pII.309.2.1–3)

This is a hallelujah lesson! *"I will not fear to look within."* We're saying, Yes. I'm done pretending I'm separate, filled with dark and scary things that can hurt. I won't be afraid of the light I find inside on the altar of my heart. I'll look within because I know it is the home of divinity, of joy and love, of my will at one God's.

Yes. I accept my inheritance, my Life in God. His peace is mine and my joy is His. Yes. I will His will for eternal happiness for me. Yes, I accept that I am His holy Christ child of love. I want no other will but this. Can I get an Amen? Amen.

How far we've come from when we began this course. Step by forgiving step, we've seen that once we look at what we fear, it disappears. And love is right there, shining bright and clear. So, now we've had some practice with this looking within stuff, and found our safety and security, our innocence and purity, our peace and joy. We have looked within and found our Self, the Christ child in us.

Today's lesson is saying we're ready to go all the way to our release from idle dreams of sin, to God's altar within, serene and undefined. The holy altar to our Self.

I remember a day watching Cole and Parker playing on the trampoline in the backyard, laughing and happy, like this was the whole world to them. My mind morphed, and what I was seeing was my Self. No longer standing watching, but the presence of this pure innocent joy, my heart bursting with love and gratitude.

Later that day, I notice the message light blinking on the answering machine, and this old haunting feeling that I'm somehow in trouble reaches right inside my bliss and gut punches me. I hadn't even listened to the message. I had no reason to feel this guilty feeling. Yet there it was intruding on my serenity.

My hand instantly goes to my heart and I turn within, quieting my energy and recalling my lesson, *"I will not fear to look within today."* The contrast was astonishing—my whole world in an instant. From the pure innocence as the Christ child filled with joy and happiness. Penetrated by a thought of fear and guilt, and gut punch!

But as quick as recognition, my hand impulsively goes to my heart, and I zero deep to the center of my being, deep into the heart of God, and like an eternal spring, my innocence and joy returns, casting the imagined fear away.

A few minutes later the boys come running in, "Mom, we had a message. It's Lin, she wants to take us for ice cream after work. Can we?" Of course, silly ego! There is nothing to fear.

We can fearlessly face down any belief because it cannot stand against the truth. We look within and find only eternal happiness.

DAY 310

(Lesson 310)

"In fearlessness and love I spend today."

(W-pII.310.1)

"This day, my Father, would I spend with You, as You have chosen all my days should be. And what I will experience is not of time at all. The joy that comes to me is not of days nor hours, for it comes from Heaven to Your Son. This day will be Your sweet reminder to remember You, Your gracious calling to Your holy Son, the sign Your grace has come to me, and that it is Your Will I be set free today."

(W-pII.310.1.1–4)

Isn't the prayer crazy beautiful? As we pray the words, we are drawn into a joyous experience of timeless awakening; the advent of Christ's all-inclusive embrace of safety and release, making fear impossible. Our decision for this state must be wholehearted.

We can't keep just a little of our day to our own self-initiated plans, little fears and worries and live this day in fearlessness and love. Love is all inclusive. So, as we enter into our prayer, we bring all our little-me fears and give them to the Holy Spirit for correction, so we can enter fully, wholeheartedly into this state of love, where fear has no meaning.

The course teaches us that the way we let truth dawn upon our mind is through relationship here. Today, we are looking at our relationship with life. Just as when we see the love in our brother as his only identity, today, we are looking at our relationship with our life and realizing the timelessness of atonement.

Our life reflects our state of being. If we are fearful, that is the world we encounter. In deciding to live in fearlessness and love, we're deciding to be in a state of happy fulfillment as the light of the world. We are joyously free. Simply being. There is nothing to fear, for we have become willing to remember that only love is real.

The quality of our attention is the currency we have to spend on this day. Will we spend it with love and unity as the lesson invites?

When Lucas he was around eleven, there was a kid who lived next door that was always bulling his brother. I'd hear the conflict going on in their back yard. I don't like it. So, naturally, I tell Lucas not to befriend the kid, because he'd just end up getting hurt.

He looks at me, with tears in his eyes, like I'm some kind of alien. I say, "What is it, honey?" Lucas, innocent love all over his face, says, "Mom, are you asking me not to be friends with him because I should be afraid of him?"

I say, "Yes. You've heard how mean he is. I don't want you to get hurt."

Lucas, being the consummate forgiver, says, "But, if he is being mean, isn't friendship what he needs? I don't think he's really mean. It's just hurt, right?" I humbled into love and fearlessness, awakened to the lesson alive in me.

Lucas continues, "I think he is afraid nobody can really love him, so he pushes them away. I know, can I have him over for a sleepover?"

How could I say no, with my Lucas guru shining the way for me? Of course, by now, I'm on the love and fearlessness light track. We invite him for a sleepover, and it's like he never leaves. He's nothing like fear told me. He's part of our yummy extended family. He and Lucas are still friends today. *"In fearlessness and love I spend today."*

DAY 311
(Lesson 311)

"I judge all things as I would have them be."

(W-pII.311.1)

*"Father, we wait with open mind today, to hear Your Judgment of the Son
You love. We do not know him, and we cannot judge. And so we let Your
Love decide what he whom You created as Your Son must be."*

(W-pII.311.2.1–3)

Today we begin a new theme which we'll consider with the next ten lessons, *"What is the Last Judgment?"* When I first read this definition of the last judgment, it was like Whew! I realized I still had a fearful belief attached to the idea of a last judgment, from childhood programing. Even after working with the course. It was one of those sneaky hideaway beliefs tucked away and labeled "To be looked at upon death." But, that's the mind-training. Nothing gets left out of the chance to review with love, now.

That's what the last judgment really is: it is a review by our Self with Christ vision, where we look on everyone and everything with unity and love, knowing it is all God. We're doing it with our training. We're no longer seeing differences, distinctions, or comparing one thing to another. Christ's vision sees a forgiven world of union and wholeness. So, whew!

Today's lesson, *"I judge all things as I would have them be,"* is a call to see with love. What seems to be happening directly reflects our state of mind. When we're judging according to a personal self, our energy tightens and contacts around what we think we want, yes? If we're letting the Holy Spirit within our mind judge for us, we flow with life, releasing each moment as it passes by, allowing us to be present here and now. We can totally tell by the way we feel.

Yesterday is a perfect example. I spent much of the day meditating and writing and feeling "in the zone." As I finish and save, what I'd written disappears from my computer. I try all the things I know to retrieve it, but to no avail. Shit man—I was totally in the zone, too! I try the same things again. Nada! Wait, isn't that the definition of insanity, doing the same thing expecting different results?

Not accepting the actuality of the present moment is fertile ground for judgment to take root. "What the fuck? What did I do wrong? I don't want to lose that writing . . . I'm screwed." (Some zone.)

The shift from my yummy in-the-zone energy to icky rock-in-my-gut is immediate. Realizing my insanity, I stop, relax my mind, recalling today's lesson, and laugh. *"I judge all things as I would have them be,"* I let laughter roll through me, loving the release—which is total and immediate. I let it roll through my whole body and release the past. It feels delicious!

Now I am free to let my holy Self judge, and I feel it in the wholehearted acceptance and joy of this moment, here and now. What's great is I'm back to ground zero, knowing nothing is really "mine" to keep. I can't lose what must give its gifts and continue flowing. It is my appreciation that keeps my heart full and flowing with life.

The day's writing experience was a gift of grace. The words were only mine as they flowed from the Source of communication—mine to appreciate for the moments my fingers touched the keyboard, while I let myself be a vessel. Glorious. This is the judgment I prefer. One of appreciation, joy, and letting go.

DAY 312

(Lesson 312)

"I see all things as I would have them be."

(W-pII.312.1)

*"I have no purpose for today except to look upon a liberated world,
set free from all the judgments I have made. Father, this is Your Will
for me today. and therefore it must be my goal as well."*

(W-pII.312.2.1–2)

Today we are choosing to look upon a liberated world set free from judgments we have made. We're freeing our minds from thinking we know what should happen. We're accepting all things exactly as they are, with an open mind and heart. So, where we saw attack or fear, now we see innocence, we see a call for love and forgiveness, both in ourselves and others.

We're paying attention to when we feel tempted to feel frustrated, seek pleasure, are afraid, doubtful, worried, attacked, or attacking—anything that disturbs our peace. We're recognizing types of feelings come because we have judged what's happening as something we want or don't want. But now we want to see a forgiven world where innocence, peace and love reign. We choose again, and we open to present awareness and can see the part we can play which will best serve the whole.

The thing that I've found most curious is my preferences. Preferences can be sneaky "good" judgments—the choice to exclude the rest from my experience of love and union.

Notice the subtle ways we judge everything according to our chosen identity—self or Self. We assign meaning according to what it means to me, the separate, individual, personal self. Or, we let the Holy Spirit within our minds, judge for us. This influences how we look upon what we see.

The instant I judge for a specific, I limit myself to seeing only what supports my decision and reject everything else. Let's use a time judgment as an example. "I'm busy." Because I'm busy I feel hurried. The phone rings as I'm going out the door. I see the call as an interference to my agenda, and my taking time for the call will take something away from me. Yes? The freeway is seemingly full of inconsiderate people, cutting me off and driving too slowly. Appreciation for Divine flow goes out the window.

We've all had those times when our point of view differs from another and how difficult it is to persuade them to see the situation differently than the one they hold. They're every bit as convinced their perception is right as we are. Yes? Today we willingly give up our investment in being right, so we can see with innocent eyes where love unites and happiness just is.

Today's idea lets us be wrong in the sweetest way.

Here's an example from back when. There's this a colleague at work, whom I didn't really know. I'd heard rumors—narcissistic, opinionated. I was to meet with him, and dread oozed in my gut. But I'd put today's lesson out front in my mind, so, I notice I'm judging him as a self-protective mechanism—I'm afraid I'll fail myself in an interaction with him.

Is this how I would have it be? No. Right then, I know there is no failure in love. I choose to set us both free and accept what happens as just as it is, free from resistance. I can be present and be a light of joy and understanding.

When I meet with this guy, the first thing I notice are his clear blue eyes. Eyes of compassion and determination. I listen to him and his passion for understanding his patients, and not just treating them as a diagnosis. We're totally aligned. In fact, I can't imagine he got a rep as difficult. We quickly become trusted colleagues and friends. Yes, this is how I would have it be.

CHAPTER TWO HUNDRED FIFTY

DAY 313

(Lesson 313)

"Now let a new perception come to me."

(W-pII.313.1)

"Father, there is a vision which beholds all things as sinless, so that fear has gone, and where it was is love invited in. And love will come wherever it is asked. This vision is Your gift. The eyes of Christ look on a world forgiven. In His sight are all its sins forgiven, for He sees no sin in anything He looks upon. Now let His true perception come to me, that I may waken from the dream of sin and look within upon my sinlessness, which You have kept completely undefiled upon the altar to Your holy Son, the Self with which I would identify."

(W-pII.313.1.1–6)

With today's lesson, *"Now let a new perception come to me,"* we're acknowledging that we are the determiner of our experience, not the victim of forces outside ourselves. We are the dreamer of the dream we call our life. We will with God's Will, the happy dream forgiveness brings.

The new perception is seen through Christ's vision which is our true sight. This sight sees no sin, but only holiness. The new perception is available only now. It is one of unity and love—love looks out and seeing only love, recognizes itself. Whether it be love extending or the call for love, we see a unified whole. Through Christ vision we look upon a forgiven would, for judgment has been replaced by unity.

Here's an example of a moment, when I realize how crucial this clean slate is for true perception. I'd been doing the lessons. I was experiencing peace and joy and I was seeing people and situations differently, in a more loving and less judgmental way. I was actively looking for the innocence and holiness in myself and others, so I felt pretty good about how things were going.

A radio host, whom I had met at an Avatar event, asks me to be a guest on her show. I felt excited and nervous. I had a week to prepare. She hadn't given me any specific guidelines for what we'd be discussing, just that she would be asking me questions about myself and the work I was doing.

I went over notes from workshops, client sessions, and my journals. But the more I prepared, the more anxious I felt. By the time the interview commenced, I was so far removed from the awareness of my true Self, that I didn't even want to do the interview anymore.

As the interview gets underway, I'm fixated on remembering all the important points I had decided on throughout the previous week, which made it impossible for me to be present. I feel horribly icky.

That's my flip-switch. It's like I'm watching this image of this girl so nervous and so unlike myself—the Self which had met this woman spontaneously filled with joy for life; so much so, she'd called me "infectious with joy!" The woman she wanted to share with her audience.

In that realization, I'm immediately present. Instantly I feel released of the burden of me, knowing nothing from my past could possibly prepare me for this present moment—but Divinity can. I lean back and trust. Today's lesson plays like a background music, *"Now let a new perception come to me."*

Our conversation flows joyfully. As calls come in, we invite everyone into a deeper conversation about purpose and meaning. We're totally relaxed and having fun. Everyone is a part of the miracle taking place live, on the radio, all joining a new perception.

Only in the present can we truly see.

Today we are inviting that new perception to come, and we trust what we are given.

DAY 314
(Lesson 314)

"I seek a future different from the past."

(W-pII.314.1)

"Father, we were mistaken in the past, and choose to use the present to be free. Now do we leave the future in Your Hands, leaving behind our past mistakes, and sure that You will keep Your present promises, and guide the future in their holy light."

(W-pII.314.2.1–2)

I love the progression of these lessons. Remember that the theme we are working with these ten lessons is *"What is the Last Judgment?"* The final paragraph is a summation of its message and the perception necessary for us to see a future different from the past. It says, *"This is God's Final Judgment: ;You are still My holy Son, forever innocent, forever loving and forever loved, as limitless as your Creator, and completely changeless and forever pure. Therefore awaken and return to Me. I am Your Father and you are My Son"* (W-pII.10.5). Feel it?

We're looking at our responsibility for sight from a present moment perspective. Released from the judgments of the past, we leave judgment to the Holy Spirit, which brings a present perception of what is now.

We have invited this new perception, so we're not using past learning to see what is happening. We're inviting our Christ vision to see for us. From this new perception, the future collapses into now. Our stories from the past are not present, so they can't cast shadows on this clean and present moment extending. Without the past, fear and guilt are gone.

We are present to our Self as God created us. Our presence is our gift to the future. Being present to what is, void of judgment, lets our holy identity find relationship with all that arises in our experience, making each encounter holy.

This new perception of the future collapsing into now is bright and clear for me as I gathered with loved ones for Mother's Day brunch yesterday.

The last few times I have been with Lucas and his family, I felt disconnected from Lucas. I blamed it on him. He'd changed. He wasn't as present as he used to be when we regularly joined in spiritual discourse about our knowing our Self and extending us into the world. As he remarried and his life took him in less proximity to me, I didn't join in his expansion. I thought it was him. Not so much negatively, just disconnected.

Now, brought to the light of awareness, I see it differently. I realize the responsibility for a change in relationship is mine. I'm the one making shit up. I was seeking the past and judging a possible future based on the change of scenery. I was not being present with what actually is.

I was looking for the past and could not see the gift, present now. I change my mind, applying these past few lessons to reinforce my responsibility for sight, I am reminding myself first that I am only love, and love is always present. So, if I feel disconnected, I have chosen not to love. Period.

This is my restoration to sanity. In seeing this, I feel only the present eternal yumminess that is our holy relationship, beyond time. I see he *is* sharing his spiritual journey as it is now, in his yummy fatherhood experience. Now I am present—I am a part of the experience. The mom's day outing is free, and we join easily. Conversation flows innocently from one topic to the next from politics to the children's activities—each a spiritual discourse to an open mind.

Each moment is a fresh gift of union. Happy Mother's Day to me!

DAY 315

(Lesson 315)

"All gifts my brothers give belong to me."

(W-pII.315.1)

"I thank You, Father, for the many gifts that come to me today and every day from every Son of God. My brothers are unlimited in all their gifts to me. Now may I offer them my thankfulness, that gratitude to them may lead me on to my Creator and His memory."

(W-pII.2.1–3)

Today's idea invites the mind to open wide and receive, aligning heart and mind in wholeheartedness. Just contemplate this first line, *"Each day a thousand treasures come to me with every passing moment."* Yummy, yes? That's every smile, every kind word or gentle touch, every expression of gratitude or mercy from one to another throughout the entire world is a gift to us. It's incredible.

Like each time someone turns within, lifts their heart to the Divine, they are our savior. We receive what we are open to receive. Our gratitude opens us even more to receiving. We start seeing expressions of love everywhere—whether as a call for love or another answering—it's all we want to see.

Here's an example that still busts my heart wide open when I recall it.

The boys and I are taking the bus to the mini speedway. Our car is in the shop, so we decide half the adventure will be getting there and taking public transportation. We get on this bus and the seats are already filled.

So, we're standing in the aisle and this guy gets up and offers us his seat. He's this big guy with a bald head, a goatee, and tattoos for sleeves, and he's got this amazingly warm and friendly face. My heart swells with gratitude as we thank him, and Parker and Cole take the seat.

At the next stop, an elderly couple gets on and the boys jump up and offer them their seat. Several others seated do the same. It's like a fun game we've all decided to play.

I look around at my yummy comrades on this public transport, and it's like the bus to heaven. I see a woman holding another's hands and comforting the one who is crying silently. I'm blessed by this tenderness. In another row, a man has his hand on the back of his son's neck, gently stroking it. My heart swells.

Toward the back, a mom starts tickling her toddler. He's laughing and it catches on like a virus. Those closest them start laughing and this makes the kid laugh even more. This joy busts me up. The boys too. Then, like a wave, others start laughing and pretty soon the bus is filled with laughter and joy.

Every time someone new gets on, people jump up to surrender their seats in the spirit of this blessed exchange. This link of generosity continues until we arrive at our destination. Love is the best gift—it touches everyone!

Can today get any better than that? I'm overflowing, feeling blessed and honored through every exchange of smiles and joy and generosity of spirit. It's today's idea, vibrant and alive. *"All gifts my brothers give belong to me."*

That's just one snippet from a day. Today's lesson is talking about the millions of moments where love leads! Each moment the heart of love is lifted, and the mind is given freedom from fear in anyone, anywhere—Huge.

Each time we see a smile or an act of kindness from one brother to another, can we allow the gratitude that beckons from our heart to open it and join in union? Can we expand to include those we cannot see, but are ours as well? Can we realize in the quiet of our mind lifted to our Father, a thousand minds who are listening to the call Home? Can we let our heart fill with gratitude, thanking them as savior and join in the glad crusade? Yep.

DAY 316

(Lesson 316)

"All gifts I give my brothers are my own."

(W-pII.316.1)

"Father, I would accept Your gifts today. I do not recognize them. Yet I trust that You Who gave them will provide the means by which I can behold them, see their worth, and cherish only them as what I want."

(W-pII.316.2.1–3)

Our turn. The law of love is "what I give my brother is my gift to me." Just like yesterday's lesson, all gifts given from anyone are gifts to everyone. Every time I forgive and see you differently, I remember I am love. Each time I honor your holiness, I accept the holiness I am as God created me. The lesson says God's grace is given me in every gift a brother has received throughout all time. Wow! That's abundance.

I love the image from the lesson of a treasure house full of the gifts God gave us, with angels watching its doors and not one gift is lost, and only more are added. We can't ever lose. You'd think we'd be running around giving everything to everyone, all the time. Yes?

Here's a beautiful example. Back when we had the Vision Center, I'd been asked to speak at a nearby women's shelter. The women gave their full attention, and I felt honored and graced to be with them. After I spoke, we sat together in a circle of couches, talking and sharing ourselves with each other. Several of the residents asked about our services at the Center and what they cost.

I'm sitting with these beautiful, courageous women, and I look into their faces and I see the innocent Christ child in each one. They are giving me their love and attention and gratitude. I feel so blessed and honored I say, "I'd love to gift you all a weekend workshop, in appreciation for this lovely evening." They heartedly agree.

I remember walking away from the shelter, and my heart was so full, I felt I would burst. It's like today's lesson is the beating rhythm of my heart, *"All gifts I give my brother are my gifts to me."* I skip up the street filled with joy and gratitude, knowing the women are feeling the same.

The following weekend we have the workshop. What make it so remarkable is that I truly feel the mutual gifting. As the women share hard lives of courage, I am humbled by their raw openness, and love and trust. They just open themselves up and let their fears and heartaches spill out into the center of our love, trusting me to handle them with care.

It's like angels do the heavy lifting for me. Just the perfect initiatives come to mind, special tweaks, that make them specifically meaningful.

As the first evening comes to a close, someone suggests we turn the weekend into a vigil of forgiveness, love and courage. We light candles and bring in blankets and pillows. The women stay on sight all weekend, some stay awake, keeping the flame of forgiveness and courage burning, while others slept, rotating roles throughout the weekend. The unadulterated care they show for each other is astonishing, and humbling. I received a thousand-fold each gift given and received.

CHAPTER TWO HUNDRED FIFTY-FOUR
DAY 317

(Lesson 317)

"I follow in the way appointed me."

(W-pII.317.1)

"Father, Your way is what I choose today. Where it would lead me do I choose to go; what it would have me do I choose to do. Your way is certain, and the end secure. The memory of You awaits me there. And all my sorrows end in Your embrace, which You have promised to Your Son, who thought mistakenly that he had wandered from the sure protection of Your loving Arms."

(W-pII.317.2.1–5)

Today's lesson is a declaration that we follow in the way appointed especially for us. We're claiming our unique role in the whole of God's plan for salvation. The Christ in us is ready. We want to be wholehearted in this decision. We must unite heart and mind.

Today, we choose wholeheartedly to follow the Divine way appointed for us. We are not looking to past experience for what to do. Our state of being tells us. We're not looking to others, comparing our path to theirs. We are taking instruction from each present moment, trusting God's plan and following our hearts and minds in union with the Holy Spirit.

Whatever arises and with anyone we encounter we meet with presence. It is our holiness that speaks to us and bears witness to their holiness, beyond time and human destiny, but within this present moment. So, it's not so much the thing we do but the state of being from which we encounter it.

For years I confused this appointed way with the context in which I felt guided to share it. I believed my appointed way was counseling. I felt I had been given this amazing gift where wisdom came to me through my heart and mind as I connected with others.

I was sure it was my purpose in life because it felt like I was actually a conduit for miracles. And this is true as far as my experience goes. See, the thing about attaching anything to form is that it's fertile ground for ego hijacking. The minute I put a label on it, I've boxed it up and identified myself with the label.

But true to my intention to let Spirit lead, at some point I realize that every label is imprisoning. Each comes with expectations—and squeezes in on my availability to let spirit rip. I started thinking it was *my* gig—and ego crept in.

Clarity comes one day while with a client. She'd been diagnosed with depression. She'd tried every kind of medication and behavioral modification, seen many therapists and doctors and now she was feeling suicidal.

I'm listening while she cries, defeated. I realize I have no idea how to reach her. I'm supposed to know how to help. My heart races. This, I realize, is fear. And not for her. No, it's me. I think I'm on my own here. That was my flip-switch.

I see my role-identity is in the way. I'm not open to the way appointed by the Divine. I thought I needed to do something. I do. I surrender—wholeheartedly. And love is right there, immediately. Oh my God—love is always the answer—just love.

I think, *"I follow in the way appointed me,"* grateful to seek beyond all constructs—to see how my counselor label is actually a barrier to my freedom to follow in the way appointed right here and now. Only in this present moment do I hear the Voice for God.

I let go of everything I thought I knew and give over my identity as a counselor to the Holy Spirit for correction. I open my full heart to this woman, and I share my present experience with her. She, too, is part of this way, and our union subscribes the way forward. Turns out, she's looking for a divine connection. Go figure. She's seeking a spiritual opening which my honesty facilitates. The happy way begins to unfold in its appointed way.

CHAPTER TWO HUNDRED FIFTY-FIVE

DAY 318

(Lesson 318)

"In me salvation's means and end are one."

(W-pII.318.1)

"Let me today, my Father, take the role You offer me in Your request that I accept Atonement for myself. For thus does what is thereby reconciled in me become as surely reconciled to You."

(W-pII.318.2.1–2)

Today's lesson is simply saying that we, the holy child as God created, is the goal for which salvation aims and the means for its accomplishment. I love this line. *"I was created as the thing I seek. I am the goal the world is searching for."* It doesn't leave a lot to be confused about.

But let me break it down. Because, believe me, I have imprisoned myself in confusion and delayed my happiness lots. Remember, the goal is God. It is to realize our identity as love, extended from God's love, creating and returning to God. We're like this unique aspect of the whole, that without each of us, would not be a masterpiece.

So, once we know the goal is "know thy Self," we turn toward it, and everything for its accomplishment is right there, already within and connected to the Source of accomplishment. Tremendous!

It is the awakening experience we have, as we forgive and release past associations of identity. It's like, OMG, that amazing all-encompassing love, I just knew was available, wasn't out there. No wonder I couldn't find it. It's within! The second we claim it as our own, it reaches its arms out wide to bring everyone into its embrace.

When we feel whole and complete, we realize our holographic relationship with everyone and all circumstances. When we come in contact with anyone, even if just in our imagination, love's impulse to extend dictates our response most often now. The response is to relate with love to all beings and in all situations. This is our part in salvation. We are in a holy relationship with all creation. It's the simple way, once we realize the means and end are one.

When I started living as my whole Self, synced with Divine flow, friends asked if I was ever going to be in a relationship again, I'd smile and say, "I am." It's like, "Wow, who would have ever guessed we don't need a special relationship?" I'd finally realized specialness cheats me of total union with all. It puts conditions on love, which I don't want. God is where salvation's means and end are one.

Love is its own ministry and living as my Self soon attracted someone perfectly suited for the holy relationship where in union means and end are one. That's the glory, the mystery and magic of trusting the Divine.

We are the means and the end. What we are *is* how we are saved. The return to the recognition of our Self as God created us, is what all our unlearning and learning is for. We are the one. We come to know our Self as we forgive what is not. Which is what we've been doing throughout this curriculum.

We accept atonement for our Self, and being one Son, everyone receives atonement too. Our willingness to place our faith in unity, trusting the Holy Spirit as the bridge that remembers the Christ within, leads us back to the Self we are, still in heaven and still in God.

We ultimately realize God's final judgment for ourselves: *"You are still My holy Son, forever innocent, forever loving and forever loved, as limitless as your Creator, and completely changeless and forever pure. Therefore awaken and return to Me. I am Your Father and you are My Son"* (W-pII.10.5.1–3). And salvation has been accomplished.

DAY 319

(Lesson 319)

"I came for the salvation of the world."

(W-pll.319.1)

*"Father, Your Will is total. And the goal which stems from it shares its totality.
What aim but the salvation of the world could You have given me? And
what but this could be the Will my Self has shared with You?"*

(W-pll.319.2.1–4)

The lesson starts by saying, *"Here is a thought from which all arrogance has been removed, and only truth remains."* Was that your response to reading this lesson? *"I came for the salvation of the world."* I admit, I wavered at first.

But could anything else be true? If God wills we be saved from the dream of separation we made, then it is so. What but our Self, who knows our union with God, could the means be?

I recall a time when a friend asks me for a miracle. She's been having a nightmare of a time with her teenaged son. She's so angry and frustrated, she feels she can't love him. Not the way he's being. She needs him to change so she can, again, feel the love she knows she has for him.

She wants a miracle, she says, and I quote, "I feel guilty times ten." She says, "You're always saying we're entitled to miracles. We just need to ask and be willing to receive. Well, I'm asking and I'm willing."

I want to start backtracking. "I didn't mean through me!" Today's lesson pops up on the screen of my mind, and I pause, *"I am here for the salvation of the world."* Hello! She is my savior, and I am hers. I take her hands and we closed our eyes. I let the story drop to the altar in my heart.

I allow divine love to rise from center of my being and expand, encompassing us both, and reaching further still. I let the image of a teenaged boy come to mind and then dissolve into this amazing ocean of love.

As we sit in this holy encounter, an ancient hate becomes a present love as this prayer spills through my lips, "Love, we come with hands empty, for we release the past and all hurt along with it. We come with hearts open to receive and give as one. Let us be aware of Your presence now, and let it fill our hearts and mind, extending into tomorrow and beyond time. May this relationship be holy as is Your will, and all that is not love be happily released. As is our will. So, it shall be. Amen."

My friend looks up with shiny eyes and says, "I feel my son with us. I do love him. What should I do now?" I say, "Trust him. Trust yourself. Trust love. It is the only thing."

As we stand and hug, her phone dings. It's a message from her son, saying, "I cleaned my room and did the dishes." My friend breaks down, tears flowing. "Oh my God! I love him so much! He's totally trying. I thought he gave up. I'm so glad I didn't when I wanted to. Thank you."

"It's all love," I say. "There's your miracle."

It is not arrogant to be as we are created to be. It is arrogant to believe we are the one special kind of problem that can't be included in God's plan. Nothing but what God wills is real. Resistance is futile.

It is our holiness joined as one that saves everyone along with us. As we come to accept our purpose as the salvation of the world, we invite our brothers to salvation with us. It is a change of mind from one of separation to one of unity and love. It is atonement.

CHAPTER TWO HUNDRED FIFTY-SEVEN
DAY 320
(Lesson 320)

"My Father gives all power unto me."
(W-pII.320.1)

"Your Will can do all things in me, and then extend to all the world as well through me. There is no limit on Your Will. And so all power has been given to Your Son."
(W-pII.320.2.1–3)

Today's lesson is the last of lessons under the theme, *"What is the Last Judgment?"* In considering today's we want to realize that we, the extension of the Source of all that is, share all the same limitless attributes as God. How could we not, if we are God's extension? If our Source is unlimited in love, strength, peace, and joy, then by birthright the power of His will must be ours as well.

If we are not in touch with these attribute as ours, we are misidentifying ourselves. Is there anything besides the All of All? Only dreams. But even dreams are ultimately sourced from the only Source of life there is—from the unlimited power of creation that is our identity.

Our work with our curriculum has brought us to this state of readiness. Do we accept our will really is one with God's? Do we accept there is no will apart from His? That we are limitless in power and in strength? That all joy and peace are ours?

The time is now. We are on our appointed way, returning to wholeness and to recognition that we and God are one. As we claim our inheritance, releasing the false, we begin to realize the power of God's will through us. Is there any place or any situation that could possibly be out of the Divine reach?

What I've seen in my own life, is when I attempt to fix rather than forgive, I reinforce my belief in limitation and powerlessness. Like when I was trying to fix my back. I resisted accepting things as they appeared right now, and that resistance left me feeling powerless. I turned to experts and tried to re-establish my former state, to no avail.

Once I offered my situation in prayer, surrendering both problem and *my* solution, the light dawned. I cannot keep my identity as a body and move beyond it. I can't identify with limitation and let the power of the Divine move through me. I have to make a choice. God is my only goal. In each present moment, free from past ideas of who or what I am, I feel the power of joy to unite and heal. Gratefully I realize the perfection of my current classroom.

So, when Lar was diagnosed with stage-4 cancer this year, I don't resist. Lar and I join in recognizing the truth of today's lesson, and through our joining align with divinity. Whatever is happening is the perfect happening. Nothing is happening by accident.

Every happening contains the gift of Divine power within it. A twinge of pain is a call for love to fill my mind with the remembrance of our identity as God created us—to extend the love called for and expect a miracle.

A million chances to extend has shown up at hospitals, the cancer center, the neighborhood. Who we are as love gives us the strength and power to bring and accept miracles—to be a light wherever we go. Healing, of course, is as inevitable as God.

DAY 321

(Lesson 321)

"Father, my freedom is in You alone."

(W--pII.321.1)

"I did not understand what made me free, nor what my freedom is, nor where to look to find it. Father, I have searched in vain until I heard Your Voice directing me. Now I would guide myself no more. For I have neither made nor understood the way to find my freedom. But I trust in You. You Who endowed me with my freedom as Your holy Son will not be lost to me. Your Voice directs me, and the way to You is opening and clear to me at last. Father, my freedom is in You alone. Father, it is my will that I return."

(W-pII.321.1.1–8)

Today we begin with a new theme from which we consider the next ten lessons. It is: *"What is Creation?"* This section is the alpha and omega *"Creation is the sum of all God's Thoughts, in number infinite, and everywhere without all limit. Only Love creates, and only like Itself. There was no time when all that it created was not there"* (W-pII.11.1). It speaks to us from this place of total inclusion, and we find the freedom that comes from God alone.

I was lucky through failure. In early adulthood, I looked for freedom in independence, competence, accolades, being recognized as an expert in my field. What happened is the more I gained these things, the more foreboding I felt. Rewards and labels created prison walls for an identity I had to maintain constantly lest it all break apart—like at any moment the other shoe could drop. The very things I thought would free me, imprisoned me.

I sought solace in drink—mini escapes to forget I was in this prison cell. I drank to erase the responsibility I felt to maintain this image.—I drank to blow it up. And blow it up I did. Thank God.

Alcoholism is the fast track to God. It was out of this a dark night of the soul period, where I finally let myself deep dive into the darkness I'd fought so hard to avoid. The darkness I believed to be myself.

At the bottom of that darkness I found a pilot light burning bright deep within—which spread throughout my being as all-encompassing love. I knew beyond doubt, it was Divinity. It was God. It was my Self.

And in that light, I saw my true face. It was without form, yet it was more real than looking in a mirror. I felt its certainty and the whole world changed around me.

Everything was touched with light, vibrant and alive. The essence of life shaping and transforming my experience of sight.

It's one of those things that once you see it, you can't un-see it. I realized I'd been wrong about everything. I'd been wrong about who I was, and what God was.

Freedom is the experience that God is. And in that, I live. My freedom lies in what I am as God created me, totally dependent on the wholeness of our creation. This is where my freedom lies.

Today's lesson reminds us that freedom is found in trust. Trusting God and all creation to be what it is. Listening to the voice for love and taking guidance given through our union with Him.

CHAPTER TWO HUNDRED FIFTY-NINE
DAY 322
(Lesson 322)

"I can give up but what was never real."
(W-pII.322.1)

"Father, to You all sacrifice remains forever inconceivable. And so I cannot sacrifice except in dreams. As You created me, I can give up nothing You gave me. What You did not give has no reality. What loss can I anticipate except the loss of fear, and the return of love into my mind?"
(W-pII.322.2.1–5)

Giving up illusion is the way we see truth. A favorite saying by author David Foster Wallace is, "Everything I've ever let go of has claw marks on it." It's like if we didn't put up a fight to hold onto what we believe belongs to us, we didn't care. We have this carefully constructed identity built to defend against attack, and we fight to the death to keep it.

So, when we first started the mind-training that's kind of how we responded, when asked to see our "story of me" as illusion. That story was our religion. We didn't want to sacrifice what took so long to construct.

Then we're told time itself is an illusion, and our whole system collapses. We learn miracles happen in an outside of time interval, which collapses time, so the shift in perception is immediate in our surrender. Its results show us a different world.

In these final workbook lessons, we are revisiting all the concepts we have practiced step by step from the beginning of our curriculum, but from a different view. We have an experience of the Divine and the unreality of fear.

As we're considering today's lesson, we are looking from the perception of our right-mind. *"I can give up but what was never real."* What is it that keeps us hanging on? The course begins in this same idea: *"Nothing real can be threatened. Nothing unreal exists. Herein lies the peace of God"* (ACIM T.in.2.2). The beginning, the end, and the means. All our practicing is really about giving up what isn't real, so we will see what's really here.

A few years back, when Cole was seventeen and Parker fourteen, they decided they wanted to move out on their own. They had an online business and were doing pretty well, and they felt like they were ready to take on more responsibility for maintaining their lifestyle.

My immediate response is resistance. It felt like loss. My mind began its defense, saying, "They're too young. They have no idea what it takes to maintain a household." But my heart said, "Life will give them the opportunity for all they need to learn. You know they come equipped to handle whatever their choices bring. The Divine's got them." I placed the situation in God's hands, leaned back and trusted. Within days everything fell perfectly in place for a move.

Since our lease on the house was up, Cole and Parker and Lar and I moved into separate apartments in the same beautiful complex. This way Lar and I could keep an eye out and assist if needed.

During the year, which we fondly refer to as *"the great apartment experiment,"* the perfection of their decision unfolded. The blessings and joy of letting go of my illusion of sacrifice, seeing love freed to be itself, were daily and constant.

The boys became a dynamic source of love and assistance for others in the apartment community. People came to them when they had computer or software problems. Others came for headshots for their acting portfolios. Several told me that they just wanted to be in Cole's calming presence or Parker's bright and happy attitude. Yep, turns out, *"I sacrifice illusions; nothing more."*

DAY 323

(Lesson 323)

"I gladly make the 'sacrifice' of fear."

(W-pII.323.1)

"Here is the only 'sacrifice' You ask of Your beloved Son; You ask him to give up all suffering, all sense of loss and sadness, all anxiety and doubt, and freely let Your Love come streaming in to his awareness, healing him of pain, and giving him Your Own eternal joy. Such is the 'sacrifice' You ask of me, and one I gladly make; the only 'cost' of restoration of Your memory to me, for the salvation of the world."

(W-pII.323.1.1–2)

Today we gladly "sacrifice" what's still standing in the way of our full return to Divinity. It sets in quotations terms we believe, kind of like "this isn't real" and then uses them to help us return home. The Holy Spirit uses everything we made in the name of fear to show us another purpose that reveals love. It's cool like that.

We give up what was never real and the truth is there, shining bright. We pay the debt we owe to truth by merely letting go of self-deceptions. Speaking of debts and payoffs, we hold on to fears only because we think it gives us something we value, protection, self-righteousness, victimhood. If we don't see a payoff in it, why haven't we let it go?

I became a metaphysical minister through the University of Metaphysics, partly because I felt I needed this "house of authority" backing me up to do the work I felt I was meant to do. I was afraid of being misperceived, just standing in the light of authority as a minister of God's love.

I'm not saying that becoming credentialed through this authority was wrong. In fact, it was wonderful, and acted as a confirmation of the deeper truth I knew through my work with *A Course in Miracles*. It's just at the time, I wasn't always clear of my motives. So, being a minister became my classroom to show me what my motives were.

Case in point, I meet with a couple to talk about vows, and the groom asks, "What kind of minister are you?" I hear, "Where do you get your authority to marry us?" Feeling suddenly defensive, I say, "I am a Metaphysical minister, licensed through the state of Nevada." My insecurity is immediately reflected in his next comment, "Oh, one of those internet ministers."

The hairs on the back of my neck stand in my defense, silently screaming, "No, I'm legit!" Luckily, I spot my flip-switch—pause, and call to mind today's lesson, "I gladly make the sacrifice of fear and pay my debt to truth."

I return to calm, before speaking, letting go, and letting love fill me with true authority. The next thing I hear myself say is, "Though I have credentialed licensure, it is my relationship with the Divine and our coming together in the name of love, for the union of your two souls, that is the *true* authority."

The power of that moment, those words, resonates deeply with each of us. So much so, the bride asks if I'll use the words in our upcoming ceremony.

In fact, the idea of true authority being the union of love became a standard expression in future ceremonies. It clarifies my role in its proper place of service. By "sacrificing" my self-deception (fear) and the images of authority I worshiped falsely (fear), love's true authority naturally flows through me.

Can we make the sacrifice of fear today and pay our debt to truth? Can we stand in the light of truth and let love stream into our consciousness and bless the world with its light?

DAY 324

(Lesson 324)

"I merely follow, for I would not lead."

(W-pII.324.1)

"Father, You are the One Who gave the plan for my salvation to me. You have set the way I am to go, the role to take, and every step in my appointed path. I cannot lose the way. I can but choose to wander off a while, and then return. Your loving Voice will always call me back, and guide my feet aright. My brothers all can follow in the way I lead them. Yet I merely follow in the way to You, as You direct me and would have me go."

(W-pII.324.1.1–7)

Today we follow the way of love. Love creates its own field of energy and moves in the direction of union. We've come to a stage in our curriculum where we no longer are looking to the past for direction. We happily release our fear, and with it, lack and suffering. We've realized that everything is an idea, a thought in the mind, so we let go of our attachment to things of this world in favor of remembering that only love is real.

We want only God's will. To follow in the way appointed by Him. But how? We have severed our connection to moving from fear or achievement as a motivator. So, we wait in peace, and trust, and the way lights up before us.

I had an experience in 2003 (no fault of my own), where my mind cracked open and the light of truth was all there was. I rarely talk about it, because it is indescribable—beyond anything, yet completely whole. Divine love was all there was, and I was that. Indivisible.

What I want to talk about is what happened in the days and weeks that followed. I felt like I was dancing around, curiously reacquainting myself with life from this new state of being. Though my actions looked much the same in everyday life, the remarkable thing was how quiet my mind was, how full my Self was with life and love. I felt an inner Divine compass directing me. That's what today's lesson is inviting us to trust.

Each day lit up before me as I awoke. I seemed to live today's lesson effortlessly. I no longer was trying to get something from life. I felt whole, merely following the way appointed for me. My mind-training with the Course became alive in me.

Over time, the poignancy of that experience diminished, but the brightness of life breathing into creation moment by moment still astounds me. A deep sense of trust in love as the only true voice remains.

Not that I don't doze off and forget. I do. It's just that I have this inner trust it's all going according to plan. I can lean back and trust—flowing with Divine flow. The same seeming issues and problems present themselves—chances to forgive and surrender.

I just don't *do* problems anymore. I see the gift of awareness peeking out at me from beneath their skirts. I take its hand and follow its lead. Even when seemingly big things happen, like breaking my back or Lar's cancer, it's merely a chance for full offering. I know deep within this is a necessary classroom right now, forgive, and follow joy.

It's fun, in fact, to see what my ego mind gets up to when there is a block in the flow of joy—to realize I have placed resistance on the altar where only God belongs, and also to see that it is not the truth. I simply follow divinity, for I would not lead. At least, not for long.

DAY 325

(Lesson 325)

"All things I think I see reflect ideas."
(W-pII.325.1)

"Our Father, Your ideas reflect the truth, and mine apart from Yours but make up dreams.
Let me behold what only Yours reflect, for Yours and Yours alone establish truth."
(W-pII.325.2.1–2)

We're beginning to see our transformation in how the world appears to us. Through forgiving our false beliefs and opening to a new perception of everyone and everything, the edges have softened in radiant presence.

Have I told you how much I love metaphysics? The minute I was introduced to the ideas, they felt familiar. It answered the questions that had been free-floating in my psyche all my life. It's like the puzzle pieces, once dumped out on the table, finally began to form into a picture.

As soon as I learned that it was my thinking, and my faith in beliefs that were behind everything that appeared in my life, it's like something inside said, "Yep! I knew it!" We know.

So, if our lives are a reflection of what's in our mind, then that's the source of the problems we see. But also, the source of our solutions and the source of our happiness, when we reach toward true Source. Thinking comes first, then the appearance. What is showing up in our life right now, is really already gone. The thinking that put it there is in the past.

If we want a future different than the past, I must choose to think in a different way. Not from the same pool of thoughts from the past. The lesson says, "The things *I think* I see." We're just *thinking* we see a thing. What we're seeing is the image of an idea we want to see. Because we value it gets projected outward and claimed as ours. Today's lesson calls this process salvation's keynote.

I've had an amazing year. I've traveled a lot, moved homes, and my life has been filled with brand new experiences and people. One thing remains constant. It's all yummy—joy, love. I feel incredibly grateful, blessed by holiness and bursting at the seams with joy.

In the midst of all this, I have also been had huge lessons in forgiving my body identity. But here's the thing, I am grateful for each and every thing that arises because it shows me my state of mind. Gratitude makes me forgive easily. I trust that miracles are happening, my life reflects it. That's all I can see.

Earlier today I'm picking up dry-cleaning and the attendant that greets me has this wonderful energy. She tells me she is blessed—I feel that cha-chinch, knowing we're blessing each other. It lifts us simultaneously into a magical communion. Right there at the dry cleaners, we are having this holy encounter, all under the guise of dry-cleaning.

Back in the day, I thought dry-cleaning was for the purpose of getting my clothes cleaned. But my thought pool premise has changed. I am looking from love for love. I am looking for the truth and union. *"From forgiving thoughts, a gentle world comes forth . . ."* It's freakin' happening for us!

Today we hold in our mind what we really want. We're not trying to change what's already appearing, except to check it and see if our forgiveness is complete. Then forget about it. It's already the past. Our premise is Divinity, and it in this we choose our thoughts. And we see Divinity reflected here. We are merely claiming our inheritance. We choose to behold the truth.

DAY 326

(Lesson 326)

"I am forever an Effect of God."

(W-pll.326.1)

"Father, I was created in Your Mind, a holy Thought that never left its home. I am forever Your Effect, and You forever and forever are my Cause. As You created me I have remained. Where You established me I still abide. And all Your attributes abide in me, because it is Your Will to have a Son so like his Cause that Cause and Its Effect are indistinguishable. Let me know that I am an Effect of God, and so I have the power to create like You. And as it is in Heaven, so on earth. Your plan I follow here, and at the end I know that You will gather Your effects into the tranquil Heaven of Your Love, where earth will vanish, and all separate thoughts unite in glory as the Son of God."

(W-pll.326.1.1–8)

Today's lesson, *"I am forever an Effect of God,"* takes us right back to the cause for our being. This idea takes us beyond this world where we are the cause and what we project is the effect. It's taking us to true cause, God, where we are the effect. That means we are just like Him.

Whatever the cause, the effect can only contain the elements of the cause. Like if I plant a lettuce seed, the effect is going to be lettuce. I'm not going to get a strawberry. We are love because our Cause is Love. We are the heart of creation.

Once we've taken responsibility for being the cause of what we think we see, we are ready to move beyond it to true cause. It can't be said too much—God is love. Love which created us is what we are.

Only illusion can appear as something other than love. Love is the raw material of creation. Nothing that is not love actually exists. No effect can be different than its cause. So, cause and effect are actually identical. This identical identity is what we are acknowledging with today's lesson.

I love how this plays out in my life now. The effect is identical to the love I am holding as my identity. I acknowledge that I have the attributes of God, so I trust that what I need for miracles is given in each present moment. I trust that I am part of creation unfolding.

Like the other day I'm a driving down the street, and I see this woman in one of those wheelchair scooters, stuck halfway on the road and halfway on the curb. I pull over to help. As I approach, a man from another direction approaches as well. We are joined in seeing the opportunity to extend love. We pick her up and set her on her way.

I ask her if she wants a ride. She touches my hand and says, "Thank you but I enjoy riding around and appreciating the beauty, and people just living their lives." I feel that appreciation as my own. I thank her and say, "I love it. I'm with you, girl. You're beautiful."

These holy encounters are the life blood of my days now. I find them everywhere, or maybe they find me, because that is all I want.

It is God's will that we are so like Him that cause and effect are indistinguishable. We're beginning to realize that we need do nothing, because the cause of what we are moves through us. We are the heaven here on earth, one with all creation.

DAY 327

(Lesson 327)

"I need but call and You will answer me."

(W-pII.327.1)

"Father, I thank You that Your promises will never fail in my experience, if I but test them out. Let me attempt therefore to try them, and to judge them not. Your Word is one with You. You give the means whereby conviction comes, and surety of Your abiding Love is gained at last."

(W-pII.327.2.1–3)

This lesson has been proved to me so often and in so many ways, I find it hard to believe it isn't my first immediate response to everything. But that's what the lesson is saying. God is asking us to put it to the test. It says, *"Let me but learn from my experience that this is true, and faith in Him must surely come to me."*

Back when my faith wasn't quite so strong, and I was just beginning to trust that God was actually always with me, I recall an experience when the boys were little. We were on our way from Albuquerque to visit with family in Utah and we get a flat tire.

We're in the middle of nowhere and the spare turns out to be flat too. My mind starts reeling, reprimanding me for not getting new tires before the trip—for not getting the spare fixed since the last flat. I feel panic rising, with no civilization in sight and few cars on this section of freeway. As often happens with the mind-training, today's lesson was my lesson for the day.

Back then I set a timer on the hour to help me return my mind to the idea the lesson is teaching. The boys and I are just standing there staring at these two flat tires and my phone alarm buzzes. I nearly burst into tears as I recall the lesson. *"I need but call and You will answer."*

I start praying like crazy. "God, I am here, and I've got a situation. I need help. I am afraid and I feel guilty. I want see innocence and not guilt. I want to see your answer and not my problem. Please show me the purpose for this happening. Restore my mind to sanity so I can see through the eyes of love instead of fear. Can you bring some help? Thank you for the peaceful outcome that is sure."

Instantly, my heart settles. Cole casually says, "There's no chance the wrong thing is happening." That's like our family's mantra. It's an instant flip-switch out of powerlessness. I smile and breathe a sigh of relief. Remembering we have roadside assistance, I call. They say it'll be a couple of hours before anyone can get to us, so we decide to settle in and picnic in the back of the van.

Minutes later a car passes, U-turns, and comes back to help. They're from a town a little way back. When our "good Samaritan" sees our situation, he calls his son who owns a service station and tells him the kind of tire we need.

His son rounds up a used tire that'll work, and within an hour he's putting it on our car for us. We have a holy encounter with this man, his wife, and his son. They share pictures of their grandkids. We're all grateful and blessed by the encounter. As we're driving away, Parker says, "I love those guys!" It's like a confirmation of today's lesson's truth.

That's the simplicity of today's lesson practice. We call on God and in calling, we realize we trust. We are developing the habit of engaging with God. We are learning to not let our mind slip away from God, from love. We learn to count on it.

DAY 328

(Lesson 328)

"I choose the second place to gain the first."

(W-pII.328.1)

"There is no will but Yours. And I am glad that nothing I imagine contradicts what You would have me be. It is Your Will that I be wholly safe, eternally at peace. And happily I share that Will which You, my Father, gave as part of me."

(W-pII.328.2.1–4)

I really didn't get this lesson at first. I thought, "I choose the second place to gain the first? Does it mean I accept myself as the effect and God as First cause? How do I practice this in my life?" In the culture I grew up in, it was an unspoken rule to be first. To be right. It is in my DNA.

So, the idea of stepping back, not knowing the answer, not being first with my opinion, felt like betrayal to my people. Luckily, by the time I found this lesson, I'd forgiven "my people." But the desire to be the first to respond was bred into me. Surrender only came through practice.

At the time, I was doing counseling for a living, so my perspective seemed pretty important. I'd think I was integrating the lesson idea during my morning practice and then I'd notice myself jumping in with my specialness all over the place.

But I guess you could say the lesson was working on me. It was taking the scenic route through all the ways I was still inserting "me," where I could have had the Divine. Where I could have been in the flow of creation, I was only getting mine. Thank you very much.

It was during a staff meeting that I finally saw the light. There was a discussion happening about a patient that I case managed. She'd come in to get her meds stabilized so I didn't have a lot of influence as far as prescribing treatment. I felt uneasy.

My mind starts telling me she's appropriate for a group I facilitate. But before jumping in, my lesson drops into my mind. *"I take the second place to gain the first."* Bingo. I can see the flow of creation happening, and my desire to resist it—to jump in and highjack the conversation in a direction I feel comfortable with. Instead, I ease back into the pulse of God, flowing with, instead of trying to direct the flow.

As I sit back listening to the psychiatrist and social worker talk about her diagnosis and meds, I'm at peace. I feel gifted by their exchange. I see I'm still part of, through my presence. The difference is tactile. I see the patient and the entire team in a new light. It turns out this patient isn't appropriate for my group after all. How often have I missed the gifts right before me, by inserting "me"?

The lesson says, *"To join with His is but to find our own. And since our will is His, it is to Him that we must go to recognize our will."*

To know our true will, we need help from a mind that is not tethered to the dream. We need a completely new point of reference, outside of time and space. We need a perspective that, being from truth, is nearer to our hearts.

We have to let go of the idea that we know what the situation needs—that something within our frame of reference of this world is going to give us the answer that serves love. We let go of any idea that we find can answer with the same perspective that sees a problem. We choose the second place to gain the first.

DAY 329

(Lesson 329)

"I have already chosen what You will."

(W-pII.329.1)

"Father, I thought I wandered from Your Will, defied it, broke its laws, and interposed a second will more powerful than Yours. Yet what I am in truth is but Your Will, extended and extending. This am I, and this will never change. As You are One, so am I one with You. And this I chose in my creation, where my will became forever one with Yours. That choice was made for all eternity. It cannot change, and be in opposition to itself. Father, my will is Yours. And I am safe, untroubled and serene, in endless joy, because it is Your Will that it be so."

(W-pII.329.1.1–6)

We've all had those experiences where, in the midst of a conflict, we realize, "Wait a minute. This is not what I really want. This is not my real will." We feel like a puppet on a string to our ego conditioning. But deep within a light flashes, reminding us, "This is not my will."

I was at that skate park with Parker one day when this realization hit me, and I actually listened. I realized it had happened many times before, but I was too busy making my point—too busy being right—to be happy. But this day, I had the fortune of today's lesson on speed-dial in my awareness as my practice for the day.

Parker's skating and a couple of older kids keep cutting in front of him. Parker's having a blast. He's totally present. His great big smile and carefree attitude aren't affected at all by these kids. But I'm afraid they'll crash and he'll get hurt. I start getting pissed. I start planning my intervention.

But I feel love's nudge and a tiny light of awareness speaks, "This is not my will." I stop, and state my lesson, *"I have already chosen what You will."* And in an instant, I forgive. My former perception dissolves into acceptance and trust. I see with new eyes as I look again at the skate park and all the skaters.

All I see is the joy and happiness of kids enjoying each other. The conflict is gone. My energy flows with these guys. I feel joyous, realizing happiness is my only will. God's will and mine are one in the same!

We are love, and ultimately love seeks only itself. Whatever bullshit we have interposed upon our mind to obscure our full remembrance of God and our identity in Him, goes up in smoke, when faced with the blazing light of Truth.

The temporary stint in insanity was already done, before pretending began. The false is not stable when looked at straight on with eyes of love. Insanity cannot hold up against the sanity of love. This is atonement.

The dream of wandering away from God, playing the prodigal son, is not our reality. Thinking we have usurped the power of God was the nightmare from which we are now awakening. We are the dreamer and not the dream. We have not been dreamed up by something outside ourselves in a scenario imprisoning us in time and space.

We have all the power of creation. We can, and have, used it to dream. Today we accept that only the truth could be true. And all power is given us to awaken. Now.

It takes but an instant to return our minds to true will—the will of love, of joy, and of happiness now.

DAY 330

(Lesson 330)

"I will not hurt myself again today."

(W-pII.330.1)

"Father, Your Son can not be hurt. And if we think we suffer, we but fail to know our one Identity we share with You. We would return to It today, to be made free forever from all our mistakes, and to be saved from what we thought we were."

(W-pII.330.2.1–3)

Today's lesson is the last of the lessons under the theme, *"What is Creation?"* What but forgiveness can restore us to the realization that we are creation? Anytime we think that we are less than God created us to be, we hurt ourselves. We have attacked our mind, and the results feels utterly real. In truth, hurt and attack are impossible because God's Son is forever invulnerable.

Today we return our minds to this state of invulnerability and remember our shared identity with our Creator. We're making a commitment to this union today. *"I will not hurt myself again today."* The mind-training has taught us to distinguish between the voice of the fear and the voice of love.

Fear is always talking to us as a body. It's the voice that tells us something is wrong and then starts planning ways to fix it. Love speaks from a recognition that we are love, already whole and perfect as we were created. It reminds us of our invulnerability as God's treasured child. Love reminds us that we are the light. We are spirit. Today we are simply declaring we're done listening to insanity.

You know those experiences when you just want a do-over? Something happens and we don't want to accept it. We keep thinking of what we could have done differently, as if somehow that would change anything. By the time it happens, it is already past.

This resistance to letting all things be exactly as they are is the way we hurt ourselves. Forgiveness lets us see that what happened was the best possible happening to bring our minds to surrender, where we remember we are not the happening. It is our perfect chance for changing our mind to see with love.

I love how life always gives us the fertile ground for planting the seed for the change of mind through practicing the lesson for the day.

The other day I caught myself in a train of thought, and I noticed I was attacking my state of peace and joy. I'd gone to a website to RSVP for an upcoming writer gathering. I'd made my plans for travel such that I would be able to attend. But, when I went to the site, it looked like the meeting had changed to another day. Immediately I resist.

I'm on the phone with Lin while doing this, and I'm telling her about it. Saying, if I'd known, I'd have left earlier for my trip. I see the insane script pulling at me, when Lin says, "Well, there is no chance the wrong thing is happening, right?" I burst out laughing. The release is immediate. I see how I'm hurting myself by resisting. Honestly, I don't care what happens. I am interested in being present with whatever shows up.

There is something magical about seeing insanity with a witness that holds the truth for us. It's so powerful. Holy relationships expedite sanity. Whoever is saner at the time becomes a more powerful magnetic force restoring us to joy. That's the simplicity of salvation. It just takes an instant to see the unreality of hurt and choose joy instead.

CHAPTER TWO HUNDRED SIXTY-EIGHT

DAY 331

(Lesson 331)

"There is no conflict, for my will is Yours."

(W-pII.331.1)

"How foolish, Father, to believe Your Son could cause himself to suffer! Could he make a plan for his damnation, and be left without a certain way to his release? You love me, Father. You could never leave me desolate, to die within a world of pain and cruelty. How could I think that Love has left Itself? There is no will except the Will of Love. Fear is a dream, and has no will that can conflict with Yours. Conflict is sleep, and peace awakening. Death is illusion; life, eternal truth. There is no opposition to Your Will. There is no conflict, for my will is Yours."

(W-pII.331.1.1–10)

Today we begin a new theme from which we consider the next ten lessons: *"What Is the Ego?"* A favorite definition of the ego comes from chapter 4 in the text. It says, *"The ego is nothing more than a part of your belief about yourself. Your other life has continued without interruption, and has been and always will be totally unaffected by your attempts to dissociate it"* (T.4.5.1).

I like this definition because it puts the ego in its proper place. It is just part of our belief—a bunch of false ideas we call ourselves. This is the belief we have been undoing through forgiveness and the application of the lesson ideas, to the life this belief dreamed up. We have come to a place where we have accepted that our will is the same as God's, which is pure love and perfect happiness. Now we're just cleaning the remains of sleep from our eyes.

We're noticing the ways we still allow ourselves to be tempted to hurt ourselves and realize this is not our real will. We forgive and feel the freedom that is our birthright. We are learning the power of presence. The practice today is to stay in the frequency of joy, recognizing only the will of love is real. We've got forgiveness at the ready if we start to doze off.

The course tells us that the ego's range is somewhere between suspicious and vicious. The closer we get to seeing it is a bullshit belief, and not anything to do with who we really are, it pulls out the big guns.

Case in point, breaking my back. I am not a body, right? At first I felt this experience with my back was in conflict with what I had come to recognize as my Self as love. Although my first impulse was to just trust and let go, I let fear creep in, which bound me to a problem.

So, naturally, I took the problem to the experts, further cementing my vulnerability. The feelings of guilt and unworthiness that came up surprised me. They seemed to conflict with my spiritual identity. But the thing is, if they are there, I put them there! A deep forgiveness—the body identity—was in order.

What I see now, is nothing, but something completely unexpected, and seemingly impossible, could have disarmed this core identity belief, and released me into the freedom, peace, and gratitude I live now. This is the gift of awakening to our will, one with God's. There is no conflict in love. Period.

DAY 332

(Lesson 332)

"Fear binds the world. Forgiveness sets it free."

(W-pII.332.1)

"We would not bind the world again today. Fear holds it prisoner. And yet Your Love has given us the means to set it free. Father, we would release it now. For as we offer freedom, it is given us. And we would not remain as prisoners, while You are holding freedom out to us."

(W-pII.332.2.1–6)

Fear is the crazy glue that keeps the idea of separation pieced together into a semblance of a whole world. The course tells us it isn't love we're seeking through the mind-training. Love is. We're seeking out the barriers we've placed in our mind, that block our awareness of love's presence. That's fear.

Without the belief in fear, the world we see disappears. In its place a new world appears. In the face of truth, fear is gone. That's what forgiveness does. Like the lesson says, *"Forgiveness bid this presence enter in, and take its rightful place within the mind."*

The choice to release fear is up to us. No one can do it for us. We put it there because we wanted it. Once we realize it is keeping us in chains, binding us to guilt and attack, we realize we don't want it. We want the truth to replace the error of fear in our minds.

It is through our willingness to change our mind that we employ forgiveness to see past the error and into the heart of love. Now we see fear arise, and rather than let it take us down the road to doom, we notice our peace has been disturbed and invite the Holy Spirit to reinterpret through love.

Like the other day on the freeway, a semitruck starts changing lanes right on top of my little car. I'm surrounded by cars and it seems like there was nothing I can do to not be part of a crash. Fear seems immediate.

But, just as immediate, love's answer steps in. My mind stills to my heart center, beyond body-identity, and takes the wheel. I keep driving, accepting whatever happens, trusting my invulnerability. And, no shit, it's like the parting of the Red Sea, a path seems to spontaneously clear before me. By forgiving my fear response, I'm able to see the synchronicity around me rather than confusion.

We have moments like this every day, a thousand times a day. Now we are learning to look past the fearful fantasy the ego mind projects and trust the synchronicity of union through love. We are, after all, the relationship we are choosing to have with whatever shows up in our lives. Is it going to be a relationship of fear or the joyous one of love? Are we going to bind ourselves to fear? Or release ourselves through forgiveness?

In contrast, years ago, I recall another time driving on the freeway, when a car started moving over into my lane. I was terrified. I started honking and waving my hands before I even looked to see if I could avoid a collision.

Only by survival instinct, I swerved off onto the shoulder. The guy in the other car passes, yelling obscenities and waving a bird finger at me. It totally wrecked my day. Everywhere I went I told the story of my victimhood, which kept me bound by fear, and that tethered me to a victim reality for months to come.

One day while sitting with a friend and recanting the story, I realized I was still hurting myself with this fantasy. In that realization, I finally forgave. Actually, this is the first time I have recalled this event since. Fear bound me. Forgiveness set me free. Free to be in a different world when a similar event occurs.

DAY 333
(Lesson 333)

"Forgiveness ends the dream of conflict here."

(W-pII.333.1)

"Father, forgiveness is the light You chose to shine away all conflict and all doubt, and light the way for our return to You. No light but this can end our evil dream. No light but this can save the world. For this alone will never fail in anything, being Your gift to Your beloved Son."

(W-pII.3332.1–5)

We are coming close to completing our yearlong curriculum. We're revisiting ideas from the first lessons, but from a new state of mind, where we are now. We're realizing that forgiveness is the only way to end the conflict brought on by our fear-based thought system.

We can't just add true ideas, like affirmations, try as we might. The only way is to turn around, and, with the Holy Spirit, face what we were afraid to look at, see it's just a faulty perception, and let it go.

We realize we can't ignore what we have come to believe. We have to look at it square on. The crazy thing is that once we do, we easily see that they are just perceptions. And perceptions can be changed. That's forgiveness. Forgiveness is the light from our true Self, which shines away the conflict and doubt, and lights the way for our return to love.

Today we reinforce our will to not stop short of our goal. We have learned that when we look, we see that our fears are a boogieman. But that boogieman haunts us, until we turn around and stare it down.

As I began the mind-training, I realized I was afraid of myself. Something seemingly dark lurked beneath the surface and I needed to stay ahead of it. As I started pulling the covers back on what I believed about myself, what I noticed was how erroneous these beliefs were, how when faced, they weren't what I thought.

It was the anticipation of fear that kept me from looking. I started watching my mind very closely and realized that there was a program based in fear that ran continuously in my mind. I felt this indeterminate defense going on all the time, just beneath the surface. Something would happen and the program would start up and I'd feel guilty, then start worrying, and so on.

The funny thing was, as I caught my mind in the act, something shifted in my feelings about it, and it lost its weight, and the next time I saw it come up, it didn't feel that real. That's the whole deal—and the kingdom of happiness is ours!

This kind of experience happens again and again as we look at the conflicts in our life and forgive. We learn to trust the transformation back to love, and the feeling of defensiveness is gone. Now when we feel a contraction in the flow of happiness, we know we've dozed off. We get still, look at what has entered our mind causing the conflict, forgive, and remember love is what we are. Happiness is already ours.

DAY 334

(Lesson 334)

"Today I claim the gifts forgiveness gives."

(W-pII.334.1)

"I seek but the eternal. For Your Son can be content with nothing less than this. What, then, can be his solace but what You are offering to his bewildered mind and frightened heart, to give him certainty and bring him peace? Today I would behold my brother sinless. This Your Will for me, for so will I behold my sinlessness."

(W-pII.334.2.1–5)

Today we claim the gifts forgiveness gives. No one can do this for us, and it doesn't happen on its own. We claim them. We're not waiting around for something to happen. We've seen the freedom and joy forgiveness brings, and today, we claim this state as all we want.

We have to decide we're done with letting ego insert itself. We're deciding for the eternal. We are deciding to be in present love. In claiming the gifts forgiveness brings, we're not claiming them as something we personally own, or a way to increase our specialness. That's separation.

When we claim the gifts forgiveness brings, it is a gift to the whole. We claim in order to reclaim our Self. What we are claiming ultimately is our true identity as God created us. We're leaving the ego behind. Why wait? Claiming the gifts forgiveness gives is merely to claim our inheritance as God's holy kid.

Today's lesson speaks from the urgency many of us feel at this stage of the curriculum. We're not willing to put up with interference to our happy state of being. When we feel constricted, we instruct our minds look, forgive, and shift to gratitude, and let love fill our hearts.

We're saying we want only the real. We seek but the eternal. The eternal is found instantly in being present, as the love that we are. We're not going to accept gifts of false perception anymore. We are interested only in the treasures God has laid before us as we claim our true identity.

Yesterday I came to Utah to visit family and, after driving all day, I notice the pull of mind to going to a story about being tired and tempting me away from the excited bliss I really feel. I love how clear it is now. The difference between temptation to doze off, and actually dreaming myself a character in the dream of fear or tiredness.

The happy expression of my Self with my other Selfs is the only experience I really want. When I feel that false pull, I stop it in its tracks. I know better. Like the badass, goddess of a woman Trinity in the Matrix says, "I've been down that road and I know where it leads." I'm not interested in ignorance anymore. Tired is false. The ego is the only weariness. Self is alive awareness.

So, I take the red pill and recalled the truth. "I am the happy outcome I want." My happiness infects everyone around me, and their joy infects me.

Today, we claim the gifts forgiveness gives; the treasures our Father has laid before us. There is nothing standing in our way but our unwillingness to completely release our personal story of guilt.

We have come far in our curriculum and we are no longer insane. We have put illusion to the test of perfect peace through application of our lessons, and seen how malleable its images are.

We have seen just how unstable the foundation of a world of pain and fear is. It has nothing solid to anchor to, for it is illusion. We've become willing to bring everything to the alchemy touchstone. Forgiveness, and the entire world, transforms to one of love and present happiness.

DAY 335

(Lesson 335)

"I choose to see my brother's sinlessness."

(W-pII.335.1)

"What could restore Your memory to me, except to see my brother's sinlessness? His holiness reminds me that he was created one with me, and like myself. In him I find my Self, and in Your Son I find the memory of You as well."

(W-pII.335.2.1–3)

Today's lesson reminds us that the way to know our Self, is by seeing everyone sinless. Period. This is the way we realize our own innocence. We only see what we wish to see reflected in each other. And, what we see shows us what we believe we are. That's why it is so crucial to choose what we want to see.

If we still value specialness, we can't see the innocence in our brother. We need a comparison. It's the stories of the past that give us the material for judgment. Choosing to see each other sinless lets us be present and see what is now. Love rushes into the present. Forgiveness is the choice to see only sinlessness. When we do, we feel the effects of that choice, in the way we see ourselves as well, holding us both in the light

We want to see our brother's sinlessness, because we realize that what we choose to see in them, sets the limits on how we see ourselves. We realize our oneness, and we know we cannot hold one brother out of forgiveness's light and be awake to who we are in truth. We cannot wish unhappiness on another and live in the state joy and happiness which is our birthright. Our desire for the truth and only the truth has been activated. And nothing else will satisfy.

I had a date with my hairdresser yesterday. As I'm driving there, I have today's lesson in my mind. I stop to get gas, and the woman in the car next to mine at the gas pump starts yelling at the attendant over the intercom about her card not going through.

I feel that twinge to judge, but softened my mind with today's idea, *"I choose to see my sister's sinlessness."* Compassion flows and I see it's fear motivating her attack and forgive her, seeing how truly innocent she is. I know the trap of fear and choose her release.

I'm smiling, holding her in my heart, as I gas up my car, and I feel a tap on my shoulder. It's the woman. She asks, "Do we know each other? I saw you looking at me and it felt like you knew me." I stop and look into her eyes, seeing her innocence, and say, "I don't think we've met before."

She says, "Are you sure?" I say, "Nope, but how great is this? We stop to get gas and meet a new friend." She proceeds to share a story about how frustrating her day has been thus far, like everything just seemed to be working against her. I tell her she can try what I do, choosing unconditional happiness up front each day, and how it changed the way I see situations that arise.

Like, I say, "When I noticed your frustration at the pump, I sent peace and happiness your way." She shrugs and smiles a knowing smile. "I guess that's why I was feeling we knew each other." We hug and go on our way. Every encounter is a chance for a holy encounter when sinlessness is what we want to see.

DAY 336

(Lesson 336)

"Forgiveness lets me know that all minds are joined."

(W-pII.336.1)

"In quiet may forgiveness wipe away my dreams of separation and of sin. Then let me, Father, look within, and find Your promise of my sinlessness is kept; Your Word remains unchanged within my mind, Your Love is still abiding in my heart."

(W-pII.336.2.1–2)

The world we made is one of distorted perceptions where separate, individual, and guilty persons come to compete in the game of survival of the fittest, where everyone eventually loses to death. Yuck. These perceptions stem from purpose held in the mind. The purpose of separation is what made the world of fear, problems, loss, and pain.

But we are learning that these perceptions can easily change, because they are not actually real. When we change the purpose to atonement, the effects of separation begin to disappear.

We're looking for union through the love we share as one. Seeing you sinless lets me realize that the sins I held against myself are but misperceptions based in a false identity and are easily released. Because of the peace and joy I feel in seeing your holiness and innocence, I realize this peace is mine. This joy and abundant love coming from, and through me are what I am. The experience is real, it is whole, and I naturally feel connected to you. Once we get a taste of it, nothing else compares.

Here's an example. Recently, I ran into an old frenemy. We were bitch buddies back in our early twenties, and that was our common bond. We had a falling out over a "who's right" situation that never got resolved. What struck me, seeing her after all these years, is that she had merely reflected my insecurities and shame back to me, and I attacked her for it.

We spotted each other across the room at a coffee shop we both use to frequent. I hadn't been there in years either. No surprise here. Like returning to the scene of the crime. Yet with a new purpose, I was seeing her through the eyes of forgiveness.

As our eyes meet, she quickly looks away. As for me, I'm keenly aware of a forgiveness opportunity. Immediately I forgive the past and feel joyed to see her. Like it was choreographed, as I actively forgive, she lifts her head, and looks at me.

It seems the same shift is happening in her as well. As I walk toward her, I want only a sinless mind. I see her inner light and my heart fills with love and compassion for the shadow girls we were before. She moves in my direction, a smile spreading across her face, matching my own. We greet with a long honest hug. Looking into each other's eyes, we both start talking at once, saying, "I've missed you."

Forgiveness lets me know that minds are joined. When we give everything to forgiveness, we see how without judgment our oneness is obvious. Everything effects the whole. We experience love rising within us, and there is nowhere it ends and another love begins.

Love is all-inclusive. The other that was once outside our self is brought into our heart as the reflection of our innocence. And we see it in her eyes. Joy is sure to follow.

DAY 337

(Lesson 337)

"My sinlessness protects me from all harm."

(W-pII.337.1)

"You Who created me in sinlessness are not mistaken about what I am. I was mistaken when I thought I sinned, but I accept Atonement for myself. Father, my dream is ended now. Amen."

(W-pII.337.2.1–3)

When our minds are still, the story of me let's go, and we're in a state of everlasting love. It's the most incredible awareness to realize that if we don't interfere, happiness just is. If we're not bothering ourselves with the fear program, we experience peace and happiness.

The more we forgive, the less the ego's lies have any hold on our mind. The more we're having an experience of Self, the more we feel free from suffering and loss. Happiness is right here, the instant we do nothing to get it.

Today's lesson is telling us there is only one thing that we *must* do. We *"must accept atonement for [ourselves], and nothing more."* We were mistaken about what we thought we were. But now that dream comes to an end. Isn't that amazing? Joy is our vocation! The means for its accomplishment is accepting atonement for ourselves. Nothing else. Our sinlessness protects us when the ego starts dancing.

It's incredible the resistance the ego throws up, though, isn't it? It'll pull out all the tricks of its trade to keep us from quietude, where the truth is already present. Atonement is that call we have felt deep within our whole lives that beckons us toward happiness.

Unhappiness is merely denial of the truth. Happiness is our true state of being. Unhappiness comes when we block the awareness of love's presence. That's why forgiveness is central in our mind-training. Forgiveness is the transition from fear to love. This is atonement.

When I decided on the path of unconditional, present happiness as my chosen spiritual path, and I came to today's lesson, I saw how simple the path could really be. While working at a neuropsychiatric hospital, I practiced in earnest. All around me were mental problems.

Each day seemed fraught with a pervasive feeling of fear, of un-safety, of the possibility of being harmed. As I began to see that the insanity was in my mind, I practice with this lesson a lot, *"[Our] sinlessness protects [us] from all harm."* It served as an instant flip-switch to forgive, anytime I noticed my happy matrix glitch.

I witnessed the release reflected everywhere I looked. In patients and staff, and mostly in my ability to see with love, sinlessness, and compassion, which healed the images of fear and unsafety from my mind.

Every encounter is a chance to see our innate sinlessness. To forgive our mistaken ideas and be happy, awake, and present.

CHAPTER TWO HUNDRED SEVENTY-FIVE

DAY 338

(Lesson 338)

"I am affected only by my thoughts."

(W-pII.338.1)

"Your plan is sure, my Father—only Yours. All other plans will fail. And I will have thoughts that will frighten me, until I learn that You have given me the only Thought that leads me to salvation. Mine alone will fail, and lead me nowhere. But the Thought You gave me promises to lead me home, because it holds Your promise to Your Son."

(W-pII.338.2.1–5)

This is the single idea that changed my life completely. It is why I am happy no matter what! Because it is 100 percent up to me! I love to feel yummy, inspired, at peace with everyone and all that happens. It is bliss to be the face of happiness and light.

Today's idea, accepted wholeheartedly, is the reason we can be supremely happy and spreading that joy every moment of every day. It is an uncompromising choice for love; to allow life to move through us and from our true Self as God created us. Because we are affected only by our thoughts. And we can always think of God.

Today's lesson idea, truly taken to heart, proves itself out. We are affected 100 percent only by our own thoughts. The amazing thing I have found is that with practice, when I let go of fear-based thoughts, love thoughts are immediately present in my mind.

Something occurs, and the ego, which always speaks first and loudest, jumps in with fix-it-or-else ideas. But now I see the temptation to go there and choose love instead. By accepting what occurs exactly as it is, love and joy begin to stabilize as predominate.

Here's an example from just yesterday. The family gathered together at Lucas and Sarah's place for a fun barbecue, visiting and playing games. Totally yummy! On the way back to our hotel, the check engine light comes on and there's no gas acceleration.

Immediately my ego jumps in, tempting me to close my heart. "Hey, listen to me! You've got a car problem! Get worried!" The thing is, I know when I feel that contraction in my joy, and I remember, *"I am affected only by my thoughts."* When I notice a fearful thought has entered my mind, I know, I am the solution. The situation is never a cause. Only my thoughts. So, I accept the situation with love and enthusiasm. "Awesome. This is exactly what I wanted." And I know it's true.

I look at the thought of resistance and see where I'd set up the glitch. I'd told Cole he could use my car for work while his was in the shop, and I felt responsible to him. I forgive in a breath and happily call Cole. He, of course, says, "Hey, there's no chance the wrong thing happened. It goes how it goes. We'll deal with it." In accepting the situation exactly as it was and trusting God's plan, I get that tingly feeling that a miracle is in the works.

Back to the hotel I check online and find a forum for Scion IQ and several people had said that it was just that the gas cap wasn't on tight. I'm laughing out loud by now—how simple—how grateful. I re-screw the gas cap, get in the car and it runs perfectly, with full acceleration.

I call Cole and say, "You know how everything goes my way, and miracles happen constantly? Well . . ." He interrupts, "The car's back to normal, right?" Right. Miracles are the natural expression of thinking with love.

DAY 339

(Lesson 339)

"I will receive whatever I request."

(W-pII.339.1)

"Father, this is Your day. It is a day in which I would do nothing by myself, but hear Your Voice in everything I do; requesting only what You offer me, accepting only Thoughts You share with me."

(W-pII.339.2.1–2)

The prayer from today's lesson is a guide for how we want all our days to be. We always get what we request. It's just so often we're unconscious to what we are asking. Resistance to loving what is, is asking for experiences we resist. Reacting with judgment to a brother is asking to feel judged.

If we look around and see what we've been receiving in our lives, we see what we've been asking for. We are 100 percent responsible for what shows up in our lives. We can deceive ourselves, but the facts prove out. We only need to look around us and check how we feel. If we're not happy and excited, we've asked for pain.

The groovy part is that the second we take responsibility for it, we can see that we've received what we were asking for and make another choice. I like to say, "Awesome. This is exactly what I wanted." It's like a fast-track, catch-n-release, forgiveness reboot.

Usually an image or train of previously unconscious thoughts become present in my mind. Some fearful worry I didn't catch and release, or a judgment I still felt justified in keeping which is now playing out in my life. I pull the thread and let it unravel, as I forgive and choose again. It's fun. Or like I like to say, "It's the only game in town."

The tricky part is that often we're confused about what we want. We want pleasure and we get pain. We've all had this experience. We actually feel threatened by too much happiness. Check it for yourself. This sneakily little idea creeps in like we're waiting for the other shoe to drop. Right? We've all thought it. "This is too good to last." And boom! The road to its destruction has entered our mind. We receive what we ask.

I experienced this not long ago. I wanted a day of rest. So, that was my request to life. Then I, by myself, decided how that should look. I thought I needed some alone time. I wanted to be in my own little world with God and spend a day in solitude. (Self-initiated plan.)

My phone keeps ringing. I'd answer the phone, but then I'd feel irritated and I'd make like I was okay with it and join in the conversation. But afterward I'd feel like something was being taken away from me. After the second call, I stopped myself. "Wait a minute. This is awesome. It's exactly what I wanted." With joy I realize that it was rest from my own thinking that I really wanted before I dubbed "my plan" over it, thinking I needed "alone time." It's actually in joining, where I find rest.

Now I'm laughing. This is awesome. I am never alone. God is always with me. Rest cannot be found in withdrawal, only union. Here is rest. Everyone and everything is an extension of my mind. There's no escape. I whisper the prayer from today's lesson, steeped in the stillness and rest only God's will can bring.

Today's prayer bypasses confusion. It's like an instruction manual:

1. Devote the day to God.
2. Decide to do nothing by yourself.
3. Listen for the Voice for God.
4. Follow His direction in everything.
5. Request only what God offers.
6. Accept only the thoughts God shares with us.

DAY 340

(Lesson 340)

"I can be free of suffering today."

(W-pII.340.1)

"Father, I thank You for today, and for the freedom I am certain it will bring. This day is holy, for today Your Son will be redeemed. His suffering is done. For he will hear Your Voice directing him to find Christ's vision through forgiveness, and be free forever from all suffering. Thanks for today, my Father. I was born into this world but to achieve this day, and what it holds in joy and freedom for Your holy Son and for the world he made, which is released along with him today."

(W-ppI.340.1.1–6)

Aren't these latter lessons so beautiful and comforting? We are ready to receive the joyous freedom they bring. We have opened through our willingness to gladly hold the joy and gratitude all our forgiveness brings. This day is holy. Our suffering is over.

We have one voice which shows us through Christ's vision, the true way before us. This is what we were born for. This day. To be free from suffering forever. It has already been accomplished by God. So, it's really already ours. Accepting and receiving is the choice we make. Today's the day. We lay down our arms and trust fall into God's.

It's perfect too that today's lesson comes on our last day with the theme, *What Is the Ego?* Like we're done with it. Period. We're done with suffering. We're ready for perfect happiness. It is our natural state of being when fear is gone. No one can give it to us, nor take it away. It is ours. *[We] can be free of suffering today.*

We've already seen how if we're still suffering somewhere in our lives, we ask for it, and received as we have asked. It is crucial that we take full responsibility. So, like if I'm in pain. "Awesome. This is exactly what I wanted." You say something mean to me. "Awesome. This is exactly what I wanted." It shows me what's in my mind that is in conflict with what I am in truth, which is pure love and joy. I take full responsibility for all the effects of my thoughts and let the truth of who I am shine through.

I'm watching the sunrise, sitting on my yoga trapeze in my backyard, in the stillness of love. It's one of those perfect moments where I feel one with the universe. I feel my Self as creator. Like nothing could intrude upon my still mind at one with creation, right?

A bee starts buzzing around. At first, I watch it move from one plant to the next, but as it gets closer, I swallow, and my heart speeds up. I try to relax and just let what will be, be. I remind myself of my invulnerability as a child of God. The bee lands on my shoulder. Shit! Where's that equanimity I had a minute ago?

Wow. I'm suddenly so small, and the fear of a little bee, so big. Turning my mind inward, I see how the whole body-fear-identity buzzes around in my psyche, looking for a place to land. And gratefully I give it one—the heart of forgiveness.

I remind myself, *"I can be free from suffering today,"* and breathe deeply the peace it brings. A smile rises from this inner altar, spreading wide on my face—joy bubbling up until I'm laughing. Laughing is full-body forgiveness, releasing everything that went before this holy moment. It also tips me out of the trapeze and onto the ground, where I sit a minute and watch the bee fly off to a nearby flower.

It seems like a little thing. But often, it's the little things that can show us the whole of creation, the joy in surrender and everlasting peace, free of suffering, now.

DAY 341

(Lesson 341)

*"I can attack but my own sinlessness,
and it is only that which keeps me safe."*

(W-pII.341.1)

"Father, Your Son is holy. I am he on whom You smile in love and tenderness so dear and deep and still the universe smiles back on You, and shares Your Holiness. How pure, how safe, how holy, then, are we, abiding in Your Smile, with all Your Love bestowed upon us, living one with You, in brotherhood and Fatherhood complete; in sinlessness so perfect that the Lord of Sinlessness conceives us as His Son, a universe of Thought completing Him."

(W-pII.341.1.1–3)

We begin a new theme today, by which we consider today's lesson and the next nine. It is *"What Is a Miracle?"* It says, *"A miracle is a correction. It does not create, nor really change at all. It merely looks on devastation, and reminds the mind that what it sees is false"* (W-pII.13.1). Each forgiveness brings a miracle to take the place of the error in our mind. Each contains the gift of grace. Forgiveness is the portal to recognizing the hand of grace in our lives.

Every attack thought is an attack on our own sinlessness. Liberating, yes? No one else can touch my sinlessness. I am the gatekeeper. On one level, it's easy to see that if I have judgments against anyone, I am seeing sin and believing it is real. But, what about the subtle ways we attack our sinlessness? Each resistance to seeing with love is an attack on our sinlessness. Each time we turn away because we think something to horrific, too mean, too pathetic, we're attacking our sinlessness and all creation.

Last night, Lin and I share a lengthy conversation about "the new feminism." Ultimately, we're discussing leaving no one out of sinlessness.

Lin's passion for equality, her unique view and vigilant willingness to look deeply at the hurt, anger, and despair in the world, then her own belief system, is always enlightening and humbling for me. We discuss the subtle, and not so subtle, ways we actually reinforce our sinfulness by excluding anyone from our purview.

We use different terms, but for me, I see today's lesson written all over in our conversation. A homeless man is asking for help—do I give him the dignity of looking in his eyes and seeing his holiness, or do I contract and turn away? Someone is bulling another, do I see both, equally innocent, both under the spell of fear and confusion? Or do I judge one and feel sorry for the other. Both responses make sin real in my mind. Both equally attack our sinlessness.

Lin's an activist. She is passionate about supporting true equality in every aspect of human living, for all. It's her spiritual path. She's alive with light and the spirit of sinlessness as she shares all that she is learning and how she's challenging her long-held beliefs; seeing the subtle ways she has benefited from white privilege, due to ignorance.

I look at myself as she shares, and see myself in her, and see my own complicity. I forgive and join. I'm humbled and blessed by how she is forgiving, by not looking away, but immersing herself in the thick of it through communication and love. I'm inspired by her uncompromising willingness to completely invest herself.

Lin uses the word "intersectional," which means the point or common line where everything is the same. This is sinlessness. I choose to have the willingness to see the intersection where you and I meet in truth—our sinless identity, as God created us. Anything else is an attack on my sinlessness.

CHAPTER TWO HUNDRED SEVENTY-NINE

DAY 342

(Lesson 342)

"I let forgiveness rest upon all things,
for thus forgiveness will be given me."

(W-pII.342.1)

"I thank You, Father, for Your plan to save me from the hell I made. It is not real. And You have given me the means to prove its unreality to me. The key is in my hand, and I have reached the door beyond which lies the end of dreams. I stand before the gate of Heaven, wondering if I should enter in and be at home. Let me not wait again today. Let me forgive all things, and let creation be as You would have it be and as it is. Let me remember that I am Your Son, and opening the door at last, forget illusions in the blazing light of truth, as memory of You returns to me."

(W-pII.342.1.1–8)

I *let forgiveness rest upon all things"* means that we wholeheartedly accept it all. Every happening and each brother, completely. We let the past be gone, fear be gone, for love is all there is—we are the love which lets illusion pass. *"For thus forgiveness will given me."*

I love the imagery in today's lesson and how the prayer starts with gratitude. Thank You, God, that we have been given everything already, that the answer is already present with each seeming problem. We have this key in our hand, given us by God, that lets us leave the world of fear behind through forgiveness, which unlocks the door where we escape to reality at last.

It's like we've got forgiveness's key in one hand and unforgiveness in the other hand. We're standing there at the gates of heaven, the flames of hell nipping at our feet, and we're balancing these two opposing things in our hands. "Okay, do I want to finally release my hostages, and go home to heaven, to love, my Self? Or do I want to keep them prisoner and keep myself imprisoned as jailer with them? God or death? Back and forth. Right?"

It's what we do each time we come to a place where we have a choice to condemn or forgive. God's world is innocent. Today we forgive whatever still tethers us to illusions and turn the key to full release and supreme happiness. The choice is ours to open the door and enter in. Are we willing? Will we forgive it all so we can forgive ourselves?

Lin and I watched a documentary called *13th* about mass incarceration, racism, the history of white supremacy, slavery, and the progression that brought about the state of the prison industrial complex that exists today.

I can't think of a better depiction of hell. It is the epitome of the ego dream upon the world. Every being is imprisoned by the thought system that enabled condemnation of one being, and privilege of another. In my case, I see I'm imprisoned because of my desire to look away from what I am complicit in making—by my ignorance, I have been a silent participant.

When Lin invited me to watch with her, I knew I was being given a miracle. I could feel my heart and mind aligning in forgiveness's light before I even knew what I was about to see. Like I was standing at the gate, the forgiveness key in hand, reviewing what I had still not forgiven.

I decide to turn the key, and bid all my brothers take my hand and enter with me as I watch, forgiving each grip in my heart, as the clips of horrors appear on the screen, accepting my complicity, and letting holiness wash over the mind that made the images become real. I let fear come up, and faced it down with love, *Brother, forgive me now. I come to you to take you home with me."*

CHAPTER TWO HUNDRED EIGHTY

DAY 343

(Lesson 343)

*"I am not asked to make a sacrifice, to find
the mercy and the peace of God."*

(W-pII.343.1)

"The end of suffering can not be loss. The gift of everything can be but gain. You only give. You never take away. And You created me to be like You, so sacrifice becomes impossible for me as well as You. I, too, must give. And so all things are given unto me forever and forever. As I was created I remain. Your Son can make no sacrifice, for he must be complete, having the function of completing You. I am complete because I am Your Son. I cannot lose, for I can only give, and everything is mine eternally."

(W-pII.343.1.1–11)

Today's lesson is about living from grace. Mercy and the peace of God are already ours. We're not asked to make a sacrifice because what we let go of is not real. It was the virus implanted by ego in the software of creation imposing a false will. I pressed the "I accept" button. I could have laughed, like I do now, when I see it spamming my inbox, and press delete. That's forgiveness. Nothing can intrude upon my holy love mind, unless I want it. I don't.

The lesson says, *"Salvation has no cost. It is a gift that must be freely given and received."* When we value things of this world, believing we need them for our happiness, the very valuing of them makes salvation feel like a sacrifice.

Here is an example I saw play out in my work as a minister years ago, which I was reminded of last night in a holy encounter at dinner with my nephew and his fiancée. They have gifted me the opportunity of officiating their wedding this fall, and I am gifting them right back. Grace.

When I first started officiating weddings, I was living in Vegas, where weddings are big business. My first opportunities to officiate came from a minister at Excalibur Hotel and Casino. I felt blessed and honored that he would extend his trust to me. It was a mutually beneficial arrangement where both of us received equal financial compensation.

That relationship informed another with a local ranch, because I knew how to ride and couples wanted to be married on horseback. I felt the grace of miracles and I was in the flow of giving and receiving. Each wedding was a blessing. I felt my heart open wide, and spirit flowed through me joining with the union of each couple.

However, I still believed in scarcity and the idea of earning and sacrifice. So, as time went on, the gift of mutual giving and receiving miracles started to fade. Friends encouraged me to charge more for my services, to lend more credibility to my value as a minister. I did. I lost sight of true value, and didn't see I was defending the very thing I thought I wanted to lose—scarcity.

I love how relentlessly God's mercy brings my life to a state of readiness. Invitations to officiate all but dried up. Duh. Mired in shame and unworthiness, I finally see my faulty premise. Being a minister is a gift of grace of which I am steward. I feel the tightness constricting my heart let go.

My heart opens and I feel the abundance of love—*"I am not asked to make a sacrifice to find the mercy and the peace of God."* The grace of mercy, total forgiveness and the peace of God wash over me.

Now, in the grace of God's mercy and peace, I gratefully gift my services as officiate whenever the chance arises. I get all the gifts!

DAY 344

(Lesson 344)

*"Today I learn the law of love; that what I
give my brother is my gift to me."*

(W-pll.344.1)

*"This is Your law, my Father, not my own. I have not understood what giving means, and thought
to save what I desired for myself alone. And as I looked upon the treasure that I thought I had,
I found an empty place where nothing ever was or is or will be. Who can share a dream?
And what can an illusion offer me? Yet he whom I forgive will give me gifts beyond the worth
of anything on earth. Let my forgiven brothers fill my store with Heaven's treasures, which
alone are real. Thus is the law of love fulfilled. And thus Your Son arises and returns to You."*

(W-pll.344.1.1–7)

Notice how the lessons now are mostly a prayer of gratitude and confirmation of our decision to follow in the way of redemption God appointed for us? Can't you just feel how close we are? The union of love we have found with each other, and with God? Yummy.

It's what today's lesson talks about. The law of love: that what I give you is my gift to me. We're really seeing that our brother is our Self. Now we are keenly aware when we withhold. Any time we want to keep something for ourselves, we lose touch with the love we are as one.

We feel the glitch. It doesn't feel yummy. It's like we're trading everything for that thing we don't want to share—which is nothing. Because sharing is life. Union is life. Union is living in the law of love. Everything is a relationship.

"Who can share a dream?" The ego dances alone in the end. That glitch—that's our business. It is the call for love. It is the flip-switch to forgive.

I've got this awesome little car. I loaned it to Cole to use for the week, not recalling I'd set a lunch date with my friend, Patricia. Patricia was my first consciously chosen holy relationship. Both course students, we chose in, in holiness.

It's been incredible. Often, in my morning time with the Divine, her presence is palpable. Union—it's divine. That was twenty something years ago. It's totally having lunch with Christ when we're together.

I love how everything operates with such synchronicity under the law of love. I'm thinking, "Wow, I'll call Patricia, and make different arrangements," and my phone rings. It's Cole: "Hey, do you need a ride anywhere before I take off for work?" Union, through the law of love, forms an ongoing communion behind the scenes, alerting us to each other.

By way of contrast, and using the car scenario, when Lin first started driving, I'd just bought a new-for-me car. I had reservations about letting her drive. I wanted to trust her, but I was afraid my car would get damaged and I wouldn't have it for myself.

Disregarding my conflicted mind, because I wanted to have faith in her, I let her drive. That's not the law of love. That's begging. The law of love is wholehearted. It is giving without reservation. Forgiving what I think I want and trusting love has a better plan for me to receive the storehouse of gifts it has to give.

Anyway, the first time Lin takes the car by herself, she runs over a boulder and basically totals the car. Now we both have guilt, and no car.

As she stands before me crying, keys in hand, telling the story of what happened—the tiny dog that ran into the road she swerved to miss—my heart melts. I see clearly that my so-called gift was empty. My heart was missing from it.

I'd withheld the only thing that mattered—wholehearted trust. Now, I have another chance to give, and to receive, and I forgive easily. Serial car adventures became a love symbol of my gift of trust from and in Lin. *"And thus is the law of love fulfilled."*

DAY 345

(Lesson 345)

"I offer only miracles today,
for I would have them be returned to me."

(W-pII.345.1)

"Father, a miracle reflects Your gifts to me, Your Son. And every one I give returns to me, reminding me the law of love is universal. Even here, it takes a form which can be recognized and seen to work. The miracles I give are given back in just the form I need to help me with the problems I perceive. Father, in Heaven it is different, for there, there are no needs. But here on earth, the miracle is closer to Your gifts than any other gift that I can give. Then let me give this gift alone today, which, born of true forgiveness, lights the way that I must travel to remember You."

(W-pII.345.1.1–7)

I was taught that miracles looked like the parting of the Red Sea, and turning water into wine, or raising the dead. This fear-based training caused me to be unconscious of the miracles available and even happening in my life.

That's like looking at a vast ocean and seeing only the couple amazing waves, admiring the surfer riding them out and discounting the ocean itself, surrounding me and making the waves possible.

I grew up learning that miracle working was a right of only the elite spiritual guys. Average Joe, and I, were not miracle worker material.

I couldn't have been more wrong. Turns out, miracle working is our profession as children of love. When I first started reading the principles of miracles at the beginning of the course, something clicked—the truth. I felt instantly included in the essence of what was being said. It was an experience of unity I couldn't deny.

We can absolutely offer only miracles, today and every day. Miracles are our ministry. As love, miracles are our holy exchange with life. Life is love. And joining brings miracles. No other identity fits!

Love is the ever-present divine thought in the mind. Noticing and letting it rip is a habit we develop, by forgiving any interference that arises. That's the light today's lesson talks about. We offer miracles continually by being what we are and awakening the sleeping world we see.

One day last week, I had an agenda to write all day. But life had other plans. I decided to make a green drink, and found I needed to go to the store. Offering miracles is the principle agenda, so, *my agenda* is flexible.

I take a quick trip to the grocery store and a woman backs up and barely bumps my car. It didn't leave a scratch. She jumps out of her car. I get out of mine. She's obviously gripped with fear and remorse, apologizing profusely for, "not paying attention—should have been looking where I was going—in a hurry to get . . .'"

I smile and bring her into an embrace, where her restlessness quiets and love joins our hearts. It takes just a few minutes to bless us both with a miracle. And we're off to share our miracle with the next guy.

This kind of "offering a miracle response" becomes our way of being in the world, once we have an experience of what today's lesson is saying. *I offer only miracles today, for I would have them returned to me.*

It is the simplicity of living in joy and trust, knowing that all that we give is returned in the most delightful of ways.

DAY 346

(Lesson 346)

"Today the peace of God envelops me,
and I forget all things except His Love."

(W-pII.346.1)

"Father, I wake today with miracles correcting my perception of all things. And so begins the day I share with You as I will share eternity, for time has stepped aside today. I do not seek the things of time, and so I will not look upon them. What I seek today transcends all laws of time and things perceived in time. I would forget all things except Your Love. I would abide in You, and know no laws except Your law of love. And I would find the peace which You created for Your Son, forgetting all the foolish toys I made as I behold Your glory and my own."

(W-pII.346.1.1–7)

Today's lesson is a model for how we want all our days to be. We begin the day in God's love, enveloped in His peace, with today's prayer on our hearts. It is a prayer of gratitude, walking our minds right into the eternal stillness and peace within, where we know we are loved, and we are love. *"Today the peace of God envelops me, and I forget all things except His Love."* This is the state from which we embark our day. *"And when the evening comes today, we will remember nothing but the peace of God."*

I love how this plays out in my daily life. Being a love center, filled with the joy and peace of God, creates a magnetic field that others respond to. We want to be close; we're drawn to the light. It is the call to recognize the eternal Self we share as one.

Cole just came and snuggled next to me as I write this, sitting on Lin's bed. The quiet is so deep and penetrating, extending forever, synchronizing our breathing, our hearts beating as one, it brings tears of joy to my eyes. A blessing of present love, enveloping us in this amazing peace of God.

We are always this center of God's love. We just get distracted by the shiny objects of the ego; like aspirations in the world of form, self-initiated plans, or problems to fix. When we go there, our energy literally sucks in around that focus. That's why lessons like today's, that remind us to practice our identity enveloped in God's peace, are so wonderful and practical. We make a habit of remembering our identity as love.

Case in point, just now. Cole asks if I'd like to go get breakfast. I shake my head no. I'm writing—got an agenda. Before the thought fully forms, I feel it tightening my energy field. I pause. I release. I love. Imagine, an invitation from Christ, "Come join me for breakfast," and refusing?

I look at Cole. Yep, an invitation from Christ Cole. I say, "I mean, yes! I'd love to go to breakfast with you." I let go of the things of time and receive this miracle of present happiness. What but joining in love could matter? What would I let be more important?

It's these little glitches that are so important for me to catch now. They are disturbances in my conscious contact with the peace of God in which I live. I recognize the disturbance, forgive, and I'm back home, enveloped in the peace of God. I forget all things except His love.

DAY 347

(Lesson 347)

"Anger must come from judgment. Judgment is the weapon I would use against myself, to keep the miracle away from me."

(W-pII.347.1)

"Father, I want what goes against my will, and do not want what is my will to have. Straighten my mind, my Father. It is sick. But You have offered freedom, and I choose to claim Your gift today. And so I give all judgment to the One You gave to me to judge for me. He sees what I behold, and yet He knows the truth. He looks on pain, and yet He understands it is not real, and in His understanding it is healed. He gives the miracles my dreams would hide from my awareness. Let Him judge today. I do not know my will, but He is sure it is Your Own. And He will speak for me, and call Your miracles to come to me."

(W-pII.347.1.1–10)

Listen today. Be very still, and hear the gentle Voice for God assuring you that He has judged you as the Son He loves." Today, we spend in stillness, and listen for the Voice for God. There is no reason to allow upset to linger anymore. We've given our minds to the Holy Spirit throughout the course of this year's curriculum, and sanity has returned.

If we're angry or upset at what seems to be happening, we are dealing with illusion. We are judging. And we are hurting ourselves. Judgment is the weapon we use against ourselves to keep us from realizing the miracle we are.

Even the slightest judgment simply doesn't feel okay anymore. We can no longer get the cheap satisfaction of being right, which use to reinforce and justify anger, right? We know we are only attacking our own mind. We pick up the key of forgiveness, open the door of love, and let the law of love guide us as to what to say or do instead.

Our part is to be still and listen. We listen heart to heart in divine love—and hear the gentle Voice of God—of love assuring us that we are a child of love. It's the only judgment that is legit.

Here's an example from a conversation I had with a colleague back in the day. She was angry about a new policy being enacted by the hospital. She thought it would limit our freedom. I spontaneously, say, "Being angry about it, only keeps us from seeing the ways it can benefit us."

She raises her voice. "No. Anger is the feeling that lets us know we are being violated." That sounded reasonable. I feel myself aligning with this idea. "Yeah, we should have a voice." I start feeling angry about the policy too.

As I'm walking away, I feel sick with judgment—that's my flip-switch. "Wait a minute. This is not who I am." Today's prayer comes like a peace-offering. *"Anger must come from judgment. Judgment is the weapon I use against myself to keep the miracle away from me."*

The scene with my colleague replays before me. It's like I see the miracle coming at me and I how deflected it with judgment. My colleague was clearly asking for a miracle. It only asks that I be still and listen.

Now I see her call for love and my own. I pray, "Straighten my mind, my father, I receive your gift of freedom and release. I claim it now for my sister and myself and allow truth to penetrate our minds and the situation at hand." I forgive the falsehood of judgment and let my mind quiet. I allow the stillness to speak.

The release feels incredible. "What if this new policy provides even more freedom, by defining new parameters from which to work with clients?" I hold this state of miracle-mindedness for all of us.

DAY 348

(Lesson 348)

"I have no cause for anger or for fear, for You surround me.
And in every need that I perceive, Your grace suffices me."

(W-pII.348.1)

"Father, let me remember You are here, and I am not alone. Surrounding me is everlasting
Love. I have no cause for anything except the perfect peace and joy I share with You.
What need have I for anger or for fear? Surrounding me is perfect safety. Can I be
afraid, when Your eternal promise goes with me? Surrounding me is perfect sinlessness.
What can I fear, when You created me in holiness as perfect as Your Own?"

(W-pII.348.1.1–7)

God's grace suffices. It amazes me. Everything is happening in the gentle flow of God's grace. Like just a minute ago. I'm thinking about this darling friend that works at the fitness center, and my heart is filled with love for her. My phone rings. Yes, it's her. She's calling to arrange a time to meet. I tell her I was just thinking of her. She says, "Me too! I need a yummy boost." "Me too," is like, "I see my Self in you!"

When we live in sync with God's grace, it's infectious. With no fear or anger interfering, love flows, and we see our love-self in each other. God's got this. His grace suffices. *"Every need that I perceive, Your grace suffices me."*

God's grace suffices us. Everything is perfect, and so is everything else. We are the center of God's love. What we need to fulfill the law of love gets beamed out and picked up by the other in need of a miracle and brought back to us in miracles.

It doesn't matter how seemingly insignificant the situation, our love is essential to its transformation from a possible problem, to a miracle. The only time when fear or anger seem reasonable is when we've forgotten who we are. We think we're alone. That's scary. It is the definition of the separation. There's no real cause.

God is Cause. Love is cause. It is the truth to remember. If we feel afraid or angry, it's signaling us—we've dozed off. Stillness is waking. As we pause into the stillness beneath the fray, the stillness penetrates us with God's love and peace, surrounding us and the situation at hand. We feel His grace, and everything is perfectly fine.

Here's example from the other day. I get lost driving in my car. I thought I knew where I was going. Apparently not. Google, my GPS guru, isn't giving me any answers. I pull to the side of the road and look around. Nothing looks familiar.

I'm out of the city. I'm tempted to be afraid or mad at myself for not paying close enough to attention, and at Google for abandoning me.

Instead, I presence myself with my surroundings, appreciating the beauty and quiet of this moment. Joy rises and fills me with the essence of miracles. I know I am safe, surrounded by God's ever-present love. I remember there is never any cause for anger or fear because love's GPS is guiding me. As I rest in this abundant peace a memory fills my mind.

Parker's driving while the boys and I explore our new surroundings last year. I remember that he'd taken a turn just back a little way that led directly back to the freeway. Ha! "Thanks God!" I turn my car around and drive with joy and gratitude, in the grace of God's GPS.

His grace suffices us for everything that He would have us do.

CHAPTER TWO HUNDRED EIGHTY-SIX

DAY 349

(Lesson 349)

"Today I let Christ's vision look upon all things for me and judge them not, but give each one a miracle of love instead."

(W-pII.349.1)

"So would I liberate all things I see, and give to them the freedom that I seek. For thus do I obey the law of love, and give what I would find and make my own. It will be given me, because I have chosen it as the gift I want to give. Father, Your gifts are mine. Each one that I accept gives me a miracle to give. And giving as I would receive, I learn Your healing miracles belong to me."

(W-pII.349.1.1–6)

Love and judgment cannot occupy the mind at the same time. It's one or the other, but never both. We're choosing love. Judgment is blindness. It transposes the past onto the present moment and makes it impossible to see present happiness.

We're done with that. We will with God. By choosing to let Christ's vision take charge of our sight, love flows easily, and we see where we can bring a miracle.

Remember that the law of love is: What I give my brother is my gift to me. Giving miracles is the way we realize that they are ours. Christ's vision sees wholeness, healing the separation, judgment brought into the mind. Thought and action are aligned in love. As we accept God's gifts, they become ours to give.

This is our ministry. God's grace is with us. We're seeing that it goes before us, making clear our path for bringing miracles.

Recently, I swung by the post office to mail a package. The line is nearly at the door when I walk in. I feel the temptation to judge, "I don't have time to wait in line." I love it, because it's like even the most seemingly "innocent" judgments are like a buzzing noise in my energy field, interfering with the flow of joy and love.

I notice and choose to let Christ's vision see the situation for me. I let love look around me, silently thanking each person for their holiness and blessing them. Excellent use of time.

In front of me is a guy in a suit, with a briefcase in one hand and a package in the other. He's tapping his foot and looking at his watch. A smile spreads across my face, and I see my chance to give a miracle. I strike up a conversation with him. He tells me that he works at a bank, but at heart, he is a poet.

The package he is holding is a selection of poems he is submitting to a magazine. He says, "I'm afraid I'm going to be late for work, but I've got to get this sent today because of a deadline."

I ask if he'd like to share one of his poems with me. His face lights up, "Are you sure?" I say, "Absolutely. There is nothing I'd like more right now. In fact, I think that's why we're standing in this line together."

With a big smile, and a hushed voice, which only makes his sharing seem all the more sacred, he begins reciting a beautiful poem. It's about watching his child sleep, and how the world and time disappear, and there's only this peaceful child opening his heart to beauty.

Tears spill as I thank him for sharing. "Look," I say, "you're next." The line had moved gracefully along while we attended to love. Neither of us were going to be late. God's grace suffices.

DAY 350

(Lesson 350)

"Miracles mirror God's eternal Love. To offer them is to remember Him, and through His memory to save the world."

(W-pII.350.1)

"What we forgive becomes a part of us, as we perceive ourselves. The Son of God incorporates all things within himself as You created him. Your memory depends on his forgiveness. What he is, is unaffected by his thoughts. But what he looks upon is their direct result. Therefore, my Father, I would turn to You. Only Your memory will set me free. And only my forgiveness teaches me to let Your memory return to me, and give it to the world in thankfulness."

(W-pII.350.1.1–8)

Today's lesson is alive in us now. This past ten lessons with the theme of miracles have been reinforcing forgiveness and miracles are one in the same. We're looking at our judgments and the miracle reminds us that what we see is false. You'd think we'd be hunting down opportunities left and right to forgive and offer a miracle so we could have it, and with it, the memory of God. Right?

That's how I feel. I'm on alert for where miracles are needed. My holiness takes care of the how. We are the Christ child come to play. We bring miracles to the world. That's the thought we want with us as we move into each day.

It feels freeing and open to let go of an agenda and forgive. It feels amazing to see the person and situation in a way that connects us and feels loving and happy! It's bliss to give up grievances! We are having an experience of God's grace going before us. And gratitude beats our hearts.

While I was in Salt Lake City last week, I ran into an old friend. She's a social worker, and she tells me about budget cuts and how it's becoming very difficult to give good care to people who need it most. I remember thinking all the same thoughts a million years ago when I worked in the mental health field.

I've been down that road, changed my mind, and received a miracle. As she talks, I look past her story to her innocence and offer a miracle. I tell her about a day, back in the day, when I felt a similar frustration.

I remember walking down the hall of the hospital after a staff meeting. I'm totally pissed off. "It's bull shit, all the hoops we have to jump through just to sit with a patient and assist in healing." By the grace of God, I realized the split mind from which I was seeing, and in that moment, it was actually comical, it was so obvious. I was choosing victimhood, and I needed a miracle.

It's like my mind turns back in on itself. I was aware of the stillness surrounding and permeating everything, cutting through the hospital noise and my thoughts. I listened into the silence, and I heard one thought loud and clear, "You do not work for the system, you work for God." I grab on to the miracle like a lifeline and forgive the system and everyone in it.

My friend says, "Oh my God! You're so right. That's just what I needed to hear right now. I'm in social work because it is a calling. That's all I need to focus on."

No one is exempt from forgiveness's light; each invites a miracle. That includes the "system" and everyone in it. Forgiveness is inclusion. Giving and receiving *are* the same. We are in the flow of the law of love.

"Miracles mirror God's eternal Love. To offer them is to remember Him, and through His memory to save the world." Everything that shows up in the day is the perfect chance to offer a miracle.

CHAPTER TWO HUNDRED EIGHTY-EIGHT

DAY 351

(Lesson 351)

"My sinless brother is my guide to peace.
My sinful brother is my guide to pain.
And which I choose to see I will behold."

(W-pII.351.1)

"Who is my brother but Your holy Son? And if I see him sinful I proclaim myself a sinner,
not a Son of God; alone and friendless in a fearful world. Yet this perception is a
choice I make, and can relinquish. I can also see my brother sinless, as Your holy Son.
And with this choice I see my sinlessness, my everlasting Comforter and Friend
beside me, and my way secure and clear. Choose, then, for me, my Father,
through Your Voice. For He alone gives judgment in Your Name."

(W-pII.351.1–6)

We offer this prayer together, now, and hold it in our hearts throughout the day. Today begins our last theme by which we consider the next ten lessons. It is *"Who am I?"* This section begins with my favorite passage in *A Course in Miracles.*

It's my favorite passage because, when I first read it, I had an experience of its truth. In a holy instant, as I read, a blazing light of truth cut through everything I thought I was, and left me pure and innocent, full and whole, wanting nothing.

I immediately, committed the passage to memory, in honor of the gift I had just received; the total recognition I want to hold next to my heart. This is the invitation made to us today, to join heart and mind wholeheartedly, in the realization of *who we are in truth,* as we read these words.

I am God's Son, complete and healed and whole, shining in the reflection of His Love. In me is His creation sanc-
tified and guaranteed eternal life. In me is love perfected, fear impossible, and joy established without opposite. I
am the holy home of God Himself. I am the Heaven where His Love resides. I am His holy Sinlessness Itself, for in
my purity abides His Own. (W-pII.14.1.1–6)

This has been my mantra, backgrounding my life ever since. Adopt it for yourself, own it, and know that you are God's Son, complete and healed and whole, shining in the reflection of God's love. Now and eternally.

It's perfect that we are given this description of what we are, right now, as we are coming to the completion of our year given to God through application of these workbook lessons. We have awoken from our slumber of fear and false identity, and now we claim the truth of our divinity.

Today's lesson is one of unity with each other, as brothers. *"My sinless brother is my guide to peace."* This idea goes before us lighting each encounter with the innocence we share.

Recently, there was an incident in the news about a bombing in Manchester England, killing twenty-two and injuring over a hundred. One young brother, with a suicide bomb, confused and afraid, walked into the Manchester arena and detonated.

He is reported to have called his mother shortly before, and what he said, is what each of us have felt many times. He said, "Please forgive me for anything I did wrong."

Isn't this call, our call? Please forgive me for anything I did wrong. His call for love is our call to all brothers, for all brothers. My heart broke for this young man, along with each and all of us. I forgive—seeing his confusion and behind it, his sinlessness. I forgive it all—the belief in sin, attack, fear, and death. I choose to see only sinlessness and rest in peace.

DAY 352

(Lesson 352)

*"Judgment and love are opposites.
From one come all the sorrows of the world.
But from the other comes the peace of God Himself."*

(W-pII.352.1)

"Forgiveness looks on sinlessness alone, and judges not. Through this I come to You. Judgment will bind my eyes and make me blind. Yet love, reflected in forgiveness here, reminds me You have given me a way to find Your peace again. I am redeemed when I elect to follow in this way. You have not left me comfortless. I have within me both the memory of You, and One Who leads me to it. Father, I would hear Your Voice and find Your peace today. For I would love my own Identity, and find in It the memory of You."

(W-pII.352.1–10)

Our lessons now are all in the form of prayers. We are learning to live in constant communion with God, listening to His voice and letting Christ's vision rest upon all things. I love the simplicity of these final lessons. It's all or nothing. No compromise. Love or judgment? Sorrow or the peace of God?

Will we be blinded by judgment or will we see with Christ's vision? Is it a hard question?

"Yet love, reflected in forgiveness here, reminds me You have given me a way to find Your peace again. I am redeemed when I elect to follow in this way." So simple. So powerful. That's why forgiveness is our function; it releases the light of love that was blocked by judgment.

We have not been left comfortless. God is with us. We are part of Him. We forgive and feel the love of God as our home, and see love reflected everywhere and in everyone. God's peace is inevitable. As we forgive, we extend the love from our own identity as one, and we recall the memory of God. We are the bringers of light.

I look back on where I started. I was totally immersed in the thought system of fear, defending and judging, worrying and planning for future happiness. It's like reviewing a movie of a life I'm not identified with, except in whatever way the transformation through forgiveness serves the healing of us all.

Immersed in the thought system of love, I happily bringing light and love, comfort and peace wherever the Divine would have me go. I am fine-tuned to catch the glitches in my flow of love and joy and employ forgiveness easily, reminding myself that judgment and love are opposites—I choose peace and joy.

The first time I did the lessons and came to this stage, I still had a lot of mistrust in myself. I feared that not having a daily lesson to follow, to keep at the center of my day as a guide, might leave me vulnerable to losing myself again.

I needn't have concerned myself. We cannot lose what we are in truth. That's the ego. It jumps in with fear if we give it an opening. I realized that this fear and mistrust I was having were exactly what I still needed to forgive, so I could feel the comfort that is promised in this lesson. I gave myself in trust.

There was still a lot to uncover and forgive, and I have wavered. But the instant I am willing to take full responsibility for everything, I see God's grace.

Each experience is our classroom for forgiveness. We can't lose our Self. We can forgive and escape illusions. Forgiveness is our way home to our Self—to the peace of God Himself.

DAY 353

(Lesson 353)

"My eyes, my tongue, my hands, my feet today have but one purpose; to be given Christ to use to bless the world with miracles."

(W-pII.353.1)

"Father, I give all that is mine today to Christ, to use in any way that best will serve the purpose that I share with Him. Nothing is mine alone, for He and I have joined in purpose. Thus has learning come almost to its appointed end. A while I work with Him to serve His purpose. Then I lose myself in my Identity, and recognize that Christ is but my Self."

(W-pII.353.1–5)

We have one purpose—to give ourselves to Christ to bless the world with miracles. We've come to a place where we see that our bodies are neutral and take instruction from our minds. It is our presence that animates the body. It's meant to be used to serve the purpose of miracles.

First, we had to see that we are not our body; that our identity is beyond form or time and space. Now the body can be used by the Christ, to bless the world with holiness and joy. Today's lesson is a commitment we make to the Christ Self we share as one. So, everything we do, now serves this one purpose.

It simplifies all our choices. They belong to truth. They are to use for miracles. It is our pledge. We're trusting that we always have whatever is needed to serve love's purpose.

When recent body challenges brought everything I thought I believed and practiced up for review and forgiveness on a new level, I realized I still had deep-seated body identity beliefs that needed to be looked at and dislodged.

Trust in the Divine and forgiveness has been key. It's been a powerful witness for me through the experiences of what seemed like a broken body, to see that when I am on purpose and present to what shows up in my life, I experience only the union through love, and my body symptoms slip from my mind. They literally are not there when I am present to my identity as God created me. The Christ in me steps forward and moves though me, using everything in joy and union.

The body, made for separation and fear, has been given a new purpose. This year has been the witness to giving my body to the service of Christ. I am always able to do what I am called to do. I have a new love and appreciation for my body. It is the human vessel through which I connect and join with my brother as my Self in Christ.

Our ministry is Christ's service, to bring miracles to the world. We are the light and joy of miracles. The circumstances may be vastly diverse, but our purpose is one. We give all that we have to the purpose of atonement we share, uniting us with each other in our identity with Christ.

We have become companions, vessels for miracles in everything we do. That's the practice today. We give ourselves completely to Christ in service to the world. We lose ourselves in our identity and *"recognize that Christ is but our Self."*

DAY 354

(Lesson 354)

"We stand together, Christ and I,
in peace and certainty of purpose.
And in Him is His Creator, as He is in me."

(W-pII.354.1)

"My oneness with the Christ establishes me as Your Son, beyond the reach of time, and wholly free of every law but Yours. I have no self except the Christ in me. I have no purpose but His Own. And He is like His Father. Thus must I be one with You as well as Him. For who is Christ except Your Son as You created Him? And what am I except the Christ in me?"

(W-pII.354.1–7)

Our mission now is to take our stand, together, as our Christ identity. We're living the law of love. Our lives, like our lessons now, are a prayer of gratitude for the Christ we recognize as us.

It's wild to remember how I resisted taking this stand in the beginning. I thought, "I'm not there yet. I still lose myself in my old identity. I can't honestly say I stand together, Christ and I, in peace and certainty of purpose."

Taking our stand in faith, declaring our identity as Christ, is the readiness. I was still looking at myself from within the dream. What's amazing is just in giving myself to the lesson, letting my mind still into the quiet of divine mind, I am lifted above the dream story of time and into God's eternal presence now.

We are in the heart of God, and from here we stand with Christ, as one Self. The present moment is our portal to miracles—to Christ consciousness, and from there we have all that need to serve Christ's purpose.

The ego-fear identity can't survive in its presence. When Love-Christ identity is present in our mind and heart, there is no cross section where they intersect. One is true and the other false. It really is uncompromising. Each day is an adventure in miracles.

Case in point, a few minutes ago a friend from Albuquerque called. She's been wanting to move and has been accepted into a community she's been wanting to live in for some time. She called for counsel because something didn't feel right. Ours is a holy relationship.

She knows I will be the voice of sanity, seeing the Christ in her, and reminding her of the truth she knows in her heart. She tells me what's going on, and I look with her to the Christ within.

She tells me she is afraid she won't be able to get everything lined up before her window of opportunity closes. She's devising a plan to try to control the outcome. It's wonderful to step back with her and let Christ step forward. There's no time stamp on Divine window of opportunity. If it's for us, it will be open. If not, it's not our window.

Within minutes, she sees the flaw in her plan. Fear and scarcity had slipped in, making plans from the laws of fear, when only the law of love would bring her peace. Joyfully, she declares, "I'm giving up my plan and trusting God's. Whatever the outcome is, I accept as the best for me." The peace and joy surrounding us is eternal, cutting through the miles between us in time and space.

The simplicity of salvation is right here, always, as we stand with Christ as our only identity. Christ's certainty and purpose flow through us, from the center where we are one with God. Today we stand with Christ as our one identity, our only purpose, living the law of love.

DAY 355

(Lesson 355)

*"There is no end to all the peace and joy,
and all the miracles that I will give,
when I accept God's Word. Why not today?"*

(W-pII.355.1)

*"Why should I wait, my Father, for the joy You promised me? For You will keep Your Word
You gave Your Son in exile. I am sure my treasure waits for me, and I need but reach
out my hand to find it. Even now my fingers touch it. It is very close. I need not wait an
instant more to be at peace forever. It is You I choose, and my Identity along with You.
Your Son would be Himself, and know You as his Father and Creator, and his Love."*

(W-pII.355.1–7)

The first line of the prayer today is, *"Why should I wait, my Father, for the joy You promised me?"* It's the honest request from our hearts. Yes? Why wait, when our life is sourced totally from the Divine through our state of mind? God is the decision we make. Unequivocally.

For me, it's almost a physical shift in my energy. Like the door closes behind me. Now, from this identity in Him, we're filled with Source for our life. We're experiencing the treasures miracles bring, through forgiveness, as we release our self from the self-imposed exile of fear and confused identity, so why wait?

Why not stand in our identity as Christ now? We only have the responsibility of this moment. For this instant, why not be the happiness we wish to have at all times. It is an honest inquiry.

When we are ready, no past ideas can offer defense. All we want *is* what we are. And that creates its own purpose which includes and serves the world.

I love this line, *"Even now my fingers touch it. It is very close."* Can you feel it? So close, we feel its touch as we complete this final stage of our year given to God. We feel the reality of our Self, the joy and grace flowing through us and bringing miracles.

What is holding us back from totally stepping in and closing the door on fear and conflict forever? *"[We] need not wait an instant more to be at peace forever."* This moment, now, we choose only God and our identity in Him. We are our Self—the love and light of the world.

As we come to the close of these lessons, doubt often creeps in, "Maybe I didn't do the lessons perfectly, spend enough time, whatever." But the thing is, they are just forgiveness opportunities to bring the light we are to mind and let a miracle shine through. So what?

If it's still disturbing my mind, it's in the mind of the one Son we share. So, awesome. My seeing that little glitch, forgiving, and choosing love and joy instead, heals everyone who still harbors doubt and uncertainty, right?

Why should it keep me from the fullness of my identity as Christ, my eternal oneness with God, right here, right now? I am anyway. The truth is true, and nothing but the truth is true. Why delay an instant longer? By standing with Christ, owning that all God's gifts are ours to give, the odds that we will see where love is needed and answer its call, becomes available to us in way that is blocked when we waver and let doubt occupy our mind. Right?

It is an unequivocal decision. This is what I am. Christ, one with my Father and united with all creation. The resistance is nothing compared to the power of love. The ego is really nothing. Its reign is over. Today is the day. Why wait?

DAY 356

(Lesson 356)

"Sickness is but another name for sin.
Healing is but another name for God.
The miracle is thus a call to Him."

(W-pII.356.1)

"Father, You promised You would never fail to answer any call Your Son might make to You.
It does not matter where he is, what seems to be his problem, nor what he believes he has
become. He is Your Son, and You will answer him. The miracle reflects Your Love, and thus it
answers him. Your Name replaces every thought of sin, and who is sinless cannot suffer pain.
Your Name gives answer to Your Son, because to call Your Name is but to call his own."

(W-pII.356.1–6)

Sickness is another name for sin. It equates both, as the same error in our mind. We are sick when we believe we are guilty because sinlessness and innocence are part of our identity in truth. It has nothing to do with the body. The body is neutral. Used by the ego, it traps us in a false identity as frail and weak, at the mercy of outside forces. Given to the Holy Spirit, it is a means of communicating miracles.

We are spirit. So, if you read this like, "Shit, if I'm sick, I'm guilty"—then you're just off the mark in your thinking. We are not a body. This lesson is about our one identity with God. When we feel guilty, our awareness of our sinlessness is clouded over by the error called sin. It isn't real and it has no real power.

All power is of God. We give everything all the meaning it has for us. When we feel guilty, or see sin in someone else, the ego's syphoning that power from the power of God within us to give it meaning. We are creators. We can mis-create, and it can seem very real. But only in dreams. Who we are has not been touched by it at all.

Yes, we often see many physical changes as we change our minds about our Self. Healing is the natural outcome of miracles. But it is paramount to leave the circumstances of what that outcome is in the hands of God.

Changing the state of the body is never the concern with the course. In fact, at one place in the text it says, "*The body is insignificant.*" It is useful only to serve the purpose of atonement. Any particular bodily state, even paralysis, cannot intrude upon our purpose. So, leave it be. Forgive when we can't seem to leave it alone and surrender into the space in our hearts beyond body identity.

The state of the body is irrelevant to atonement. If I am crippled, that doesn't mean I am guilty and punishing myself (an error I have made in the past). It is a chance to see beyond it, directly to God and my Self as Christ.

Crippled or fit is irrelevant to fulfilling my purpose as the light of the world. Noticing the temptation for guilt and body-identification, to lose sight of my purpose, brings forgiveness. I call on God, on love, and choose the truth of my identity as Christ, one with God. We're not trying to fix anything in the world anymore.

The truth stands. It is but a call away. Healing is another name for God. The instant we remember God, we are back in our right mind. The miracle takes no time at all. The instant we recall God to mind, we have also called our Self to mind. And in God everything is already accomplished.

DAY 357

(Lesson 357)

*"Truth answers every call we make to God,
responding first with miracles,
and then returning unto us to be itself."*

(W-pII.357.1)

*"Forgiveness, truth's reflection, tells me how to offer miracles, and thus escape the
prison house in which I think I live. Your holy Son is pointed out to me, first in my brother;
then in me. Your Voice instructs me patiently to hear Your Word, and give as I receive.
And as I look upon Your Son today, I hear Your Voice instructing me to find the way to You,
as You appointed that the way shall be: 'Behold his sinlessness, and be you healed.'"*

(W-pII.357.1–4)

Cole and I are out delivering product for one of his entrepreneurial businesses the other day. At one stop, the guy is angry and starts yelling that the order should have been delivered over a week ago. We're just standing there with big smiles, beaming joy and light on the situation.

I see this brother's confusion, and fear that he won't get his needs met. I stand peacefully, quietly, blessing him with love, expecting a miracle. Cole, too, just stands there smiling, while the guy releases his rant.

It's a great example of seeing how forgiveness even in situations that seemingly don't affect me, bring miracles. As he rants on, my physical senses activate, heat rising up in incurring anger. In the past I'd have been afraid and defensive; explaining, complaining, or blaming. What I witness now is a call for love. I breathe deeply into the love and I feel one with this brother.

As he talks, I realize he thinks we were from a completely different company with which he placed an order. Cole realized it immediately. But rather than react, we listen, giving him our attention and presence. Once his energy is spent, he chuckles a little embarrassedly, "Wait a minute, are you guys from . . . ? [naming a company, not Cole's.] You're not, are you?" We all bust up.

It was awesome because, none of us needed anything to be different. The perfect thing happened. When he realizes who Cole is, and that he's getting product from Cole earlier than expected, he says, "It's funny how you get something in your head, and that's all you can see. Sorry about that, man." Cole says, "No worries, man. Glad we could do that for you."

Christ's vision looks on everything with love. It is infectious.

That's what today's lesson is about. Truth answers every call we make to God. By seeing our brother as our self, we call on God. It's instantaneous. We are one. Instead of reacting, we see the chance to bring a miracle into our joined mind by seeing with love. God, too, is there.

That is the simplicity of practicing today's idea. We give what we want to receive. Forgiveness reflects the truth, and how to bring a miracle shows up as we listen patiently for God's word, and the encounter is holy.

Today is a day of sinlessness and celebration. Whomever we meet we see the light of Christ, and we see them sinless. To each we hold one thought in mind, *"I behold [your] sinlessness, and [I am] healed."* Have fun giving miracles today.

DAY 358

(Lesson 358)

"No call to God can be unheard nor left unanswered.
And of this I can be sure; His answer is the one I really want."

(W-pII.358.1)

"You Who remember what I really am alone remember what I really want. You speak for God, and so You speak for me. And what You give me comes from God Himself. Your Voice, my Father, then is mine as well, and all I want is what You offer me, in just the form You choose that it be mine. Let me remember all I do not know, and let my voice be still, remembering. But let me not forget Your Love and care, keeping Your promise to Your Son in my awareness always. Let me not forget myself is nothing, but my Self is all."

(W-pII.358.1–6)

No call to God can be unheard, nor left unanswered, because God is what we are. Calling to God is calling to our whole Self. God is the wholeness of all creation, and we are that. Wholeness and love are one in the same.

Love would be not be itself if it favored anything that would separate, split apart, or place hierarchies. Anything that diminishes full recognition of the power and presence of love now, will not allow us to recognize our true Self. We are what we are praying for. As long as we believe that God is somewhere "out there," we don't realize that His voice is ours as well.

I've had a daily devotional practice, spending my first waking hours with the Divine, for over thirty years—praying, meditating, and reading *A Course in Miracles* and other inspirational material, and writing.

At first, I kept a journal to fix myself. But, as I practiced the lessons in the course, fixing gave way to love. I saw that only my thoughts can hurt me. In changing my thoughts, I was having an experience of joy and peace. This experience transformed what I wanted to write about. Like, God is within me and I cannot be without Him.

I've had some incredible, indescribable awakening experiences during these devotional times. My mind has burst wide open by light, by sublime love and gratitude.

However, the thing that ultimately shifted my paradigm is the practice of choosing love in answer to everything. By applying the new ideas given through the lesson, even when I didn't understand—that faith, called upon my Self that did understand the language of the Divine, transforming my paradigm.

I quit journaling when I quit trying to fix myself. My writing became more like love letters of gratitude. Over the years I've come to realize that devotion itself is the experience of God within, loving Itself—reaching for and answering in love.

The experience of God came quietly into my mind as a constant communion, through paying intense and honest attention to what I am thinking, feeling, and believing.

As long as my inner world was more or less on auto pilot, it remained unconscious, and I could not experience the true power of changing my mind. Being willing to look at my thinking and calling on love to replace what feared and hurt, I see it reflected everywhere and my world changes. I feel Divinity's wholeness.

There is something available, an infinite source of love and possibility, beyond what can be contained within this world, yet a part of what we are. As we expand to reach It, It reaches back, and brings that infinite possibility into our world of form.

What we really want is a return to recognition of our Divine wholeness—to heal this limitation belief in our mind. We want the experience of infinite love, Divine union—God. What serves that purpose is always given.

DAY 359

(Lesson 359)

"God's answer is some form of peace. All pain is healed;
all misery replaced with joy. All prison doors are opened.
And all sin is understood as merely a mistake."

(W-pII.359.1)

"Father, today we will forgive Your world, and let creation be Your Own.
We have misunderstood all things. But we have not made sinners of the holy Sons of God.
What You created sinless so abides forever and forever. Such are we. And we rejoice to learn
that we have made mistakes which have no real effects on us. Sin is impossible, and on
this fact forgiveness rests upon a certain base more solid than the shadow world we see.
Help us forgive, for we would be redeemed. Help us forgive, for we would be at peace."

(W-pII.359.1–7)

The experience of peace was one of my first realizations that my prayers were being answered. Praying used to be like begging. "Please help me. Help me get what I want. Please recognize my illusion and fix it for me." Then, *A Course in Miracles* came into my life. It actually suggested that true prayer was forgetting the things I think I want and letting God teach me what it is I truly want.

The course says its goal is the attainment and keeping of peace and happiness. I realize that everything in my life ultimately boils down to this same goal.

As I started the mind-training, my prayers shifted to a single-minded purpose—an experience of peace in whatever difficulty I had in my life. I'd see my judgments, lay them on the altar of my mind and release them, asking to see things differently. Time and time again, with amazing consistency, I felt immediate peace.

I'd ask for guidance in what to do and get on with life before me. It was the results that showed me if I was actually paying attention to the guidance, or still trying to get the outcome I thought I needed. For me, guidance often comes as an intimate, peaceful feeling, saying "yes" to what is present in my life—saying "yes" to what will bring forgiveness, healing, and union. Sometimes quite potently.

When Lin was a teenager she went through this brief phase where she was identifying herself as a gothic—wearing black lipstick, black clothes, and even tinted her naturally platinum blonde hair black. It seemed to me like she was immersing herself in a culture of darkness, depression, and despair. I feared for her. I wanted her to see reason. My reason.

I justified my fear judgments using metaphysics—our thoughts create our reality and our predominate thoughts play out as the experiences in our lives. I wanted her to see that she needed to protect herself from negative thoughts. Like I knew?

How could I know when fear had a hold of my mind? By the grace of God, I went to Him rather than bombard her with my fears. I intuitively knew I could only see what I put there. I was doing exactly what I was accusing Lin of doing—immersing myself in a culture of darkness and despair.

I offered my judgments and fears, my call for love, in prayer. I asked for forgiveness. I asked for peace. I asked to forget what I thought needed to happen and see what love would teach me. I felt immediate release and peace filled my being.

Later that day I overhear Lin speaking with a client, "Being gothic is saying I am willing to face my dark beliefs and make a choice. Plus, I like the look—all dark and mysterious. There is really nothing to be afraid of."

Pow! Nothing to be afraid of. Wow. The answer to my call to God. Total peace. Total joy. Lin's a guru.

CHAPTER TWO HUNDRED NINETY-SEVEN

DAY 360

(Lesson 360)

"Peace be to me, the holy Son of God.
Peace to my brother, who is one with me.
Let all the world be blessed with peace through us."

(W-pII.360.1)

"Father, it is Your peace that I would give, receiving it of You. I am Your Son, forever just as You
created me, for the Great Rays remain forever still and undisturbed within me. I would reach
to them in silence and in certainty, for nowhere else can certainty be found. Peace be to
me, and peace to all the world. In holiness were we created, and in holiness do we remain.
Your Son is like to You in perfect sinlessness. And with this thought we gladly say 'Amen.'"

(W-pII.360.1–7)

Today's lesson reads like an acceptance letter as ministers of God. *"Peace be to me, the holy Son of God."* First, we claim eternal peace through our true identity. Then, extend God's peace through what we are, and though our union we bless the world with peace.

This is really the culmination of all the lessons we've been considering with the theme, *"What am I?"* I love that we are completing with this lesson of peace. It's like it all comes full circle with the goal of the course, the attainment and keeping of peace. From this stillness where our self abides, the Great Rays of Self, forever still and undisturbed within us, bring light to the world.

Yesterday I had a decompression clinic. I look through the glass doors before entering. The place is packed, crazy busy, trying to fit everyone in after the holiday. Today's lesson is the perfect antidote gift for me to give. I pause before entering and offer a prayer. "Let me be the presence of eternal peace and joy and let peace still any chaos and let love reign." I enter filled with joy, my smile wide, radiating the light of peace and union.

Immediately there's a hug fest with the staff. "I'm so glad you're here, bringing your yumminess." I'm with half a dozen patrons waiting at the desk to sign in. I start giving each a little namaste, nod, and a smile. It's yummy. Everyone smiles back with a namaste.

When staff comes to explain about the overflow due to the holiday and thanks us for our patience, I say, "Looks like a well-oiled machine to me, moving peacefully along." And it is. It's more like a party. Lots of jovial conversation and laughter. It's like being there for treatment is secondary to enjoying each other. Peace and joy are the content. The setting provides the context for the content of peace, joy, love, and union.

How often have we been in these kinds of situations, where we have the opportunity to be the center of peace extending to include everyone, but chose to resist instead, losing ourselves in the fray of chaos?

Look for these opportunities today, whether it be with one other you join, with two, or with a crowd. In the grocery store, on the bus, or watching television with family. Let peace be your first and final goal. It proves itself out. We are God's Son of peace and love, untied we bring peace to all minds as one.

DAYS 361–365

(Lesson 361–365)

*"This holy instant would I give to You.
Be You in charge. For I would follow You,
certain that Your direction gives me peace."*

(W-pII.361–365.1)

*"And if I need a word to help me, He will give it to me. If I need a thought,
that will He also give. And if I need but stillness and a tranquil, open mind,
these are the gifts I will receive of Him. He is in charge by my request. And He will
hear and answer me, because He speaks for God my Father and His holy Son."*

(W-pII.361–365.2)

Today begins our final five days sharing this year we have given to God through this curriculum—but our lives are forever entwined. Our minds are joined, and every forgiveness, every call or extension of love, blesses the whole mind of God's Son. Thank you, from the depths of my open heart.

These five day we repeat the same lesson. This is the prayer of our hearts as we go forward, trusting the Divine in all that we do. We begin with a set of instructions which help us in our final release to God, fully accepting our ministry as Christ, trusting His Voice and guidance as our own.

Our final lessons will be left as free of words as possible. We use them but at the beginning of our practicing, and only to remind us that we seek to go beyond them. Let us turn to Him Who leads the way and makes our footsteps sure. To Him we leave these lessons, as to Him we give our lives henceforth. For we would not return again to the belief in sin that made the world seem ugly and unsafe, attacking and destroying, dangerous in all its ways, and treacherous beyond the hope of trust and the escape from pain. (W-pII.fl.in.1–5)

So, each day we're simply joining in a holy instant with the Divine. In the stillness of our whole mind, we're letting everything else drop away. We offer the prayer given us to imprint on our hearts.

This holy instant would I give to You. Be You In charge. For I would follow You, certain Your direction gives me peace.

Trust in this relationship, this constant communion with the Divine, hearing Its voice as our own. Trust will handle every seeming problem that arises. Trust lets us see where to bring a miracle and just what is needed at the time.

Not long ago a package was left on my doorstep. It was addressed to someone a couple houses away. Left here by mistake? Nope. I check the address again, grab a post-it note pad and pen, and walk to the neighbor. Why did I bring the notepad? A little tickle in my heart prompted.

When I arrive at the address, no one is home. I leave a little note saying, "Your package was left mistakenly on my doorstep. Have a yummy day." I set the package inside the screen and leave with a blessing in my heart.

The next day, my doorbell rings. My neighbor, new best friend of the moment, is beaming with joy, her eyes glistening with gratitude. She says, "Are you the angel that brought my package to my door? When it didn't arrive last week, I called, and they said it had been delivered. I was heartbroken."

Tears fill her eyes as she shares her miracle with me. "This means so much to me, this . . ." She opens her hand, and in it is an ornate brass locket. "This is a rare locket. Made in Poland. It is just like the one my mother had when I was a girl. I found it online as part of an auction.

"Anyway, when I saw the locket, it felt like a gift from God. You see, I lost my mother's locket just after she passed, when I was a young mother myself. I've always regretted it. I've often wished I had it. How wonderful to pass it on to my daughter. Since it's identical to my mother's, well, it's a miracle."

I agree wholeheartedly. Indeed, it is a miracle and sharing it with me shines the miracle on me too.

Take today's lesson for a test drive. Everything we need is within us, now, in our relationship with the Divine. We need but give each moment to this relationship of love.

"And if I need a word to help me, He will give it to me. If I need a thought, that will He also give. And if I need but stillness and a tranquil, open mind, these are the gifts I will receive of Him. He is in charge by my request. And He will hear and answer me, because He speaks for God my Father and His holy Son."

For the remaining days of our year together, I join you purely in spirit. I encourage you to witness to your own experience of trust—to the presence of our final lesson in your life. Write your own stories of miracles, to return to in the moments when you forget. This prayer waits for you to make it yours. I am with you. We are one.

AUTHOR'S NOTE

Dear Reader,

Thank you for reading *Coffee With The Divine: A Yummy Guide to Daily Miracles*. I hope this book helps you on your own life's journey in some small way. We're all in this together, after all. Online reviews are always appreciated but no pressure. If you'd like to connect, here's where you can find me:

Facebook: https://www.facebook.com/danetpalmerauthor
Pinterest: https://www.pinterest.com/danet_theyummyway/
Instagram: https://www.instagram.com/danetpalmer_theyummyway/
Podcast: https://theyummyway.buzzsprout.com/
Website: https://theyummyway.com/

On the website you can also sign up for my newsletter and receive a free copy of *The Yummy-Stat Playbook: Your Guide to Living from Love and Wholeness*.

In infinite Joy and Love, Danét

ABOUT THE AUTHOR

35 years ago, Danét made an appointment with divinity. It turned out to be the single most life-changing decision of her life — to dedicate her first few wakening moments to The Divine, and her own spiritual awakening. To open to Love and keep her heart open no matter what — to make unconditional love and present joy her spiritual path.

She has kept this daily appointment ever since, and by surrendering her thoughts and emotions to Divine Love, she learned that Divine Love is the true nature of who she is and who we all are. From this base, she attracted the theosophy of A Course in Miracles where she learned to forgive false beliefs and embody the truth of innate worth in herself and everyone. She has nurtured this philosophy that joy is the way of love and the practice of aligning our thinking with love.

She practices and teaches and that we can change our thought system from fear-based thinking to thoughts that are governed by love and goodwill toward others, always.

Danét has lived an astonishingly happy and fulfilling personal life with her marriage to who she proudly calls her life mate. As a mother, she has reveled in raising her four incredibly fabulous children and likes to think herself as a catalyst for them to learn to follow their own hearts and grow as individuals.

While the children have since grown into fine adults and have left home in pursuit of their careers, now, Danét loves being Grammy Nay to her three adorable grandkids.

Danét has lived a life that's been guided by the dictates of her own Divine guidance. This has also led her to live a non-traditional and extremely interesting life, which has taken her from working in a psychiatric institute for some years to serving in the military, to performing ministerial duties in Las Vegas.

A Metaphysical Minister by profession, Danét has worked as an inspirational pragmatic or psycho-spiritual coach/counselor for many years. During that time, she has helped create and facilitate intensive workshops and has also facilitated groups as well as individual and couples counseling.

As a psycho-spiritual coach, Danét has indulged in a therapeutic technique called experiential therapy that uses certain expressive tools and activities to help her clients re-interpret emotional situations from their recent and past relationships.

It was while helping people as a psycho-spiritual coach that Danét realized her own calling and earned a BA from the University of Metaphysics. Danét is also a licensed minister who occasionally provides ministry services for weddings or counseling.

She remains passionate about spreading the message of inspiration through joy — articulating and sharing wisdom in a joyful, synchronizing way. As a professional author and podcaster, Danét is also passionate about creating a 'Yummy Way Movement' with a worldwide community committed to living joy and has another book on the way. So, stay tuned!

Made in the USA
Middletown, DE
18 February 2022

61294891R00203